Lawrenceville Press

An Introduction to Computing Using AppleWorks

versions 2 and 3

Second Edition

Bruce Presley
William Freitas

First Edition published 1989
Second Edition published 1991
Copyright © 1991
by

Second Edition

ISBN **0–931717–92–2**   (softcover)
ISBN **0–931717–93–0**   (hardcover)

Printed in the United States of America

All orders, including educational, Canadian, foreign, FPO and APO addresses may be placed by contacting:

Lawrenceville Press
P.O. Box 704
Pennington, NJ 08534-0704
(609) 737-1148
FAX: (609) 737-8564

This text is available in both hardcover and softcover editions.

16 15 14 13 12 11 10 9 8 7 6 5 4 3 2 1

This text is written and published by Lawrenceville Press, Inc. and is in no way connected with Apple Computer, Inc. or the Claris Corporation.

Apple®, Apple II®, Applesoft® and ProDOS® are registered trademarks of Apple Computer, Inc. AppleWorks® is a registered trademark of Apple Computer, Inc. licensed to Claris Corporation.

PREFACE

W e believe the best way to introduce students to computing is with an introductory course that covers a brief history of computing, applications software (word processing, database, and spreadsheet), and a discussion of the role computers play in modern society. These goals are accomplished by this text which is designed to serve both the needs of students who will complete only an applications course, as well as those who will go on to take subsequent computer courses. The emphasis of this text is on the concepts of computing and problem solving using AppleWorks so that students learn how computers can be applied to a wide range of problems. The text is written for a one or two-term course for the high school or college student. No previous computer experience is assumed.

Design and Features

FORMAT — Each chapter contains numerous examples and diagrams printed in a two color format to help students visualize new concepts.

OBJECTIVES — An outline of the significant topics that should be emphasized is presented at the beginning of each chapter.

CONCEPTS of APPLICATION — Each of the application areas begins with an introductory section which describes the application and its uses. In this way, students are taught the purpose of the application without being overly concerned with the specific software. If the student then goes on to use another software package, he or she will fully understand the general concepts behind each application.

HANDS-ON PRACTICE — In the applications chapters each new concept is presented, discussed and then followed by a hands-on practice which requires the student to test newly learned skills on the computer. The practice sections also serve as excellent reference guides to review applications commands.

VOCABULARY — A vocabulary section which defines the new terms used is given at the end of each chapter.

CHAPTER SUMMARY — At the end of each chapter is an outline that briefly discusses the concepts covered in the chapter.

REVIEW PROBLEMS — Numerous review problems are presented for each section of the chapter, providing immediate reinforcement of new concepts. Answers to all review problems are included in the Teacher's Resource Package described below.

EXERCISES — Each of the applications chapters includes a set of exercises of varying difficulty, making them appropriate for students with a wide range of abilities. Answers to all exercises are included in the Teacher's Resource Package described below.

HISTORY of COMPUTING   Before learning to use the applications software, Chapter 1 introduces students to a history of computing and the vocabulary needed to understand concepts presented in later chapters.

PROGRAMMING   Chapter 10 offers an introduction to programming in Applesoft BASIC. This introduction is sufficient to illustrate the problem-solving concepts involved in writing a program.

SOCIAL and ETHICAL IMPLICATIONS   Because computers play such an important role in modern society, Chapter 11 discusses the social and ethical consequences of living in a computerized society. Advances in computer related technology that will impact on the student's world are also discussed.

CAREERS in COMPUTING   It is hoped that many students will become interested in careers in computing based upon their experience in this introductory course. A section in Chapter 11 outlines different computer careers and the educational requirements needed to pursue them.

APPENDICES   Summaries of AppleWorks and ProDOS commands are presented in appendices at the end of the text for easy reference.

Teacher's Resource Package

When used with this text, the Lawrenceville Press Teacher's Resource Package provides all the additional material required to offer students an excellent introductory computer applications course. These materials, along with the text, place a strong emphasis on developing student problem-solving skills. The Package divides each of the chapters in the text into a series of lessons which contain the following features:

- **ASSIGNMENTS** - Reading and problem assignments are suggested for each lesson.

- **DISCUSSION TOPICS** - Additional material is provided which supplements the text and can be used in leading classroom discussions. Often this includes explanations of more advanced commands or concepts not covered in the text.

- **TRANSPARENCY MASTERS** - Most lessons contain transparency masters which often present diagrams of the different applications screens.

- **WORKSHEETS** - Included in each lesson is a worksheet containing problems which are meant to be completed in the computer lab. These problems supplement those in the text, giving students additional reinforcement of the concepts they have just learned. Many of these problems make use of the data files included on the Master Diskette described below.

- **MASTER DISKETTE** - A Master Diskette that contains files to be used in conjunction with text problems and worksheets is included in the Teacher's Resource Package. These files are especially helpful in allowing students to work with large amounts of data without first having to type it into the computer. Student diskettes can be easily made by following the directions included with the Master Diskette. The Master Diskette is available in either 5 1/4" or 3 1/2" formats.

In addition to the material in the lessons, the following features are found at the end of each chapter:

- **TESTS** - Comprehensive end of chapter tests are provided as well as a mid-term and final examination. A full set of answers and a grading key are also included.

- **ANSWERS** - Complete answers are provided for the Review and Exercise problems presented in the text. Where appropriate, answers have also been included on the Master Diskette.

As an added feature, the above material is contained in a 3-ring binder. This not only enables pages to be removed for duplication but also for the insertion of additional teacher notes.

Acknowledgments

The authors would like to thank the following people whose talents contributed to the production of this text.

For their careful review of the text while it was being written we are especially grateful to Arlene Yolles of Ridgefield High School in Ridgefield, Connecticut, Clyde Knowlton of the Horseheads Central School District in Horseheads, New York, Pat Reisdorf of the Foxcroft School in Middleburg, Virginia and Eric Neufer of the Hun School in Princeton, New Jersey. Many of their suggestions have been incorporated in this text.

The imaginative graphics designs were produced by Gregg Schwinn. Marge Vining, of the Rhode Island School of Design, drew the clever cartoons. We very much appreciate both their effort and willingness to work under demanding deadlines.

Thanks are due the staffs at Supertype of the Palm Beaches and Heffernan Press, Inc., especially Bill Daley who was responsible for the printing of the text. For their help with the AppleWorks software we wish to thank Allison Elliot and Elisa Nakata at Claris Corporation.

The success of this and many of our other texts is due to the efforts of Heidi Crane, Vice President of Marketing at Lawrenceville Press. She has developed the promotional material which has been so well received by schools around the world. We are also indebted to the staff and sales force at Delmar Publishers who so effectively market Lawrenceville Press books.

We would like to thank the St. Andrew's School for allowing us the flexible schedules to produce this text. A very special note of appreciation is due our colleague in the Computer Science department and friend, Ruth Wagy, who has generously shared with us materials developed in her applications courses. She has also helped test this text in her classes and has offered many valuable suggestions on ways in which it could be improved. David Attis, one of our most talented students, was helpful in reviewing this text.

Finally, we would like to thank our students, for whom and with whom this text was written. Their candid evaluation of each lesson and their refusal to accept anything less than perfect clarity in explanation have been the driving forces behind the creation of *An Introduction to Computing Using AppleWorks*.

About the Authors

Bruce W. Presley, a graduate of Yale University, taught computer science and physics at The Lawrenceville School in Lawrenceville, New Jersey for twenty-four years where he served as the director of the Karl Corby Computer and Mathematics Center. Mr. Presley was a member of the founding committee of the Advanced Placement Computer Science examination and continues to serve as a consultant to the College Entrance Examination Board. Presently Mr. Presley, author of more than a dozen computer text books, is president of Lawrenceville Press and teaches computing applications and physics at the St. Andrew's School in Boca Raton, Florida.

William R. Freitas, a graduate in computer science of Rutgers University, is director of development at Lawrenceville Press where he has co-authored several programming texts as well as a number of Teacher's Resource Packages. Mr. Freitas currently teaches computing applications and Advanced Placement Computer Science at the St. Andrew's School in Boca Raton, Florida.

Table of Contents

Chapter Nine - Integrating the Word Processor, Data Base and Spreadsheet

Chapter Ten - An Introduction to Programming Using Applesoft

Chapter Eleven - The Future of Computing: Social and Ethical Implications

Appendix A - AppleWorks Commands and Functions

Appendix B - Using the 'Other Activities' Menu

Chapter 1

The History of Computing

_____

_____

_____

_____

_____

_____

_____

Objectives

After completing this chapter you will be able to:

1. Define what a computer is.

2. Discuss the history of computers.

3. Understand how computers work.

4. Name the components of a modern computer system.

5. Understand the advantages of using a computer.

6. Know what software and hardware are.

*T*his text is about computers: their history, how they process and store data, how they can be programmed and the role they play in modern society. We will employ a popular computer program named AppleWorks to teach you how to use the computer to word process and produce data bases and spreadsheets. Each of these applications will be explained as we proceed.

There are three reasons for learning how to use a computer. The first and most important is to develop problem-solving skills. This is done by learning how to analyze a problem carefully, developing a step-by-step solution, and then using the computer as a tool to produce a solution.

A second reason for learning about computers is to become acquainted with their capabilities and limitations. Because you are a part of a society which is becoming increasingly computerized, learning to use a computer is probably the best way to become familiar with one.

Finally, using a computer can be fun. The intellectual challenge of controlling the operations of a computer is not only rewarding but also an invaluable skill. The techniques learned in this class can be applied to your other subjects, and to your personal and business life as well.

1.1 What is a Computer?

A computer is an electronic machine that accepts information, processes it according to specific instructions, and provides the results as new information. It can store and move large quantities of data at very high speed and even though it cannot think, it can make simple decisions and comparisons. For example, a computer can decide which of two numbers is larger or which of two names comes first alphabetically and then act upon that decision. Although the computer can help to solve a wide variety of problems, it is merely a machine and cannot solve problems on its own. It must be provided with instructions in the form of a computer "program".

A program is a list of instructions written in a special language that the computer understands. It tells the computer which operations to perform and in what sequence to perform them. In this text we will use a computer program called AppleWorks and will also learn how to write our own programs in the BASIC language.

THE HISTORY OF COMPUTERS

Many of the advances made by science and technology are dependent upon the ability to perform complex mathematical calculations and to process large amounts of data. It is therefore not surprising that for thousands of years mathematicians, scientists and business people have searched for "computing" machines that could perform calculations and analyze data quickly and accurately.

1.2 Ancient Counting Machines

As civilizations began to develop, they created both written languages and number systems. These number systems were not originally meant to do mathematical calculations, but rather were designed to record measurements. Roman numerals are a good example of this. Few of us would want to carry out even the simplest arithmetic operations using Roman numerals. How then were calculations performed thousands of years ago?

Calculations were carried out with a device known as an abacus which was used in ancient Babylon, China and throughout Europe until the late middle-ages. Many parts of the world, especially in the Orient, still make use of the abacus. The abacus works by sliding beads back and forth on a frame with the beads on the top of the frame representing fives and on the bottom ones. After a calculation is made the result is written down.

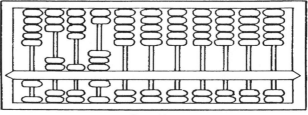

The Abacus

1.3 Arabic Numerals

Toward the end of the middle ages, Roman numerals were replaced by a new number system borrowed from the Arabs, therefore called Arabic numerals. This system uses ten digits and is the system we still use today. Because the Arabic system made calculations with pencil and paper easier, the abacus and other such counting devices became less common. Although calculations were now easier to perform, operations such as multiplication and division were able to be done by only those few mathematicians who were well educated.

1.4 The Pascaline

One of the earliest mechanical devices for calculating was the Pascaline, invented by the French philosopher and mathematician Blaise Pascal in 1642. At that time Pascal was employed in the recording of taxes for the French government. The task was tedious and kept him up until the early hours of the morning day after day. Being a gifted thinker, Pascal thought that the task of adding numbers should be able to be done by a mechanism that would resemble the way a clock keeps time.

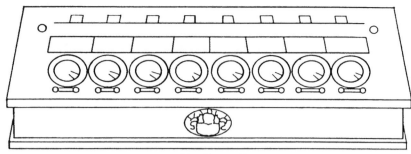

The Pascaline

The Pascaline he invented was a complicated set of gears which could only be used to perform addition and not at all for multiplication or division. Unfortunately, Pascal never got the device to work properly.

1.5 The Stepped Reckoner

Later in the 17th century, Gottfried Wilhelm von Leibniz, a famous mathematician who is credited with being one of the developers of the calculus, invented a device that was supposed to be able to add and subtract, as well as multiply, divide and extract square roots. His device, the Stepped Reckoner, included a cylindrical wheel called the Leibniz wheel and a moveable carriage that was used to enter the number of digits in the multiplicand.

Though both Pascal's and Leibniz's machines held great promise, they did not work well because the craftsmen of their time were unable to make machined parts that were accurate enough to carry out the inventor's design. Because of mechanically unreliable parts, the devices tended to jam and malfunction.

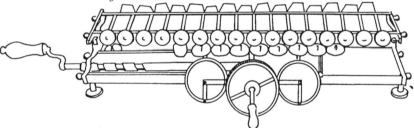

The Stepped Reckoner

1.6 The Punched Card

In 1810 Joseph Jacquard, a French weaver, made a revolutionary discovery. He realized that the weaving instructions for his looms could be stored on cards with holes punched in them. As the cards passed through the loom in sequence, needles passed through the holes and then picked up threads of the correct color or texture. By rearranging the cards, a weaver could change the pattern being woven without stopping the machine to change threads.

Jacquard's Loom

The weaving industry would seem to have little in common with the computer industry, but the idea that information could be stored by punching holes on a card was to be of great use in the later development of the computer.

1.7 Babbage's Difference and Analytical Engines

In 1822 Charles Babbage began work on the Difference Engine. His hope was that this device would calculate numbers to the twentieth place and then print them at forty-four digits a minute. The original purpose of this machine was to produce tables of numbers that would be used by ship's navigators. At the time navigation tables were often highly inaccurate due to calculation errors. In fact, several ships were known to have been lost at sea because of these errors. Again because of the mechanical problems that had plagued Pascal and Leibniz, the Difference Engine never worked properly.

Undaunted, Babbage later planned and began work on a considerably more advanced machine, called the Analytical Engine. This machine was to perform a variety of calculations by following a set of instructions or program entered into it using punched cards similar to the ones used by Joseph Jacquard. During processing, the Analytical Engine was to store information in a memory unit that would allow it to make decisions and then carry out instructions based on those decisions. For example, in comparing two numbers it could be programmed to determine which was larger and then follow different sets of instructions. The Analytical Engine was no more successful than its predecessors, but its design was to serve as a model for the modern computer.

Analytical Engine

Babbage's chief collaborator on the Analytical Engine was Lady Ada Augusta, Countess of Lovelace, the daughter of Lord Byron. Interested in mathematics, Lady Lovelace was a sponsor of the Engine and one of the first people to realize its power and significance. She also tested the device and wrote of its achievements in order to gain support for it. Because of her involvement she is often called the first programmer.

Babbage had hoped that the Analytical Engine would be able to play chess, thinking out and making brilliant moves. Lady Lovelace, however, said that the Engine could never "originate anything", meaning that she did not believe that a machine, no matter how powerful, could think. To this day her statement about computing machines remains true.

1.8 The Electronic Tabulating Machine

By the end of the 19th century, U.S. Census officials were concerned about the time it took to tabulate the count of the continuously increasing number of Americans. This counting was done every ten years, as required by the Constitution. The Census of 1880, however, took nine years to compile, making the figures highly inaccurate by the time they were published.

To solve the problem, Herman Hollerith invented a calculating machine that used electricity rather than mechanical gears. Holes representing information to be tabulated were punched in cards similar to those used in Jacquard's loom, with the location of each hole representing a specific piece of information (male, female, age, etc.). The cards were then inserted into the machine and metal pins used to open and close electrical circuits. If a circuit was closed, a counter was increased by one.

Hollerith's machine was immensely successful. The general count of the population, then 63 million, took only six weeks to calculate, while full statistical analysis took seven years. This may not sound like much of an improvement over the nine years of the previous census, but Hollerith's machine enabled the Census Bureau to make a far more detailed and useful study of the population than had previously been possible. Based on the success of his invention, Hollerith and some friends formed a company that sold his invention all over the world. The company eventually became known as International Business Machines (IBM).

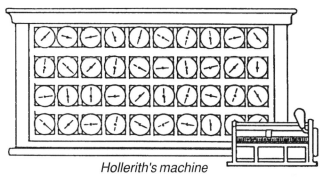

Hollerith's machine

1.9 The Electro-Mechanical Computer

By the 1930's, key-operated mechanical adding machines had been developed which used a complicated assortment of gears and levers. Scientists, engineers and business people, however, needed machines more powerful than adding machines; machines capable of making simple decisions such as determining which of two numbers was larger and then acting upon the decision. A machine with this capability is called a computer rather than a calculator. A calculator can perform calculations, but it can not make decisions.

The first computer-like machine is generally thought to be the Mark I, which was built by a team from IBM and Harvard University under the leadership of Howard Aiken. The Mark I used mechanical telephone relay switches to store information and accepted data on punched cards, processed it and then output the data. Because it could not make decisions about the data it processed, the Mark I was not, however, a real computer but was instead a highly sophisticated calculator. It was, nevertheless, impressive, measuring over 51 feet in length and weighing 5 tons! It also had over 750,000 parts, many of them moving mechanical parts which made the Mark I not only huge but unreliable.

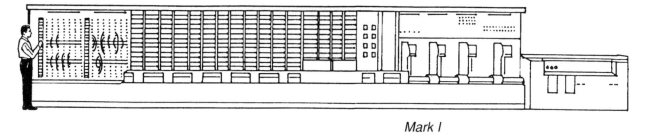

Mark I

1.10 ENIAC, the First Electronic Computer

In June 1943, John Mauchly and J. Prosper Eckert began work on the Electronic Numerical Integration and Calculator, or ENIAC. It was originally a secret military project which began during World War II to calculate the trajectory of artillery shells. Built at the University of Pennsylvania, it was not finished until 1946, after the war had ended. But the great effort put into the ENIAC was not wasted. In one of its first demonstrations it was given a problem that would have taken a team of mathematicians three days to solve. It solved the problem in twenty seconds.

ENIAC was different from the Mark I in several important ways. First, it occupied 1500 square feet, which is the same area taken up by the average three bedroom house and it weighed 30 tons. Second, it used vacuum tubes instead of relay switches. It contained over 17,000 of these tubes, which were the same kind used in radio sets. Because the tubes consumed huge amounts of electricity the computer produced a tremendous amount of heat and required special fans to cool the room where it was installed. Most importantly, because it was able to make decisions, it was the first true computer.

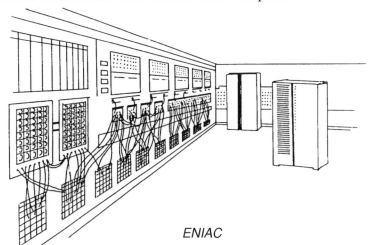

ENIAC

ENIAC had two major weaknesses. First, it was difficult to change its instructions to allow the computer to solve different problems. It had originally been designed only to compute artillery trajectory tables, but when it needed to work on another problem it could take up to three days of wire pulling, replugging and switch-flipping to change instructions. Second, because the tubes it contained were constantly burning out, the ENIAC was unreliable.

1.11 The Stored Program Computer

In the late 1940's, John von Neumann considered the idea of storing computer instructions in a central processing unit, or CPU. This unit would control all the functions of the computer electronically so that it would not be necessary to flip switches or pull wires to change the instructions. Now it would be possible to solve many different problems by simply typing in new instructions at a keyboard. Together with Mauchly and Eckert, von Neumann designed and built the EDVAC (Electronic Discrete Variable Automatic Computer) and the EDSAC (Electronic Discrete Storage Automatic Computer).

With the development of the concept of stored instructions or "programs", the modern computer age was ready to begin. Since then the development of new computers has progressed rapidly, but von Neumann's concept has remained, for the most part, unchanged.

The next computer to employ von Neumann's concepts was the UNIVersal Automatic Computer, called UNIVAC, built by Mauchly and Eckert. The first one was sold to the U.S. Census Bureau in 1951.

Computers at this time continued to use many vacuum tubes which made them large and expensive. UNIVAC weighed 35 tons. These computers were so expensive to purchase and run that only the largest corporations and the U.S. government could afford them. Their ability, however, to calculate at speeds of 1000 calculations per second made them popular.

1.12 The Transistor

It was the invention of the transistor that made smaller and less expensive computers possible, with increased calculating speeds of up to 10,000 calculations per second. Although the size of the computers shrank, they were still large and expensive. In 1963, IBM, using ideas it had learned while working on projects for the military, introduced the first medium-sized computer named the model 650. It was still expensive, but it was capable of handling the flood of paper work produced by many government agencies and businesses. Such organizations provided a ready market for the 650, making it popular in spite of its cost.

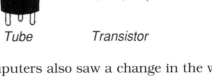

Tube   Transistor

These new computers also saw a change in the way data was stored. Punched cards were replaced by magnetic tape and high speed reel-to-reel tape machines. Using magnetic tape gave computers the ability to read (access) and write (store) data quickly and reliably.

Another important advance occurring at this time was the development of programming languages. Previously, computers had to be programmed by setting different switches to their On or Off positions. The first programming languages were very similar, being strings of 1's and 0's representing the status of the switches (1 for On and 0 for Off). These were called "low-level" languages. Languages such as FORTRAN (FORmula TRANslator), which was the first popular "high-level" language, allowed programmers to write in English-like instructions that had commands like READ and WRITE. With them, it was possible to type instructions directly into the computer, eliminating the time consuming task of re-wiring.

The most widely used high-level programming language today is COBOL. COBOL was first developed by the Department of Defense in 1959 to provide a common language for use on all computers. In fact, COBOL stands for COmmon Business Oriented Language. The designer of COBOL was Grace Murray Hopper, a Commodore in the Navy at the time. Commodore Hopper was the first person to apply the term "debug" to the computer. While working on the Mark II computer in 1945, a moth flew into the circuitry, causing an electrical short which halted the computer. While removing the dead moth, she said that the program would be running again after the computer had been "debugged". Today, the process of removing errors from programs is still called debugging.

A number of new high-level languages have been developed since that time: *BASIC* is a popular language used on microcomputers. You will be introduced to BASIC programming in Chapter 10. *C* is a language designed by Bell Labs for programming large systems and is available on many computers today. Developed by the Swiss computer scientist Niklaus Wirth to teach the fundamentals of programming, *Pascal* is a language used by many schools and universities. The latest language developed by the Department of Defense is named *Ada*, after the first programmer, Ada Augusta the Countess of Lovelace.

1.13 Integrated Circuits

The next major technological advancement was the replacement of transistors by tiny integrated circuits or "chips". Chips are blocks of silicon with logic circuits etched into their surface. They are smaller and cheaper than transistors and can contain thousands of circuits on a single chip. Integrated circuits also give computers tremendous speed allowing them to process information at a rate of 1,000,000 calculations per second.

One of the most important benefits of using integrated circuits is to decrease the cost and size of computers. The IBM System 360 was one of the first computers to use integrated circuits and it was so popular with businesses that IBM had difficulty keeping up with the demand. Computers had come down in size and price to such a point that smaller organizations such as schools and hospitals could now afford them.

1.14 The Microprocessor

The most important advance to occur in the early 70's was the invention of the microprocessor, an entire CPU on a chip. In 1970, Marcian Hoff, an engineer at Intel Corporation, designed the first of these chips. As a result, in 1975 the ALTAIR microcomputer was born. In 1977, working originally out of a garage, Stephen Wozniak and Steven Jobs designed and built the first Apple computer. Microcomputers were now inexpensive and therefore available to many people. Because of these advances almost anyone could own a machine that had more computing power and was faster and more reliable than either the ENIAC or UNIVAC. As a comparison, if the cost of a sports car had dropped as quickly as that of a computer, a new Porsche would now cost about one dollar.

1.15 Mainframe, Mini and Microcomputers

There are three general size categories by which computers are classified. The choice of which size computer to use depends on what tasks are planned for it and how much data it must store.

Mainframe computers are large computer systems costing many hundreds of thousands, if not millions, of dollars. Because they are so large, mainframes can carry out many different tasks at the same time. They are used by large corporations, banks, government agencies and universities. Mainframes can calculate a payroll, keep the records for a bank, handle the reservations for an airline or store student information for a university - tasks requiring the storage and processing of huge amounts of information.

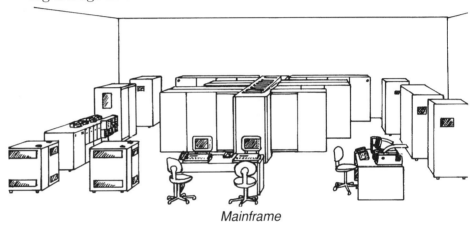

Mainframe

Minicomputers are smaller than mainframes, usually taking up the space of one or two small bookcases. They are also less expensive, costing from about ten thousand to about one hundred thousand dollars. Minicomputers are used by smaller businesses, schools and research institutions. Like mainframes, minicomputers can do more than one task at a time. Although minicomputers store large amounts of data, they cannot store as much as a mainframe or process it as fast.

Minicomputer

Most people using mainframe and minicomputers communicate with them by using "terminals". A terminal consists of a keyboard where commands and data are entered and monitors which display the output produced by the computer. The terminal is connected by wires to the computer, which may be located on a different floor or in a different building a few blocks away. Some mainframe computers have over a hundred terminals attached and working at the same time.

Microcomputers are small and usually inexpensive. Often called "personal computers" or PC's, they can cost as little as one hundred dollars and fit on a desk top. Unlike mainframes and mini-computers, most microcomputers can only carry out one task at a time. During the past few years the processing speed and ability of micro-computers to store large quantities of data has increased at such a rapid rate that some of them now rival both mini and mainframe computers. The computer you will use is a microcomputer. In a microcomputer, the monitor and keyboard are attached to the computer allowing only one person to use it at a time.

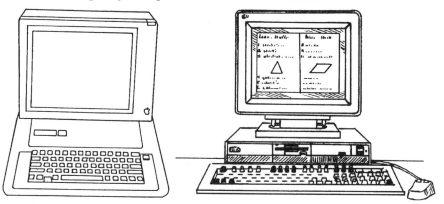

Modern microcomputers

1.16 How Computers Work

All computers process information, or "data". This data may be in the form of numbers, letters, words, pictures or symbols.

In order to process data, a computer must carry out four specific activities:

1. Input data
2. Store data while it is being processed
3. Process data according to specific instructions
4. Output the results in the form of new data

As an example of computer processing, it is possible to input a list containing the names and addresses of one hundred thousand people and then ask the computer to search through this data and print only the names and addresses of those people who live in Florida. Another example would be to ask the computer to add all integers from 1 to 1000 and print their sum (i.e. $1 + 2 + 3... + 1000 = ?$). In each of these examples, data must be input so that it may be processed by the computer. In the first case, the data is a list of names and addresses, while in the second, a list of numbers.

1.17 The Components of a Computer

Computers contain four major components. Each component performs one of the four tasks we have described:

1. Input Device: a device from which the computer can accept data. Keyboards and disk drives are examples of input devices.

2. Memory: an area inside the computer where data can be stored electronically.

3. Central Processing Unit (CPU): processes data and controls the flow of data between the computer's other units. It is here that the computer makes decisions.

4. Output Device: a device that displays or stores processed data. Monitors and printers are the most common visual output devices while disks drives are the most common storage devices.

The following diagram illustrates the direction in which data flows between the separate units:

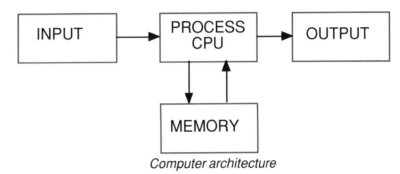

Computer architecture

Notice that all information first flows through the CPU. Because one of the tasks of the CPU is to control the order in which tasks are completed, it is often referred to as the "brain" of the computer. This comparison with the human brain, however, has an important flaw. The CPU only executes tasks according to the instructions it has been given; it cannot think for itself.

1.18 Advantages of a Computer

Although computers cannot think, they do have some advantages over the human brain. For example, suppose you were read a list of ten numbers (input) and were asked to first, remember them (memory), second, calculate the average (process), and third, write down the average (output). In so doing, you would carry out the same four tasks as a computer. Now suppose you were read 100 or 1000 numbers and asked to calculate the average. Chances are you would get confused and tired performing all the calculations. The computer would have none of these problems. It would accurately remember all of the data and be able to quickly calculate the answers. The computer, therefore, has three important advantages over the human brain:

1. Reliable memory, with the ability to store and recall large amounts of data over long periods of time.

2. Speed, which enables it to process data quickly.

3. The ability to work 24 hours a day without rest.

Remember, however, that as reliable and fast as a computer is, it is only as "smart" as the instructions it is given by its program.

1.19 Hardware and Software

A computer requires both "hardware" and "software" to make it work. Hardware refers to the physical parts that make up a computer system and include keyboards, printers, memory units, CPU's, monitors, and disk drives. Software, on the other hand, describes the instructions or the program that is given the computer. Some software is made a permanent part of most computers, so that the tasks a computer must always be ready to perform can be carried out easily. Other software is entered into the computer only when a specific task is required. In this text we will make use of applications software written to perform a number of different tasks.

1.20 Memory

Most computers have two types of memory contained on chips, ROM and RAM. Read Only Memory or ROM contains the most basic operating instructions for the computer. It is made a permanent part of the computer and cannot be changed. The instructions in ROM enable the computer to complete simple jobs such as placing a character on the screen or checking the keyboard to see if any keys have been pressed.

Random Access Memory or RAM is temporary memory where data and instructions can be stored. Data stored here can be changed or erased. When the computer is first turned on this part of memory is empty and when turned off, any data it stores is lost. Because RAM storage is temporary, computers use disks as auxiliary memory storage. Before turning the computer off, the data stored in RAM can be saved as output on a disk so that it can be used again at a later time.

1.21 Central Processing Unit

The Central Processing Unit (CPU) directs all the activities of the computer. It can only follow instructions that it receives either from ROM or from a program stored in RAM. In following these instructions, the CPU guides the processing of information throughout the computer.

The Arithmetic Logic Unit, or ALU, is the part of the CPU where the "intelligence" of the computer is located. It can perform only two operations. It can add numbers and compare numbers. Then the question is: How does the computer subtract, multiply or divide numbers? The answer is by first turning problems like multiplication and division into addition problems. This would seem to be a very inefficient way of doing things, but it works because the ALU is so fast. For example, to solve the problem 5 x 2, the computer adds 5 two's, 2 + 2 + 2 + 2 + 2 to calculate the answer, 10. The time it takes the ALU to carry out a single addition of this type is measured in nanoseconds (billionths of a second). The other job of the ALU is to compare numbers and then decide whether a number is greater than, less than or equal to another number. This ability is the basis of the computer's decision-making power.

1.22 How the Computer Follows Instructions

Memory storage, both RAM and ROM, and the CPU are made of tiny chips of silicon. These chips are so small that they must be housed in special plastic cases that have metal pins coming out of them. The pins allow the chips to be plugged into circuit boards that have their wiring printed on them.

Chips are covered by intricate circuits that have been etched into their surface and then coated with a metallic oxide that fills in the etched circuit patterns. This enables the chips to conduct electricity along the many paths of its circuits. Because there are as many as millions of circuits on a single chip, the chips are called integrated circuits.

The electrical circuits on a chip have one of two states, OFF or ON. Therefore, a system was developed that uses only two numbers, 0 and 1: 0 representing OFF and 1 representing ON. A light switch is similar to a single computer circuit. If the light is off, it represents a 0, and if on, a 1. This number system, which uses only two digits, is called the "binary" (base 2) system.

Humans find a system with ten digits, 0 to 9, easier to use primarily because we have ten fingers. The computer uses binary digits to express not only numbers, but all information, including letters of the alphabet. Because of this a special code had to be established to translate numbers, letters and characters into binary digits. This code has been standardized for computers as the American Standard Code for Information Interchange, or ASCII. In this code, each letter of the alphabet, both upper and lower case, and each symbol, digit and control function used by the computer is represented by a number. The name JIM, for example, is translated by the computer into the ASCII numbers 74, 73, 77. In turn these numbers are then stored by the computer in binary form:

Letter	ASCII	Binary code
J	74	01001010
I	73	01001001
M	77	01001101

1.23 Bits and Bytes

Each 0 or 1 in the binary code is called a "bit" (BInary digiT) and these bits are grouped by the computer into 8 bit units called "bytes". Each ASCII code is one byte in length. Note how eight 0's and 1's are used to represent each letter in JIM in binary form.

The size of the memory of a computer is measured by the number of bytes that make up its RAM. A computer might have, for example, 64K of RAM. In computers and electronics, K represents 2^{10} which equals 1024. The letter K comes from the word kilo, which means 1000, and although 1024 is more than 1000, K is still used as the abbreviation. 64K of memory, therefore, is really 64×2^{10} which is 65536 bytes.

It is possible to give a computer its instructions directly in binary code, typing in 0's and 1's using what is called "machine language". This is extremely difficult to do, which is the reason that high-level programming languages have been developed. The English word instructions from these languages are translated by the computer into binary code. The software we will use in the applications chapters of this text to do word processing, data base and spreadsheet applications has already been programmed making it easy for us to use.

1.24 Applications Software

One of the most useful ways in which a computer can be used is to run commercially produced "applications software". This is software written by professional programmers to perform specific applications or tasks. In this text we will use an applications program named AppleWorks which includes three applications: word processing, data base and spreadsheet.

Word processing allows us to enter text from the keyboard into the computer and then manipulate it electronically. We will be able to insert and delete text, correct mistakes, move text and perform numerous other functions all on the computer screen. The text will then be able to be printed.

Data bases allow us to store and manipulate large quantities of data using the computer. For example, a data base can store the names, addresses, grades and extra-curricular activities for all of the students in a school. It will be possible to add or delete data and produce printed reports using the data base.

Spreadsheets primarily store numeric data which can then be used in calculations. We will use a spreadsheet to store a teacher's grades and then calculate student averages. The primary advantage of a computerized spreadsheet is its ability to redo the calculations should the data it stores be changed.

One common factor shared by these three applications is their ability to store data on disk in a "file". A file is simply a collection of data stored on a disk in a form the computer can read. Unlike the computer's RAM memory, data placed in a file is not erased when the computer's power is turned off. This way, the applications program can access the information again and again.

A major advantage of AppleWorks is that it is an "integrated" program. This means that a single program performs all three applications, allowing data stored in a file by one application to be transferred to another. Later in this course you will produce a data base file of names and addresses and then use this file in conjunction with a word processor file to produce personalized letters to everyone in the data base file.

Besides integrated programs like AppleWorks there are numerous other applications programs available. There are programs that can be used by musicians to produce musical scores and then play them on a synthesizer, programs that assist an architect in designing a building, programs that produce the special effects graphics that you see in the movies and on television, and much more. This book, for example, has been created and typeset using applications software.

As we progress in this text the usefulness of applications software will become increasingly obvious. With computers becoming more widely used in almost every facet of professional life, applications software is being written to assist people in all professions. Learning AppleWorks will give you an idea of how the computer and applications software can be applied to help solve many types of problems.

Chapter Summary

Man has searched for a machine to calculate and record data for thousands of years. The earliest of these devices were mechanical, requiring gears, wheels and levers, and were often unreliable. The advent of electricity brought about machines which used vacuum tubes, and were capable of performing thousands of calculations a minute. The unreliability of the vacuum tube lead to the development of the transistor and integrated circuit. Computers based on these devices were smaller, faster, more reliable and less expensive than before.

All computers have several parts in common: (1) an input device which allows data and commands to be entered into it, (2) some way of storing commands and data, (3) a Processing Unit which controls the processing, and (4) some way of returning the processed information in the form of output. In general, a computer is a machine which accepts information, processes it according to some specific instructions called a program, and then returns new information as output.

Today's microcomputer makes use of a CPU on a chip, the microprocessor which controls the actions of the computer. Based on von Neumann's concept, the computer stores both data and instruction in its memory at the same time. Memory comes in two forms, RAM chips which can be erased and used over, and ROM chips, which is permanent. Keyboards and disk drives are used to input data. Monitors and printers are used to output data. Because the contents of RAM are lost when the computer's power is turned off, disks are used to store data. The CPU contains a special device called the Arithmetic Logic Unit (ALU) which performs any math or comparison operations.

Vocabulary

ALU - Arithmetic Logic Unit, the part of the CPU that handles math operations.

ASCII - American Standard Code for Information Interchange, the code used for representing characters in the computer.

Bit - Binary Digit, a single 0 or 1 in a binary number.

Byte - A group of 8 bits.

CPU - Central Processing Unit, the device which electronically controls the functions of the computer.

Data - Information either entered into or produced by the computer.

Hardware - Physical devices which make up the computer and its peripherals.

Input - Data used by the computer.

K, kilobyte - Measurement of computer memory capacity, 1024 bytes.

Keyboard - Device resembling a typewriter used for inputting data into a computer.

Memory - Electronic storage used by the computer.

Microprocessor - CPU on a single chip.

Monitor - Television-like device used to display computer output.

Output - Data produced by a computer program.

Peripheral - Secondary hardware device connected to a computer such as a printer, monitor or disk drive.

Program - Series of instructions written in a special language directing the computer to perform certain tasks.

PC - Personal Computer, a small computer employing a microprocessor.

RAM - Random Access Memory, memory which the computer can both read and write

ROM - Read Only Memory, memory from which the computer can read only.

Software - Computer programs.

Reviews

Sections 1.1-1.10

1. What is the primary difference between a computer and a calculator?

2. What is a computer program?

3. Why did early calculating devices not work well?

4. Was Pascal's Pascaline a computer? Why or why not?

5. If successful, could Babbage's Analytical Engine been considered a computer? Why or why not?

6. a) What was the first calculating machine to make use of punched cards?
   b) What were the cards used for?

7. Why did scientists and business people want computers rather than calculators?

8. a) The Mark I was considered a calculator rather than a computer. Why?
   b) Why was the Mark I unreliable?
   c) What was the most important difference between the ENIAC and Mark I?

Sections 1.11-1.15

9. John von Neumann made one of the most important contributions to the development of modern computers. What was this contribution and why was it so important?

10. What made early computers so expensive?

11. What two innovations made the IBM Model 650 superior to earlier computers?

12. High level programming languages such as FORTRAN and BASIC were developed in the 1960's. Why were they important?

13. a) What is an integrated circuit?
    b) In what ways is it superior to a transistor?

14. What invention made the microcomputer possible?

15. Compare a microcomputer like the Apple with ENIAC. What advantages does the microcomputer have?

16. List three jobs which could best be performed on each of the following computers:

    a) mainframe computer
    b) minicomputer
    c) microcomputer

17. Suppose you were to use a computer to store the names of all the students in your school and then print only those names beginning with the letter "P". Explain how each of the four activities needed to process data would be performed.

Sections 1.16-1.24 18. List three tasks for which a computer would be better than a human working without a computer.

19. a) What is computer hardware?
    b) What is software?

20. Which of the four major components of a computer would be used to perform each of the following tasks?

    a) display a column of grade averages
    b) calculate grade averages
    c) store electronically a set of grades
    d) type in a set of grades
    e) decide which of two grades was higher
    f) store a set of grades outside of the computer

21. What is the primary difference between the two types of memory contained in a computer?

22. How would the computer solve the problem 138 x 29?

23. Why does the computer use binary numbers?

24. How does the computer store a person's name in memory?

25. a) What is a bit?
    b) A byte?
    c) A K?

26. How many bytes of memory does a 256K computer contain?

27. What is applications software?

Chapter 2

Introducing the Word Processor

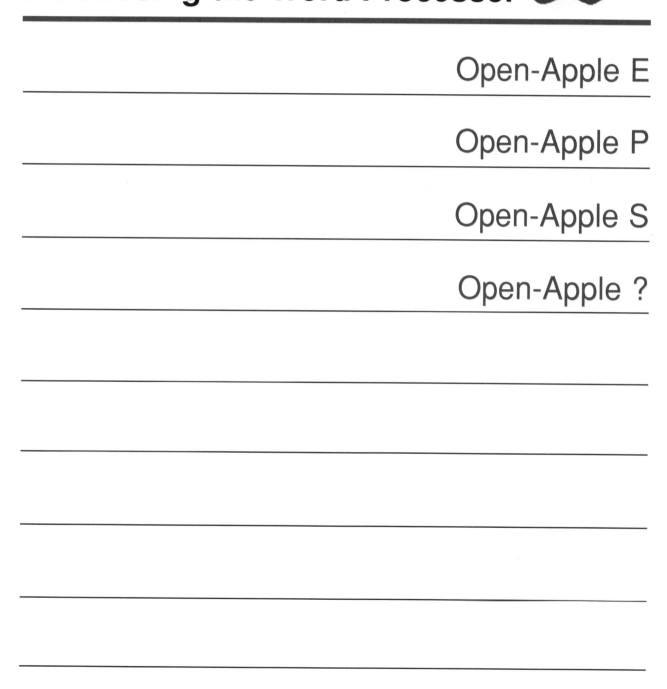

Open-Apple E

Open-Apple P

Open-Apple S

Open-Apple ?

Objectives

After completing this chapter you will be able to:

1. Describe what a word processor is.

2. Explain the capabilities that a word processor has that makes it more powerful than a typewriter.

3. Start AppleWorks and enter the date.

4. Select menus from the Main Menu and choose different options from them.

5. Create a new word processor file from scratch.

6. Use the Word Processor to enter and modify text in a document.

7. Save a document on the disk.

8. Load a previously saved document from the disk to the Desktop.

9. Print a word processed document

10. Exit AppleWorks properly.

*T*his chapter describes what a word processor is, and why it is a powerful tool for preparing documents. Directions for starting the computer, using floppy disks and running the AppleWorks program are given. You will use the word processor to create, edit, print and save a document.

2.1 What is a Word Processor?

A word processor is basically a computerized typewriter. Therefore, using a typewriter and a word processor are alike in some important ways. Both use similar keyboards to enter data and both produce easy to read, professional looking documents. A word processor, however, has some powerful capabilities not shared by a typewriter. One of the most useful of these is the ability to easily make changes in a document.

The superiority of a word processor over a typewriter can be demonstrated by comparing their abilities to correct mistakes. When a typist makes a mistake on a typewriter, the error is immediately printed on the page. If the error is simple, an eraser or white-out can be used to eliminate it. If the error is large, involving many words, the typist may decide to throw the page away and start over.

When a word processor is used, the words typed are transferred from the keyboard into the computer's memory rather than on to paper. This allows the document to be edited electronically on the screen before it is printed. Instead of being forced to re-type an entire page to correct a simple error or make an editing change, a word processor allows only those words requiring changes to be re-typed. Words, phrases and even whole paragraphs can be inserted, changed or deleted. The computer automatically adjusts the position of words in the document, pushing them forward or backward as needed to accommodate the changes. Pieces of the document can also be moved or copied from one place to another. The word processor allows the document to be continually refined by making changes until what has been written truly reflects what you wish to say. This process is helpful in improving the quality of your writing.

Another useful feature of word processing is the flexibility it provides when deciding how a document is to look. Does the document look better with a half inch margin or an inch margin? Should a paper be double spaced or single spaced? Word processed documents can be displayed in different formats on the screen and compared without any re-typing. When the desired format has been determined, the document may be printed.

What immediately distinguishes word processors from even the most sophisticated typewriter is that a word processor can save an entire document on a disk. The saved document can then be recalled at any time, and another copy printed or changes made. It is also possible to combine pieces of one document with another, so that lengthy paragraphs and even whole pages can be included in a new document without their having to be re-typed.

GETTING STARTED ON THE COMPUTER

You are now ready to start using the computer. This chapter will take a "hands on" the computer approach to introduce word processing and editing skills. You will learn how to start the computer and run the AppleWorks program. Simple "text" (characters, words and phrases) will be entered in the word processor to demonstrate how it may be edited, printed and saved.

2.2 Using Disks

Disks will be used both to start the computer and to save any files that you create. It is important to handle the disks carefully because they store large quantities of data in a magnetic format that is vulnerable to dirt and heat. Observing the following rules will help to insure that your disks give you trouble free service:

1. Keep disks away from electrical and magnetic devices such as computer monitors, television sets, stereos and any type of magnet.

2. Make sure that your disks are not exposed to either extreme cold or heat. Being made of plastic they are sensitive to temperature.

3. Be careful not to allow dust, dirt, or moisture to penetrate the disk by keeping it in its sleeve when not in use.

4. Never touch the disk except by the edges of its jacket. Touching the disk's magnetic surface will usually damage it, destroying valuable data.

5. Do not bend or crimp the disk and never place paper clips on it.

2.3 How To Use This Text

Throughout this text new commands and procedures will be introduced in a two-step process. First, the command or procedure will be discussed. You will be told what the command does and how to apply it, but will not use the computer at this time. Second, the discussion will be followed by a section titled *Practice*. Each Practice will lead you through a step-by-step example of how to use the command on the computer. You should actually perform the steps given in a Practice on the computer using AppleWorks. Practices also serve as reviews of the steps required to perform specific tasks. Because the discussion sections explain the details of what is to be demonstrated, you should read them carefully before proceeding to the Practice.

2.4 Starting the Computer

Before using AppleWorks, it is first necessary to load the disk operating system (ProDOS) into the computer's memory. ProDOS contains special programs that the computer needs in order to run. The process of transferring ProDOS from disk to computer memory is called "booting". The following instructions assume that you have two disks, one that contains ProDOS and AppleWorks (STARTUP), and another for storing the files you create (DATA). Your STARTUP disk has been prepared so that ProDOS will load automatically. After ProDOS has booted, the AppleWorks program will automatically run.

Practice 1

In this Practice, you will turn on the computer, boot ProDOS and start the AppleWorks program. The date will be entered if your computer does not have a built-in clock.

1) BOOT PRODOS AND START APPLEWORKS

   a. Place the STARTUP disk carefully in drive 1 (normally the top drive or left hand drive) with its label up and towards you as shown in the diagram:

Be careful when placing disks into the computer

   b. Place your DATA disk in drive 2.
   c. Close the drive door and then turn on both the computer and the monitor. After a few seconds, the red "in use" light on the disk drive will come on and the computer will automatically load ProDOS from the disk. Never open the drive door when the light is on because this may damage the disk.

After ProDOS has been loaded, the AppleWorks program will run and you will see a copyright screen similar to the following:

```
                          TM
                 AppleWorks
              Integrated Software




      By R.J. Lissner and CLARIS Corporation
   Enhanced by Alan Bird, Randy Brandt and Bob Renstrom

      Copyright CLARIS Corporation   1983-89   V3.0
   Portions copyright CLARIS Corp, Alan Bird, and Beagle Bros, Inc.
              All Rights Reserved

   ---------------------------------------------------------------
```

   d. Press the Space Bar to continue.

2) ENTER THE DATE

If your computer does not have a built-in clock, you will be prompted to enter today's date using the form shown on the screen:

Type today's date or press Return: 6/27/91

Enter today's date and press the key marked Return. (Note that on some computers this key is marked "Enter".) Pressing the Return key enters whatever has been typed into the computer's memory. If you make a mistake when entering the date, press the key marked Esc and start over. AppleWorks will not accept an invalid date.

If you have a computer with extra memory, such as the IIGS, a portion of the AppleWorks program may be loaded into the extra memory. If so, you will see the message:

Preloading AppleWorks

2.5 The Main Menu

After it has been loaded, AppleWorks displays the following screen, which is called the "Main Menu". A menu is a list of options from which you may choose:

```
Disk: Disk 2 (Slot 6)                   MAIN MENU
_____

        _____
       |   Main Menu       |_____
       |                                                    |
       |    1. Add files to the Desktop                     |
       |                                                    |
       |    2. Work with one of the files on the Desktop    |
       |                                                    |
       |    3. Save Desktop files to disk                   |
       |                                                    |
       |    4. Remove files from the Desktop                |
       |                                                    |
       |    5. Other Activities                             |
       |                                                    |
       |    6. Quit                                         |
       |_____|


_____
Type number, or use arrows, then press Return      ⌘-? for Help
```

Available options on a menu are numbered. To select an option, either type its number or use the up and down-arrow keys (↑,↓) to highlight it and then press the Return key. Because 'Add files to the Desktop' is already highlighted, simply pressing Return will select it.

AppleWorks has a number of other menus besides the Main Menu. In most of these menus, an initial selection called the "default" will already be highlighted (like 'Add files' in the menu above). If that selection is the one you desire, all that need be done is to press the Return key. If another selection is desired it must be highlighted using the arrow keys, or the corresponding number typed, and then Return pressed. As you progress in using AppleWorks you will have the opportunity to work with the other menu options.

2.6 The AppleWorks Desktop

AppleWorks is set up to work like an office. In an office, different business documents are stored in "files" in a filing cabinet. Before a file may be used, it must be taken from the cabinet and placed on a desk. In AppleWorks, each word processed document, data base and spreadsheet is stored in a different file on a disk. (Data base and spreadsheet files will be explained later in this text.) Before a file may be used, it must be electronically transferred from the disk to the computer's memory. AppleWorks refers to the area of memory containing files to be worked on as the "Desktop". In order to create a new Word Processor document, a new, empty file must first be added to the Desktop.

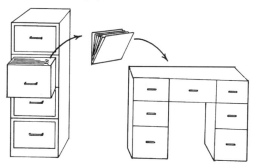

2.7 Adding Files to the Desktop

Files are placed on the Desktop using the first option in the Main Menu, 'Add files to the Desktop'. Because this option is already highlighted, pressing the Return key will execute it and display the Add Files menu:

```
Disk: Disk 2 (Slot 6)            ADD FILES            Escape: Main Menu
_____

       _____
      |   Main Menu            |_____
      |                                                               |
      |   _____                                    |
      |  |   Add Files           |_____|__
      |  |                                                                |
      |  |                                                                |
      |  |   Get files from:                                              |
      |  |                                                                |
      |  |   1. The current disk: Disk 2 (Slot 6)                         |
      |  |   2. A different disk                                          |
      |  |                                                                |
      |  |   Make a new file for the:                                     |
      |  |                                                                |
      |  |   3. Word Processor                                            |
      |__|   4. Data Base                                                 |
      |      5. Spreadsheet                                               |
      |_____|


Type number, or use arrows, then press Return              348K Avail.
```

Option 3 is used to create a new file for the Word Processor. Note that the outline of the Main Menu is shown behind the Add Files menu. As you choose different options, new menus will be shown "stacked" on top of the previous ones. This allows you to see the different "levels" of the menus, showing their relationship to the options previously chosen. Should you display a menu by mistake, the menu directly behind it can be reached by pressing the key marked Esc (for "escape"). This is noted in the upper right-hand corner of the screen which says that pressing the Escape key at this point will return you to the Main Menu.

AppleWorks has two different ways to create a Word Processor file. To create a new file, the 'From scratch' option is used. Because this is the default, pressing the Return key will select it. The second method will not be discussed in this text.

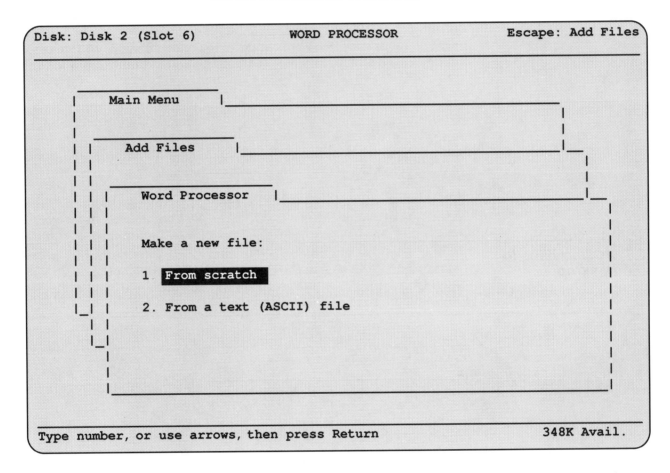

AppleWorks requires that all files be given names. This is necessary so that it can distinguish one file from another. Before AppleWorks can create a new Word Processor file you must first name the file. After selecting 'From scratch' from the Word Processor menu, AppleWorks asks "Type a name for this new file:". At this point the name is entered and Return pressed. Questions such as this are called "prompts" because AppleWorks is prompting you to enter some information, in this case the name of a file.

2.8 The Word Processor Screen

After the Word Processor menu option is selected and a file name supplied (in this case the name Example was used) the following screen appears:

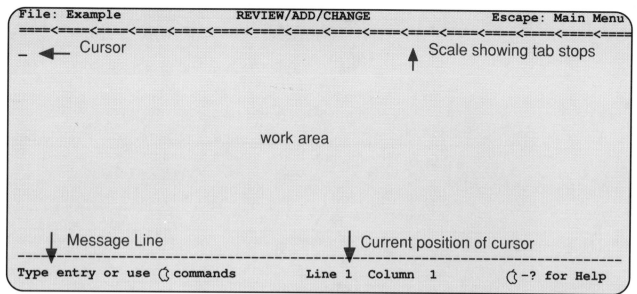

The Word Processor screen contains several features that will be important as you learn to use the word processor. Note the Message Line at the bottom of the screen which is used to display various messages about the current status of AppleWorks. AppleWorks also uses the Message Line to inform you of the actions that may be taken. The current message says that text may be typed into the word processor or that "Open-Apple commands" may be used. Open-Apple commands are used to access AppleWorks functions and will be discussed as we proceed. The center of the screen is called the work area. Any text typed into the word processor appears in this area. The blinking underline at the top left-hand side of the screen is called the "cursor". It shows where characters typed into the word processor will appear. The Message Line also shows the position of the cursor, currently in column 1 of line 1.

Whenever the Word Processor screen is displayed it is possible to enter text (characters, words and phrases) into the file whose name appears in the upper left-hand corner. Any text typed on the keyboard will appear on the screen at the current position of the cursor. As we will see later, after text has been entered it is possible to make changes to it and perform several powerful operations on it.

Practice 2

The following instructions assume that both ProDOS and AppleWorks have been loaded as described in Practice 1. You should have the AppleWorks Main Menu on the screen.

1) SELECT 'ADD FILES TO THE DESKTOP' FROM THE MAIN MENU

   Because 'Add Files' is the default option and has already been highlighted, simply press Return to select it.

2) SELECT 'MAKE A NEW WORD PROCESSOR FILE' FROM THE ADD FILES MENU

   a. Press 3. Note that the highlight moves to the 'Make a new Word Processor file' option.
   b. Press Return to execute this option.

3) SELECT 'FROM SCRATCH' FROM THE WORD PROCESSOR MENU

'From Scratch' is the default option so press Return.

4) SUPPLY A NAME FOR THE NEW WORD PROCESSOR FILE

The prompt

`Type a name for this new file:`

is shown on the Message Line. Type the name Example and press Return. If you make a mistake while entering the file name, press the Escape key and start over.

<u>Check</u> - The Word Processor screen should appear with the file name Example in the upper left-hand corner:

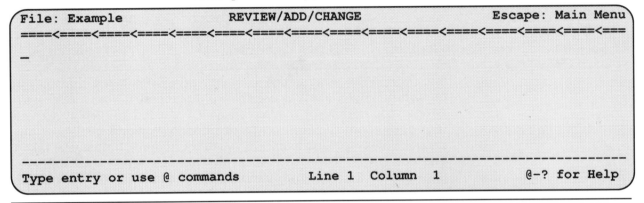

2.9 The Computer Keyboard and Word Processing

Before proceeding, take time to familiarize yourself with some of the keys needed to do word processing. Most of the keys work just as they do on a typewriter, but some have special features. Information will be provided on additional keys as they are needed.

<u>Cursor control "arrow" Keys</u>:
When the Word Processor screen is first displayed, a small blinking underline called the "cursor" appears in the upper left corner of the work area. The cursor can be moved around the screen, without erasing or entering text, using the cursor control keys which are marked with arrows (up, down, left and right). To move the cursor down one line press the key marked with a down-arrow. Similarly, to move the cursor up, left or right, use the keys marked with the appropriate arrows. Each of these keys is a repeat key, meaning that it will continue moving the cursor as long as it is held down. As the cursor is moved, the numbers in the Message Line at the bottom of the screen change to show its position.

<u>Delete and insert</u>:
The Delete key is used to erase a character. Pressing Delete erases the character directly to the left of the cursor. When a character is deleted any characters to its right are automatically moved over to close the gap left by the deleted character.

To insert text the cursor is first placed where the new material is to appear using the cursor control keys and the new material typed. AppleWorks will automatically insert the characters you type at the current cursor position. Any material following the insertion is moved to the right to accommodate the insertion. Deleting and inserting are powerful text editing features. They allow almost any type of change to be made to a document.

Escape:
Esc is used to terminate (escape from) the computer's current operation. The specific effect that pressing the Escape key will have is usually
shown in the upper right-hand corner of the screen. For example,
pressing the Escape key from the Word Processor screen will return you
to the Main Menu.

Return:
Return is used to instruct AppleWorks to accept a menu choice. In the
Word Processor the Return key is also used to end a paragraph or any
line which terminates before it reaches the right-hand side of the
screen, and move the cursor on to the next line.

Practice 3

AppleWorks should still be loaded and the Word Processor
screen displayed from Practice 2. This Practice will direct you to enter
some text into the Example file and then edit it. It also demonstrates the
use of the arrow and Delete keys to insert and delete characters.

1) TYPE THE FOLLOWING LINE INTO THE EXAMPLE FILE

    Use the Shift key to generate the capital letters:

    `Hello, World!`

    Do not press Return yet. Note that the cursor is currently on
    line 1 in column 14.

2) ERASE THE EXCLAMATION POINT (!)

    Press the Delete key once to erase the character to the left of the
    cursor, the exclamation point (!). AppleWorks automatically
    moves the cursor into the space formerly occupied by the
    erased character.

3) MOVE THE CURSOR WITHOUT ERASING ANY TEXT

    Move the cursor under the letter "l" by pressing the left-arrow
    key twice. Note that the left-arrow and the Delete keys both
    move the cursor one place to the left but the Delete key erases
    a character each time it is pressed, while the left-arrow key does
    not.

4) DELETE THE LETTER "r"

    Press the Delete key once. The screen now contains the letters
    "Hello, Wold" with the "l" moving over to occupy the space
    where the "r" was.

5) INSERT A CHARACTER

    Press the `r` key. An "r" is inserted into the line and the "ld"
    characters moved to the right to make room, creating "Hello,
    World".

6) MOVE THE CURSOR WITHOUT ERASING ANY TEXT

    Press the left-arrow key until the cursor is under the "H" in
    "Hello". Press left-arrow again a few times. Note that the cursor
    may not be moved off the work area.

7) DELETE ALL OF THE LETTERS

   a. Move the cursor to column 13 using the right-arrow key.
   b. Continue to press Delete until all of the letters have been deleted.

8) TYPE THE FOLLOWING POEM PRESSING THE RETURN KEY AT THE END OF EACH LINE:

   ```
   Jack and Jill went up the hill,
   to fetch a pail of water.
   Jack fell down and broke his crown
   and Jill came tumbling after.
   ```

   Return is pressed at the end of each line because the lines do not reach the right side of the screen. Use the Delete and arrow keys to correct any typing errors that you may have made.

9) EDIT THE POEM

   Use the Delete and arrow keys and insert new text as necessary to make the following changes in the poem:

   a) insert "BIG" and a space before the word "pail"
   b) change the word "water" to "gold"
   c) change the word "crown" to "arm"
   d) change "came tumbling after" to "stood up and laughed"

Check - The screen should now show the edited poem:

```
File: Example              REVIEW/ADD/CHANGE              Escape: Main Menu
====<====<====<====<====<====<====<====<====<====<====<====<====<====<===
Jack and Jill went up the hill,
to fetch a BIG pail of gold.
Jack fell down and broke his arm
and Jill stood up and laughed._




-----------------------------------------------------------------------
Type entry or use @ commands       Line 4  Column  31        @-? for Help
```

2.10 Saving a Document on Disk

Saving documents on disk is an important part of using a word processor. Because the computer's memory can only store information while the power is on, any data in memory is lost when the power is turned off. However, if a copy of the document is saved on disk before the power is shut off, the document can later be retrieved from the disk and loaded into memory. Unfinished documents, as well as those that might need future editing or re-printing should always be saved.

Another important reason for saving documents is to prevent their accidental loss. A momentary power interruption will wipe everything out of the computer's memory. Even bumping the power cord can sometimes cause the memory to be cleared. It is therefore a good practice, especially when working on long documents, to save the document repeatedly. Then should a power failure occur, the document can be restored from the disk at the point where it was last saved. It is also important to save a document on disk before you attempt to print it because a problem involving the printer could cause the document to be lost if it had not previously been saved.

When a document is saved a copy of what is currently stored in the computer's memory is placed on the disk. It is important to realize that the computer also retains the document in memory so that there are now two copies, one in memory and one on the disk. The copy in memory will be erased when the computer is turned off, but the copy on the disk is permanent and can be recovered at any time.

Documents stored on disk are called "files", and files must be given names by which they can be identified. This name can be up to 15 characters long but may only contain letters, numbers and spaces. Examples of legal file names are LETTER, CHAPTER 2, and CHEM REPORT. It is important to give a file a name that describes what it contains. For example, a file containing a letter to Suzy Jones might better be named SUZY JONES or SUZY LETTER rather than just LETTER. When a new Word Processor file is first created, AppleWorks asks you to supply a name for it. For example, in Practice 2 the file name used was "Example". When that file is saved on disk, AppleWorks uses Example to name that file.

To save a document the Save Desktop Files option from the Main Menu is executed. A copy of the document in the computer's memory is then placed on the disk, using the name that was given when the file was first created.

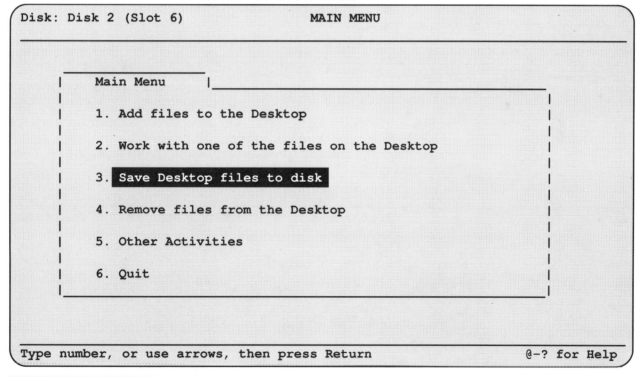

```
Disk: Disk 2 (Slot 6)                    MAIN MENU


     |   Main Menu     |
     |                                                                |
     |   1. Add files to the Desktop                                  |
     |                                                                |
     |   2. Work with one of the files on the Desktop                 |
     |                                                                |
     |   3. Save Desktop files to disk                                |
     |                                                                |
     |   4. Remove files from the Desktop                             |
     |                                                                |
     |   5. Other Activities                                          |
     |                                                                |
     |   6. Quit                                                      |
     |                                                                |


Type number, or use arrows, then press Return          @-? for Help
```

2.11 Quitting AppleWorks

One of the most important procedures to learn is how to quit AppleWorks properly. Whenever you want to stop using AppleWorks either so that another program can be run or the computer turned off, the quit procedure should be performed. If AppleWorks is not properly exited any files that you have created can be damaged or lost. Quitting is accomplished by selecting the 'Quit' option from the Main Menu.

The upper right-hand corner of the Word Processor screen says Escape: Main Menu. This means that pressing the Escape key will display the Main Menu. Option 6 on this menu is Quit, and is selected to exit AppleWorks. Never just turn the computer off before following the Quit procedure. After quitting it is necessary to again boot ProDOS and run the AppleWorks program if you wish to continue working with it.

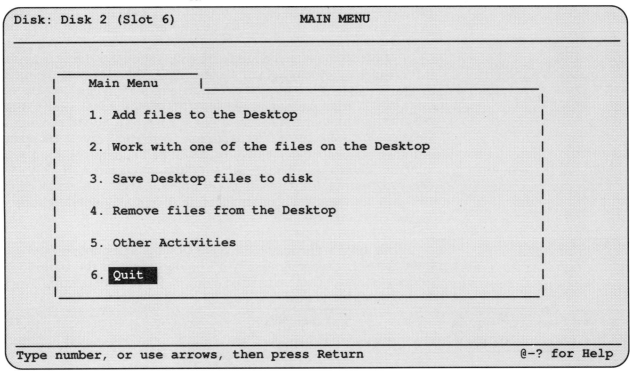

```
Disk: Disk 2 (Slot 6)                    MAIN MENU
 _____
|                                                                    |
    _____
|  | Main Menu     |_____       |
|  |                                                        |        |
|  |  1. Add files to the Desktop                           |        |
|  |                                                        |        |
|  |  2. Work with one of the files on the Desktop          |        |
|  |                                                        |        |
|  |  3. Save Desktop files to disk                         |        |
|  |                                                        |        |
|  |  4. Remove files from the Desktop                      |        |
|  |                                                        |        |
|  |  5. Other Activities                                   |        |
|  |                                                        |        |
|  |  6. Quit                                               |        |
|  |_____|        |
|                                                                    |
 --------------------------------------------------------------------
 Type number, or use arrows, then press Return         @-? for Help
```

If you have created a new file, or made editing changes to a previously created file, AppleWorks will inform you that any new information will be lost if you do not save the file before quitting. If you wish to retain the changes, save the file on disk. If you do not wish to save the new information you may throw out the file and any previously saved version will remain on the disk unchanged.

Practice 4

This Practice saves the Example file created in the previous Practices on disk.

1) RETURN TO THE MAIN MENU

Press Escape to exit the Word Processor screen.

2) CHOOSE THE 'SAVE DESKTOP FILES' OPTION FROM THE MAIN MENU

Type 3 and press Return.

3) SELECT THE FILE NAME FROM THE SAVE FILES MENU

The Save Files menu shows a list of files on the current Desktop. Example should be the only file on your Desktop, so press Return.

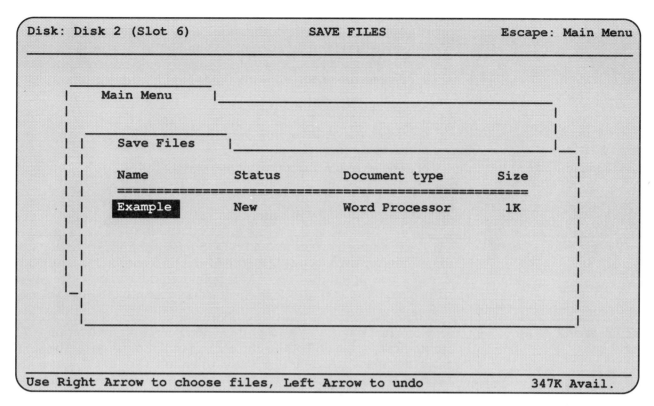

```
Disk: Disk 2 (Slot 6)              SAVE FILES          Escape: Main Menu
_____

     _____
    |   Main Menu        |_____
    |    _____|                                           |
    |   |                                                            |
    |   |  Save Files     |_____|__
    |   |                                                              |
    |   |  Name           Status        Document type        Size      |
    |   |  =========================================================   |
    |   | [Example]       New           Word Processor        1K       |
    |   |                                                              |
    |   |                                                              |
    |   |                                                              |
    |   |                                                              |
    |   |                                                              |
    |   |                                                              |
    |  |_|                                                            |
    |                                                                 |
    |_____|


Use Right Arrow to choose files, Left Arrow to undo         347K Avail.
```

4)   VERIFY THAT EXAMPLE SHOULD BE SAVED ON THE CURRENT DISK

AppleWorks will tell you that you created this file and asks where the file should be saved. Because we want to save the file on the current disk, which is the default, simply press Return.

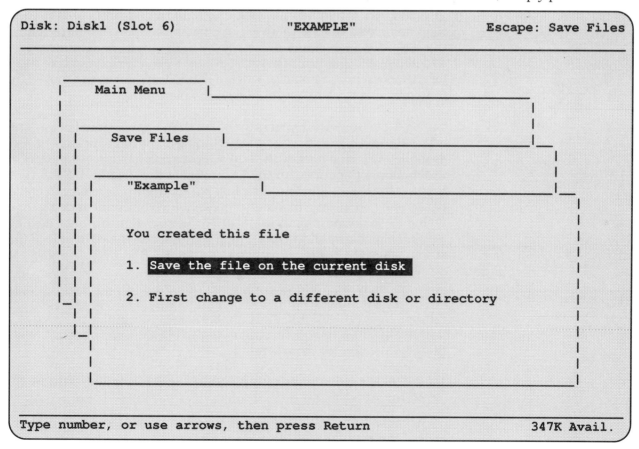

```
Disk: Disk1 (Slot 6)               "EXAMPLE"          Escape: Save Files
_____

       _____
      |   Main Menu        |_____
      |    _____|                                         |
      | |                                                            |
      | |  Save Files     |_____|_
      | |                                                              |
      | |   _____                                        |
      | | |  "Example"        |_____|_
      | | |                                                            |
      | | |                                                            |
      | | |  You created this file                                     |
      | | |                                                            |
      | | |  1. [Save the file on the current disk]                    |
      | | |                                                            |
      |_| |  2. First change to a different disk or directory          |
       | |                                                             |
       |_|                                                             |
        |                                                              |
        |_____|


Type number, or use arrows, then press Return              347K Avail.
```

AppleWorks displays the message "Carefully saving this file", saves the file on the current disk and returns to the Main Menu. Pressing the Escape key at this point would return to the Word Processor screen, allowing the file to be further edited.

5) PROPERLY QUIT APPLEWORKS

    a. Select the 'Quit' option from the Main Menu by typing 6 and pressing Return.

    b. The Message Line displays the prompt:

       `Do you really want to do this?` **No** `Yes`

    Press the Y key to signify Yes.

The screen clears and a ProDOS message appears letting you know that AppleWorks has been exited and the computer is now ready to run a new program. Only at this point can the computer be safely turned off. If you wish to reload AppleWorks you must reboot ProDOS.

2.12 Word Wrap

When using a typewriter it is often necessary to determine if a word will fit on the end of the current line or if it must go on the next. Such decisions are not necessary when using a word processor because the computer will determine if there is sufficient room for a word at the end of a line. If not, the word will automatically be moved to the beginning of the next line in a process called "word wrap" or "wrap around".

One of the advantages of allowing AppleWorks to determine the arrangement of the words on a line can be seen when deleting or inserting text. When new words are added to a line, any words to their right are moved over. If there is not enough room on the current line, those words which do not fit are moved to the next line. There may be a "domino" effect as words move from one line to the next to make room for the added text. Similarly, when deleting text, words are moved up from previous lines to accommodate the change.

Sometimes the typist rather than the computer must determine where the end of one line and the beginning of the next are located. For example, you must specify the end of a paragraph by pressing Return, which moves the cursor to the beginning of the next line. Each time Return is pressed again a blank line is produced. Therefore, to end a paragraph and insert a blank line, press Return twice and then resume typing at the beginning of the next paragraph. Return must also be pressed to end any short lines which do not reach the right side of the screen, as in the poem you entered in Practice 3.

Practice 5

This Practice demonstrates word wrap and how paragraphs are created. Boot ProDOS and start AppleWorks as described in Practice 1 if you have not already done so. A new Word Processor file named News Story will be created from scratch.

1) CREATE A NEW WORD PROCESSOR FILE FROM THE ADD FILES MENU

    a. Select the 'Add files' option from the Main Menu.

    b. Make a new Word Processor file, option 3.

   c. Select the 'From scratch' option.
   d. At the prompt

```
Type a name for this new file:
```

   type `News Story` and press Return.

2) ENTER THE FOLLOWING STORY

Type in the story below, allowing the computer to determine the end of lines. Press Return only at the end of a paragraph or a line which does not reach the right margin:

```
The Senior Prom will be held in the main ballroom of the
downtown Hilton, at 7:30 PM next Saturday night. Music for dancing
will be provided by the Tom Steves Trio. All Juniors and Seniors and
their dates are invited, and tickets are $25.00 per couple.

The menu for the evening's event will be:

    Fruit cup
    Roast Duck a l'Orange with Wild Rice stuffing
    Garden salad
    Mint parfait

After dinner, dancing will continue until 11:30 PM. An after-
Prom party will take place in the school's cafeteria immediately
following.
```

3) SAVE THE FILE ON DISK

   a. Press Escape to return to the Main Menu.
   b. Select the 'Save Desktop files to disk' option and press Return.
   c. Press Return to accept the default of saving News Story.
   d. Press Return to accept the default of saving the file on the current disk. When the Main Menu appears, press Escape to return to the Word Processor screen.

4) EDIT THE STORY

Use the Delete and arrow keys, and insert new text as necessary to make the following changes:

   (a) Insert the name of your school before the words "Senior Prom". Note how the rest of the paragraph is adjusted to make room.
   (b) The dessert has been changed from Mint parfaits to Double Chocolate Chip ice cream.
   (c) The Prom will end at 11:00 PM and not 11:30.
   (d) The location has been changed from the downtown Hilton to the Eastside Sheraton.

5) CREATE A NEW PARAGRAPH

   a. Place the cursor on the first letter of the sentence which begins "All Juniors and Seniors" and press Return twice.
   b. Indent the new paragraph five spaces and add the following sentence to the end of the new paragraph:

```
Tickets are available from Mrs. Mitchell in the Student Affairs
office during school hours.
```

6)   ADD A HEADLINE TO THE STORY

a.   Move the cursor to the beginning of the document and add the following headline. Use 15 spaces before typing the word "PROM" to center the title:

```
PROM TO BE HELD AT EASTSIDE SHERATON
```

The rest of the text moves to the right to make room for the headline.

b.   Press Return twice to terminate the headline and insert a blank line between it and the rest of the story.

7)   SAVE THE FILE AGAIN TO RETAIN THE EDITING CHANGES

a.   Press Escape to return to the Main Menu.
b.   Select the 'Save Desktop files to disk' option and press Return.
c.   Press Return to accept the default of saving News Story.
d.   There is already a file named News Story on your disk from when it was saved in step 3 above. Because of this, AppleWorks displays the message:

```
This file already exists on
Disk 2 (Slot 6)
```

1. **Let the new information replace the old.**

2. Save with a different name.

Press Return to accept the default of saving the new information on the current disk, replacing the old. The old file is now erased and cannot be recovered.

e.   Press Escape when the Main Menu appears to return to the Word Processor screen.

Check - The completed story should be similar to:

```
File: News Story              REVIEW/ADD/CHANGE            Escape: Main Menu
====<====<====<====<====<====<====<====<====<====<====<====<====<====<====<===
                   PROM TO BE HELD AT EASTSIDE SHERATON

     The Lawrenceville School Senior Prom will be held in
the main ballroom of the Eastside Sheraton, at 7:30 PM next
Saturday night. Music for dancing will be provided by the
Tom Steves Trio.

     All Juniors and Seniors and their dates are invited,
and tickets are $25.00 per couple. Tickets are available
from Mrs. Mitchell in the Student Affairs office during
school hours.

     The menu for the evening's event will be:

          Fruit cup
          Roast Duck a l'Orange with Wild Rice stuffing
          Garden salad
          Double Chocolate Chip ice cream

     After dinner, dancing will continue until 11:00 PM. An
-------------------------------------------------------------------------
Type entry or use @ commands        Line 1  Column  1        @-? for Help
```

8) PROPERLY QUIT APPLEWORKS

a. Press Escape to return to the Main Menu.
b. Select 'Quit', option 6, and press Return.
c. Confirm that you wish to quit by pressing Y.

2.13 Loading a Previously Saved File from the Disk

Before a previously saved file may be edited it must first be added to the Desktop. This is accomplished by selecting the 'Add Files' option from the Main Menu. The default option on the Add Files menu is to load a file from the current disk. Pressing Return will show a list of the names of previously saved files from which you may select. The list also includes additional information which will be of use later.

To select a file to be added to the Desktop, the cursor is placed on the file's name using the up and down-arrow keys. Once the file's name has been highlighted pressing the Return key will place it on the Desktop, where it may then be edited. Note that you may see different files on this menu depending on what has been saved on your disk:

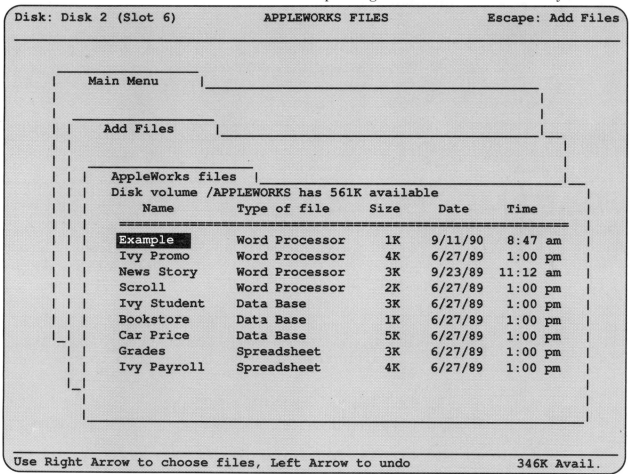

```
Disk: Disk 2 (Slot 6)         APPLEWORKS FILES          Escape: Add Files
_____

      _____
     |  Main Menu     |_____
     |                |                                                |
     |   _____  |                                                |
     | |   Add Files  |_____|_
     | |              |                                                 |
     | |              |                                                 |
     | |   _____                                           |
     | | |  AppleWorks files  |_____|_
     | | |  Disk volume /APPLEWORKS has 561K available                 |
     | | |      Name          Type of file    Size    Date     Time    |
     | | |     ========================================================|
     | | |     Example        Word Processor    1K    9/11/90   8:47 am |
     | | |     Ivy Promo       Word Processor    4K    6/27/89   1:00 pm |
     | | |     News Story      Word Processor    3K    9/23/89  11:12 am |
     | | |     Scroll          Word Processor    2K    6/27/89   1:00 pm |
     | | |     Ivy Student     Data Base         3K    6/27/89   1:00 pm |
     | | |     Bookstore       Data Base         1K    6/27/89   1:00 pm |
     |_| |     Car Price       Data Base         5K    6/27/89   1:00 pm |
       | |     Grades          Spreadsheet       3K    6/27/89   1:00 pm |
       | |     Ivy Payroll     Spreadsheet       4K    6/27/89   1:00 pm |
       |_|                                                              |
         |                                                              |
         |_____|

_____
Use Right Arrow to choose files, Left Arrow to undo            346K Avail.
```

It is important to realize that any editing changes made to a previously saved file will not be stored on the disk unless the file is again saved. It is also important to realize that saving an edited document replaces the original file on the disk, erasing the original.

2.14 Shortcuts: Using the Open-Apple Commands

AppleWorks can execute certain commands from within the word processor by using "Open-Apple commands". These are commands that cannot be executed using the menus, or are shortcuts that execute a menu command without having to leave the word processor screen. Each Open-Apple command is executed by holding down the Open-Apple key ( ) and pressing a letter. A full list of Open-Apple commands is given on the inside covers of this text. In this chapter several of the most common Open-Apple commands are discussed.

Another way to get a listing of the Open-Apple commands is to press Open-Apple ? from the word processor screen. This Help command clears the screen and displays a list of Open-Apple command which you can scroll through using the arrow keys. Pressing Escape from the Help screen returns you to the word processor.

2.15 Saving Files from within the Word Processor

To save a Word Processor file by the method previously explained it has been necessary to Escape from the word processor, and select the proper options from the different menus. Using an Open-Apple command it is possible to save the current file directly from the Word Processor screen by holding down the Open-Apple key and pressing S (for **S**ave).

Pressing Open-Apple S automatically saves whatever file is displayed on the Word Processor screen on the current disk. You will see the menus used in the previous method displayed on the screen, and AppleWorks will automatically select the options required to save the file.

2.16 Faster Modifications using Exchange Mode

AppleWorks normally assumes that any characters typed are to be inserted at the current cursor position. However, it is often the case with large corrections that you would prefer to simply type over the old text, erasing it as the new characters are entered. In order to change from inserting text to overwriting it, hold down the Open-Apple key and press E (for **E**xchange characters). The cursor changes from an underline to a blinking block to indicate that the word processor is now in overwrite or "exchange" mode. Any characters now typed will replace those already on the screen, rather than being inserted between them. To switch back to insert mode, press Open-Apple E again.

Practice 6

In this Practice the News Story file will be transferred from the disk into the computer's memory, edited and then re-saved in its new form. If you did not quit AppleWorks at the end of Practice 5 you should do so now.

1) BOOT PRODOS AND START APPLEWORKS

Boot ProDOS and start AppleWorks as described in Practice 1.

2) ADD A FILE TO THE DESKTOP

From the Main Menu, press Return to select the default option 'Add Files'. The Add Files menu will be shown.

3) SELECT THE GET FILES FROM 'THE CURRENT DISK' OPTION

Because this is the default, press Return.

4) SELECT THE FILE TO LOAD FROM THE APPLEWORKS FILES LIST

a. Use the up and down-arrow keys to move the cursor in the listing of previously saved files. Highlight News Story.

b. Press Return. When the desired file name (in this case News Story) is highlighted, pressing Return will transfer that file from the disk to the Desktop.

5) EDIT THE FILE

Insert and delete text and use Exchange mode (Open-Apple E) where necessary. The Prom Committee has made the following changes:

The Prom will start at 7:00 PM.
The Amazing Schmenge Brothers, not the Tom Steves Trio, will provide the evening's entertainment.
Guests will have the choice of Fruit cup or Lime sherbet for an appetizer.

6) SAVE THE MODIFIED FILE ON DISK

Press Open-Apple S. The file is saved on disk exactly as if the Save files option had been chosen from the Main Menu.

Check - When complete, the modified file should be similar to:

```
File: News Story          REVIEW/ADD/CHANGE          Escape: Main Menu
====<====<====<====<====<====<====<====<====<====<====<====<====<====<===
             PROM TO BE HELD AT EASTSIDE SHERATON

     The Lawrenceville School Senior Prom will be held in
the main ballroom of the Eastside Sheraton, at 7:00 PM next
Saturday night. Music for dancing will be provided by the
Amazing Schmenge Brothers.

     All Juniors and Seniors and their dates are invited,
and tickets are $25.00 per couple. Tickets are available
from Mrs. Mitchell in the Student Affairs office during
school hours.

     The menu for the evening's event will be:

     Fruit cup or lime sherbet
     Roast Duck a l'Orange with Wild Rice stuffing
     Garden salad
     Double Chocolate Chip ice cream


     After dinner, dancing will continue until 11:00 PM. An
------------------------------------------------------------------------
Type entry or use @ commands          Line 1  Column  1          @-? for Help
```

2.17 Printing a Document

Printing involves sending a copy of a document from the computer's memory to the printer. First, make sure that your computer is connected to a printer. Then check to be sure that the printer is turned on, is "on line" and that paper is positioned at the top of the page. Before printing any document it should first be saved on disk so that, should an error occur and the document be erased from the computer's memory, it could be restored from the disk.

To print a document hold down the Open-Apple key and press P (for **P**rint) when in the word processor. The Print command requires you to specify which pages to print, the printer to use, and how many copies to print. Because the default values are the most normally used, simply press Return for each of the three questions and then printing will begin. If you wish to change any of the default options, select the desired choice by using the arrow keys. If more than one copy of the document is to be printed, type the number required and press Return.

AppleWorks uses a menu to display the possible printer choices:

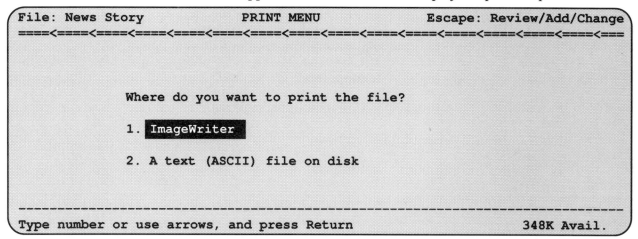

```
File: News Story              PRINT MENU           Escape: Review/Add/Change
====<====<====<====<====<====<====<====<====<====<====<====<====<====<===



          Where do you want to print the file?

          1. ImageWriter

          2. A text (ASCII) file on disk



------------------------------------------------------------------------
Type number or use arrows, and press Return                    348K Avail.
```

You may have different printer options on this menu depending on the printers available. Check to find out which printer your computer is connected to before printing.

Practice 7

The following Practice demonstrates how a Word Processor document may be printed and should only be attempted if you have a printer connected to your computer. Start AppleWorks if you have not already done so and add the News Story file created in the previous Practices to the Desktop.

1) EXECUTE THE PRINT COMMAND

Press Open-Apple P.

2) INDICATE WHICH TEXT IS TO BE PRINTED

From the prompt

Print from? **Beginning** This page   Cursor

accept the default option of 'Beginning' by pressing Return to print the entire file.

3) CHOOSE THE PRINTER

Select the proper printer for your computer and press Return.

4) ENTER THE NUMBER OF COPIES

From the prompt

How many copies? **1**

press Return to accept the default of 1 copy. The computer returns to the Word Processor screen when printing is completed, or you may press Escape to terminate printing and return immediately to the Word Processor screen.

2.18 Screen Scroll

Most documents have more than one page, and are too long to be displayed on a single screen. The AppleWorks screen is like a window that displays only a portion of a document, 20 lines at a time. To bring unseen parts into view the screen window can be moved up and down through the document. This is referred to as "screen scroll".

The cursor control keys are used to move the screen window in a document. Up-arrow and down-arrow move the cursor one line at a time. Open-Apple up-arrow and Open-Apple down-arrow move the window one screen (20 lines) at a time. When working with long documents it can be time consuming to move the cursor in such small increments. AppleWorks can move the cursor directly to the first character in a document by holding down the Open-Apple key and pressing 1 (Open-Apple 1). Holding down Open-Apple and pressing 9 (Open-Apple 9) moves the cursor directly to the last line in the document. In addition, Open-Apple 5 moves the cursor to the middle of the document, and the other number keys work similarly. Actions of the cursor control keys are summarized in the table below:

Key	Cursor Action
up-arrow	Moves up one line
Open-Apple up-arrow	Moves up one screen, 20 lines
Open-Apple 1	Moves to first character in document
down-arrow	Moves down one line
Open-Apple down-arrow	Moves down one screen, 20 lines
Open-Apple 9	Moves to last character in document
Open-Apple 5	Moves to the middle of the document
left-arrow	Moves one character to the left
Open-Apple left-arrow	Moves to beginning of previous word
Open-Apple < (less than)	Moves to beginning of current line
right-arrow	Moves one character to the right
Open-Apple right-arrow	Moves to beginning of the next word
Open-Apple > (greater than)	Moves to end of current line

Practice 8

This Practice demonstrates screen scroll and cursor movement. Boot ProDOS and start AppleWorks if you have not already done so. A Word Processor file named SCROLL will be added to the Desktop. Each line in SCROLL is numbered to help demonstrate screen movements.

1) ADD THE FILE NAMED "SCROLL" TO THE DESKTOP

   Select 'Add files' from the Main Menu and add the Word Processor file named Scroll from your data disk to the Desktop.

2) MOVE THE CURSOR TO THE BOTTOM OF THE SCREEN

   Press down-arrow 19 times. Notice the position of the cursor as given on the Message Line at the bottom of the screen.

3) SCROLL DOWN 1 LINE

   Press down-arrow again. Notice that line 1 disappears off the top of the screen and line 21 appears from the bottom.

4) SCROLL DOWN 5 LINES

> Press down-arrow 5 times. Note that each time down-arrow is pressed another line scrolls off the top of the screen, and the next line in the document appears from the bottom.

5) JUMP TO THE LAST LINE IN THE DOCUMENT

> Press Open-Apple 9. The cursor moves immediately to the last line in the document, line number 80 in this file.

6) JUMP TO THE FIRST LINE IN THE DOCUMENT

> Hold down the Open-Apple key and press 1. The cursor moves directly to the first line in the document, much faster than using the up-arrow key.

7) MOVE DOWN ONE SCREEN

> Press Open-Apple down-arrow. The cursor immediately moves down 20 lines, to the bottom of the screen.

8) MOVE TO THE LAST LINE IN THE DOCUMENT

> Press Open-Apple down-arrow until the cursor is on the last line in the document, line 80. Try pressing down-arrow again a few times. AppleWorks will move the cursor to the next line, but no further.

9) JUMP TO THE TOP OF THE CURRENT SCREEN

> Press Open-Apple up-arrow. The cursor jumps to the first line on the current screen, line 62.

10) JUMP TO THE MIDDLE OF THE DOCUMENT

> Press Open-Apple 5. The cursor jumps to line 41, the middle line of the document.

Check - The cursor should be on the middle line of SCROLL:

```
File: Scroll                    REVIEW/ADD/CHANGE                Escape: Main Menu
====<====<====<====<====<====<====<====<====<====<====<====<====<====<===
33
34
35
36
37
38
39
40
41
42
43
44
45
46
47
49
49
50
51
52
------------------------------------------------------------------------
Type entry or use @ commands          Line 41  Column  1          @-? for Help
```

11) QUIT APPLEWORKS

    a. Press Escape to return to the Main Menu.
    b. Choose 'Quit', option 6.
    c. Press Y to confirm that you wish to quit AppleWorks.

Chapter Summary

A word processor is basically a computerized typewriter, with the addition of several powerful features. Documents ranging from research papers to business letters can be produced quickly and efficiently using a word processor. Word processing allows documents to be changed easily. Text can be inserted, deleted or modified without re-typing the entire document. Formatting options allow the appearance of text on the page to be changed. By saving the document in a file on disk, it can later be recalled, edited and printed.

The computer uses ProDOS to start up. AppleWorks will then automatically load and display an opening copyright screen. (You may be asked to enter the date.) When AppleWorks has loaded, the Main Menu is displayed. The Main Menu controls access to files and the Desktop.

AppleWorks uses menus to access word processor options. Each option in a menu is numbered. Pressing the corresponding number and then the Return key executes the option. The up and down-arrow keys can also be used to select an option from a menu. Pressing the Return key then executes the selected option. Certain options display another menu which is shown stacked on top of the previous one. Some menu options may be executed directly from the Word Processor screen by using Open-Apple commands.

This Chapter discussed the options and procedures necessary for the production of word processed documents using AppleWorks. The major steps in producing such a document are:

1) Boot ProDOS and load the AppleWorks program from the disk into the computer's memory.
2) Place the file to be word processed on the Desktop - either by creating a new file from scratch or loading a previously saved file from the disk.
3) Enter or edit the document.
4) Save the document on disk.
5) Print the document.
6) Properly exit AppleWorks.

When editing a document, pressing Open-Apple E causes the characters then typed to replace any characters currently in the document. Saving a document is accomplished by pressing Open-Apple S from the word processor screen. Pressing Open-Apple P prints a document.

The AppleWorks screen is like a window which displays 20 lines of a document at a time. The window may be moved through the document using the cursor control keys in a process called screen scroll. Open-Apple 1 moves the cursor directly to the first character in a document and Open-Apple 9 to the last.

Vocabulary

Add Files option - Option used to create new files or load previously saved files from the disk.

Arrow keys - Four keys that move the cursor up, down, right and left on the screen without changing any text. The arrow keys are also used to select options from menus.

Boot - To turn on the computer and load the operating system (ProDOS).

Character - Any letter, number or symbol which can be displayed on the computer screen or typed on the keyboard.

Cursor - A blinking line on the screen which indicates where characters entered from the keyboard will be placed.

Cursor control keys - Keys used to move the cursor without having any effect on the text. See Arrow keys.

Default - An option that is selected automatically by pressing Return if no other option is chosen.

Delete key - A key that erases the character to the left of the current cursor position.

Delete text - The removal of a character or group of characters from a document.

Desktop - An area in the computer's memory holding files that may be used by AppleWorks.

Document - Any material that can be typed in the word processor, such as a letter, paper or story.

Esc key - Key used to terminate (escape from) an option or to quit a menu.

Exchange mode - Option used to switch between insert and overwrite modes: `Open-Apple E`.

File - Information created by AppleWorks which is stored on a disk.

File name - A name for a file stored on disk.

Format - The arrangement of text on a page.

Get Files option - Main Menu option used to place a previously created disk file on the Desktop.

Insert text - Adding words or characters to a document.

Main Menu - Menu containing options for manipulating different files and the Desktop.

Make New File option - Option to create a new file.

Menu - A list of options that are available at a particular point.

Open-Apple commands - Commands executed directly from the Word Processor screen by holding down the Open-Apple key and pressing another key. Some Open-Apple commands are shortcuts for menu options, others do not appear on any menu.

Open-Apple key - Key on the lower-left of the keyboard marked with an apple. Used to execute Open-Apple commands.

Print command - Command which prints the file currently on the screen: `Open-Apple P`.

ProDOS - Disk operating system programs that the computer needs to start up.

Prompt - A message displayed on the screen by AppleWorks asking for information to be typed.

Quit option - Main Menu option used to exit AppleWorks.

Return key - Key used to indicate the end of an entry such as an option or response to a question, or to choose from a menu. In word processing Return is used at the end of each paragraph.

Save command - Command used to save a document on disk: `Open-Apple S`.

Screen scroll - Moving through a document, the screen acts as a window showing only part (20 lines) of the document.
Text - Any character or group of characters in a document.
Word processor - A computer application that allows text to be manipulated and stored.
Word wrap - When the computer decides whether to keep a word on the current line, or move it to the next based on the amount of space left on the line.

Reviews

Sections 2.1-2.4

1. What are three advantage of using a word processor rather than a typewriter to produce a letter?

2. How can using a word processor improve the quality of your writing?

3. Name three different businesses that could benefit from using word processors. Explain how each would benefit.

4. a) Why is it important to take good care of a disk?
   b) What should be avoided when handling or storing a disk?

5. What is ProDOS and what is it used for?

6. What is meant by the term "booting" the computer?

7. What purpose does the Return key serve?

8. What is a menu and what is it used for?

Sections 2.5-2.7

9. a) How many options does the Main Menu offer?
   b) What two methods may be used to select one of its options?

10. What is meant by a default option?

11. a) What is the Desktop?
    b) What steps are used to place a new word processing file on the Desktop?

12. How can you go from the menu currently displayed on the screen to one shown behind it?

13. What purpose do file names serve?

14. What type of messages are displayed on the message line?

15. How do you know at what position the cursor is located on the Word Processor screen?

Sections 2.8-2.10

16. a) Why is it important to exit AppleWorks properly?
    b) List the steps required to exit AppleWorks starting from the Word Processor screen so that the file currently being worked on is saved.

17. How can the cursor be moved down 3 lines and then 10 spaces to the right?

Sections 2.11-2.13   18. What is a "repeat key"?

19. Describe the operations necessary to change the word "men" to "people" in the sentence:

```
Now is the time for all good men to come to the
aid of the party.
```

20. What does pressing the Return key do when working in the Word Processor?

21. What is the difference between pressing the Delete key or the left arrow key four times while the cursor is located in the middle of a line of text?

22. Give three reasons why it is useful to save a word processor file on disk.

23. If you are working on a word processor document when the power is turned off, how can you retrieve the document if it has not been previously saved on disk?

24. a) Which of the following are legal file names?

```
RICH$
Letter to John Willibee
** FUN **
Rhonda Letter
My Poetry
```

b) What should be considered when selecting the file name of a word processor document?

25. When a file is saved where does it go? Is it removed from the computer's memory?

26. What is "word wrap"?

Sections 2.14-2.15   27. What must be done to end a paragraph and start a new one?

28. a) If a previously saved file is edited will the changes be automatically made to the file on disk, or must the file be saved again?
b) What happens to an original file if an edited version of it is saved?

Sections 2.16-2.17   29. a) Why is it important to save a document before printing it?
b) What command is used to print a document?

30. What is an advantage of using Open-Apple commands rather than menu commands when using the word processor?

31. What is the difference between insert and exchange modes?

Exercises

1. a) Enter the following letter in the word processor in a new file named Marge:

                              September 26, 1989

    Mrs. Margaret Livingston
    123 Main St.
    Reedsburg, WI 53959

    Dear Margaret,

        I am writing to let you know how much I am enjoying my new word
    processor. It has so many advantages over my old typewriter.

        One thing that I will never miss is white-out. For years we used
    it to make corrections and it left a thick patch on the page.

        Now corrections are handled on the computer screen so that no one
    knows about my mistakes. Once I ended up re-typing an 8 page letter to
    correct the misspelling of the bank director's name. With my word
    processor it would have taken about 1 minute to retrieve the letter
    from a floppy disk and make the changes on the screen. The revised
    letter could then have been printing while I got a cup of coffee.

        Thanks again for all your help.

                              Sincerely,

                              A. Secretary

    b) Save Marge on your data disk.

    c) Print a copy of Marge on the printer.

    d) Edit the letter as follows:

    Delete the word "old" in the last line of paragraph one.
    Delete the sentence "One thing that I will never miss is white-out."
    Change "For years we used it" to "For years we used white-out".
    Change "so that no one knows about my mistakes" to "so that my mistakes are invisible"
    Replace "A. Secretary" with your name.
    Add the following lines to the beginning of the third paragraph:

    "My boss likes to make several revisions of each letter and memo that leaves the office. That means that each has to be re-typed, often several times."

    e) Save the modified Marge letter on your data disk.

    f) Print the revised letter.

2. Word processors can be used to create documents which store a variety of different information.

   a) Enter each of the following sayings into the word processor leaving a blank line between each. Name the file Benjamin in honor of Benjamin Franklin who wrote many famous sayings in Poor Richard's Almanac:

   An apple a day keeps the doctor away.

   A penny for your thoughts.

   Every cloud has a silver lining.

   A penny saved is a penny earned.

   Early to bed, early to rise, makes a man healthy, wealthy and wise.

   b) Save Benjamin on your data disk.

   c) Print a copy of Benjamin on the printer.

   d) Edit the saying on each line as follows:

   (1) change apple to orange
   (2) change penny to dollar
   (3) change silver to gold
   (4) change penny to quarter (twice)
   (5) change man to person

   e) Save the modified Benjamin file on your data disk.

   f) Print the modified Benjamin file.

3. You are thinking of applying to several colleges around the country.

   a) Use the word processor to create a file named Apply which contains a letter requesting information and an application from a college. Use the following as a guide, substituting your own information:

```
September 28, 1989

Ivy University
Admissions Department
1 College Court
Newton, IA 63343

Dear Sirs:

I am interested in attending Ivy University. I will graduate in 1990 and
plan to major in medical communications. I have been president of the
Student Congress for 4 years and captain of the Debate Team for 2 years.
I have varsity letters in three sports and was a member of the All-state
gymnastics and swim teams. My current grade point average is 3.95.

Please send a course catalog and application to me at this address:

     A. Student
     223 Main Street
     Anytown, USA 11111

Thank you very much.

Sincerely,

A. Student
```

b) Save the Apply letter on your data disk.

c) Print the Apply letter.

d) The good news is that the new grades are out and you finally got that 4.0. Change your GPA in Apply.

e) The bad news is that you lost the recent Student Congress election. Change the file to read "3 and a half years".

f) Change the name and address of Ivy University to a school you would like to attend and print the new letter. Be sure to change the school's name in the first sentence as well.

g) Save the updated letter.

4. Your cousin is visiting you from out of town. Using the word processor, create and print lists of directions in a file name Directions that your cousin can follow to go from your house to the following places:

a) Your school. Be sure to describe what time school gets out and where your cousin should meet you.

b) The local fast food restaurant.

c) The closest grocery store to your house.

d) Your video rental club. Be sure to include your membership number in the directions so that your cousin can rent some videos.

e) Your cousin is not the brightest person in the world. Leave complete instructions describing how to use the VCR to play a video.

5. Your school newspaper has an opening for an arts critic. Use the word processor to create and print a review of the last movie or concert you attended in a file named Art Critic. Save and print a copy of Art Critic.

6. A word processor can be used as a diary. Create a new file named Diary and make a journal entry describing what you did last week. Be sure to include your plans for the upcoming weekend. Save and print a copy of your diary page.

7. Your English teacher has asked you to write an essay entitled "How I spent my summer vacation". Use the word processor to create and print a small version of this essay. Save the essay on disk in a file named Essay and then print it.

8. Use the word processor to produce an advertisement for an upcoming dance or other special event. Save the file on your data disk under the name Advertise and print a copy.

Chapter 3
Manipulating Text with the Word Processor

Open-Apple C

Open-Apple D

Open-Apple F

Open-Apple K

Open-Apple O

Open-Apple R

Open-Apple T

Open-Apple Y

Open-Apple V

Open-Apple Z

Objectives

After completing this chapter you will be able to:

1. Use formatting to control the placement of text on the page.

2. Create tables in documents using margins and tabs.

3. Emphasize areas of text using underlining, bold characters and line spacing.

4. Move text from one position to another.

5. Copy text in a document.

6. Use the Find and Replace commands.

7. Create headers and footers for printed documents.

8. Use the spelling checker to verify spelling in a document.

*C*hapter 2 introduced the options necessary to create, edit, save and print Word Processor documents. In this chapter techniques that improve the appearance and readability of such documents are covered. Included are:

- formatting features that control the arrangement of text on the page, such as margins, paragraph alignment (flush left, justified, right justified or centered), tabs and pagination (how text is divided into pages).

- options that manipulate blocks of text, including cut-and-paste features that move and copy text from one place to another.

- techniques to search for specific text in a document, and replace it with different text.

Many of the word processing options discussed in this chapter are powerful tools, capable of manipulating text in ways that go far beyond what a typewriter can do. After familiarizing yourself with these tools, you will understand why word processing has achieved such popularity.

3.1 Tabs and Tab Stops

Tab stops are used to position text within a line or to create tables of data. AppleWorks has default tab stops at every fifth space, with the first stop appearing at the sixth space. Pressing the Tab key moves the cursor to the next tab stop to the right. Do not confuse tab stops with tabs themselves. Tabs are actual characters that are placed in a document using the tab key. Tab stops are only locations specifying the length of the tab character (how far it will move the cursor). While default tabs are initially set to every five spaces, they can be changed to any interval desired.

Default tabs are generally used for indenting text from the margin. When beginning a new paragraph, press Tab once to indent the first line six spaces before entering text. When creating the heading of a letter, your address and the date should be aligned near the right side of the page. By using the same number of tabs, the cursor may easily be placed at the desired spot before each line is typed.

Although tabs move the cursor more than one space, they are generated by a single keystroke and may be inserted into text or deleted from text as any other character. In AppleWorks, pressing the tab key does not actually insert the number of individual space characters needed to move the cursor to the next tab stop. Instead, a code is placed in the text which tells the computer to move to the next tab stop. When the Zoom command is used, this code is displayed on the screen as a caret (^). Even when the Zoom mode is off, placing the cursor on a tab character displays the word "Tab" on the message line. Deleting a tab requires that only the code be deleted. The text will automatically be moved to the left to fill the space created by removing the tab.

In AppleWorks, it is possible to insert a Tab into a previously entered line of text. After a line has been typed, positioning the cursor in the line and pressing Tab will move the characters to the right of the tab to the next tab stop.

Note: In earlier versions of AppleWorks, the tab key actually inserts spaces into the document instead of the special tab character used in version 3.0. Pushing tab at the beginning of a line of text when using an earlier version inserts five spaces into the document and not a special code telling the cursor to move to the next tab stop. This means that if the tab stops are later changed it will not affect the tabs that were previously entered since they are simply strings of space characters. This type of tab cannot be inserted in a previously entered line of text. Pushing the tab key in the middle of a line of text simply moves the cursor to the next tab stop without affecting the text itself. These "space" tabs in earlier versions must be deleted as individual spaces.

3.2 The Screen Scale

Directly above the work area is a scale that is used to measure distances from the left side of the page. This scale gauges the placement of horizontal formatting features including tabs and margins (to be discussed later in this chapter). Stretched across the screen to the right are less than signs (<) marking the position of each tab stop. Each equals sign on the scale represents one space on the line.

3.3 Individual Tab Stops

In addition to the defaults, AppleWorks allows individual tab stops to be set anywhere on the tab ruler. These new tab stops differ from default tab stops in that, rather than appearing at regular intervals, individual tab stops can be inserted anywhere on the line. Individually set tab stops are marked by characters on the scale line.

There are several different types of tab stops in AppleWorks. The default tab stop alignment is Left-aligned, meaning that text entered at that stop will be aligned at the stop's left. Left-aligned stops are marked with a less than sign (<) on the ruler. It is also possible to create right-, center-, and decimal-aligned tab stops which are marked with a greater than sign (>), caret (^) and decimal point (.) respectively. A right tab aligns the end of the text at the stop while a center tab centers the text equidistant over the stop. Decimal tabs are used with numbers and align the numbers with the decimal point at the stop. Earlier versions of AppleWorks use only the left-aligned stop. Examples of each stop are shown on the next page with the corresponding ruler:

```
=<==================>========^=============.==
  Left stop     Right     Centered  Decimal
  Name          Jason      Weston        27.1
  Address   Amsterdam    Netherlands      3.14
```

Individual tab stops are set using the `Open-Apple T` (for Tabs) command. When `Open-Apple T` is pressed, the following message appears.

Tab Ruler?   **Modify current**   Create New

Using the Modify Current command, the default ruler can be modified. The changes made then apply to the whole document. If the tabs are to be changed only for the parts of the document below the cursor the Create New command is selected. The position of the new ruler is marked in Zoom mode like this:

`-----Tab Ruler`

The new ruler will be in effect for all of the document below the cursor or until you create another new ruler.

After choosing one of the two options, the cursor moves to the scale line and the following prompt appears in the Message Line:

```
Tabs:  L:Left   R:Right   D:Decimal   C:Center
U:Undo tab  N:No tabs (Column 1)
```

To create a new stop, the cursor is moved along the scale using the left- and right-arrow keys. The cursor's current position from the left side of the page is shown by the number following Column. Pressing the L, R, D, or C keys will set a new stop of the specified type at the cursor's position, and the character corresponding to that type of stop will be shown on the scale. To clear a stop, the cursor is moved to the stop's character and the U key pressed. All of the stops may be cleared by pressing the N key. Pressing Escape completes the procedure and returns the cursor to the work area. Any tab stops set or cleared are retained when the file is saved on disk, so that the next time it is loaded, the file will have the same stops.

3.4 Deleting Text

It is often necessary to remove lines of text from a document when editing. In the last chapter the Delete key was used to remove text one character at a time. This is cumbersome when the amount of text to be deleted is more than a word or two. To speed deleting, AppleWorks uses the `Open-Apple Y` command to delete all of the text from the cursor's current position to the end of the line. This command makes it easy to remove a number of lines by first moving the cursor to the first line to be deleted and then pressing `Open-Apple Y` to delete each line. Be careful when using this command because, should a line be deleted by accident, it cannot be restored and must be retyped.

In Version 3.0 pressing `Open-Apple Delete` deletes the character directly above the cursor.

Practice 1

This Practice demonstrates how to use tabs, set and remove tab stops and delete text.

1) BOOT PRODOS AND START APPLEWORKS

Following the directions given in Chapter 2 to start Apple-Works.

2) ADD A NEW WORD PROCESSOR FILE NAMED "TAB TEST" TO THE DESKTOP FROM SCRATCH

a. Select 'Add files' from the Main Menu.
b. Select 'Word Processor' from the Add Files menu and then 'From scratch'.
c. Enter the name `Tab Test` and press Return. Because this is a new file the default tab stops are automatically set at each fifth character.

3) ENTER THE FOLLOWING TEXT

Type: `This is a test sentence.`

4) INDENT THE SENTENCE USING A TAB

a. Press `Open-Apple` < to return to the beginning of the line.
b. Press the Tab key to insert a tab. The sentence is indented by five spaces, so that the first letter of the sentence starts in column 6, directly below the tab marker in the screen scale.

5) SET LEFT-ALIGNED TAB STOPS AT COLUMNS 10 AND 30

a. Press `Open-Apple T` and choose the default selection, 'Modify current'. The cursor moves to the scale line.
b. Press the `N` key to remove all of the default tab stops. To show that no tab stops are set, the scale changes to all equal signs.
c. Move the cursor to column 10 using the arrow keys and press `L`. A less than sign is displayed in the scale.
d. Move the cursor to column 30 and press `L`. A less than sign is again displayed.
e. Press Escape to return to the Word Processor work area. Two less than signs are shown in the ruler marking the position of the left-aligned tab stops just set. Notice that since the first tab stop is now at column 10, the sentence is now indented 9 and not 5 spaces.

6) ENTER THE FOLLOWING TABLE

a. Press `Open-Apple` > to move the cursor to the end of the current line. Press Return 2 times.
b. Press Tab once to start the following table at line three, column 10. Use Tab to move from column to column, pressing Return at the end of each line:

```
Semester           GPA
Fall, 1988         3.0
Spring, 1988       3.1
Fall, 1989         3.05
Sprimg, 1989       3.2
```

7) DELETE THE FIRST LINE FROM THE FILE

    a. Press `Open-Apple 1` to move the cursor to the beginning of the file.

    b. Press `Open-Apple Y`. The entire line is removed from the screen much faster than using the Delete key, leaving an empty line.

8) MOVE TO THE END OF THE DOCUMENT AND CREATE A NEW RULER

    a. Press `Open-Apple 9` to move the cursor to the end of the document.

    b. Press `Open-Apple T` and choose 'Create New'.

    c. Press `N` to clear the new ruler and move the cursor to column 5 and press `L` to create a left-aligned tab stop.

    d. Press `R` in column 30 for a right-aligned tab stop, `C` in column 42 for a centered tab stop and `D` in column 57 for a decimal-aligned tab stop.

    e. Press Escape to return to the work area.

9) ENTER THE FOLLOWING TABLE

Enter the following table starting at line 11, column 5. Press Tab to move from column to column, pressing Return at the end of each line:

```
Last Name     First Name      State    Balance
Lee                Alice    Missouri    $165.45
Dunham              Rich    Illinois      $5.90
Baber              Julie       Texas     $47.75
```

10) USE ZOOM MODE TO SEE NEW TAB RULER

    a. Press `Open-Apple Z`. All tabs are displayed as carets (^) in the text. A marker showing the position of the new ruler appears on the screen. Tabs above the line are set for the first table, while the tabs below the line are set for the second table.

    b. Press `Open-Apple Z` to remove Zoom mode.

<u>Check</u> - Your document and scale should be similar to:

```
 File: Tab Test              REVIEW/ADD/CHANGE            Escape: Main Menu
===<====================>==============^==============.=====================

        Semester         GPA
        Fall, 1988       3.0
        Spring, 1988     3.1
        Fall, 1989       3.05
        Spring, 1989     3.2


    Last Name       First Name         State    Balance
    Lee                  Alice      Missouri    $165.45
    Dunham                Rich      Illinois      $5.90
    Baber                Julie         Texas     $47.75


-------------------------------------------------------------------------
Type entry or use @ commands          Line 14  Column 60       @-? for Help
```

11) SAVE THE FILE

    a. Press `Open-Apple S`. Tab stops in the first section and all of the tab stops in the second section are retained in the file.

    b. Press Escape to return to the Main Menu.

3.5 Formatting Text

Books, newspapers and other printed materials use a variety of techniques to arrange text on a page. While you may not recognize the terms that are used to describe such techniques, you are familiar with the techniques themselves from publications you have seen.

Arrangements of text are called "formats." A document's format includes the size of its margins, how various parts of a document line up within those margins, the spacing between lines and paragraphs, and how the document is divided into pages. Format also includes the arrangement of text into tables composed of columns and methods of emphasizing text such as underlined or boldface (darker) letters.

3.6 Setting Margins

One way to affect the appearance of a document is by setting margins. Margins are the blank spaces between the edges of the paper and the text. AppleWorks' default settings are one inch for both the left and right margins, two inches for the bottom, and no margin at the top for an 8 inch by 11 inch page:

Text is printed in this area of the page only.

Left Margin: 1 inch   Right Margin: 1 inch

Bottom Margin: 2 inches

Margins can be widened or narrowed as desired. Changes to the margin settings have a corresponding effect on the number of characters that will fit on a line. Widening a margin decreases the amount of text that a line can contain, while narrowing a margin increases the line's capacity.

The length of a line of text that will fit across a page is determined by subtracting the size of left and right margins from the width of the page. Using the default margins of 1" on a 8" page yields a line 6" long (8" - 1" - 1" = 6").

Options for setting margins are displayed by pressing `Open-Apple O` (for Options). When pressed, `Open-Apple O` displays a menu of over thirty different options, each one of which has an effect on a document's format. While that seems like a large number, most are rarely used so it is not necessary to learn all of them, only the five or six most commonly used. Current settings for some of the most common options are shown in the bold line at the top of the menu:

PW=8.0   LM=1.0   RM=1.0   CI=10   UJ   PL=11.0   TM=0.0   BM=2.0   LI=6   SS

```
Option: _                   CN: Centered          GB: Group Begin       +B: Superscript Beg
                            RJ: Right Justified   GE: Group End         +E: Superscript End
PW: Platen Width            PL: Paper Length      HE: Page Header        -B: Subscript Begin
LM: Left Margin             TM: Top Margin        FO: Page Footer        -E: Subscript End
RM: Right Margin            BM: Bottom Margin     SK: Skip Lines        UB: Underline Begin
CI: Chars per Inch LI: Lines per Inch  PE: Pause Each page   UE: Underline End
P1: Proportional-1 SS: Single Space     PH: Pause Here        PP: Print Page No.
P2: Proportional-2 DS: Double Space     SM: Set a Marker      PD: Print Date
IN: Indent                  TS: Triple Space      SC: Special Code      PT: Print Time
JU: Justified               NP: New Page          BB: Boldface Begin    EK: Enter Keyboard
UJ: Unjustified             PN: Page Number       BE: Boldface End      MM: Mail Merge
```

Top, bottom, left and right margins each have their own two-letter code. For example, to change the left margin of a document, type LM from the Options menu and press Return. AppleWorks will then prompt you to enter the size of the new margin in inches. When the size of a left or right margin is changed, the screen display is adjusted to reflect the new settings. Margin settings can be easily changed to experiment with different formats. Pressing Escape removes the Options menu from the screen and returns the cursor to the work area with the new margins set.

It is important to realize that a document's margins may change from paragraph to paragraph. For example, one paragraph may use the defaults, while the next may have larger or smaller margins. When a margin is changed through the Options menu, the change affects only the current paragraph and any text <u>below</u> the current cursor position to the end of the document. Therefore, to set margins for the entire document, the cursor must first be placed at the very beginning of the document (Open-Apple 1) before the Option command is executed. Any margins set are retained when the file is saved on disk.

Practice 2

To demonstrate the different formatting options, the following Practice sessions in this chapter use Ivy University's promotional file named Ivy Promo which is stored on your data disk.

In this Practice margin widths will be set and changed. Pay attention to how each margin change affects the number of lines in the paragraphs and the length of lines in reference to the scale. Boot ProDOS and start AppleWorks if you have not already done so, and add the Ivy Promo Word Processor file from your data disk to the Desktop.

1) MOVE THE CURSOR TO THE BEGINNING OF PARAGRAPH TO BE CHANGED

Move the cursor to the first character of the second paragraph, the "L" in "Located".

2) DISPLAY THE OPTIONS MENU

Press Open-Apple O. The Options menu appears with the settings for the most common options shown in bold along the top of the menu. Note the position of the prompt asking for "Option:".

3)   SELECT THE LEFT MARGIN OPTION

The current value of the left margin is shown in the bold line, LM=1.0. This means that the left margin is currently set to the default of 1 inch. Type the code for left margin, LM, and press Return.

4)   ENTER A LEFT MARGIN OF 2 INCHES

The prompt

`Inches:`

appears directly below the Option prompt. Type 2 and press Return. Text on the screen is reformatted to show the new left margin and a marker is temporarily displayed in the work area showing where the new margin takes effect.

5)   RETURN TO THE WORK AREA

Press Escape. Note that the paragraph is indented to show the new margin, and that the marker has disappeared. Scroll down to verify that the left margin has been changed for all paragraphs below the second.

6)   MOVE THE CURSOR TO THE BEGINNING OF THE PARAGRAPH TO BE CHANGED

Move the cursor to the beginning of the line which reads "OUR CONTRIBUTION TO AMERICA".

7)   SET THE RIGHT MARGIN TO 1.5 INCHES

a.   Press `Open-Apple O`. The Options menu appears. Note that the setting for left margin is now set to 2 inches (LM=2.0) from step 4. The current setting for the right margin is the default of 1 inch (RM=1.0).

b.   Type the code for right margin, RM, and press Return.

c.   The prompt

`Inches:`

appears. Type `1.5` and press Return. Text on the screen is reformatted and a temporary marker is displayed showing where the new margin begins. This paragraph and all paragraphs below it now have left margins of 2 inches and right margins of 1.5 inches.

d.   Press Escape to return to the work area. Note that all paragraphs below this one now have a right margin of 1.5 inches.

e.   Press `Open-Apple S` to save this modified version on disk.

<u>Check</u> - Margins have been changed as shown by the text on the screen:

```
File: Ivy Promo            REVIEW/ADD/CHANGE           Escape: Main Menu
=====<====<====<====<====<====<====<====<====<====<====<====<====<====<==
                Located in bucolic Leaf County, the 50 acre
           wooded setting is ideal for students wishing to
           major in biology, botany, and related fields. If
           you are considering entering one of these areas of
           study, we hope that you will pay us a visit. There
           is a reaction many get from visiting our campus
           that cannot be communicated with words or
           pictures. At Ivy University we are willing to help
           you in any way we can. Please feel free to contact
           us should you have any questions.

           OUR CONTRIBUTION TO AMERICA

                As one of the premier educational
           institutions in the country, Ivy University
           has long been recognized as a national
           treasure. Many leaders in industry, science,
           sports and government are alumni of Ivy
           University. Graduates of Ivy University have
           always excelled, and we are proud to point to
-------------------------------------------------------------------------
Type entry or use @ commands        Line 25 Column 11        @-? for Help
```

3.7 Zoom Mode

It is often difficult to determine the exact margin settings for a document simply by looking at the Word Processor screen. This is especially true when a document has several different formats. Apple-Works can be made to display more information about a document by using "Zoom" mode, Open-Apple Z. In Zoom mode the temporary markers shown when a margin is first set from the Options menu are made visible again. In addition, the position of each Return character is indicated by a rectangular "blotch" mark.

Practice 3

The Ivy Promo file modified in the last Practice should still be displayed. Zoom mode will be used to display the current margin settings.

1) MOVE THE CURSOR TO THE BEGINNING OF THE DOCUMENT

   Press Open-Apple 1.

2) SWITCH TO ZOOM MODE

   Press Open-Apple Z. Margin markers appear. Note that the margin is set from the position of the marker to the end of the document, or until another marker for that option appears. The rectangular "blotch" marks at the end of each paragraph indicate where the Return key has been pressed. These markers are not shown when the document is printed.

3) SWITCH BETWEEN NORMAL AND ZOOM MODE

    a. Press `Open-Apple Z` again. The margin and Return markers disappear.

    b. Press `Open-Apple Z` again to return to Zoom mode. Because of the extra formatting information that it provides, a document is best formatted in Zoom mode.

<u>Check</u> - Margins and Return markers are shown on the screen in Zoom mode:

```
File: Ivy Promo            REVIEW/ADD/CHANGE            Escape: Main Menu
=====<====<====<====<====<====<====<====<====<====<====<====<====<==
----------Left Margin:  2.0 inches
                Located in bucolic Leaf County, the 50 acre
        wooded setting is ideal for students wishing to
        major in biology, botany, and related fields. If
        you are considering entering one of these areas of
        study, we hope that you will pay us a visit. There
        is a reaction many get from visiting our campus
        that cannot be communicated with words or
        pictures. At Ivy University we are willing to help
        you in any way we can. Please feel free to contact
        us should you have any questions.

----------Right Margin:  1.5 inches
        OUR CONTRIBUTION TO AMERICA

                As one of the premier educational
        institutions in the country, Ivy University
        has long been recognized as a national
        treasure. Many leaders in industry, science,
        sports and government are alumni of Ivy
------------------------------------------------------------------------
Type entry or use @ commands       Line 25 Column 11       @-? for Help
```

3.8 Double and Single Spacing

Single spacing places text on each line of the printed page while double spacing inserts a blank line between lines of text. Double spacing can make a document more readable and leaves room for notes to be written between lines, which is especially helpful while rewriting a document. Examples of both formats are given below:

Single Spaced:

This paragraph is single spaced. There is little room between the lines for notes or comments, but more information can be placed on each page. Most printed text, including this book, is single spaced.

Double Spaced:

This paragraph is double spaced. Note how room is left between each line for notes or comments. Double spacing is used mostly for academic papers and drafts.

Single and double spacing are selected from the Options menu, and can be applied to specific paragraphs. One paragraph in a document can be single spaced and the next double spaced. Single spacing is the default. To sct double spacing, place the cursor in the first paragraph to be double spaced and select DS from the Options menu.

The current paragraph and all below it will be double spaced, leaving the paragraphs above unchanged. To switch back to single spacing, move the cursor to the desired paragraph and select SS from the Options menu. All paragraphs after the cursor to the end of the document are then single-spaced. AppleWorks also allows text to be triple spaced (Open-Apple O TS), a rarely used format. Any spacing options set are retained when the file is saved on disk.

Unlike left and right margins, double spaced text is not displayed on the screen. In order to tell if a paragraph has been double spaced, Zoom mode (Open-Apple Z) must be used to display the Option markers. All text after the Double Space marker will be double spaced when printed.

Practice 4

This Practice demonstrates the use of double spacing. Boot ProDOS and load AppleWorks if you have not already done so, and add the Word Processor document named Ivy Promo to the Desktop. The first paragraph only is to be double spaced.

1) PLACE THE CURSOR IN THE PARAGRAPH TO BE DOUBLE SPACED

Move the cursor into the paragraph which begins "Ivy University is one of...".

2) DISPLAY THE OPTIONS MENU

Press Open-Apple O.

3) DOUBLE SPACE THE PARAGRAPH

a. Type DS and press Return. AppleWorks will automatically double space the current paragraph and all below it.
b. Press Escape to return to the work area.
c. If you are not already in it, switch to Zoom mode by pressing Open-Apple Z to verify that the paragraph has been double spaced by displaying the Double Space marker.

4) SINGLE SPACE THE SECOND PARAGRAPH

a. Move the cursor into the second paragraph which begins "Located in...".
b. Press Open-Apple O to display the Options menu.
c. Type SS and Return. AppleWorks will single space the rest of the document from this paragraph on.
d. Press Escape to return to the work area.

5) SAVE AND PRINT THE FILE

a. Press Open-Apple S to save the modified file on disk.
b. Make sure that your computer is connected to a printer, and that the printer is on line with the paper positioned at the top of a new page. Press Open-Apple P and accept the default for where to begin, choose your printer and enter 1 after the How many copies? prompt. Note the double and single spaced text produced in the printed copy.

Check - Display the document in Zoom mode to verify the double and single space markers. Remember, double spacing is not shown on the screen, but appears when the document is printed:

```
File: Ivy Promo              REVIEW/ADD/CHANGE            Escape: Main Menu
=====<=====<=====<=====<=====<=====<=====<=====<=====<=====<=====<=====<=====<==
———————Double Space
     Ivy University is one of our nation's most prestigious
private universities. Undergraduate study is offered in an
intellectually invigorating and challenging climate. School
colors are leafy green and neon pink. With world famous
faculty members, high standards and a down to earth
practicality, you can be assured of obtaining the best
possible education.

———————Left Margin:  2.0 inches
———————Single Space
             Located in bucolic Leaf County, the 50 acre
            wooded setting is ideal for students wishing to
            major in biology, botany, and related fields. If
            you are considering entering one of these areas of
            study, we hope that you will pay us a visit. There
            is a reaction many get from visiting our campus
            that cannot be communicated with words or
            pictures. At Ivy University we are willing to help
            you in any way we can. Please feel free to contact
---------------------------------------------------------------------------
Type entry or use @ commands         Line 15 Column  1         @-? for Help
```

3.9 Paragraph Alignment

AppleWorks provides four ways to align text in a paragraph relative to the margins: justified, unjustified, centered and right justified. Each of these options is selected by entering the desired code from the Options menu, Open-Apple O. Justified alignment (JU from the Options menu) creates straight paragraph borders at both margins. To justify a paragraph, the computer automatically places extra spaces between words to fill up each line. As a result the rightmost word in each line is pushed over to the right margin. Justified formats are common in newspaper columns and books; this text book for example. Like double spacing, justified text is not displayed on the screen as it will be printed, therefore Zoom mode must be used to determine if a paragraph is justified or not.

Unjustified (UJ from the Options menu) means that words are lined up at the left hand margin. The resulting right margin is jagged, which is the default alignment. This is the format produced by a typewriter.

Centering (CN from the Options menu) is an alignment most often used for headings and titles. It involves positioning a line so that it is equidistant from the left and right margins. AppleWorks automatically calculates the position of the line and then centers it. Centered text is shown properly on the screen.

AppleWorks version 3.0 also allows text to be right justified (RJ from the Options menu). With this seldom used format the right margin is straight, but the left is jagged. Examples of these alignments are shown on the next page:

Justified: This paragraph is justified. Each of the
lines is extended to reach the right margin.
The effect of justifying a paragraph is that
the borders on each margin appear straight.
Note the extra spaces between some words that
are used to extend the lines to the right
margin.

Unjustified: This paragraph is unjustified. Notice
how the length of each line is different.
The effect of an unjustified paragraph is
that the right margin on each line appears
jagged. This format is often called "ragged
right" for this reason.

Centered: This paragraph is centered. Each line is
placed halfway between the margins.
Centered text is often used for titles.

Right Justified: This paragraph is right justified. Each of
the lines is flush with the right margin,
while the left side is ragged.

Practice 5

This Practice demonstrates each of the three most common text alignments. Boot ProDOS and start AppleWorks if you have not already done so, and add the Ivy Promo Word Processor file to the Desktop. You will modify the file by centering the two heading lines and justifying the rest of the text.

1) PLACE THE CURSOR ON THE LINE TO BE CENTERED

Place the cursor on the first line in the document, the heading which reads "Ivy University".

2) DISPLAY THE OPTIONS MENU

Press Open-Apple O. Note that the default format shown in the bold line is "UJ" for unjustified.

3) SELECT THE CENTER COMMAND

a. Type CN and press Return to execute the Center command. Notice how the first line and all below it are moved over to the centered position.
b. Press Escape to return to the work area.

4) MOVE THE CURSOR TO THE PARAGRAPH TO BE JUSTIFIED

Place the cursor at the beginning of the paragraph that begins "Ivy University is one of...".

5) JUSTIFY THE PARAGRAPH

a. Display the Options menu by pressing Open-Apple O.
b. Select the justified command, JU, press Return.
c. Press Escape to return to the work area.

Selecting justified text for this paragraph removes the centering and sets all paragraphs below it to justified as well. Note that the text does not appear justified on the screen, only when printed.

6) SAVE AND PRINT THE MODIFIED FILE

    a. Press `Open-Apple S`. When Ivy Promo is next loaded, the titles will be centered and the rest of the document justified.

    b. Press `Open-Apple P` and select the proper options to print the document. The titles are centered and the body of the text is justified in the printed copy.

<u>Check</u> - Display the document in Zoom mode to verify that the title is centered and the paragraph justified:

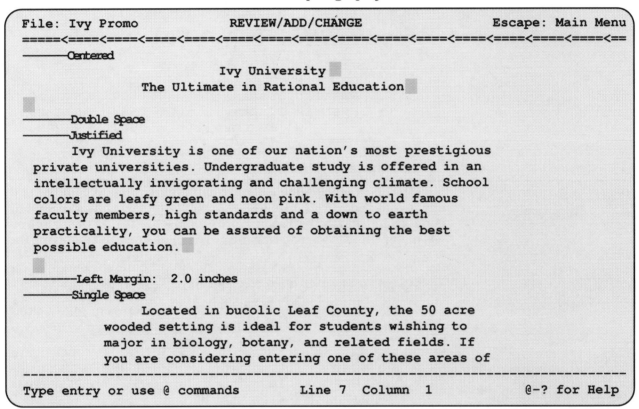

```
File: Ivy Promo              REVIEW/ADD/CHANGE              Escape: Main Menu
=====<=====<=====<=====<=====<=====<=====<=====<=====<=====<=====<=====<==
--------Centered

                      Ivy University
              The Ultimate in Rational Education


--------Double Space
--------Justified
      Ivy University is one of our nation's most prestigious
private universities. Undergraduate study is offered in an
intellectually invigorating and challenging climate. School
colors are leafy green and neon pink. With world famous
faculty members, high standards and a down to earth
practicality, you can be assured of obtaining the best
possible education.


--------Left Margin:  2.0 inches
--------Single Space
                Located in bucolic Leaf County, the 50 acre
                wooded setting is ideal for students wishing to
                major in biology, botany, and related fields. If
                you are considering entering one of these areas of
-----------------------------------------------------------------------

Type entry or use @ commands        Line 7  Column  1        @-? for Help
```

3.10 Pagination

Pagination is the division of a document into page-sized sections for printing. Using the specifications for page length and margins, AppleWorks calculates the number of lines that fit on each printed page. Do not confuse screen pages which contain 20 lines of text with printed pages which usually contain 50 to 60 lines.

A "page break" is the location in a document where one printed page ends and another begins. To have AppleWorks display the positions of page breaks, the command `Open-Apple K` (for Kalculate) is used. AppleWorks first asks you to select your printer from a menu. Broken lines are then displayed on the screen indicating where the page breaks will occur when the document is printed. The page number is also shown. Page break markers disappear when any editing change is made because the change may affect the pagination of the document. To recalculate and display the location of the page breaks, `Open-Apple K` must be used again.

Some types of material call for starting a new page before completing the previous one: the beginning of a new chapter, a change in subject matter, or the presentation of a table are three examples. You can cause AppleWorks to advance to the next page regardless of the number of lines left on the current page by creating a "manual page break." To do this place the cursor where the new page is to start and select the New Page (NP) command from the Options menu. Manual page breaks can be removed by placing the cursor on the New Page marker and pressing `Open-Apple D` (for Delete) and then Return.

Practice 6

This Practice demonstrates automatic and manual page breaks. Start AppleWorks if you have not already done so and add the Ivy Promo Word Processor file to the Desktop.

1) CALCULATE THE PAGE BREAKS

    a. Press `Open-Apple K`. After clearing the screen AppleWorks displays a menu listing the available printers.

    b. Choose your printer and press Return.

2) LOCATE THE PAGE BREAK MARKERS

    a. Scroll through the document until the page break marker for the first page is visible:

– – – – – – – – – – – -End of Page 1- – – – – – – – – – – –

    b. Press `Open-Apple down-arrow` until the second page break marker is visible:

– – – – – – – – – – – -End of Page 2- – – – – – – – – – –

3) INSERT A MANUAL PAGE BREAK

    a. Move the cursor up until it reaches the end of the first paragraph directly below the first page break marker.

    b. Press `Open-Apple O` and select the new page command by typing NP and Return. A New Page marker appears on the screen to indicate the position of the manual page break.

    c. Press Escape to return to the work area. Any page break markers previously displayed are removed from the display.

    d. If not already in Zoom mode, press `Open-Apple Z` to view the New Page marker.

4) RECALCULATE THE PAGE BREAKS

    Press `Open-Apple K` and select your printer. Note that page 2 now contains only one paragraph.

5) DELETE THE MANUAL PAGE BREAK AND RECALCULATE

    a. Move the cursor to the New Page marker and press `Open-Apple D` and Return. The marker disappears, indicating that the page break has been deleted.

    b. Recalculate the page breaks by pressing `Open-Apple K` and selecting your printer from the displayed menu.

    c. Press `Open-Apple S` to save the file on disk.

3.11 Selecting a Block

Some formatting options do not apply either to the whole document or to specific paragraphs, but to "blocks" of text. Once defined, these blocks may be deleted, moved from one part of the document to another, or copied over again. The first step in defining a block is to highlight it. When a block of text is highlighted, it is said to be "selected." Once selected, one of the three block operations can be performed on it. To perform a block operation, the following steps are used:

1. Place the cursor on the first character in the block to be selected.
2. Issue the command affecting the block.
3. Use the arrow keys to move the cursor to the last character in the block.
4. Execute the command by pressing Return.

Moving the cursor after one of the block commands has been issued creates a highlighted block. Any cursor control key may be used to highlight the block, including the Tab and Open-Apple arrow combinations. A block remains highlighted until the command is executed or Escape pressed to cancel it. When creating a block, the name of the command appears at the top of the screen in place of REVIEW/ADD/CHANGE.

3.12 Deleting a Block

You already know how to delete text one character at a time using the Delete key and one line at a time using Open-Apple Y. There are times, however, when the amount of text to be deleted is large enough to make using either approach cumbersome. A more efficient method is to issue the Delete command (Open-Apple D), select the area to be deleted as a block and then delete it by pressing Return.

When deleting a block, it is helpful to select not only the text to be deleted but the surrounding spaces and punctuation as well. Thus if a phrase to be deleted is surrounded by commas, including the commas in the highlighted block will insure that they are deleted too. If a sentence is being deleted, eliminate the period and the following spaces by selecting them as part of the block.

The Delete command is the only way to remove the formatting option markers inserted into a document from the Options menu. Deleting blocks is easiest in Zoom mode because the Return blotches and options markers are displayed.

Practice 7

In this Practice the block delete command will be used to remove words and an entire paragraph from Ivy Promo. Start AppleWorks if you have not already done so and add the Ivy Promo Word Processor file to the Desktop.

1) MOVE THE CURSOR TO THE FIRST CHARACTER IN THE BLOCK TO BE DELETED

   a. Move the cursor to the first paragraph in the document which begins "Ivy University is one of...".
   b. Place the cursor under the comma that begins the phrase ", high standards".

2) ISSUE THE DELETE COMMAND

Press `Open-Apple D`. Note that DELETE TEXT is displayed above the work area at the top of the screen, and that the display temporarily switches to Zoom mode if not already selected.

3) HIGHLIGHT THE BLOCK TO BE DELETED

Use the right-arrow key to move the cursor to the final "s" in "standards".

4) DELETE THE HIGHLIGHTED BLOCK

Pressing Return deletes the block and the rest of the paragraph is automatically reformatted.

5) SELECT AN ENTIRE PARAGRAPH AS A BLOCK TO BE DELETED

a. Place the cursor at the beginning of the first line of the first paragraph which begins "Ivy University is one of...".
b. Press `Open-Apple D` and then down-arrow until the entire paragraph is highlighted, including the blotch marker on the line <u>after</u> the paragraph.
c. Press Return to delete the paragraph. Note how the next paragraph moves up take its place.
d. Press `Open-Apple S` to save this modified version on disk.

6) DELETE AN OPTION MARKER

a. Move the cursor to the Double Space marker.
b. Press `Open-Apple D`. The entire line is highlighted.
c. Pressing Return deletes the marker and the document is automatically reformatted.

<u>Check</u> - The paragraph and option marker should be deleted:

```
/ File: Ivy Promo          REVIEW/ADD/CHANGE          Escape: Main Menu \
 =====<====<====<====<====<====<====<====<====<====<====<====<====<====<==
 ────────Centered
                         Ivy University▓
                The Ultimate in Rational Education▓
 ▓
 ────────Justified
 ────────Left Margin:  2.0 inches
 ────────Single Space
              Located in bucolic Leaf County, the 50 acre
           wooded setting is ideal for students wishing to
           major in biology, botany, and related fields. If
           you are considering entering one of these areas of
           study, we hope that you will pay us a visit. There
           is a reaction many get from visiting our campus
           that cannot be communicated with words or
           pictures. At Ivy University we are willing to help
           you in any way we can. Please feel free to contact
           us should you have any questions.▓

 ────────Right Margin:  1.5 inches
 OUR CONTRIBUTION TO AMERICA▓
 ─────────────────────────────────────────────────────────────────────────
 \ Type entry or use @ commands        Line 5  Column  1       @-? for Help /
```

3.13 Moving a Block

One of the most useful editing tools that a word processor provides is the ability to move pieces of text from one area of a document to another. For example, a sentence can be moved from one paragraph and placed on the next page. Text moved can be as small as a single character or word or as large as an entire page or even a group of pages. AppleWorks neatly closes the space that formerly held the moved text and opens new space to receive it, rearranging the rest of the document to accommodate the change. Whole paragraphs or groups of paragraphs can similarly be re-positioned by moving them from one place in a document to another.

AppleWorks expands this capability by allowing the text to be moved outside of the document to a special area in memory called the "Clipboard." The Clipboard can be accessed from other Word Processor files, allowing text to be moved from one document to another. This is useful when large blocks of identical text must appear in two documents. Instructions for using the Clipboard are given in Chapter 9.

Moving a block of text is a five step process:

1. Move the cursor to the first character in the block to be moved.
2. Issue the Move command, `Open-Apple M`. MOVE TEXT appears above the work area to indicate that the Move command is being performed.
3. AppleWorks must then be told if the text is to be moved to a new position in the document, or placed on the Clipboard.
4. The block to be moved is selected by moving the cursor to the last character in the block and pressing Return.
5. Place the cursor at the new location for the block of text using the arrow keys and then press Return.

When Return is pressed the block is moved from its old position to the position of the cursor. AppleWorks temporarily switches to Zoom mode during a move, making it easy to include the Option and Return markers in the block to be moved.

3.14 Copying a Block

AppleWorks can also copy blocks of text. While the Move command deletes a block from its original position and reproduces it in another location, Copy retains the original and creates an exact duplicate in a new location. Blocks may also be copied to the Clipboard.

The procedure for copying is similar to that for moving blocks. To copy a block of text, the Copy command `Open-Apple C` is used. A block is then selected and the cursor moved to the new position. When Return is pressed the block will be copied.

Practice 8

This Practice demonstrates the use of block move and copy within a document. Start AppleWorks if you have not already done so and add the Ivy Promo Word Processor file to the Desktop. A block consisting of a sentence will be moved and then an entire paragraph copied.

1)   POSITION THE CURSOR AT THE BLOCK TO BE MOVED

You will move the sentence about contacting the school from the first paragraph to the second. Place the cursor on the space before the "P" in "Please feel free...".

2)   ISSUE THE MOVE COMMAND

a.   Press `Open-Apple M`. MOVE TEXT appears above the work area and the prompt

`Move Text?` **Within document**   `To clipboard   From clipboard`

is shown on the Message Line.

b.   Press Return to accept the default of moving the block to a new position within the same document. The display temporarily changes to Zoom mode if it was not in it already to aid in the block selection.

3)   SELECT THE BLOCK TO BE MOVED

With the cursor on the space before "Please", press right-arrow and move the cursor to the sentence's period. (Do not include the blotch marker at the end of the paragraph.) The selected block is shown in highlighted letters. Press Return to indicate that the block has been selected.

4)   PLACE THE CURSOR AT THE NEW POSITION FOR THE BLOCK

AppleWorks displays the prompt:

`Select new location, then press Return`

Move the cursor to the blotch marker at the end of the paragraph which begins "As one of..." and press Return. The sentence is moved from one paragraph to another.

5)   POSITION THE CURSOR AT THE BLOCK TO BE COPIED

You will produce a copy of the first paragraph at the end of the document. Place the cursor on the first letter in the paragraph, the "L" in "Located in...".

6)   ISSUE THE COPY COMMAND

a.   Press `Open-Apple C`. COPY TEXT appears above the work area and the prompt

`Copy Text?` **Within document**   `To clipboard   From clipboard`

is shown on the Message Line.

b.   Press Return to accept the default of copying the block to a new position within the current document. The display is temporarily changed to Zoom mode if it was not in it already.

7)   SELECT THE BLOCK TO BE COPIED

Move the cursor to the "blotch" marker after the final sentence's period. The entire paragraph should be shown in highlighted letters. Press Return to indicate that the block has been selected.

8) PLACE THE CURSOR AT THE NEW POSITION FOR THE BLOCK

    a. Move the cursor on the last line in the document by pressing `Open-Apple 9`.

    b. Press Return to copy the block. A copy of the first paragraph is placed at the cursor position.

    c. Insert spaces at the beginning of the paragraph to properly indent it.

    d. Jump back to the top of the document using `Open-Apple 1` and verify that the original paragraph is still there.

    e. Press `Open-Apple S` to save the modified version on disk.

<u>Check</u> - A copy of the first paragraph should be at the bottom of the document and the sentence about contacting the school moved to the second paragraph.

3.15 Text Formats

AppleWorks' Options menu has a number of commands which affect the way that individual characters appear when printed. Two of the most common are Underline and Boldface, which are used to emphasize different parts of a document.

The following steps are required to create emphasized text:

1. The cursor is moved to the first character of the text to be emphasized.
2. The Options menu is displayed by pressing `Open-Apple O`.
3. The two letter code for the command to begin the emphasis (boldface, underline or another) is entered and Escape pressed to return to the work area.
4. The cursor is moved to the end of the text to be emphasized.
5. The Options menu is again displayed by pressing `Open-Apple O`.
6. The two letter code for the command to end the emphasis is entered and Escape pressed to return to the work area. All characters between the begin emphasis command and the end emphasis command will be emphasized when printed.

Underlined and boldfaced text are not differentiated in any way on the screen. However, a caret symbol (^) is placed on the screen as a marker at the beginning and end of the emphasized block. The type of emphasis may be determined by moving the cursor to the caret and checking the status line at the bottom of the screen where a message indicating the type of emphasis is displayed.

Underline:

To underline a block of text, move the cursor to the first character in the block and issue the Underline Begin command, Open-Apple O UB. Return to the work area with Escape, move the cursor to the last character in the block and issue the Underline End command, `Open-Apple O UE`. Carets are shown on the screen marking the emphasized block.

Boldface:

Boldface text is printed darker than plain text so that words and phrases printed in bold stand out on the page. It is most frequently used for titles and headings.

To boldface a block of text, move the cursor to the first character in the block and issue the Boldface Begin command, `Open-Apple O BB`. Return to the work area, move the cursor to the last character in the block and enter the Boldface End command, `Open-Apple O BE`. As with underlined text, carets are shown on the screen marking the block. To distinguish underlined text from boldface text, move the cursor to the caret. A message describing the option will appear at the bottom of the screen: Boldface Begin, Boldface End, Underline Begin, etc.

AppleWorks also has shortcuts for these formatting options which make use of the Control key. With these shortcuts the Options Menu can be bypassed completely. For example, text can be underlined by simply moving the cursor to the beginning of the block to be underlined, pressing `Control-L`, moving the cursor to the end of the block and pressing `Control-L` again. Formatting options such as centering can also be used by pushing `Control-C`. All of the text following that point will be centered. These shortcuts are summarized in the following chart:

Formatting Control Key Shortcuts

`Control-B`	Begin or End Boldface
`Control-L`	Begin or End Underline
`Control-C`	Center the following text
`Control-F`	Justify the following text
`Control-N`	Unjustify the following text
`Control-R`	Right Justify the following text
`Control-P`	Insert a manual Page Break

Earlier versions of AppleWorks only use the `Control-B` and `Control-L` shortcuts.

Practice 9

This Practice demonstrates the use of underlined and boldface text. Start AppleWorks if you have not already done so and add the Ivy Promo file to the Desktop. Students may follow these instructions or use the Control key shortcuts. Note: AppleWorks version 2.0 uses the Control key shortcuts only for underlining and boldfacing.

1) POSITION THE CURSOR AT THE FIRST CHARACTER TO BE BOLD-FACE

    Move the cursor to the "I" in the first "Ivy University" in the title at the top of the document.

2) SELECT THE BOLDFACE BEGIN COMMAND FROM THE OPTIONS MENU

    a. Press `Open-Apple O`.
    b. Type the Boldface Begin code, BB and press Return. A caret (^) is placed before the I.
    c. Press Escape to return to the work area. Press the left-arrow to move the cursor to the caret. Note the Boldface Begin in the Message Line.

3) SELECT THE BOLDFACE END COMMAND

a. Move the cursor to the space after the "y" in "University" on the same line.
b. Press Open-Apple O.
c. Type the Boldface End code, BE and press Return. A caret is placed after the y.
d. Press Escape to return to the work area. Move the cursor to the caret and note the Boldface End in the Message Line.

4) UNDERLINE THE NEXT LINE

a. Move the cursor to the first "T" in the next line.
b. Press Open-Apple O.
c. Type the Underline Begin code, UB and press Return.
d. Press Escape to return to the work area. Press the left-arrow to move the cursor to the caret. Note the Underline Begin in the Message Line.
e. Move the cursor one space to the right of the "n" at the end of the line.
f. Press Open-Apple O.
g. Type the Underline End code, UE and press Return.
h. Press Escape to return to the work area. Press the left-arrow to move the cursor to the caret. Note the Underline End in the Message Line. The second line will now print as underlined.

5) PRINT THE DOCUMENT

Press Open-Apple P, select 'This Page' and your printer from the menu. Print one copy. The Ivy University in the title should be in boldface, and the next line underlined.

6) SAVE THE MODIFIED FILE

Press Open-Apple S and save the file. The next time Ivy Promo is loaded the bold and underline commands will be present.

Check - On the screen the titles are surrounded by carets:

```
^Ivy University^
^The Ultimate in Rational Education^
```

3.16 Finding Text in a Document

The Find command operates differently than the commands you have studied so far. Open-Apple F (for **F**ind) does not involve entering text or editing it. Rather the computer scans a document looking for a particular combination of letters called the "search text." Search text may be a single letter, a word or a phrase and is entered at the Find what text? prompt. Starting from the current cursor position, the computer moves through the document looking for a sequence of letters that matches the search text. If a match is found the scanning stops, allowing the document to be read or edited. The search can then be repeated until all occurrences of the search text have been found. Find is useful when trying to locate a specific word or passage in a large document.

Note that Find begins its search at the current cursor position. To search the entire document the cursor must first be moved to the beginning (Open-Apple 1) before executing the Find command.

When entering the search text, any old text may be first removed by pressing Open-Apple Y.

Find has a number of different options. AppleWorks can be told to search for specific text, a certain page number, or a marker set by the Options command. Normally, AppleWorks ignores case differences (i.e. upper and lower case) during a search. If the search text is "Dog" AppleWorks will find "dog", "Dog", "DOG", etc. The 'Case sensitive text' option tells AppleWorks to find only text with the same capitalization as the search text. For example, a case sensitive search for "Cat" will not find "CAT" or "cat".

It is important to realize that a match is also considered to be found when the search text is located within another word. For example, specifying a search text of "the" will not only find "the" but also "they", "theory", "another", etc. Such "false finds" can be eliminated by carefully specifying the search text. For example, specifying "the " ("the" plus a space) will eliminate most false finds.

Practice 10

This Practice demonstrates the Find command. If you have not already done so, start AppleWorks and add Ivy Promo to the Desktop. You will search for each occurrence of the word "bandage".

1) ISSUE THE FIND TEXT COMMAND

   a. Move the cursor to the top of the document by pressing Open-Apple 1.
   b. Press Open-Apple F. FIND appears above the work area.

2) CHOOSE THE TEXT OPTION

Because Text is the default

Find?   **Text**   Page Marker Case sensitive text Options for printer

pressing Return will accept it.

3) ENTER THE SEARCH TEXT

At the prompt

Find what text?

type the word bandage and press Return. The first "bandage" found is in the course description for class 101.

4) REPEAT THE SEARCH USING THE SAME SEARCH TEXT

AppleWorks will prompt with:

Find next occurrence?   **No**   Yes

To repeat the search using the same search text, press the Y key. The cursor will move to the next occurrence of bandage. (Pressing Return would halt the search and the cursor would return to the work area.)

5) FIND THE REST OF THE OCCURRENCES OF BANDAGE

Press Y until all occurrences of "bandage" have been found. How many did you find?

Check - When all occurrences of the search text have been found, AppleWorks displays the following message. Press the Space Bar to continue.

```
Not found, press Space Bar to continue.
```

3.17 Replacing Text

The Replace command (Open-Apple R) locates text in a document, just as the Search command does, but then replaces it with another piece of text that you supply. This makes it easy to create different versions of the same document which have some specified differences. For example, AppleWorks could be used to create a letter requesting a college interview with Ivy University. After printing the letter, the Replace command could be used to change each occurrence of "Ivy University" to "Trenton State" and then to "New Brunswick College" and so on. Thus all the letters needed could easily be created without having to type each one separately; the master letter is typed once and the name of the school changed using Replace.

The Replace command can be dangerous. If the search text is not clearly defined unwanted replacements may be made. For example, a search text of "the" will not only affect every occurrence of "the", but also any word that contains "the", such as "they", "theory", "another", etc. One way to avoid unwanted replacements is to define the search text very carefully. For example, specifying "the " ("the" followed by a space) as the search text will avoid the replacements described above.

Like the Find command, Replace starts its search from the current cursor position and can be made case sensitive. However, it cannot be used to change any Options that have been set. Replace also has the option of replacing every occurrence with the new text, or one at a time, prompting you to verify that each change should be made. It is usually advisable to verify each replacement before it is made, thereby avoiding unwanted changes. When entering the search and replace text, any old text may be first deleted using Open-Apple Y.

Practice 11

Ivy University is considering updating its image by changing its name. This Practice will use the Replace command to change each occurrence of "Ivy University" to "Modern College" in the Ivy Promo file. This will allow the administration to see how the document looks with the new name. If you have not already done so, start AppleWorks and add the Ivy Promo file to the Desktop.

1) MOVE THE CURSOR TO THE BEGINNING OF THE DOCUMENT

    Press Open-Apple 1.

2) ISSUE THE REPLACE COMMAND AND SELECT NON-CASE SENSITIVE

    a. Press Open-Apple R. REPLACE appears above the work area at the top of the screen.
    b. At the prompt

    Replace? **Text**   Case sensitive text

    press Return to accept the default of Text.

3)   ENTER THE SEARCH TEXT

At the prompt

`Replace what?`

type `Ivy University` and press Return. (Use `Open-Apple Y` to delete any previous search text if necessary.)

4)   ENTER THE REPLACE TEXT

At the prompt

`Replace with what?`

type `Modern College` and press Return.

5)   SELECT THE 'ONE AT A TIME' OPTION

a.   From the prompt

`Replace?`   **One at a time**   `All`

press Return to accept the default and execute the command.

b.   AppleWorks moves the cursor to the first occurrence of Ivy University. From the prompt

`Replace this one?` **No**   `Yes`

press `Y` to replace it with Modern College.

c.   AppleWorks asks:

`Find next occurrence?` **No**   `Yes`

Press `Y` to continue.

d.   Repeat steps (b) and (c) for each occurrence of Ivy University.

e.   Press `Open-Apple S` to save the modified version on disk.

<u>Check</u> - When AppleWorks has completed the Replace command, it will leave the cursor at the position where the last replacement was made and display the message:

`Not found, press Space Bar to continue.`

Press the Space Bar. Scroll through the file to verify that each occurrence of Ivy University has been changed to Modern College.

3.18 Headers, Footers and Page Numbers

AppleWorks can place a message at the top and bottom of each page when a document is printed. This message is often used to indicate the current page number, date or time. A message which is automatically printed at the top of each page is called a "header." Similarly, a message which is printed at the bottom of each page is called a "footer." Headers and footers are created by using the Options command, `Open-Apple O`.

To create a header or footer for a document the cursor is placed at the top of the document and the Options menu displayed using `Open-Apple O`. Entering the code `HE` places Page Header begin and Page Header End markers in the work area. Pressing Escape returns the cursor to the work area, and a message may be entered between these markers. When the document is printed, the message between the markers will automatically be printed at the top of each page. Creating a footer is a similar process: the code FO is entered from the Options menu, producing Page Footer begin and Page Footer End markers in the work area. A message typed between these markers will automatically be printed at the bottom of each page. The page footer can be placed anywhere in the document before the end of the first page, but it is a good idea to place both the header and footer together at the very top of the document so that they are easy to locate.

The current page number, time or date may be printed in a document's header or footer. This is accomplished by placing the cursor at the desired position in between the begin and end markers of a Page Header or Page Footer and entering the code from the Options menu, PP for page number, PD for the date, or PT for the time. A caret is then displayed on the screen, but the actual page number, time or date will be printed. Any headers or footers created will be retained when the document is saved on disk. To delete a header or footer from a document, the Delete command Open-Apple D is used and the entire header or footer is highlighted.

Note that in earlier versions of AppleWorks, only one line can be printed for a header or a footer. Also, the date and time options are not available, only the page number option.

Practice 12

In this Practice you will create a header and footer for the Ivy Promo document. The footer will contain the page number, and the header will contain the date and time. If you have not already done so, start AppleWorks and add the Ivy Promo file to the Desktop.

1) SWITCH TO ZOOM MODE AND PLACE THE CURSOR AT THE TOP OF THE DOCUMENT

   a. Switch to Zoom mode using Open-Apple Z if you have not already done so.
   b. Press Open-Apple 1.

2) DISPLAY THE OPTIONS MENU

   Press Open-Apple O.

3) SELECT THE PAGE HEADER COMMAND

   a. Type HE and press Return. Page Header markers are shown in the document:

      --------Page Header

      --------Page Header End

   b. Press Escape to return to the work area.

4) ENTER THE TEXT FOR THE HEADER

   a. With the cursor in the area between the Page Header and Page Header End markers, type Promotional Information and a space, and then press Return.
   b. Press Open-Apple O to display the Options menu.
   c. Type PT and press Return to have AppleWorks print the current time when the document is printed.

d. Type `PD` and press Return to have AppleWorks print the current date when the document is printed.

e. Press Escape to return to the work area, and enter a space between the carets representing Print Time and Print Date. Move the cursor to each caret and note the "Print Time" and "Print Date" messages displayed at the bottom of the screen.

f. Push the down arrow twice to move the cursor below the Page Header area.

5) CREATE A PAGE FOOTER

a. Press `Open-Apple O`.

b. Type `FO` and press Return. Page Footer begin and end markers appear in the document.

c. Press Escape to return to the work area.

d. Type `Page` on the line between the footer begin and end markers and press the Space Bar.

6) ADD A PAGE NUMBER TO THE FOOTER

a. Press `Open-Apple O`.

b. Type `PP` and press Return. A caret appears in the footer text which will be replaced by the actual page number when the document is printed.

c. Press Escape to return to the work area.

d. Move the cursor to the caret and note the "Print Page No." message at the bottom of the screen.

Check - Your header and footer sections should be similar to:

```
--------Page Header
Promotional Information ^ ^
--------Page Header End
--------Page Footer
Page ^
--------Page Footer End
```

7) PRINT THE DOCUMENT

Make sure that your computer is connected to a printer and that the printer is on line with the paper positioned at the top of a page. Press `Open-Apple P` and select 'Beginning', choose your printer and print 1 copy. Each page of the printed copy should contain the header with proper date and time and footer with proper page number.

8) SAVE THE MODIFIED FILE

Press `Open-Apple S`. The header and footer will be retained in the document file.

3.19 Using the Spelling Checker

One of the most useful features of today's word processors is the ability to have the computer check the spelling of the words in a document. In AppleWorks, this is accomplished by executing the Verify Spelling command, `Open-Apple V`. When this command is executed, AppleWorks compares the words in a document to a dictionary file.

There are several options with the spelling checker. After pressing `Open-Apple V`, the following is displayed:

`Verify Spelling?` **`All`** `  Word   Block   Dictionary   Options`

'All' checks all of the words in a document, 'Word' checks only the word next to the cursor, and 'Block' allows a highlighted block to be defined which will be checked. After selecting an option, AppleWorks scans the document and loads its dictionary files. (You may be requested to load a dictionary disk.)

During the spelling check, words not found in the dictionary are highlighted, and the following prompt is displayed:

`Unknown word?` **`Replace`** `Add to dictionary Ignore Skip Get suggestions`

'Replace' allows you to type a correction, 'Add to dictionary' places the word in the dictionary file so that it will not be marked as misspelled again. This option would be used for common words such as your name or address. 'Ignore' ignores all future occurrences of the highlighted word in the document. 'Skip' skips this occurrence of the word only; if it appears later in the document it will be marked as unknown again. 'Get suggestions' displays the misspelled word and has AppleWorks produce a list of suggested spellings from which you may select:

`Suggested spellings for "UNVERSITY"`

`1. UNIVERSITY`
`2. ADVERSITY`

`Type number, or use arrows, then press Return`

After selecting an option, pressing Return replaces the misspelled word with the suggestion. The spelling checker also locates double words and gives you the opportunity to remove them. For example, after verifying a document which contained the sentence

`Paris in the the Spring.`

AppleWorks would display the sentence with the doubled word highlighted and ask:

`Paris in the` **`the`** `Spring.`

`Remove?` **`Yes`** `  No`

Practice 13

Ivy University is about to have 50,000 copies printed of its promotional file. This practice will use the Verify Spelling command to check the spelling in the document before sending it to the print shop. If you have not already done so, start AppleWorks and open the IVY PROMO file.

1) EXECUTE THE VERIFY SPELLING COMMAND

Press `Open-Apple V` and choose 'All'. There is a pause as AppleWorks checks the spelling. AppleWorks finds a questionable word in the course description section and highlights it, displaying the options for the word on the message line.

2) CORRECT THE MISSPELLED WORD

    a. AppleWorks finds the word "proffessional". Press G to have AppleWorks get suggestions for the spelling. AppleWorks checks the dictionary and displays the most likely spelling.

    b. Because the suggested spelling is correct, press Return to accept the suggestion and have it replace the misspelled word in the file. AppleWorks continues to the next word that is misspelled.

3) IGNORE THE MISSPELLED WORD

    Because "20th" is spelled correctly, press I to ignore this word. AppleWorks continues to the next word that is misspelled.

4) IGNORE THE NEXT MISSPELLED WORD

    Because the abbreviation "AABA" is spelled correctly, press I to ignore it.

5) CORRECT THE NEXT MISSPELLED WORD

    a. Press G to have AppleWorks suggest a spelling for "feld". AppleWorks checks the dictionary and displays the most likely spelling as the default on the list of spelling options.

    b. Because the suggestion is not the one we want, type a number or use the arrow keys to highlight the correct spelling, "field".

    c. Press Return to replace the misspelled word with the highlighted spelling from the Suggest Spelling list. AppleWorks then continues to check the spelling.

6) IGNORE THE NAMES

    a. Press I to ignore the spelling of any proper names.

    b. When the spelling check is finished, AppleWorks returns the cursor to the work area.

7) SAVE THE CORRECTED FILE

    Press Open-Apple S to save the corrected file.

3.20 Superscripts and Subscripts

Many times a word processed document must contain a "superscript" or "subscript." A superscript is a section of text which is raised slightly above the current line. A subscript is printed slightly below the current line. Superscripts and subscripts are most often used to indicate footnotes or other reference material in research papers or in mathematical and scientific formulas. For example:

Dr. Sulfuric[4] proved that the formula for water is H_2O.

The "4" after Dr. Sulfuric is a superscript representing a footnote reference, and the "2" in H_2O is a subscript. It is possible to emphasize more than one character in a superscript or subscript. The following line has the word "super" as a superscript and the word "sub" as a subscript:

This is a ^{super}script and this is a $_{sub}$script.

Both superscripts and subscripts are created from the Options menu in a process similar to making bold or underlined text. First, the cursor is moved to the beginning of the text to be emphasized. Then the Options menu is displayed by pressing `Open-Apple O`. The code to create a superscript or subscript is then entered: +B begins a superscript and −B a subscript. The end of a superscript or subscript is indicated by moving the cursor to the desired location in the text and entering the appropriate code from the Options menu: +E to end a superscript and −E to end a subscript.

Like most print options the beginning and ending of a superscript or subscript is indicated in the text on the screen by a caret (^). When the cursor is placed on the caret the type of emphasis is shown at the bottom of the screen: Subscript Begin, Superscript End, etc.

Practice 14

In this Practice you will create the superscripts and subscripts shown in the examples in Section 3.19 above. Start AppleWorks If you have not already done so.

1) CREATE A NEW DOCUMENT

 a. Select 'Add files' from the Main Menu.
 b. Select 'Word Processor' from the Add Files menu and choose 'From scratch'.
 c. Enter the name `Script Test` and press Return.

2) ADD TEXT TO THE DOCUMENT

Type the following two lines into the document, leaving a blank line between them:

`Dr. Sulfuric4 proved that the formula for water is H2O.`

`This is a superscript, and this is a subscript.`

3) CREATE THE FOOTNOTE SUPERSCRIPT

 a. Move the cursor to the "4" after Dr. Sulfuric's name.
 b. Press `Open-Apple O` to display the Options menu.
 c. Type +B and Return to begin the superscript. A caret (^) is displayed in front of the "4".
 d. Press Escape to exit the Options menu.
 e. Move the cursor to the blank after the "4".
 f. Press `Open-Apple O` to display the Options menu.
 g. Type +E and Return to end the superscript. A caret is displayed after the "4".
 h. Press Escape to exit the Options menu.

4) CREATE THE FORMULA SUBSCRIPT

 a. Place the cursor on the "2" in "H2O".
 b. Press `Open-Apple O` to display the Options menu.
 c. Type −B and Return to begin the subscript. A caret is displayed before the "2".
 d. Press Escape to exit the Options menu.
 e. Move the cursor to the "O" in "H^2O".
 f. Press `Open-Apple O` to display the Options menu.
 g. Type −E and Return to end the subscript. A caret is displayed after the "2".
 h. Press Escape to exit the Options menu.

5) CREATE THE "SUPER" SUPERSCRIPT

    a. Move the cursor to the line which begins "This is a superscript ...".
    b. Place the cursor on the first "s" in "superscript".
    c. Press `Open-Apple O` to display the Options menu.
    d. Type +B and Return to begin the superscript.
    e. Press Escape to exit the Options menu.
    f. Move the cursor to the second "s" in "superscript".
    g. Press `Open-Apple O` to display the Options menu.
    h. Type +E and Return to end the superscript.
    i. Press Escape to exit the Options menu.

6) CREATE THE "SUB" SUBSCRIPT

    a. Place the cursor on the first "s" in "subscript".
    b. Press `Open-Apple O` to display the Options menu.
    c. Type −B and Return to begin the subscript.
    d. Press Escape to exit the Options menu.
    e. Place the cursor on the second "s" in "subscript".
    f. Press `Open-Apple O` to display the Options menu.
    g. Type −E and Return to end the subscript.
    h. Press Escape to exit the Options menu.

<u>Check</u> - On the screen the lines should appear with carets:

```
Dr. Sulfuric^4^ proved that the formula for water is H^2^O.

This is a ^super^script and this is a ^sub^script.
```

7) SAVE AND PRINT THE FILE

    a. Press `Open-Apple S` to save the modified file on disk.
    b. Press `Open-Apple P` and print the file. Both lines should print as shown in Section 3.20 above:

```
Dr. Sulfuric⁴ proved that the formula for water is H₂O.
```

This is a ^{super}script and this is a $_{sub}$script.

3.21 Where can you go from here?

The last two chapters have introduced you to the concepts of word processing. You can now create, edit, print, format and verify the spelling of documents using the word processor. AppleWorks has several other word processing options available that you may wish to learn about. The best place to begin is by reading the word processor sections of the AppleWorks manuals supplied by Claris with your software.

For many users, the ability to word process justifies the expense of purchasing a personal computer because it saves time and makes revisions easier. There are dozens word processing software packages available, many of which have features and options not included in AppleWorks. Some of the most popular are WordStar, Microsoft Word and Word Perfect. Because you have learned the AppleWorks word processor, it will be easy for you to learn and use another word processing package such as the ones named above. Word processing is a valuable skill, not only for school work but in your personal and business life as well.

Chapter Summary

This chapter explained how text can be formatted in a Word Processor document to improve its appearance and readability. Apple-Works has default tab stops at every fifth space. Individual tab stops may be set by pressing Open-Apple T, choosing to create a new ruler or modify the current ruler and then pressing L, R, D, or C for left aligned, right aligned, decimal aligned or centered tabs respectively. Specific stops may be cleared by pressing U, and all stops cleared by pressing N.

Text can be deleted from the cursor's current position to the end of the line by pressing Open-Apple Y.

Margins are the blank spaces between the edges of the paper and text. AppleWork's default settings can be changed using the Options menu, Open-Apple O. When a margin is changed it affects all of the document from the cursor position to the end of the document.

Zoom mode, Open-Apple Z, is used to view the end of paragraph marks, option markers and margin settings.

Single and double spacing are selected from the options menu, Open-Apple O. When spacing is set it affects all text from the cursor location to the end of the document. To determine which text is double spaced Zoom mode is used.

AppleWorks also provides four ways to align text using the Options menu: justified, unjustified, right justified and centered. Justified alignment creates straight borders at both margins. Unjustified alignment creates a straight left border and a jagged right border. Right justified creates a straight right and jagged left border. Centering positions a line equidistant from the left and right margins.

Pagination is the division of a document into page-sized sections for printing. Open-Apple K will display the position of page breaks allowing you to determine how text will be divided at the page breaks.

Blocks are used to delete, move or copy specified amounts of text. A block of text is deleted using Open-Apple D. To move a block of text from one location within a document to another, Open-Apple M is used. To copy a block of text so that it appears both at its original location and at a new location, Open-Apple C is used.

Text may be made bold or underlined using the Options menu or in version 3.0 with the Control key shortcuts.

The Find command, Open-Apple F, allows a document to be searched for a particular combination of letters called the search text. The Replace command, Open-Apple R, locates a search text in a document and replaces it with different text.

A message called a header can be printed at the top of each page, or a footer at the bottom of each page using the Options menu. Page numbers, the current date and the current time can be included in either headers or footers.

One of the most powerful features of the AppleWorks Word Processor is the Verify Spelling command, Open-Apple V. Apple-Works compares the words typed in a document to a dictionary file. If a word is found which is not in the dictionary, AppleWorks can replace it with the correct spelling or allow you to type a correction.

Vocabulary

Block - A highlighted section of text which may contain anything from a single letter or phrase to a paragraph or several pages. Once highlighted, operations such as Copy and Move may be performed using the block.

Block Copy - Creates an exact copy of a highlighted block in a new location: Open-Apple C.

Block Delete - Removes a highlighted block or option marker from a document: Open-Apple D.

Block Move - Removes a highlighted block from its current position and places it in a new one: Open-Apple M.

Boldface - Darker letters, used for emphasis.

Centered - Text positioned evenly between the left and right margins.

Double Space - Leaving a blank line between each line of text when a document is printed.

Find - The computer searches a document for specified text: Open-Apple F.

Format - The way that text appears on a page, including options such as margins, emphasized text, and headers and footers.

Footer - Message which is printed at the bottom of each page.

Header - Message which is printed at the top of each page.

Justified - Paragraph format in which each line of text is made to extend from the left margin to the right by adding extra space between words.

Margin - Blank spaces on a printed page which surround text.

Option marker - A marker placed by AppleWorks in the text to indicate the beginning or ending of a formatting option. Markers are not printed.

Options menu - Menu from which formatting options such as bold, underline and margins are set from: Open-Apple O.

Pagination - The computer calculates and displays markers showing where text will be broken into pages when printed.

Paragraph alignment - How text is printed in relation to the margins: unjustified, justified, right justified or centered.

Paragraph format - Use of options affecting a paragraph including alignment, spacing, tabs and margins.

Replace command - The computer replaces one specified section of text with another: Open-Apple R.

Scale - Line at the top of the work area showing placement of tab stops.

Search text - Text entered by user to be found or replaced.

Subscript - Text printed slightly below the normal line.

Superscript - Text printed slightly above the normal line.

Tab stop - Position(s), shown on the scale, where the cursor jumps to when the Tab key is pressed. Used to create columns or indent text.

Text alignment - See paragraph alignment.

Unjustified - Left-aligned text, with the right side jagged.

Verify Spelling - Compares words in document to a dictionary file to locate and correct misspellings: Open-Apple V.

Zoom mode - Used to display Option and Return markers on the screen: Open-Apple Z.

Reviews

Sections 3.1-3.4

1. List three ways that a word processor can manipulate text that cannot be done on a typewriter.

2. a) What are tabs used for?
   b) What are default tabs?

3. What is the screen scale/ruler and what is it used for?

4. Explain what each of the following tab stops does and give examples:

   a) left-aligned
   b) right-aligned
   c) center-aligned
   d) decimal-aligned

5. a) List the steps required to set a center-aligned tab at column 20. Start by removing the default tabs.
   b) When working on the word processor screen, how can you tell where tabs have been set?

6. a) What is the easiest way to delete an entire line of text?
   b) If a line of text was deleted by mistake, how can it be restored?

Sections 3.5-3.8

7. a) What is meant by formatting text?
   b) List five publications in which you have seen formatted text and describe the formats used.

8. a) List the steps required to change the margins of a document so that the left margin is at 2 inches and the right margin at 3 inches.
   b) How long is a line of text after these margins have been set? (Assume an 8.5 x 11 inch sheet of paper.)
   c) When working on the word processor screen, how can you tell where the margins have been set?

9. a) Why might you want text to be double spaced?
   b) List the steps required to double space only the second paragraph in a document that contains five paragraphs.
   c) Will the second paragraph appear double spaced on the screen?

Sections 3.13-3.15

10. What is meant by justified text?

11. a) What is meant by centered text?
    b) What type of text is usually centered?

12. How is it possible to determine what text has been centered and what text justified?

13. a) What is meant by pagination?
    b) How can pagination be displayed on the word processor screen?
    c) Explain two situations when you might want to control the pagination in a document.

14. a) What is meant by a block of text?
    b) How can you tell what text is included in a block on the word processor screen?

15. a) List the steps required to delete the second paragraph in a five paragraph document as a block.
b) Why is it usually best to delete a block in Zoom mode?

Sections 3.13-3.15   16. a) What is meant by moving a block of text?
b) List the steps required to move the second paragraph in a document to a point directly after the fourth paragraph.

17. a) What is meant by copying a block of text?
b) What is the difference between moving and copying a block of text?

18. List the steps required to boldface the first line of text and underline the second line in a word processed document.

Sections 3.16-3.18   19. a) What is meant by finding text?
b) Give three examples where you might use the Find command.

20. List the steps required to find each location of the name "Judith Habersham" in a document.

21. Give an example of when the Case Sensitive option of the Find command might be used.

22. a) What is the Replace command used for?
b) Give three examples where the Replace command might be used.

23. a) What is a header?
b) What is a footer?

24. a) List the steps required to print the message "Bruce's Homework" at the top of each page in a document.
b) List the additional steps required to include the page number as part of this message.

Sections 3.19-3.20   25. a) Explain what steps must be taken to have AppleWorks check the spelling of a document.
b) What does AppleWorks do when it finds what it considers a spelling error?
c) Is it possible that AppleWorks might indicate an error when a word is spelled correctly?

26. Can you add words to the AppleWorks dictionary? If so, how?

27. a) What is a superscript and a subscript?
b) Give examples of where a superscript and a subscript would be used.
c) How is a superscript created?

Exercises

1. The file on your data disk named Party gives directions from the school to a party but is listed out of order. Use the block move command to reorder the list and then print a copy.

2. Exercise 8 in Chapter 2 asked you to create an advertisement for an upcoming school event in a file named Advertise.

   a) Load the Advertise file and use formatting options such as tabs, centering and boldface to make it more attractive.

   b) Verify the spelling in Advertise. Print a copy of the completed advertisement.

3. The file named Openings on your data disk contains several lines which could be used to start a short story. Choose one of the lines, delete the rest as a block and write a paragraph using the opening line. Be sure to use proper spelling. Save the story on disk and print a copy.

4. The block copy command is useful when text must be repeated in a document.

   a) Use the block copy command to create a file named MyName which contains your name 50 times, each name on a separate line. Hint: consider using a block with more than 1 line.

   b) Add a header to this file which prints the page number on each page. Save MyName on disk and then print a copy of this file.

5. Exercise 5 in Chapter 2 asked you to write a review of a recent movie or concert and save it in a file named Art Critic.

   a) Load Art Critic and add a bold, centered headline which reads "Critic's Corner."

   b) Underline any titles in the review, such as the title of the movie, an album or song title, etc.

   c) The paper's editors like all submissions to be doubled spaced. Format your review to conform with their wishes.

   d) Use the Verify Spelling command to check the spelling in your review. Make any corrections required.

   e) Justify the text in the review so that it looks more like a newspaper article. Save the modified review and print a copy of it.

6. It is often necessary to create tables in documents using tabs.

   a) Use the word processor to create the following table. Use tabs to create the columns and bold the column headings:

Opponent	**Record**
Audubon	7-4
Cherry Hill East	7-4
Cherry Hill West	4-7
Collingswood	2-8
Gulf Stream	6-5
Haddon Heights	10-1
Pine Crest	1-10

   b) Add a third column to the table named Division:

   Division
   I
   IV
   IA
   III
   IV
   V
   I

   c) Enter another table below the first creating a new tab ruler and using left, right, center and decimal aligned tab stops. Use the following data:

	MOST VALUABLE PLAYERS		
Last Name	First Name	Sport	Height
Moore	Steve	Football	5.74
Zissu	Jan	Fencing	6.1
Bisek	Veronica	Lacrosse	5.2
Chadham	Jamie	Soccer	5.96
Haupt	Doug	Hockey	6.4

   d) Save the document under the name Table and print a copy.

7. In exercise 3 in Chapter 2 you created a file named Apply which contained an application letter for a college.

   a) Correct the spelling in the document.

   b) Using the Replace command, change the name of the college in Apply to Trenton State University and print a copy of the new letter.

   c) Change the college name from Trenton State University to New Brunswick College. Print a copy of the new letter.

   d) Change the body of the letter only to double-spaced.

   e) Save and print a copy of the modified letter.

8. You are to create a two-page newsletter on any topic that you wish. The newsletter must contain the following features:

> At least 4 different stories.
> Two advertisements.
> Bold, centered headlines.
> Justified paragraphs.
> Proper spelling.
> At least 1 table.
> At least 1 superscripted footnote. Place the footnote references on the last page.
> Consider using tabs to create more than one column per page (like a newspaper).

An example newsletter design is shown below:

I.U. News   Page 1

Ivy University News - "All the News that Fits"

We Win!

Dateline Kansas City: Today the Ivy University Roaring Tigerlilies again proved that they were a force to be reckoned with as they bested the Overbrook Rams 2-1. Overbrook took the lead early on but was soon shut down by the mighty Tigerlily defense. Not to be outdone, our offense then returned with two unanswered screamers that left the Rams in total disarray. This win gives the 'Lilies a 6-0 record. Coach Riley said that "The team has never, ever, ever played better." Talk of a possible State Championship has been heard. For complete details and a rundown of other scores please see the Sports section.

Steves' Election Bid Fails

In a surprising come-from-behind victory, dark-horse candidate J.T. Willbury today defeated incumbent Thom Steves in the Student Congress presidential race. Steves, a 3 and a half year veteran, lost by a huge margin to the newcomer Willbury. Reached at his plush offices Steves had "no comment" about the election but said that he plans to continue in his roles as debate club president and captain of the swim team. The final tally was:

Candidate	Votes
Steves	57
Willbury	3,461
Undecided	289

==========

Editorial Comment - by Dana A. Clarke

It comes as no surprise to those who have followed this year's Student Congress elections that Thom Steves was not re-elected. What is surprising is the actual <u>number</u> of people who realized that for the last 3 and a half years this guy has been sandbagging it. If ever there was a case for impeachment, this was it. The well-oiled political machine that passed as Steves' campaign staff was a joke. His grandiose plans to have the cafeteria serve chocolate milk never materialized, as did the student trip to the Bahamas.   (continued)

9. The school literary magazine would like to print the essay you wrote for Chapter 2 exercise 7. Load the Essay file and make the following changes:

    a) Add a centered header showing your name.
    b) Add a footer which prints the page number.
    c) The body of the essay should be double spaced.
    d) The margins of the paper should be 1 inch on the top and bottom, 1.3 inches on the left and 1.2 inches on the right.
    e) Add a bold, centered title.
    f) Check your spelling.
    g) Save the modified file and print a copy for the magazine.

10. Load the file named Computer Ed from you data disk and make the following changes as noted below. Print a copy when the changes are complete:

Center and bold title

Computers in Education

Justify all paragraphs

Over the past ten years it has become obvious that computers will increasingly play a role in education. The invention of the microcomputer has made it possible for schools to purchase large number of computers at affordable prices. In many schools these computers have been placed in computer laboratories, while in other schools they have been distributed to classrooms. Now that the computers are available for student use, educators have been discussing how they should be used. Below are a few examples of how schools are using their computers.

Center title

Computer Aided Instruction

Underline 2ⁿᵈ sentence

A number of computer programs have become available which instruct students in different academic disciplines. These programs have been especially effective in instructing students in languages and mathematics. When used with elementary school students, computer aided instruction has been found to keep students interested in a subject while entertaining them at the same time. Mrs. Groves, a teacher at West Lawrence Grade School, said, ''When used as part of a complete learning system, computers help reinforce skills learned in the classroom.''

Center title

Applications Programs

Many students are now taking courses which introduce them to applications software. They are taught how to use word processing, data base and spreadsheet software. Most students find that knowing how to use such software can help them in their other courses. Mr. Ronald Johnson of Ivy University said, ''Our students are especially interested in learning how to use integrated software like AppleWorks and Microsoft Works.''

Center title

Writing Programs

Bold "BASIC" and "Pascal"

Students who would like to pursue careers in computing often elect to take courses which teach them how to write computer programs. The languages most often learned are BASIC and Pascal. Besides learning to program, these courses teach valuable problem-solving skills.

Chapter 4

Introducing the Data Base

_____

_____

_____

_____

_____

_____

_____

Objectives

After completing this chapter you will be able to:

1. Describe what a data base is.

2. Give examples of manual (non-computerized) and computer-ized data bases.

3. Describe common data base operations.

4. Explain why a computer is useful for manipulating a data base.

5. Define what records, categories and entries are.

6. Plan and design a layout for a computerized data base using appropriate category names.

*T*his chapter provides an introduction to data bases and how they organize and store information. Specific tasks that are performed using a data base are covered as examples. Specialized terms that describe the operations and structure of a data base are defined. Attention is given not only to understanding what a data base is, but also to the planning and design considerations that make them more efficient and easy to use.

Chapter Five provides step-by-step instructions for creating and manipulating a computerized data base using AppleWorks. Because a knowledge of data base concepts and terminology is required, it is important to thoroughly understand the material in this chapter before proceeding to the next.

4.1 What is a Data Base?

A data base is simply a group of related pieces of information. You are familiar with several different manual (non-computerized) data bases: the card catalog in a library, a recipe file box, an office "Rolodex" file for phone numbers and a filing cabinet storing a school's student records are all examples of data bases. Each item in a data base is related to each of the others in some way. For example, each card in a card catalog records some information about a specific book in a library.

One way to think of a data base is as a collection of forms, each storing the same type of information. An example of such a form would be a card in a library's card catalog which stores the reference number, title, author and publisher data for a book:

Number: SP125

Title: *Patchwork Quilts Through the Ages*
Author: Dr. Rosey Greer
Published: Scrapwork Press, New Haven, Conn., 1982

Each card is organized so that the different pieces of information appear at the same locations. A book's reference number is in the upper left corner, title on the first line of the card, author on the second line, and so on for every card in the catalog. A consistent design makes it easy for your eyes to pick out needed information when scanning through a stack of cards.

4.2 Computerized Data Bases

As you have discovered using the word processor, the computer is a powerful tool for storing and manipulating information. The speed and storage capabilities of the computer make it an ideal tool for managing large amounts of information in the form of data bases.

Today almost all businesses or organizations use computer data bases in some way. A data base can be used by a bank to store the account information of its depositors or by a school to store student records. Department and grocery stores keep track of the different items they have for sale, their prices and how many of each are in stock in a computer data base. The size of such data bases can become very large. A major advantage of using a computer is its ability to look through a large data base for a specific piece of information in a very short amount of time. In addition, because the computer can store information about thousands of items on a small disk, the amount of space needed to store a large data base is substantially reduced.

Computerized data bases can be used to organize information about virtually any area of knowledge: agriculture, biology, education, law, medicine, economics and more. It is even possible to have a data base which stores information about other data bases. Any information that can be stored in a list or on individual forms can be put into a data base. Governments maintain thousands of computer data bases on information ranging from births and deaths to taxes. Many historians refer to our present time as the "Information Age" primarily because of the ability computers and data bases have given us to store and manipulate huge amounts of information. Clearly then, because data bases are becoming more important to the world in which we live it is increasingly necessary to learn what they are and how to use them.

4.3 Data Base Terminology

Like the documents produced by the word processor, the information for a computer data base is stored on disk in a file. A data base file has its own special structure, and differs from a word processor file or a file for some other application. Information on a single item in a data base is called a "record". For example, the catalog card for *Patchwork Quilts Through the Ages* could be thought of as a single record which is different from the record or card for any other book. A data base file, therefore, is a collection of related records.

Information within a record is separated into "categories" or "fields". Author, title, and reference number are three separate categories in a single catalog card record. It is important to note that each record in a data base has the same categories, but that the data stored in each category differs from record to record. In the card catalog, each card has a place for a reference number, title, author's name, etc., but no two cards have the same reference number. The order and placement of categories in a record is called a "layout" or "form".

The data stored in an individual category in a single record is called an "entry". For example, in the card catalog Author is a category; a place for an author's name appears in each record. Rosey Greer is an entry, the author of a specific book.

Naturally, the size of a record depends on the number of categories it contains. It is not uncommon for a data base to have as few as two categories, such as a name and phone number. On the other hand, large business or scientific data bases may contain hundreds of categories in each record. The following diagram shows the differences between a record, category and entry using the card catalog as an example:

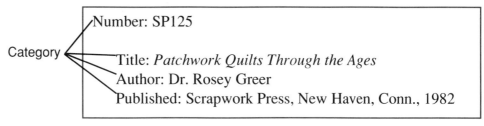

Record

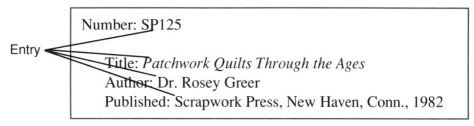

Record

4.4 Category Names and Types

To illustrate how a data base is designed and implemented on the computer we will describe how Ivy University, better known as I.U., stores its student records in a computerized data base. When storing information in a data base the computer needs to be given a specific name for each category in the record. A "category name" is required so that the computer can distinguish between the different pieces of data stored in the record.

Categories are often classified by the type of data that they store. There are a few basic category types in a computerized data base. For example, categories which store only words are called "character" categories. At I.U. the name and address for each student is stored in character categories.

Another commonly used category type is the "numeric" category. As the name implies, numeric categories store only numbers. Ivy University's data base stores student grade point averages (GPA) in a numeric category. Because numeric categories store only numbers the data they store can be used in mathematical calculations.

In addition to character and numeric, AppleWorks has a special category type called a "date category". When a category name includes the word "date", AppleWorks assumes that it is a date category and automatically converts numbers entered in that field to their corresponding date. For example, if 1/1/89 is entered into a category named "Date Hired", when Return is pressed AppleWorks will change the entry to read Jan 1 89. There are however some limitations to the date type. AppleWorks cannot distinguish between valid and invalid dates, so it is not able to determine whether dates entered into a date category have proper values. For example, the computer will accept 2/31/91 in a date category and convert it to Feb 31 91, an invalid date. Similarly, AppleWorks creates a "time category" for every category name which contains the word "time". A 1 entered into a category named "Time of Event" would be automatically changed to 1:00 PM when Return is pressed. Entering 1A in the same category would display the time 1:00 AM.

4.5 A Simple Data Base

To review what has been discussed so far, let us look at the manual system currently used by Ivy University to record student records. We will later convert this into a computerized data base. Each record currently uses the following layout:

NAME:
ADDRESS:
DATE ADMITTED:
GPA:
TUITION PAID:

All of the information above for a single student is considered to be a record. Each record contains five categories, which are defined below by describing their types and the information they store:

NAME: Student's name stored in a character category.

ADDRESS: Student's school (dorm) address stored in a character category.

DATE ADMITTED: Date the student was admitted to the University. AppleWorks will automatically make this a date category because the word DATE appears in the category name.

GPA: A numeric category which stores the student's grade point average.

TUITION PAID: Whether or not the student has paid the tuition for this semester. To save space, a code of Y will be represent Yes and a code of N will represent No.

Here are sample records for three I.U. students:

NAME: Matilda Rose
ADDRESS: 435 Frelinghuysen Hall
DATE ADMITTED: Feb 14 88
GPA: 3.4
TUITION PAID: Y

NAME: Sam Adams
ADDRESS: 121 Carey Quadrangle
DATE ADMITTED: Mar 12 79
GPA: 1.5
TUITION PAID: N

NAME: Roberta Poisson
ADDRESS: 8P Corwin Place
DATE ADMITTED: Jun 27 89
GPA: 4.0
TUITION PAID: N

Notice how each of the records has the same layout containing the same categories, but that the entries differ from record to record. It is also possible for a record to have "empty" entries; that is, a category which does not yet store any data. As an example, when new students enroll they have no value for their GPA, so that category is left blank. When their first semester is over, their record may be updated and the new GPA value stored in the category.

4.6 Common Data Base Operations

Data bases become useful when searching and sorting operations can be performed on them. The power of a computerized data base is that these operations may be performed on large quantities of data very quickly.

Find: The most common data base operation is the "Find" or "search". When users search a data base, they are asking to see all records which contain some specific text, either a letter, number, word or group of words. Each record in the data base is then checked to see if it contains the requested information in any of its categories. If it does, the record is displayed. Some examples of this type of search are:

> Show all record containing 5.
> Which records have the text Corwin in an entry?

Find is limited because it will display a record if the search text appears in any of its categories. For example, asking AppleWorks to Find 5 in the three student records above will display both Matilda Rose's record because there is a 5 in the address category, and Sam Adams' because there is a 5 in the GPA category. However, Find is useful for performing general searches like the ones described above.

Selection: Similar to Finding text, selection displays records in a data base based on certain values stored in their categories. Unlike the Find command, selection allows the search to be limited to specific categories, and can apply conditions such as 'greater than' or 'not equal to'. While Find can only display records which contain a certain value or word in any of their categories, selection makes use of "rules" to select the records to be displayed based on the contents of a specific category. For example, using the proper rules it is possible to display only records which have 4.0 in the GPA category, or all students who were admitted between May 1 87 and June 16 89. Rules can be joined together making complex conditions which limit the number of records displayed. This makes selection a powerful tool for gathering specific information from a large data base. Some example rules are:

> Which students are from Maine?
> Show all students with a GPA less than 2.0 and who were admitted before Jan 1 86.

It should be obvious that a data base can only be searched for information that it stores in its records. That is, it would be impossible to search Ivy's student data base to determine the average rainfall in New Jersey. Because it involves asking the data base a question about the data it stores, a selection rule is often referred to as a "query".

Reports: Information taken from a data base is called a "report" and contains data from specific records and categories. Reports can contain many pieces of data, or just one. For example, there may be hundreds of students from Maine, but Roberta Poisson has only one value for her current GPA. Reports generated with AppleWorks can contain titles, calculate totals and subtotals, and make use of the same printer options that the Word Processor can.

Reports can differ based on the person who is using them. Different reports may contain different information, or the same information in a different order. For example, the university's business department would need to have a report which included the tuition paid information, but is probably not interested in the student's GPA.

Arranging: It is easier to locate specific information in a data base if the records are arranged in order based on the data stored in a specific category. A student data base would be easier to search for a specific student's information if the records in it were ordered alphabetically by last name. To then find Roberta Poisson's grade point average it would not be necessary to look at every record in the file, but to simply go directly to the names beginning with "P", and search through them for "Poisson". Reports are also easier to read and understand when the information presented is in order.

Ordering records in a data base is called "arranging" or "sorting". A sort is performed based on the value of one category called the "key category" which is chosen by the user. When a data base is sorted, the position of a record in the file is changed based on the value stored in its key category. In the student records example above, the key category is the name category, so the records appear in order by name. When the computer performs a sort, it has been programmed to know that the character "A" is less than "B" and that 1 is less than 2 and so on. If the key is a date category, the data base program knows that Jan 1 89 is less than Jun 27 89, etc. This is called "chronological order". Here are the three student records sorted by date admitted:

> NAME: Sam Adams
> ADDRESS: 121 Carey Quadrangle
> DATE ADMITTED: Mar 12 79
> GPA: 1.5
> TUITION PAID: N
>
> NAME: Matilda Rose
> ADDRESS: 435 Frelinghuysen Hall
> DATE ADMITTED: Feb 14 88
> GPA: 3.4
> TUITION PAID: Y
>
> NAME: Roberta Poisson
> ADDRESS: 8P Corwin Place
> DATE ADMITTED: Jun 27 89
> GPA: 4.0
> TUITION PAID: N

It is important to realize that a computer data base file can be easily sorted on different key categories as the need arises. One report may need the data ordered by last name, and another by GPA or admit date. Here are the same three student records sorted in descending order (high to low) by GPA:

> NAME: Roberta Poisson
> ADDRESS: 8P Corwin Place
> DATE ADMITTED: Jun 27 89
> GPA: 4.0
> TUITION PAID: N
>
> NAME: Matilda Rose
> ADDRESS: 435 Frelinghuysen Hall
> DATE ADMITTED: Feb 14 88
> GPA: 3.4
> TUITION PAID: Y

NAME: Sam Adams
ADDRESS: 121 Carey Quadrangle
DATE ADMITTED: Mar 12 79
GPA: 1.5
TUITION PAID: N

In a computer data base the records may be sorted quickly using any category the user desires as the key category because the information is stored in the computer's memory, and not on paper forms. Sorting is often not possible in a manual data base without a large amount of work. For this reason most libraries must maintain two separate manual card catalogs to have their books listed by both author and subject, which often leads to errors, mis-filed cards, etc.

***Modifying*:** From time to time, data base files must be modified to be kept current: old information removed, outdated information updated, and new information added. At the end of each school year Ivy must remove any graduating seniors from its student data base. This involves "deleting" certain records from the data base file. New GPAs must be calculated for the remaining students and placed in the GPA category. Changing the information stored in a category is called "updating" the file. Finally, the names and related data of any new students who have been accepted must be added to the file.

A definite advantage of a computerized data base is the ease in which it may be modified. Like the word processor, changes made to a data base file can be made on the screen and stored electronically. When all of the desired changes have been made, the modified data base can be saved on disk for future use. A change to a manual data base would require that the appropriate record be located and then physically changed, using an eraser or by rewriting the information onto a new form.

4.7 Planning a Data Base

A great deal of time and thought should go into the planning of a data base before it is created. Carefully planning a data base will save time and eliminate frustration later. Below are listed three steps for planning a data base:

Steps for Planning a Data Base

1. Determine what data should be stored in each record. This is best accomplished by examining the needs of the different users of the data base. Start by creating a general list on paper of the data available. Eliminate any information that is not directly related to the overall purpose of the data base.

2. Examine the specific operations to be performed on the data base. Do the operations require any information that is missing from the current list? Will there be a need to separate the first name from the last? Is there a need for a complete mailing address or will a street address be enough? Make any changes required to the list produced in step 1.

3. Create a list of categories and category names using the list from step 2. Use this list to create a description of the data stored in the different categories and the operations performed with them. Produce a sample layout for a single record on paper.

Careful planning requires information about both the user of the data base and the operations that will be performed on it. Data base designers often spend a great deal of time talking to the user(s) of a proposed data base and analyzing their needs before making any decisions about categories, types, layouts, etc. It is also important to realize that most data bases are accessed by more than one user, each of whom has different requirements and will perform different operations. The time spent planning will make it easier for each user to get the fullest use from the information stored in the data base and avoid having to later make major modifications to the data base. Producing sample records and layouts on paper helps to define the data base and shows where potential errors may occur. Only after the design has been checked by hand should the computer be used to actually create the data base.

In step two it is also helpful to create examples of the reports that may be needed by sketching them on paper. This makes it easy to see what information is required by each report.

4.8 Planning Records and Categories

The two most important questions when designing a data base are "What information should be stored?" and "What operations will be performed on that information?". Deciding what information to store depends on what the data base will be used for. A student record data base would not contain any information about salaries or how many desks are in certain classrooms, only information that is directly related to the students. Each record in a student data base would probably contain the following categories at a minimum:

> *Student Name*
> *Address*
> *Date student was admitted*
> *Current GPA*
> *Has tuition been paid?*

It is important to realize that each record stores all of the information above for only one student.

Next, the operations performed on the data base should be considered. Ivy University keeps its student records in order by last name. So that the records may be sorted based on the last name only, two separate categories will have to be created to store the student name; a first name category and a last name category:

> *First name*
>
> *Last name*
>
> *Address*
>
> *Date student was admitted*
>
> *Current GPA*
>
> *Has tuition been paid?*

Finally, the administration would like to be able to send warning letters to each student who has a low GPA. In order to use the data base to produce complete mailing labels, the address category must be expanded to include separate categories for a city, state and zip code:

> *First name*
>
> *Last name*
>
> *Street address*
>
> *City*
>
> *State*
>
> *Zip code*
>
> *Date student was admitted*
>
> *Current GPA*
>
> *Has tuition been paid?*

Several problems have been avoided by carefully considering the <u>uses</u> for this data base before it is created. For example, the ability to produce mailing labels is a valuable asset of a student data base. Had this not been planned for, a great deal of work would have to be done either to later modify the data base or to create some manual system for recording student addresses. Storing a complete student mailing address in separate categories allows the university to more fully use the power of the computer data base.

4.9 Choosing Category Names

AppleWorks requires that each category have a distinct name to distinguish it from the other categories in a record. A well chosen category name describes the data stored in that category, making it easy to determine its use. Below are good examples of category names for the student record data base:

Data	**Category name**
First name	First Name
Last name	Last Name
Street address	Address
City	City
State	State
Zip code	Zip
Date student was admitted	Admit Date
Current GPA	GPA
Has tuition been paid?	Paid

Most computer data bases have a limit on the number of characters in a category name. Choosing the shortest possible name which accurately describes the contents of the category is therefore important. This is why the name Address rather than, say, Street Address, was chosen to represent the street address category. In general, a name of ten characters or less should be able to describe the data stored in any category. However, should it be required AppleWorks allows up to 20 characters per category name, including spaces and punctuation marks.

AppleWorks does not require that the type of data (character, numeric, etc.) to be stored in each category be explicitly specified. However, any name which contains the word "date" will automatically be assumed to store dates. In the record described above, Admit Date will be a date category.

4.10 *Record Layout*

The order in which the different categories appear in a record is called the "layout". Layout also includes the amount of space that a category will have when displayed on the screen. It is possible that different users of the data base will require different layouts. For example, the academic counseling department may wish to see only the name and GPA of a student, while the business office needs the full address and tuition paid categories as well. For this reason, layouts can be easily changed.

AppleWorks has two different ways of displaying record layouts on the screen. First is "single-record" format. In single record format, all of the categories for only one record are displayed. This is most often used when updating a record, or when adding a new record to the file. Below is an example of a record displayed in single record format:

```
First Name: Matilda
Last Name: Rose
Address: 435 Frelinghuysen Rd.
City: Leafville
State: NJ
Zip: 08049
Admit Date: Feb 14 88
GPA: 3.4
Paid: Y
```

The second display method is called "multiple-record" format. In multiple record format, up to 15 different records may be displayed on the screen at one time. However, because the screen is limited to a width of 80 characters, not every category may be displayed. Like the word processor, the data base screen may be scrolled up and down by moving the cursor, allowing the other records to be displayed. Listed below are three student records from the I.U. data base in multiple-record layout:

```
First Name  Last Name  Address                City          State  Zip
Matilda     Rose       435 Frelinghuysen Rd   Leafville     NJ     08049
Sam         Adams      121 Carey Quadrangle   Leaftown      PA     19717
Roberta     Poisson    8P Corwin Place        Five Points   FL     33434
```

Note that due to width restriction of the screen the Admit Date, GPA and Paid categories are not currently displayed. They are, however, still stored in the record and may be viewed by switching to single-record format. The order in which the categories appear in a format may be changed at any time, so that the records may be displayed in different formats for different uses.

After the layout has been designed it is a good idea to give some thought to the way that reports will look. Sketch sample designs of the different required reports showing category names and the amount of space to be given each category. Just as related categories should be grouped together in the layout, they should also be printed together in a report. Just as when designing the layout, it is important to consider the user of the report. As you progress you will also have to consider such points as how the data in the report should be sorted and when to print totals.

Chapter Summary

A data base is an organized collection of related information. Information in a data base is divided into records, each of which stores a complete set of data about a specific item. Different pieces of data within a record are called categories or fields and the arrangement of the categories within a record is called a layout or form.

The data stored in an individual category in a single record is called an entry. A category name is required so that the computer can distinguish between different pieces of data stored in a record. Categories which store only words are called character categories while numeric categories store only numbers. AppleWorks includes a special category called a date category which stores dates and a time category which stores times.

The speed and storage capabilities of the computer make it an ideal tool for managing large amounts of information in the form of data bases. Information in a computerized data base is stored on disk in a file. Data bases are used by many organizations (businesses, governmental agencies, educational institutions, etc.) and may become very large. They can be used to organize information about almost any area of knowledge.

Data bases become useful when searching and sorting operations can be performed on them. The most common data base operation is the find or search. When a search is performed the user asks to see all records which contain specific information. The computer then searches each record and displays only those records containing the sought information.

Records in a data base can also be selected. Unlike the find operation, selection allows the search to be limited to specific categories, and can apply conditions such as 'equal to' or 'greater than'. Selection makes use of rules to select the records to be displayed based on the contents of a specific category.

Information taken from a data base is called a report. Reports may include many pieces of data, or just one. AppleWork's reports can contain titles, calculate totals, and make use of printer options.

Ordering records in a data base is called arranging or sorting. A sort is performed based on the value of one category called the key category. When a data base is sorted, the position of a record in the file is changed based on the value stored in its key category. For example, alphabetizing the names in a data base arranges the records in alphabetical order based on the category which stores the name.

A data base may be modified: old information removed, outdated information updated and new information added. Removing records from a data base is called deleting from the file. Changing information stored in a category is called updating the file.

Before a data base is created, a great deal of planning should go into its design. Who will use the data base and how they will use it should be considered as part of the planning process. Choosing appropriate categories, category names, types and category lengths makes a data base complete and easy to use. A hastily designed data base usually requires a large amount of work to reorganize it after it has been created.

Vocabulary

Arrange - Place the records stored in a data base in order based on the value stored in one category.

Category - One specific piece of information stored in a record.

Category name - Name by which the computer identifies the different pieces of information in a record.

Character category - A category which stores only characters such as a name or address.

Data base - A collection of related information.

Data base file - A file on disk which is created by the data base application and which stores a computerized data base.

Date category - Any category with the word "date" in its name. AppleWorks automatically converts numbers entered into this category into dates.

Entry - The information stored in one category in one record.

Field - Another name for category.

Find - Operation where the computer searches through the records in a data base, displaying only those which contain specified text. See also Selection.

Form - See Layout.

Format - How the records in a data base are displayed, single-record (one at a time) or multiple-record (up to 15 at a time).

Key Category - Category which stores the data used when determining the order during a sort.

Layout - The arrangement, length and order of the categories in a data base. Also called the "form".

Modify - To change the contents of a record or entry.

Multi-record format - Up to 15 records displayed on the screen at one time.

Numeric category - A category which contains only numbers.

Query - See Selection.

Record - A complete collection of data for one item.

Report - Information extracted from a data base, usually printed on paper.

Search - See Find and Selection.

Selection - Limiting the number of records that are displayed using rules to define the criteria that displayed records must meet. Selection is based on rules which contain comparisons such as 'less than' or 'not equal to'. See also Find and Selection Rule.

Selection Rule - Description of the category to search and its contents used in a Selection. For example, "GPA less than 2.0". Rules are defined using Open-Apple R.

Single-record format - The categories for a single record displayed on the screen. Useful when updating a record.

Sort - See Arrange.

Time category - A category which contains the word "time" in its name. AppleWorks automatically converts numbers entered into these categories to times.

Update - See Modify.

Reviews

Sections 4.1-4.3

1. Why do historians refer to our present time as the Information Age?

2. a) What is a data base?
   b) What is a record?

3. a) Give two examples of manual data bases with which you are familiar.
   b) Describe the data stored in each.
   c) Describe the different categories stored by a single record in each of the manual data bases.

4. What capabilities of the computer make it an ideal tool for managing data bases?

5. What determines the size of a single record in a data base?

6. Can the following be considered to be data bases? Why or why not?

   a) a phone book.
   b) just the yellow pages in a phone book.
   c) patient files in a doctor's office.
   d) a grocery list.
   e) a school yearbook.

7. The following information is found in the white pages of a phone book:

   ```
   . . .
   Capeletti, Rod    712 Adams Ave.    212-0987
   Caputi, Jane      80 Scarlet Ct.    123-4567
   Caputi, Jane N.   255 Camden Ave.   555-1234
   Caputi, M.        77 Sunset Strip   911-1111
   . . .
   ```

   a) What information would constitute a single record?
   b) Describe the separate categories in such a record.
   c) What information does each category store?

8. How would the information stored in a doctor's patient files be broken into records? Describe some of the possible categories and the data stored in them.

9. List five governmental agencies that might use a computerized data base. Explain what each agency would store.

10. Show what a student record in your school's computer data base might look like.

Sections 4.4-4.6

11. a) What is the difference between character and numeric categories?
    b) What is a date category?

12. How many character, numeric and date categories are there in a single student record shown in Section 4.5?

13. Is it possible to enter data in to certain categories and leave others empty in the same record?

14. Choose appropriate category names for the following data:

    a) a person's name.
    b) a phone number.
    c) the color of a car.
    d) an item's price.
    e) whether an item is on sale or not.
    f) the day a person was born.

15. Answer the following questions based on the three sample student records given in Section 4.5:

    a) How many students have not paid their tuition?
    b) Which students were admitted before 1988?
    c) What are the names of the students with a GPA below 2.0?
    d) How many students live in the Carey Quadrangle?

16. a) What does it mean to search a data base?
    b) Give 3 examples of searches that could be performed on the student data base in your school's computer.

17. What is the difference between finding and selecting records?

18. Which of the following operations constitute a find and which a selection of a data base?

    a) Which records contain the name George?
    b) Which students have not paid their tuition?
    c) Which students were expelled last year?
    d) Show all records containing a 35.
    e) List all students who are over 21 years old.

19. What category are the records in a phone book arranged on?

20. Describe a situation that would require a phone book record to be:

    a) updated
    b) added
    c) deleted

21. What categories other than Name and GPA could the records in the I.U. student data base be sorted on? Give a reason for having the data base sorted this way.

Sections 4.7-4.10

22. a) What information should be stored in a computerized data base listing the cars for sale at an automobile dealership?
    b) Describe a record from such a data base, including the information to be stored in each of its categories.
    c) Give appropriate category names and a layout for the data base.

23. Why is it important to plan a data base before using the computer?

24. Why might it be better to store the first name and last name of students in separate categories rather than in the same category in the Ivy student data base?

25. a) What should be considered when choosing a category name?
    b) What is the maximum length AppleWorks allows a category name to be?

26. a) What is a data base layout?
    b) Can layouts be changed after a data base has been produced on the computer?

27. What is the difference between displaying records in single record or multiple-record format? What is the advantage of each?

Exercises

For each of the exercises below you will be asked to design a data base layout. This should be done using paper and pencil, following the steps given in Section 4.7. You should be careful to select appropriate category names, and give consideration to the types and lengths. When you have completed each design type it into the word processor and produce a printed copy. Save the printed copy so that the design can be used in the next chapter to assist in producing a computerized data base.

1. Ivy University Bookstore has decided to store their inventory information in a data base. A partial list of items, their prices and quantity in stock is displayed below. Design a data base layout for the Bookstore that includes categories for the information listed below:

Item	Quantity in stock	Price per item
Ball point pen	2,300	$0.39
Felt tip pen	3,800	$0.79
Notebook	574	$1.89
Loose leaf paper	112	$6.55
3-ring binder	743	$4.75

2. Many people use a computerized data base in place of an address book. Design a data base layout that will include the name, address, phone number and birthday for each person in such a data base. Include two additional categories which could be used to store useful information about the person.

3. Fantasy Wheels, Inc. is an automobile dealership that sells exotic used cars. They want to store their inventory of cars in a data base. Design a data base layout for them that will include all of the information listed below. Room for up to 3 accessories per car should be allocated in the design. The data for one of Fantasy's cars is shown below:

    1969 Maserati
    color: blue
    interior: black
    optional accessories: radio, 4 speed, air
    paid: $9,800
    asking price: $21,600
    date acquired: 5/9/88

4. You are to produce a questionnaire to survey a group of students in your school. In the next chapter the results of the survey will be stored in a computerized data base.

   a) Design a questionnaire using the word processor which asks students to supply the following information about themselves:

First name	List your favorite:
Last name	Course in school
Age	Rock band
Birthdate	Sport
Class	Hobby
Height	Food
Weight	Automobile
Sex	Television program

      Rate yourself as a dancer:
         Excellent, Good, Fair, Poor, Don't dance

   b) Produce 25 copies of your questionnaire and hand them out to students who are your friends and to students who you do not know well. Try to get a good mixture of boys and girls as well as students with a variety of interests.

   c) Design a data base layout for the data acquired by the survey. Be careful to group related categories and to select appropriate category names.

5. Your school is going to computerize its report card system using a data base. At a minimum, each report card will contain a student name, the names of the classes that student is enrolled in and the grades received in those classes. Acting as the data base designer, answer the following:

   a) Before a data base can be designed it is important to talk to the users of the data base. Make a list of the people you should talk to and the questions you will ask them.

   b) Design a layout that could be used to store the data base. The school would like to mail report cards directly to students' homes so be sure to include room for a complete mailing address.

   c) It will be necessary to search the report card data base from time to time. Give a list of possible queries that the school might perform on the data base. Does the layout designed in part (b) make it possible to perform these queries? Make any necessary changes to the layout.

   d) Besides the report cards themselves, give three examples of printed reports that might be produced using the data base. Does the layout designed in part (b) contain all the information needed to produce these reports? Make any necessary changes to the layout.

   e) Give three examples of when it would be necessary to update the report card data base.

6. Your local library is considering computerizing its card catalog using a data base.

   a) Give three benefits of having the card catalog stored in a data base. Can you think of any drawbacks to the computerized system? List them.

   b) Design a layout for the card catalog data base. Be sure to include all of the information currently included on the manual cards.

   c) Using the design from part (b), give three different key categories for sorting this data base. For each key category, describe why the data base might be sorted on this category.

7. Because the computerized card catalog designed in exercise 6 was such a success, the library would also like to store its lending information in a data base and keep track of its overdue books.

   a) Design a layout for a borrowed book record. Include the name of the borrower, the title and reference number of the book, the date it was borrowed and the date the book must be returned.

   b) Give three examples of printed reports that might be produced using this data base. Include a design for a report listing overdue books.

   c) Give reasons for having the data base sorted on the borrower's name, title, and due date fields.

8. Companies often use computerized data bases to keep track of their inventory.

   a) Design a data base layout for an inventory which contains three fields: the product identification code, the product name and the amount of that product "on hand" (actually in the warehouse).

   b) Often the computer is located in a different building then the warehouse where the inventory items are stored. Using the word processor, create a printed form which could be used by a warehouse worker to record the amount on hand for a specific item. Include a title describing the purpose of the form, and leave room for the product's identification code and name.

   c) The manager of purchasing needs to know when to reorder products. Using the design in part (a), create a selection rule that will display only those records with an amount on hand that is less than 100.

   d) Design a printed report for the purchasing manager showing items that need to be reordered.

   e) There is often a delay between when a product is ordered and when it arrives in the warehouse. Add a category to your layout named "Ordered" which stores the amount of a product that has been ordered, but has not yet arrived. Modify the selection rule in part (c) to display only those records for items which have an on hand amount less than 100 and have not yet been reordered.

9. Some scientific experiments require that data be recorded over a period of weeks, months or even years.

    a) Design a layout for a computerized data base to store the results of a weather experiment. Each record should contain categories which store the date, time, temperature, amount of rain fall, and sky conditions (clear, cloudy, etc.) for a single observation.

    b) Using the category names from part (a) create selection rules which display only the records which meet the following criteria:

        Sunny days only
        All cloudy days with no precipitation
        The weather on March 15, 1989
        The weather for the month of July, 1989
        All rainy days in April

Chapter 5
Creating an AppleWorks Data Base

Open-Apple D

Open-Apple F

Open-Apple I

Open-Apple L

Open-Apple R

Open-Apple S

Open-Apple Y

Open-Apple Z

Objectives

After completing this chapter you will be able to:

1. Design a record layout for a new computerized data base using AppleWorks.

2. Enter data into the new data base, record by record.

3. Save the data base in a file on disk.

4. Use the Find command to locate text in a data base.

5. Use selection rules to search for data in a specific category.

6. Change the data stored in a record or category.

7. Add records to and delete records from a data base.

8. Save an updated data base in the same file on disk.

*T*his chapter describes the steps necessary to create a computerized data base using AppleWorks and perform some common operations with it: search, select and update. A record layout will be created and records entered into the data base. The data base will then be saved on disk in a file, and searched for text. Selection rules will be used to display only the records which meet certain criteria. Commands which update and save the information stored in the data base will be introduced. Chapter 6 covers the creation of printed reports using the information in a data base and ways of ordering the records to make those reports easier to read and understand. Because of the complexity involved in producing a report, printing database information will not be discussed in this chapter.

5.1 Creating a New AppleWorks Data Base

To create a new AppleWorks data base, the 'Add Files' option is selected from the Main Menu. Option 4 on the Add Files menu allows a new Data Base file to be created from scratch. Like the Word Processor, a new Data Base file can be created from a number of different sources. We will use only the 'From scratch' option in this chapter.

Because a new data base is being created the Data Base CHANGE NAME/CATEGORY screen will appear. Each of the different screens used in the Data Base application has a title describing its purpose.

Before a new data base may be used, it must be named and the computer given information about the different categories contained in each record. You will be asked to supply the name of the new Data Base file. The CHANGE NAME/CATEGORY screen is then used to create a "layout" or "form" showing the name and placement of each category in the record:

File Name

```
/File: Student              CHANGE NAME/CATEGORY        Escape: Review/Add/Change\


Category Names
=========================================================================
Category 1
         Default Category        | Options:
         Name                    |
                                 | Change category name
                                 | Up arrow    Go to filename
                                 | Down arrow  Go to next category
                                 | @ -I        Insert new category
                                 |
                                 |
                                 |
                                 |
                                 |
-------------------------------------------------------------------------
 Type entry or use @ commands                              348K Avail.
```

Practice 1

In this Practice you will start the computer and create a new AppleWorks data base named Student from scratch.

1) BOOT PRODOS AND START APPLEWORKS

   Boot the Startup disk and enter today's date as described in Chapter 2.

2) CHOOSE THE 'ADD FILES' OPTION FROM THE MAIN MENU

   Press Return to accept the default.

3) SELECT 'MAKE A NEW DATA BASE FILE' FROM THE ADD FILES MENU

   Press 4 to highlight Data Base and press Return.

4) SELECT 'FROM SCRATCH' FROM THE DATA BASE MENU

   Press Return to accept the default.

5) ENTER A NAME FOR THE NEW FILE

   In response to the prompt

   `Type a name for this new file:`

   type `Student` and press Return.

   Check - The CHANGE NAME/CATEGORY screen shown above should be displayed.

5.2 Designing the Data Base Layout

We will design a layout for the Ivy University student data base discussed in the previous chapter. Each record stores the data for one student using the category names listed below:

Category name	Data
First Name	student's first name
Last Name	student's last name
Address	street address
City	city
State	state
Zip	zip code
Admit Date	date student was admitted
GPA	grade point average
Paid	paid tuition bill? (Y or N)

The first step in creating a new data base is to enter into the computer the names of the categories and their position in the layout. It is important to place related categories next to each other so that the layout is easier to use and understand. As an example, the category for the student's last name should be placed next to the category for the first name. Other categories that should be grouped together are Address, City, State and Zip. No data is entered at this point, only the names and positions of the different categories.

To create a layout the cursor is moved to the desired position on the CHANGE NAME/CATEGORY screen and the category name typed. After typing the category name, pressing Return enters it into the layout and moves the cursor down one line. When creating a new data base, AppleWorks supplies a default for the first category name, Category 1. Because the first category in our record is First Name, this default must be removed using `Open-Apple Y` before entering the new category name.

Practice 2

In this Practice you will create a layout for the student data base by entering the category names on the CHANGE NAME/CATEGORY screen. Note that AppleWorks has given a default name to the first category, Category 1, which you will remove. No data will be entered at this point. Only after the layout has been created can data be entered.

1) REMOVE THE DEFAULT NAME

Press `Open-Apple Y` to remove the default name supplied by AppleWorks.

2) ENTER THE NAME FOR THE FIRST CATEGORY

Type `First Name`. If you make a mistake typing the category name, use the arrow and delete keys to correct it.

3) PLACE THE FIRST NAME CATEGORY ONTO THE LAYOUT

Pressing Return places the category onto the layout at the current cursor position.

Check - Your screen should show the First Name category:

```
File: Student                 CHANGE NAME/CATEGORY        Escape: Review/Add/Change



Category Names
================================================================================
First Name                          |
                                    | Options:
_                                   |
                                    | Type category name
                                    | Up arrow   Go to previous category
                                    |
                                    |
                                    |
                                    |
                                    |
 - - - - - - - - - - - - - - - - - -|- - - - - - - - - - - - - - - - - - - - - -
Type entry or use @ commands                                348K Avail.
```

4) COMPLETE THE LAYOUT BY ENTERING THE REST OF THE CATE-
    GORIES

> Next, the category for the student's last name should be placed
> on the layout. Because the data to be stored in the Last Name
> category is related to the data stored in First Name, these
> categories should be placed next to each other on the layout.
> Using the steps described above, complete the record layout by
> adding the rest of the categories. Be sure to press Return after
> entering each category name. The completed layout should
> look like:

```
File: Student                 CHANGE NAME/CATEGORY        Escape: Review/Add/Change



Category Names
================================================================================
First Name                          |
Last Name                           | Options:
Address                             |
City                                | Type category name
State                               | Up arrow   Go to previous category
Zip                                 |
Admit Date                          |
GPA                                 |
Paid                                |
                                    |
 - - - - - - - - - - - - - - - - - -|- - - - - - - - - - - - - - - - - - - - - -
Type entry or use @ commands                                348K Avail.
```

5) TERMINATE THE LAYOUT CREATION

> After all of the categories have been entered, press Escape to
> exit the CHANGE NAME/CATEGORY screen.

5.3 Entering Records in a New Data Base

After the layout has been completed, data can be entered into
the records. When Escape is pressed AppleWorks displays the following message:

```
This file does not yet contain any information.
Therefore, you will automatically go into the
Insert New Records feature.


Press Space Bar to continue
```

Pressing the Space Bar reveals the INSERT NEW RECORDS screen:

```
File: Student              INSERT NEW RECORDS        Escape: Review/Add/Change

                    ╱ Number of Records
  Record 1 of 1 ╱ (0 selected)
  =================================================================================
  First Name: -
  Last Name: -
  Address: -
  City: - ─────── Empty Categories
  State: -
  Zip: -
  Admit Date: -
  GPA: -
  Paid: -


  --------------------------------------------------------------------------------
  Type entry or use @ commands                                      348K Avail.
```

In INSERT NEW RECORDS, each category name is displayed with space to enter data for that category. Empty categories (categories with no data stored in them) are automatically indicated by the computer with a dash (-). To enter data for a category, the cursor is moved to that category using the arrow keys and the data then typed. AppleWorks removes the dash when data is entered into a category. Pressing Return places the data into the category and moves the cursor to the next category. You must press Return to enter the data into the category before moving to the next category. If you make a mistake before pressing Return, Escape will erase the current entry and allow you to start from the beginning of that category. Appleworks will only accept enough data to reach the right side of the screen, up to a maximum of eighty characters per entry. When all of the categories in a record have been entered, pressing Return clears the screen and a new, empty record is displayed. AppleWorks keeps track of how many records have been entered and which record is currently displayed, and shows this information at the top left hand side of the screen.

5.4 Saving a Data Base File on Disk

Pressing Open-Apple S will save the current data base in a file on disk. When a data base is saved, a copy of each of the records currently in the computer's memory is made on the disk. Once a file has been saved, it may be retrieved later and the data stored in it displayed or changed. It is important to periodically save a data base when it is being worked on so that, should an accident such as a power failure occur, it would be possible to recover the file from the disk.

Practice 3

In this Practice you will enter data into three student records and save the data base in a file on disk.

1) PRESS SPACE BAR TO CLEAR THE SCREEN

Pressing the Space Bar removes the message and displays the INSERT NEW RECORDS screen.

2) TYPE A STUDENT'S FIRST NAME

Because the cursor is on the First Name category, you should enter a first name. Type Matilda and press Return. If you make a mistake, press the up-arrow key to move the cursor back to the First Name category and make the correction using the arrow and Delete keys.

3) ENTER THE STUDENT'S LAST NAME

Pressing Return moves the cursor to the next category, Last Name. Type Rose and press Return.

4) COMPLETE THE STUDENT RECORD

Enter the following data for the rest of the categories, pressing Return at the end of each category:

Address: 435 Frelinghuysen Rd
City: Leafville
State: NJ
Zip: 08049
Admit Date: 2-14-88
GPA: 3.4
Paid: Y

Note that when you press Return after entering the date, AppleWorks converts it to Feb 14 88. This is because AppleWorks treats the Admit Date category as a date field since its name contains the word "date". As discussed in Chapter 4, numbers entered into this type of category will automatically be converted into a corresponding date.

After entering the code for Paid, pressing Return enters the record into the computer's memory. The screen is cleared and a new, empty record is shown into which data may be typed.

5) ADD THE FOLLOWING TWO STUDENT RECORDS

Follow the steps above to enter the next two records into the file:

First Name: Sam
Last Name: Adams
Address: 121 Carey Quadrangle
City: Leaftown
State: PA
Zip: 19717
Admit Date: 3-12-79
GPA: 1.5
Paid: N

First Name: Roberta
Last Name: Poisson
Address: 8P Corwin Place
City: Five Points
State: FL
Zip: 33434
Admit Date: 6-27-89
GPA: 4.0
Paid: N   (Do not press Return yet.)

Check - Before the last Return is pressed, the final record entered should look like:

```
File: Student              INSERT NEW RECORDS        Escape: Review/Add/Change


Record 3 of 3   (0 selected)
===============================================================================
First Name: Roberta
Last Name: Poisson
Address: 8P Corwin Place
City: Five Points
State: FL
Zip: 33434
Admit Date: Jun 27 89
GPA: 4.0
Paid: N_


------------------------------------------------------------------------------
Type entry or use @ commands                                    348K Avail.
```

6) TERMINATE THE ENTRY OF NEW RECORDS

Press Return to complete record 3. Press Escape to terminate the entry of new records when the screen for Record 4 appears.

7) SAVE THE DATA BASE FILE ON DISK

Press `Open-Apple S` to save the Student data base containing the three new records in a file on disk.

5.5 Multi-record and Single-record Format

Pressing Escape terminates the INSERT NEW RECORDS procedure. AppleWorks then displays the contents of the data base file in multi-record format:

```
File: Student              REVIEW/ADD/CHANGE          Escape: Main Menu

Selection: All records


First Name       Last Name       Address         City            State
===============================================================================
Matilda          Rose            435 Frelinghuys Leafville        NJ
Sam              Adams           121 Carey Quadr Leaftown         PA
Roberta          Poisson         8P Corwin Place Five Points      FL




------------------------------------------------------------------------------
Type entry or use @ commands                                    @-? for Help
```

In multi-record format, the first few categories for up to fifteen records are displayed. This is important because multi-record format allows records to be compared to one another. Note that only the first fifteen characters of the data stored in a category are currently displayed (e.g., the Address category). The rest of the data is still stored in the entry, only not displayed at this time. Later we will learn how to increase the size of the category to show all of the data stored in it.

In multi-record format pressing the up and down-arrows moves the cursor from record to record. Pressing Tab moves the cursor one category to the right, and `Open-Apple Tab` one category to the left. `Open-Apple 1` moves the cursor directly to the first record in the file, `Open-Apple 9` to the last, and `Open-Apple 5` to the middle. In version 3 pressing `Open-Apple` and an arrow key scrolls the screen in the direction of the arrow, allowing other categories to be viewed.

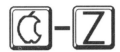

One of the difficulties with multi-record format is that all of the categories for a single record are not displayed on the screen at one time. For example, it is no longer possible to determine if Matilda Rose has paid her tuition simply by looking at the previous screen because the Paid category is no longer displayed. For this reason AppleWorks also has a single-record format similar to the INSERT NEW RECORDS screen which displays all of the categories for a single record. It is possible to switch between the multi-record format and single-record format by pressing Open-Apple Z (for **Z**oom).

```
File: Student              REVIEW/ADD/CHANGE          Escape: Main Menu

Selection: All records
                   Record Currently Displayed
Record 1 of 3   (3 selected)
=================================================================
First Name: Matilda
Last Name: Rose
Address: 435 Frelinghuysen Rd
City: Leafville
State: NJ
Zip: 08049
Admit Date: Feb 14 88
GPA: 3.4
Paid: Y

---------------------------------------------------------------
Type entry or use @ commands                        @-? for Help
```

In single record format, pressing the up- and down-arrows moves the cursor from category to category. It is possible to "scroll" from one record to the next by using the down-arrow key to move from the last category of the current record to the first category of the next record. It is also possible to scroll upwards in the file by using the up-arrow. Open-Apple 1 moves to the first record in the file, Open-Apple 9 to the last, and Open-Apple 5 to the middle.

When switching between multi- and single-record formats, the cursor always remains on the same record. For example, if the cursor is on record three in multi-record format when Open-Apple Z is pressed, the screen will display record three in single-record format. If the cursor is then moved to record one and Open-Apple Z again pressed, the screen will switch to multi-record format and the cursor will remain on record one.

5.6 Changing the Data Stored in a Category

It is possible to change the data stored in a category. Changes to the entry in a category are made by moving the cursor to the desired category, typing the new data and pressing Return. You may also use the left-arrow, right-arrow and Delete keys to edit the entry. Any old data in the category may be removed by first pressing Open-Apple Y. Changes may be made when the record is displayed in either multi-record or single-record formats. This process is called "updating" and is covered in more detail below.

It is important to remember to press Return after an update has been made. If you do not press Return the new information will not be entered into the category and the cursor may not be moved from its current position. If you choose not to make the update, pressing Escape instead of Return will erase your changes and restore the former entry.

5.7 Modifying the Screen Layout

Because multi-record format does not show the data for every category on the screen, it is often necessary to modify the layout, specifying which categories are to be displayed, and in what order. The Layout command, Open-Apple L, allows the user to change the order in which the categories are displayed on the screen. The width of each category (the amount of space it takes up on the screen) may also be changed from the default width of 15 characters. It is important to realize that modifying the screen layout in no way affects the data stored in the records, only the way in which the categories are displayed on the screen.

Pressing Open-Apple L displays the CHANGE RECORD LAYOUT screen which shows the current layout of the records:

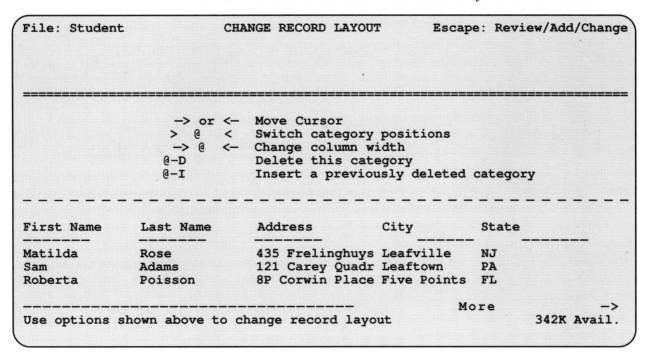

```
File: Student                CHANGE RECORD LAYOUT         Escape: Review/Add/Change
================================================================================

              -> or <-    Move Cursor
             >  @   <     Switch category positions
              -> @  <-    Change column width
          @-D             Delete this category
          @-I             Insert a previously deleted category

 - - - - - - - - - - - - - - - - - - - - - - - - - - - - - - - - - - - - - - - -

First Name        Last Name        Address        City          State
----------        ---------        -------        ------        --------
Matilda           Rose             435 Frelinghuys Leafville     NJ
Sam               Adams            121 Carey Quadr Leaftown      PA
Roberta           Poisson          8P Corwin Place Five Points   FL

-----------------------------------------               More              ->
Use options shown above to change record layout                     342K Avail.
```

Pressing the arrow keys moves the cursor from category to category. Pressing Open-Apple left-arrow reduces the current category width by one space. Similarly, Open-Apple right-arrow increases it by one. Open-Apple > (greater than sign) exchanges the current category with the one to its right. That is, pressing Open-Apple > when the cursor is on First Name would exchange First Name with Last Name, and the categories displayed would be Last Name, First Name, Address, etc. Open-Apple < (less than) switches category positions with the category to the left. It is important to note that data stored in the file may not be modified from this screen, only the appearance of the record when displayed on the screen: the order and width of the categories.

Pressing Escape returns to the REVIEW/ADD/CHANGE screen. Each time the CHANGE RECORD LAYOUT screen is exited, you are given the option of defining how the cursor will move when Return is pressed. The default is down, to the next record, but this may be changed to move the cursor right, to the next category, should you desire:

```
What direction should the cursor
go when you press Return?
```

1. **Down (Standard)**
2. Right

AppleWorks saves the layout of a data base along with the data it stores. If a data base is saved after its layout has been changed, the next time the data base is loaded it will have the new layout.

Practice 4

In this Practice you will change the record layout of the Student data base to display the GPA category after the Last Name category. Zoom mode will then be used to display all of the categories in a single record. Start AppleWorks and load the Student data base if you have not already done so.

1) DISPLAY THE CHANGE RECORD LAYOUT SCREEN

With the cursor on the REVIEW/ADD/CHANGE screen, press `Open-Apple L`.

2) MOVE THE GPA CATEGORY TO THE LEFT

a. Press `right-arrow` seven times to move the cursor to the GPA category.
b. Press `Open-Apple <`. The GPA and Admit Date categories are switched. Press `Open-Apple <` four more times until GPA is placed between Address and Last Name.

3) RETURN TO RECORD 1 ON THE REVIEW/ADD/CHANGE SCREEN

a. Press Escape. AppleWorks will prompt you to select the direction for the cursor to move when Return is pressed.
b. Press Return to accept the default of down. The multi-record format screen now displays the GPA category after the Last Name column.
c. Move to the first record by pressing `Open-Apple 1`.

4) ZOOM TO SINGLE-RECORD DISPLAY

Press `Open-Apple Z`. The first record will be displayed in single-record mode. Note that the GPA category is still displayed after Admit Date in this layout.

5) MOVE DOWN TO RECORD 3 AND SWITCH TO MULTI-RECORD DISPLAY

a. Press down-arrow until the cursor is on the First Name category of record 3.
b. Press `Open-Apple Z`. The screen will switch to multi-record display, and the cursor will be on the First Name category of record 3.

6) SAVE THE FILE AND RETURN TO THE MAIN MENU

a. Press `Open-Apple S` to save the file on disk. When next retrieved, the GPA category will be listed after Last Name in multi-record display.
b. Press Escape to exit the REVIEW/ADD/CHANGE screen and return to the Main Menu.

5.8 Finding Text in a Record

AppleWorks can be told to display only those records in a data base which contain a certain word or phrase. This operation is called "finding" and is executed by pressing Open-Apple F. You are then prompted to enter the text to be found, the "comparison information". Once entered, the computer compares that text to the data stored in each category in the file. All records for which a match is found are then displayed on the screen. When a Find command is in effect a message appears at the top left hand corner of the screen showing the comparison text. This is done so that you can tell how the records currently displayed were chosen. It is important to realize that the other records are still stored in the file, but they are not displayed because they do not contain the comparison text. Pressing Escape will return the display to showing all records. Pressing Open-Apple F again will allow you to enter a new comparison text.

When using the 'Anywhere' option and in version 2, Find does not search for text in a specific category, and a match is considered found if the comparison text is contained in any category in the record. For example, supplying "et" for the comparison text would display a record which has "Jan<u>et</u>" in the First Name category as well as all records which have the word "Str<u>eet</u>" in the Address category. Apple-Work's Find command is not affected by upper and lower case, so that entering "et" will find any combination of upper and lower case letters so long as "e" is followed by "t"; <u>Et</u>onic, be<u>et</u>s, STR<u>EET</u>, etc.

It is sometimes the case that the comparison text will not be found in any of the records in the data base. When this occurs, AppleWorks displays the message "No records match your request" and directs you to press the Space bar.

Practice 5

This Practice demonstrates the effect of the Find command with different comparison texts. To demonstrate this command on a large number of records, the Ivy Student data base file on your data disk will be used. Start AppleWorks if you have not already done so.

1) LOAD THE IVY STUDENT DATA BASE FILE FROM YOUR DATA DISK

    a. Select 'Add Files' from the Main Menu.
    b. Choose your data disk from the Get Files menu.
    c. Move the cursor to Ivy Student using the arrow keys. Press Return to load the file and view the data.

2) ISSUE THE FIND COMMAND

    a. Press Open-Apple 1 to return the cursor to the top of the file.
    b. Press Open-Apple F. AppleWorks displays the prompt:

Find text?　**Anywhere**　In a specific category

Press the Return key to accept the default of 'Anywhere'.

3) TYPE THE COMPARISON TEXT

Works prompts for the comparision text:

Type comparison information:

Type street at the prompt and press Return. All of the records now displayed have the text "street" in them somewhere. The "street" may appear in any category, including Address and Last Name. Note the message at the top of the screen which states that all of the records currently displayed contain STREET.

4) ENTER A NEW COMPARISON TEXT

    a. Press `Open-Apple F` and Return to accept 'Anywhere'.

    b. The old comparison text, STREET, appears. Press `Open-Apple Y` to delete it.

    c. Type `zzz` and press Return. Because no records are found that match the comparison text, AppleWorks displays the message:

`No records match your request`

Press the Space bar to continue.

5) TERMINATE THE FIND AND DISPLAY ALL RECORDS

Press Escape to terminate the Find and view the data base. The upper left corner of the screen now indicates "All records".

5.9 Using Selection Rules to Perform a Search

Find with 'Anywhere' (and in version 2) is limited because its searching is not restricted to a specific category. Specifying a comparison text of "Adams" not only displays Sam Adams' record, but also anyone who lives on Adams Street or comes from Adamsville, etc. Also, Find does not have the important capability of searching for more than one comparison text at a time. That is, we cannot Find the records of all students who come from Maine or Vermont in one operation.

AppleWorks can be made to display records which contain specific data by applying "selection rules". A selection rule is a description of the data that the displayed record must contain. A selection rule refers to a specific category, and may contain more than one comparison text. Rules are defined by pressing `Open-Apple R` and selecting different options from a list, similar to choosing options from a menu. The first option is the category name. AppleWorks will display all of the category names in the current data base and ask you to select the one that this rule should be applied to:

```
File: Ivy Student          SELECT RECORDS        Escape: Review/Add/Change

Selection:


=====================================================================
1.   First Name
2.   Last Name
3.   Address
4.   City
5.   State
6.   Zip
7.   Admit Date
8.   GPA
9.   Paid




---------------------------------------------------------------------
Type number, or use arrows, then press Return          348K Avail.
```

Next a list of conditions is displayed:

```
/ File: Ivy Student            SELECT RECORDS            Escape: Review/Add/Change \

  Selection:


  ================================================================================
  1.  equals
  2.  is greater than
  3.  is less than
  4.  is not equal to
  5.  is blank
  6.  is not blank
  7.  contains
  8.  begins with
  9.  ends with
  10. does not contain
  11. does not begin with
  12. does not end with



  ------------------------------------------------------------------------------
\ Type number, or use arrows, then press Return              348K Avail.        /
```

After choosing the condition, you must enter the text for the category to be compared with and press Return (similar to specifying the comparison text with the Find command). Pressing Escape then applies the rule and only records which meet the criteria defined by the rule are displayed. Like Find, the rule will be displayed in the upper left-hand corner of the screen.

Some example selection rules are:

```
First Name equals Janet
State equals ME
Last Name begins with F
```

The first rule would display every record with Janet in the First Name category only. A student who lived on Janet Street would not be displayed (unless her first name was also Janet). The second rule would display the records for every person with an address in Maine, and the third all students whose last names begin with the letter F; Amy Freitas, Barclay Fitzpatrick, Jimmy Fong but not Fran Jones. Like the Find command, selection rules ignore upper and lower case differences.

To cancel a rule, `Open-Apple R` is pressed again. AppleWorks then displays the prompt:

```
Select all records?  No   Yes
```

To remove the rule and display all of the records, press the Y key when this prompt is displayed. Pressing the Return key will accept the default of No and display the category list again, allowing you to create a new rule.

5.10 Combining Rules to Perform a Complex Search

Rules may be joined together to form ranges. Rules are joined by selecting the desired "conjunction" from a list. A conjunction is a word which joins two or more rules together to form one large rule. Available conjunctions include 'and' and 'or'. For example, it is possible to specify the rule:

```
GPA greater than 1 and GPA less than 2
```

When this rule is applied, only records with a GPA entry between 1 and 2 will be displayed. Rules may also be joined with the word 'or' to produce a rule which has different parts. When a rule is joined with 'or', records will be displayed if any of the conditions are met. For example, applying the rule

`State equals ME or State equals VE or State equals NH`

will display the records for all students from Maine, Vermont and New Hampshire.

To apply the rule, press Escape when the conjunction list is displayed on the screen. Only the records which meet the rule's criteria will then be displayed.

Practice 6

In this Practice you will apply two different selection rules to the Ivy Student data base and note their effects. Start AppleWorks and load Ivy Student if you have not already done so. We will apply the rule "PAID equals N" to get a list of all the students who have not yet paid their tuition.

1) SWITCH TO THE SELECT RECORDS SCREEN

   Press `Open-Apple R`. A list of the category names is displayed.

2) SELECT THE CATEGORY TO BE INCLUDED IN THE RULE

   Type 9 to select the Paid category and press the Return key. The partial selection rule is shown at the top of the screen:

   `Selection: Paid`

3) CHOOSE THE DESIRED COMPARISON

   A list of comparisons will be displayed. 'Equals' is the default so just press Return. The partial selection rule is shown at the top of the screen:

   `Selection: Paid equals`

4) ENTER THE COMPARISON INFORMATION

   The prompt

   `Type comparison information:`

   appears at the bottom of the screen. Type N and press Return. A list of conjunctions (ways to join rules) will be displayed. The complete rule is shown at the top of the screen:

   `Selection: Paid equals N`

5) APPLY THE RULE TO THE DATA BASE

   a. Since the rule is complete and we want no conjunction, press Escape to apply the rule to the data. Only records which have an "N" in the Paid category are now displayed. Note that the selection rule is displayed in the upper left corner of the screen.
   b. Because Paid is not currently displayed in this layout, switch to single record layout using `Open-Apple Z` and scroll through several records to verify that only records with an "N" in the Paid field are displayed.
   c. Switch back to multi-record layout using `Open-Apple Z`.

6)   SWITCH TO SELECT RECORDS TO CREATE A NEW RULE

Press `Open-Apple R`. AppleWorks will ask if all records should be displayed.

`Select all records?` **No** `Yes`

We want to apply the new rule "GPA greater than 1 and GPA less than 2" so press Return to accept the No default.

7)   SELECT THE DESIRED CATEGORY, COMPARISON AND TEXT

a.   GPA is the eighth category on the list so press 8 and the Return key.
b.   Press down-arrow and Return to select 'is greater than'.
c.   Type 1 for the comparison information and press Return.

8)   SELECT THE CONJUNCTION

A conjunction specifies how two rules will be joined. We want 'and' which is the default so just press Return.

9)   COMPLETE THE RULE AND APPLY IT TO THE DATA BASE

a.   Choose GPA from the category list.
b.   Select 'is less than' from the comparison list.
c.   Enter 2 for the comparison information and press Return.
d.   Press Escape to apply the rule to the data. All of the students now displayed have GPA entries which are greater than 1 and less than 2. Note that the rule is shown in the upper left corner of the screen.

10)   REMOVE THE RULE TO DISPLAY ALL RECORDS

a.   Press `Open-Apple R`.
b.   AppleWorks will prompt

`Select all records?` **No** `Yes`

Press Y to remove any rules and display all of the records in the data base. Note that the upper left corner of the screen now says "All records".

5.11 *Updating the Data in a Record*

Any time a data base is displayed on the REVIEW/ADD/CHANGE screen it is possible to change the contents of a category. This is called "updating a record" and is accomplished by moving the cursor to the desired record and category, typing the new data and pressing Return. If the file is then saved on disk, the new data stored in that category will be retained.

The ability to update records is important because the data stored in a data base often changes; a person may move and have a new address, the price of an inventory item may go up or down, a student receives a new GPA at the end of a semester, etc. For example, suppose Ivy University's registrar receives a check from student Bruce Bonner to pay his tuition bill. Ivy's student data base can be accessed and a "Y" stored in the Paid category of Bruce Bonner's record. Should a selection rule such as "show all records where Paid equals N" then be applied, Bruce's record would no longer be listed. It is important to realize that simply changing the value on the screen does not mean that it is changed in the file. The file must be saved on disk after the change is made. Should there be a power failure before you save the file, the change would not appear the next time the file was loaded. Therefore, you should frequently save a data base file (Open-Apple S) when updating records.

Because an update usually involves a specific record, the Find command is often used to limit the records displayed on the screen, making it easier to locate the record to be updated. In the example above, Find could be used to display all records containing the text "Bonner". The correct record would then be easy to locate and the update made directly from the FIND screen.

As we have stated before, multi-record format is limited because it often does not display all of the categories in a record. It is possible that an update may require changing the data in a category not currently displayed on the screen. When this occurs, the desired record is first located in the file (using Find or Record Selection as necessary). It is best to switch to single-record format using Open-Apple Z which displays all of the categories for that record and then make the update. This helps avoid errors such as updating the correct field but in the wrong record. In version 3 it is possible to scroll multi-record format to view categories not currently on the screen. However, updates to categories such as GPA or Paid must then be performed without the student's name being visible, which can lead to errors.

Practice 7

In this Practice you will update two records in the Ivy Student data base to reflect new information. Start AppleWorks and load Ivy Student if you have not already done so.

1) LOCATE THE DESIRED RECORD IN THE FILE

   Update: Student Jenny Lee has moved to 23 Market Street.

   a. Type Open-Apple F and find the text Lee.
   b. There are several Lee's in the file as well as someone who lives on Lee Street. Move the cursor to select Jenny Lee's record.

2) SELECT THE PROPER CATEGORY

   Press Tab until the cursor is in the Address category.

3) ENTER THE NEW DATA FOR THAT CATEGORY

   a. Press Open-Apple Y to remove the old data.
   b. Type 23 Market Street and press Return. Her new address is now stored in the category.

4) LOCATE THE DESIRED RECORD IN THE FILE

   Update: Student Bruce Bonner has paid his tuition bill.

   a. Type Open-Apple F and select 'Anywhere'.
   b. Press Open-Apple Y to delete the old comparison text. Enter Bonner and press Return.
   c. Move the cursor to Bruce Bonner's record.

5) SELECT THE PROPER CATEGORY

   a. Press Open-Apple Z to zoom to single-record format.
   b. Use the arrow keys to place the cursor in the Paid category.

6) ENTER THE NEW DATA FOR THAT CATEGORY

    a. Press Open-Apple Y to remove the old data.

    b. Type a capital Y and press Return. A "Y" is now stored in the Paid category.

7) RETURN TO MULTI-RECORD FORMAT FOR ALL STUDENTS

    a. Press Open-Apple Z to return to multi-record format.

    b. Note that the Find command is still in effect. Press Escape to cancel the Find and display all records.

8) SAVE THE FILE TO RETAIN THE UPDATES

    Press Open-Apple S to save the file on disk. Both changes will be present in the file the next time that Ivy Student is loaded.

5.12 Adding Records to a Data Base

It is often necessary to add new records to a data base; new students enroll in a school, a store adds a new item to its inventory, etc. AppleWorks allows new records to be added to a data base using Open-Apple I (for **I**nsert records). Any new records added will be placed in the file above the current cursor position. The display changes to a single-record INSERT NEW RECORDS screen where the data for the new record may be entered category by category, pressing Return after each. (This is the same screen you used to originally add records to a new data base.) After inserting the data for any new records the file must be saved on disk to retain them. Pressing Escape cancels the insert new records and switches back to multi-record format, displaying the new record.

Practice 8

A new student, Steve Rohrman, has enrolled in Ivy University and you will insert his record into the data base. Start AppleWorks and load the Ivy Student file if you have not already done so.

1) MOVE THE CURSOR TO WHERE THE NEW RECORD SHOULD BE INSERTED

    Press down-arrow until the cursor is on Matilda Rose's record.

2) ISSUE THE INSERT RECORDS COMMAND

    Press Open-Apple I. The display switches to the INSERT NEW RECORDS screen which displays a single, empty record.

3) ENTER THE DATA FOR THE NEW RECORD

    Type the following data for each category, pressing Return after each:

    First Name: Steve
    Last Name: Rohrman
    Address: 212 Phillips Ave.
    City: Magnolia
    State: NJ
    Zip: 08131
    Admit Date: 10-16-88
    GPA: 0
    Paid: Y

4) RETURN TO THE MULTI-RECORD DISPLAY

Press Escape. Note that the new student's record has been inserted above Matilda Rose's.

5) SAVE THE MODIFIED FILE

Press Open-Apple S to save the file on disk. The next time that Ivy Student is used, Steve Rohrman's record will be in the file.

5.13 Deleting Records from a Data Base

Just as it is necessary to add new records to a data base, records must often be deleted; a student graduates or drops out, a store decides to no longer carry an item, etc. In AppleWorks, Open-Apple D (for **D**elete record) will delete the current record that the cursor is on. Because of the possibility for damaging the data base by removing the wrong record, AppleWorks allows you to terminate the delete operation by pressing Escape before actually deleting the record. If Return is instead pressed, the record will be deleted from the computer's memory and erased from the screen. When the file is then saved on disk, that record will no longer be stored. As when updating a record, there is often a need to first locate the record to be deleted using the Find or Record select commands.

Practice 9

Student Bob Smallecomb has dropped out of Ivy University and you will remove his record from the data base. Start AppleWorks and load the Ivy Student file if you have not already done so.

1) LOCATE THE RECORD TO BE DELETED

Use the Find command to locate the record for Bob Smallecomb.

2) ISSUE THE DELETE RECORD COMMAND

a. With the cursor on Bob Smallecomb's record press Open-Apple D. The entire record is highlighted on the screen.
b. Press Return to delete the record, removing it from the screen. (Pressing Escape at this point would terminate the delete operation.)

3) SAVE THE FILE

Press Open-Apple S to save the file, without Bob Smallecomb's record, on disk.

Chapter Summary

This chapter covered the basics of creating and using a computerized data base in AppleWorks. Before any new data base is created on the computer it should first be carefully planned, using pencil and paper as described in Chapter 4. Once planned, the first step in creating a new computer data base is to make a new Data Base file from scratch and supply its name. Then the record layout is described to the computer on the CHANGE NAME/CATEGORY screen. AppleWorks then automatically proceeds to the INSERT NEW RECORDS screen where data may be entered into the file, record by record.

Once created, there are two ways to view an AppleWorks data base: single-record format and multi-record format. Single-record format shows all of the categories for one record while multi-record format shows only the first few categories for up to 15 records. Single-record format is useful for making changes to a record. Multi-record format makes it easy to see the relationships between the data stored in many records. It is possible to change the order in which the categories are displayed on the screen by using the Layout command, Open-Apple L. This is useful when a category not displayed in the default multi-record format must be viewed. At the same time, the amount of space each category is given on the screen (its width) may be changed.

AppleWorks has two ways of locating specific data within a data base file. The first is by using the Find command, Open-Apple F. Find performs a general search which allows a comparison text to be entered and displays all records which have that text stored in any of their categories. (In version 3 Find may be limited to a specific category.) More specific searches can be applied using the Record select command, Open-Apple R. With this command, only the records which fit certain rules are displayed. For example, using record selection it is possible to display the records for every student from Maine, or all of the students with a GPA less than 2. Both of these commands are useful because they limit the number of records displayed, helping to locate only the records desired at that time.

Because the data stored in a data base changes, AppleWorks can insert new records into a file (Open-Apple I), delete existing records from a file (Open-Apple D) and update the data stored in any category in any record. When a change has been made to a data base, the data base file must be saved on disk to ensure that the change will be present the next time the file is used. Open-Apple S saves the current file on disk and should be used after every major change.

Vocabulary

Comparison text - Text entered by the user during a Find or Record selection which records are compared to.

Delete record - To remove a record from a data base: Open-Apple D.

Find - General search which displays those records containing a comparison text in any category: Open-Apple F.

Insert record - Adds a new, empty record to the data base above the current cursor position: Open-Apple I.

Layout - The arrangement and width of categories in a record.

Multi-record format - Displays the first few categories for up to 15 records. Used when comparing records to one another.

Selection - Limiting the number of records in a data base that are displayed by using rules to define criteria that displayed records must meet.

Selection rule - Criteria for displaying records which refers to the contents of specific categories. Defined using Open-Apple R.

Single-record format - All of the categories for a single record displayed on the screen at one time. Used when updating a record.

Update a record - Changing the contents of an entry or entries in a record.

Zoom mode - Used to switch between single and multi-record formats: Open-Apple Z.

Reviews

Sections 5.1-5.4

1. a) List the steps necessary to design a new data base which stores information about the members of the Computer Club.
    b) Design a layout for the Computer Club data base. Include both the category names and a description of the data you believe the club will want to store for each of its members. Be sure to group related categories.

2. a) List the steps necessary to create the Computer Club layout on the computer from the design created in Review 1.
    b) Create sample data for one member of Computer Club and explain how it would be entered into the computer.

3. a) What should be done to place a newly entered record into the computer's memory from the INSERT NEW RECORDS screen?
    b) Why should related categories be placed together when creating a data base record layout?

Sections 5.5-5.7

4. a) Describe what will be displayed in multi-record format of a large data base. How much of each category will be displayed?
    b) How is it possible to display all of the categories in only the fifth record of a data base?

5. a) List the steps required to produce a multi-record format which displays the Last Name, Admit Date and Paid categories in the Ivy Student data base.
    b) If a file is saved after the multi-record format has been changed, what format will be displayed when the file is next accessed; the original format or the changed format?

Sections 5.8-5.10

6. a) List the steps required to display all records which contain the name Harold in the Ivy Student data base.
    b) Which records containing the following entries would be displayed?

    > John Harold
    > Judy Smarold
    > Harry T. Cat
    > 35 Harold Street
    > H. Arold Smythe
    > C. Tharold Jones
    > Heidi Smythe-Harold
    > ToDhAroldy

7. List the steps required to display all records in the Ivy Student data base for students who have not paid their tuition.

8. a) How does selection differ from Finding text?
    b) What is the purpose of a selection range?

9. Write selection rules which will display the following when applied to the Ivy Student data base:

    a) students with GPA's less than 1 and greater than 3.
    b) students from CA and OR.
    c) students with zip codes between 10016 and 11514.
    d) students whose last names begin with B and who are from FL.
    e) students who have GPA's above 3.0 and who have not paid their tuition.

Sections 5.11-5.13

10. a) What does it mean to "update" a record?
    b) Why would records be updated?

11. Sam Adams has moved to 35 Cleve Street in Lawrenceville, NJ, 08618. List the steps required to change his address in the Ivy Student data base.

12. A new student, Elise Reilly, has enrolled at Ivy University. Explain the steps required to add her to the Ivy Student data base. Because you are not sure where she fits alphabetically in the file, start by using the Find command to locate the cursor near where Elise's record should be added.

13. The Ivy University administration is discussing how to upgrade its standards by not allowing students with GPA's below 1.5 to return next year. Explain the steps that would be required to delete those students from the Ivy Student data base.

Exercises

1. In Exercise 2 of Chapter 4 you designed a data base layout that would act as an address book.

    a) Using this layout create the data base using AppleWorks and name it Address. Enter data into the file for a minimum of 10 of your friends.

    b) Using selection rules, display only the people in Address whose birthdays' are either in June or July.

    c) You've made a new friend, Amy Eppelman. Add her information to Address:

    > Amy Eppelman
    > 713 Graisbury Avenue
    > Haddonfield, NJ 08033
    > (213) 555-1324
    > Born 7/5/65

    d) Amy Eppelman has moved. Change her address and phone number to:

    > 343 Nenue Street
    > Honolulu, HI 98765
    > (767) 145-5937

    e) You have decided that the first person in the file is no longer your friend. Delete that record from Address.

    f) You would like to get some of your birthday purchases out of the way now. To prepare to buy presents, use selection rules to display only people who will have birthdays this month or next month.

2. On your data disk is a data base named Inventor which stores information about inventions: the name of the invention, the year it was invented, the name of the inventor and his or her nationality.

    a) Perform the following queries using Inventor:

    > Display all inventors who are from the United States.
    > Select all inventors from France whose inventions were produced between the years 1900 to 1930.
    > Display all inventions produced by Galileo.
    > List all inventions dealing with lights or lamps.

    b) Last week your friend Julie Fritz invented a Peanut Butter and Tunafish sandwich. Add a record to the Inventor file which chronicles this event.

3. Exercise 3 in Chapter 4 required you to design a layout for a car dealer's inventory data base.

    a) Using the layout produced in that exercise, create a data base named Fantasy that will record Fantasy Wheel's inventory. The first record should contain the car data shown in exercise 3.

    b) Add the following cars to the Fantasy data base:

    1972 Corvette
    color: red
    interior: green
    accessories: radio, automatic, air
    paid: $8,500
    asking price $25,800
    date acquired: 10/12/88

    1987 Porsche
    color: black
    interior: white
    accessories: 4 speed, air
    paid: $22,300
    asking price: $46,000
    date acquired: 5/27/89

    1985 Porsche
    color: red
    interior: blue
    accessories: radio, 4 speed
    paid: $31,000
    asking price: $62,000
    date acquired: 10/11/88

    1958 Thunderbird
    color: white
    interior: red
    accessories: radio, air
    paid: $14,500
    asking price: $31,000
    date aquired: 2/14/85

    1984 Ferrari
    color: grey
    interior: black
    accessories: 4 speed, convertible
    paid: $22,000
    asking price: $38,500
    date acquired: 7/12/84

    1975 Aston Martin
    color: red
    interior: black
    accessories: radio, air
    paid: $56,700
    asking price: $120,000
    date acquired: 10/6/87

    1988 Ferrari
    color: red
    interior: black
    accessories: radio, air, 4 speed
    paid: $72,300
    asking price: $102,000
    date acquired: 02/17/89

    1978 Triumph
    color: green
    interior: white
    accessories: 4 speed, air
    paid: $4,560
    asking price: $7,200
    date acquired: 5/18/86

    c) Fantasy Wheels has had a great day and sold the 1985 Porsche. Delete its record from the data base.

    d) A customer has come into Fantasy's show room who wants to buy a red sports car as a Valentine's day present. Produce a multi-record display which lists all of the red cars only.

    e) Fantasy has had the 1969 Maserati painted purple, replaced the radio with a CD player and raised the asking price to $29,000. Modify the record for the Maserati accordingly.

    f) Fantasy wants to modify its data base to include a category for engine horsepower. Create a new category and add the following data to it:

Automobile		Horsepower
1969	Maserati	210
1972	Corvette	245
1984	Ferrari	290
1958	Thunderbird	165
1985	Porsche	225
1987	Porsche	230
1975	Aston Martin	280
1978	Triumph	120
1988	Ferrari	310

4. Holiday Airlines has weekly flights to the Bahamas and has decided to computerize its reservation system. Holiday owns one airplane which has 20 seats numbered as shown below:

Windows   1A 1B   1C 1D   Windows

2A 2B   2C 2D

3A 3B   Aisle   3C 3D

4A 4B   4C 4D

5A 5B   5C 5D

a) Design a database layout for Holiday Airlines to store the seat number, seat location (aisle or window), whether it is in the first class section or not, name and phone number for each passenger on its plane.

b) Create the database on the computer and name it Holiday. Add an empty record for each seat on the plane. Enter the word "Empty" into the passenger name category of each record. Make all seats in rows 1 and 2 the first class section.

c) Make the following reservations by updating the proper records in the database. Use queries to locate seats for passengers with preferences:

Mr. & Mrs. A. Schwartzenegger
Phone#: 407-858-6321
Mr. Schwartzenegger: window seat, first class
Mrs. Schwartzenegger: aisle seat (next to her husband)

Mr. Bruce Presley
Phone#: 305-592-7847
aisle seat

Ms. Heidi Crane
Phone#: 609-896-9165
window seat, first class

Mr. John Heacock
Phone#: 212-885-7436
window seat

Mrs. Ruth Wagy
Phone#: 407-324-7588
No preference

Mr. & Mrs. Russell Ball
Phone#: 217-358-7671
Mrs. Ball: aisle seat, first class
Mr. Ball: window seat (next to his wife)

d) The reservation desk at Holiday needs to know the seat numbers of all empty seats. Create and apply a selection rule which does this.

e) Holiday Airlines has held a promotional contest and you have won 5 free trips to the Bahamas. Make 5 reservations using the names and phone numbers of friends.

f) The Holiday flight is about to take off for the Bahamas and the cabin staff needs to know the seat numbers and names for each passenger. Create and apply a selection rule showing only the occupied seats.

g) Passenger Presley has changed his mind and would now like a seat in the first class section. Create and apply a selection rule which lists all empty aisle seats in the first class section.

5. A Chapter 4 exercise asked you to create a layout for a company's inventory data base.

a) Using the layout designed in Chapter 4 exercise 8, create a new data base named Product which contains data for the following items:

Prod. ID	Prod. Name	On Hand	Ordered
A1000	Widgets	920	0
A2050	Wadgets	575	0
A3400	Wodgets	35	750
B1000	Flanges	330	0
B1005	Gadgets	78	0
B2005	Wonkers	2112	590
C2000	Springs	535	0
E3300	Rollers	23	444
E5000	Sanders	1778	0
F6005	Cutters	252	530
G1000	Slicers	150	0

G3350	Piercers	935	750
G4050	Smashers	575	9754
J2005	Grinders	23012	0
J3000	Punchers	578	0
K5050	Pullers	100	0
M2900	Pushers	7575	0
M6770	Washers	5	9929
N1800	Wetters	378	0
Q2505	Zonkers	942	35

b) Apply a selection rule that will display only those products with less than 100 items on hand which have not yet been reordered.

6. Exercise 9 in Chapter 4 described a data base to record weather observations.

a) Using your layout design create a new data base named Weather to store observations.

b) Add the following records to Weather:

Date	Time	Temp F	Rain	Sky
1/8/60	3:00 PM	79	0	Partly Cloudy
11/5/61	5:46 AM	67	0	Sunny
4/20/62	6:19 PM	57	1.1	Cloudy
6/5/65	5:26 PM	29	.43	Cloudy
12/21/67	10:59 PM	46	0	Clear
10/15/68	7:15 AM	81	.2	Windy
3/16/70	4:00 PM	49	0	Partly Cloudy
7/12/72	1:00 PM	78	0	Sunny
12/11/73	12:59 AM	47	0	Hazy
7/19/74	6:49 AM	56	0	Sunny
10/31/75	9:15 AM	49	.3	Windy
11/16/77	11:50 PM	74	0	Clear
1/1/80	3:43 PM	32	0	Partly Cloudy
2/6/81	6:55 PM	21	.1	Cloudy
2/27/82	8:20 PM	90	1.2	Partly Cloudy
7/19/83	5:01 AM	72	0	Partly Sunny
5/19/84	7:46 AM	62	0	Sunny
6/27/85	2:28 PM	68	.3	Cloudy
12/23/86	12:59 PM	36	0	Clear
5/19/87	2:49 AM	55	.75	Cloudy
8/24/87	5:33 AM	76	.5	Hazy
11/5/88	6:45 AM	44	.1	Windy
3/24/88	2:33 PM	66	.7	Cloudy
10/22/88	10:15 AM	83	.2	Windy

c) Add a record describing today's weather to Weather.

d) Using selection rules display only days when it rained or when the temperature was below freezing.

e) Display only those records for days when clouds were visible.

7. On your data disk is a data base named Car Price which contains information about the price of new cars. Each record contains the following categories:

   Make
   Model
   Base price
   Price with air conditioning
   Price with stereo
   Price with sunroof

   a) Which cars have a base price under $12,000?

   b) Which cars can be purchased with air conditioning for under $12,000?

   c) Your friend Bob needs a new car but does not have much money. Display a list of all cars which cost under $9,000 with a stereo.

   d) The price for a Porsche 944S with sunroof has gone up $199. Make this change in the file.

Chapter 6
Manipulating Data with the Data Base

Open-Apple A

Open-Apple D

Open-Apple I

Open-Apple J

Open-Apple N

Open-Apple P

Open-Apple T

Open-Apple V

Open-Apple ?

Objectives

After completing this chapter you will be able to:

1. Print the contents of a data base.

2. Plan and produce printed reports containing specific information from the data base.

3. Load and modify previously created report formats.

4. Use sorting to change the order in which records are displayed.

5. Create a calculated category for a report.

6. Add totals to a report.

*T*he previous two chapters described the commands and processes necessary to create and manipulate a data base using AppleWorks. It is only after a data base has been created, however, that one of its most powerful features can be employed: the ability to produce printed reports detailing the information stored in its records. In this chapter the commands necessary to produce such reports will be discussed, as well as ways of ordering the data to make the reports more readable.

6.1 The Report Styles - Table and Label

Once a computerized data base has been created its versatility becomes apparent as people access the information it stores in different ways. One of the most common ways to use the information in a data base is the printed report. AppleWorks allows a report to be organized in two general ways: "table-style" and "label-style". A table-style report prints the information from a data base in a form similar to the multi-record layout:

```
Student Listing  ─────────── Title
File:    Student ─────────── Data Base File Used                Page 1

Report:  Student List ──────── Name of Report Format            12/10/90


First Name     Last Name     Address                 City          State Zip
-----------    ----------    ----------------------  ------------  ----- -----

Matilda        Rose          435 Frelinghuysen Rd    Leafville     NJ    08049
Sam            Adams         121 Carey Quadrangle    Leaftown      PA    19717
Roberta        Poisson       8P Corwin Place         Five Points   FL    33434
```

Data from Records

In a table-style report the categories in the report are listed in columns. The report has a heading which shows the report's title, the date the report was printed, which file was used to produce it, and the page number. Each category in the report is then listed in a separate column under its name. Table reports are useful when comparing different records.

A label-style report prints the data from a file so that it can be used to produce mailing labels:

Data Base File Used ———— File: Student
Report Format Name ———— Report: Student Label   9/10/90
                Title ———— Student Mailing Labels

Date Report Printed

Data from Records

Matilda Rose
435 Frelinghuysen Rd
Leafville NJ 08049

Sam Adams
121 Carey Quadrangle
Leaftown PA 19717

Roberta Poisson
8P Corwin Place
Five Points FL 33434

This format is similar to single-record layout but without the category names (which may be included should you want them). Like the table report, a labels report begins with a heading which tells the name of data base file used to produce the report, the report name, a title describing the report's contents, and the date.

6.2 Creating a Table Report Format

Before a report may be printed its format must be described to the computer. This involves choosing which categories are to appear in the report, in what order, and how much space to use for each. This process is similar to modifying a screen layout. Pressing Open-Apple P from the data base screen displays the Report Menu:

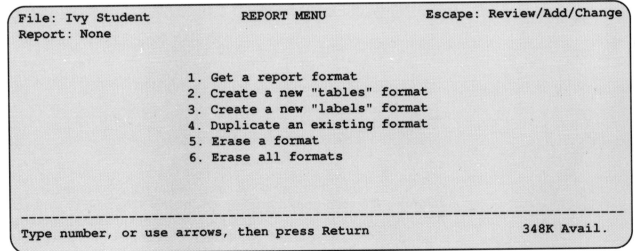

```
File: Ivy Student              REPORT MENU              Escape: Review/Add/Change
Report: None




          1. Get a report format
          2. Create a new "tables" format
          3. Create a new "labels" format
          4. Duplicate an existing format
          5. Erase a format
          6. Erase all formats



--------------------------------------------------------------------------
Type number, or use arrows, then press Return                    348K Avail.
```

As an example we will go through the steps necessary to create a new table report named "Student List". Selecting option 2 displays

Create a new "tables" format:

1. From scratch

2. From the current record layout

Selecting 'From scratch' displays a prompt for the name of the new report (version 2 proceeds directly to this prompt):

Type a name for the report:

After entering `Student List` and pressing Return, the REPORT FORMAT screen is displayed:

```
File: Ivy Student              REPORT FORMAT            Escape: Report Menu
Report: Student List
Selection: All records          ─ Report Format Name
===========================================================================

   --> or <-- Move Cursor           @-J  Right justify this category
    >  @  <   Switch category positions  @-K  Define a calculated category
   --> @ <-- Change column width     @-N  Change report name and/or title
   @-A  Arrange (sort) on this category  @-O  Printer options
   @-D  Delete this category         @-P  Print the report
   @-G  Add/remove group totals      @-R  Change record selection rules
   @-I  Insert a prev. deleted category  @-T  Add/remove category totals
   ----------------------------------------------------------------------

First Name    Last Name     Address      City         State       Zip
-A----------  -B----------  -C---------- -D---------- -E---------- -F---------
Sam           Adams         121 Carey Qu Leaftown     PA           19717
Ursala        Anderson      2112 Red Sta Dr. No Islan AZ           48039
Gill          Bates         123 Lotus La Redmond      WA           02134

   ---------------------------------------------------------------More -->
Use options shown above to change report format            348K Avail.
```

From this screen the categories to be printed in the report are chosen and their widths defined. This is similar to modifying the multi-record layout as described in the last chapter. Once the categories have been chosen, pressing `Open-Apple P` again will print the report on the printer. Before printing any file it is important to check that your computer is connected to a printer, and that the printer is on. While the report is printing, pressing Escape will terminate the printing and return you to the REPORT FORMAT screen. Pressing the Space bar will temporarily pause the printing. Space bar again will restart it.

It is important to note that a report format is saved when the data base file is saved. When first created, each report format is given a name by which it may be loaded later. After a report format has been saved it may be modified to produce a new report. This is discussed in more detail in the next section.

Practice 1

In this Practice you will print a simple table report named Student List for the Ivy Student data base.

1) BOOT PRODOS AND START APPLEWORKS

2) LOAD THE IVY STUDENT DATA BASE

    Select 'Add Files' and choose Ivy Student from your data disk.

3) DISPLAY THE REPORT MENU

    Press `Open-Apple P`.

4) CREATE A NEW TABLES REPORT NAMED STUDENT LIST

    a. Select the 'Create a new "tables" format' option from the Report Menu.

b. Select 'From scratch'.

c. In response to the prompt

`Type a name for the report:`

type `Student List` and press Return. The REPORT FORMAT screen is displayed with a default format which contains all of the categories. This format can be edited using the commands shown to produce other reports, but for now we will print it the way it is.

5) PRINT THE DEFAULT REPORT

a. Press `Open-Apple P`.

b. Select your printer from the Printer Menu.

c. In response to the prompt

`Type report date or press Return:`

type today's date in the form *mm/dd/yy*.

d. In response to the prompt

`How many copies? 1`

press Return to accept the default of 1. The report will now print.

6) SAVE THE REPORT FORMAT

After the report has printed, press `Open-Apple S`. Both the data base file and the report format will be saved on disk. When the Ivy Student data base is next loaded it will then be possible to load the Student List report format from the Report Menu and print it again.

<u>Check</u> - Reports will differ depending on the printer used but your printed report should be similar to:

```
File:   Ivy Student                                       Page 1
Report: Student List                                    12/10/90


First Name     Last Name     Address       City          State      Zip         Ad
------------   -----------   -----------   -----------   ---------   ----------  --

Sam            Adams         121 Carey Qu  Leaftown       PA         19717       Ma
Ursala         Anderson      2112 Red Sta  Dr. No Islan   AZ         48039       Ju
Gill           Bates         123 Lotus La  Redmond        WA         02134       Ju
Bruce          Bonner        35 Madison D  Newark         DE         11312       Ja
       .  .  .              Etc.
```

6.3 Modifying a Table Report

The default report format used in Practice 1 does not print all of the categories in a record and it is likely that different users will require reports showing the missing categories, or want the categories printed in a different order. For this reason it is possible to create up to twenty different report formats for each data base (any combination of label and table formats) and store them on the disk. Other reports can be created and printed as needed, but only 20 formats can be stored at any one time. Any report formats created or modified are saved on disk when the data base is saved, along with any changes that may have been made to the actual data. In this way, report formats have some of the characteristics of AppleWorks files: they have a specific name, may be loaded, modified and saved. The difference is that a report format is not a separate file, but part of a specific data base, and may only be used when that data base is loaded.

The REPORT FORMAT screen allows you to change the order and width of the categories in a report. Similar to modifying a multi-record screen layout, `Open-Apple left-arrow` decreases the size of a category by one space and `Open-Apple right-arrow` increases it by one. `Open-Apple >` and `Open-Apple <` change the order of the categories in the report. It is important to note that changing the order or width of the categories in a report format has no effect on the actual screen layout or the data stored in the records.

It is often necessary to limit the number of categories actually displayed when the report is printed. Pressing `Open-Apple D` (for **D**elete report category) deletes the category on which the cursor is currently located from the REPORT FORMAT screen. When the report is printed, that category is considered to be "hidden" and will not be printed. When a report category is deleted, the data base screen layout and the data stored in the file are not affected, only the report. It is possible to restore a previously hidden report category by pressing `Open-Apple I` (for **I**nsert report category). Once again, deleting or inserting a report category has no effect on the data stored in the data base, only on the data printed for that report.

6.4 Planning a Report

Before creating or modifying a report format it is necessary to carefully plan it. This is done by applying some of the same rules used when first creating a data base:

1. What information should be included?
2. How should that information appear on the page?

The information to be included in a report is determined by analyzing the needs of the person that the report is being created for. Including unnecessary information in a report makes it harder to find desired information. With reports, it is also important to consider how the different categories should appear when printed: in what order and how much space given to each. Both of these options are specified from the REPORT LAYOUT screen. Planning is especially important when creating label reports as we will see later.

Practice 2

In this Practice you will modify the Student List report format created in Practice 1 to produce a new report showing only the student's name and GPA. Start AppleWorks and load the Ivy Student data base if you have not already done so.

1) LOAD THE STUDENT LIST REPORT FORMAT

    a. Press `Open-Apple P` to display the Report Menu.
    b. Choose the 'Get a report format' option.
    c. Select Student List from the list of current report formats.

2) MOVE THE GPA CATEGORY AFTER LAST NAME

    a. Move the cursor to the GPA category using right-arrow.
    b. Move GPA after the Last Name category by pressing `Open-Apple <` five times.

3) DELETE THE OTHER CATEGORIES FROM THE REPORT

a. Use the arrow keys to move the cursor to Address and press `Open-Apple D`. Address will be removed from the report.

b. Use `Open-Apple D` to delete City, State, Zip, Admit Date and Paid.

4) PRINT THE NEW REPORT

a. Press `Open-Apple P`.

b. Select your printer, and enter the date and number of copies.

5) INSERT THE ADMIT DATE CATEGORY BEFORE THE GPA

After the report has been printed:

a. Move the cursor to the GPA category.

b. Press `Open-Apple I`.

c. Choose Admit Date from the menu. The Admit Date category is now placed in the report format between Last Name and GPA.

d. Press `Open-Apple P`.

e. Select your printer, and enter the date and number of copies.

6) SAVE THE NEW REPORT

Press `Open-Apple S` to save the modified Student List report format and the data base file on disk.

<u>Check</u> - The final report printed should be similar to:

```
File:   Ivy Student                              Page 1

Report: Student List                             12/10/90


First Name    Last Name     Admit Date    GPA
-----------   -----------   -----------   -----------
Sam           Adams         Mar 12 79     1.5
Ursala        Anderson      Jul 27 88     3.0
Gill          Bates         Jul  9 89     1.7
Bruce         Bonner        Jan  1 82     3.7
      . . .             Etc.
```

6.5 Using Label Report Formats

Label report formats are created and modified just like a table report. In a label report, data from different categories in a record can be displayed side by side on the same line or be spread among different lines such as:

```
Matilda Rose
435 Frelinghuysen Rd
Leafville NJ 08049
```

Label reports get their name from the fact that they can be used to produce mailing labels, but are also useful when it is necessary to display more categories than could fit on a single line in a table report. Note that unlike a table report, it is possible to remove the category names from a labels report, showing only the contents of the categories. To create a new label report format, the 'Create a new "labels" format' option is chosen from the Report Menu and a name supplied. The labels REPORT FORMAT screen is then displayed showing each category name:

```
File: Ivy Student                 REPORT FORMAT          Escape: Report Menu
Report: Student Label
Selection: All records



============================================================================
First Name
Last Name
Address
City
State
Zip
Admit Date
GPA
Paid
---------------------Each record will print  9 lines---------------------


----------------------------------------------------------------------------
Use options shown on Help Screen                            @-? for Help
```

It is possible to move categories up and down as well as left and right in a labels format. When the report is printed the data stored in each category will be printed in place of the category name.

Unlike the tables report screen, the options for modifying a labels report are not shown. AppleWorks can be told to display the options by pressing Open-Apple ?, the Help command. When issued from the labels report format screen, the Help command clears the screen and displays the following list of available options for modifying a label report format:

```
File: Ivy Student                    HELP            Escape: Report Format
Report: Student Label
Selection: All records


============================================================================
                  -->   <--      Move cursor location
                  @-arrows       Move category location
                   > @ <         Next or previous record
                  @-1...@-9      Go to beginning...end of file
                  @-A            Arrange (sort) on this category
                  @-D            Delete this spacing line or category
                  @-I            Insert a spacing line or
                                 a previously deleted category
                  @-J            Left justify this category
                  @-N            Change report name and/or title
                  @-O            Printer options
                  @-P            Print the report
                  @-R            Change record selection rules
                  @-V            Print category name AND entry
                  @-Z            Zoom between category names, entries
----------------------------------------------------------------------------
Press Space Bar to continue                                348K Avail.
```

Pressing the Space bar returns AppleWorks to the report format screen.

The arrow keys move the cursor from category to category on the format screen. Pressing Open-Apple and an arrow key moves the category that the cursor is on in the direction of the arrow. Once the desired format has been created, pressing `Open-Apple Z` displays a sample record's contents. This allows you to determine how the label will appear when printed. Pressing `Open-Apple V` causes both the category name and its contents to be printed for the current category. For all of these commands the cursor must be placed on the first letter of the category name, and then the command given.

Practice 3

In this Practice you will create a format for and print a labels report similar to the one shown in Section 6.5 above. Start AppleWorks and load Ivy Student if you have not already done so.

1) CREATE A NEW LABELS REPORT FORMAT NAMED STUDENT LABEL

    a. Press `Open-Apple P` to display the Report Menu.
    b. Select the 'Create a new "labels" format' option.
    c. Select 'From scratch'.
    d. Name the report Student Label and press Return.

2) MOVE LAST NAME TO THE SAME LINE AS FIRST NAME

    a. Place the cursor on the "L" in Last Name.
    b. Move Last Name to the middle of the screen using `Open-Apple right-arrow`.
    c. Press `Open-Apple up-arrow` to move Last Name to the same line as First Name.

3) MOVE STATE AND ZIP TO THE SAME LINE AS CITY

    Follow the steps above to move the categories.

4) DELETE THE UNNECESSARY CATEGORIES FROM THE REPORT

    a. Move the cursor to Admit Date.
    b. Press `Open-Apple D`. Admit Date is removed from the report but a blank line remains in the format.
    c. Press `Open-Apple D` again to remove the blank line.
    d. Repeat steps a through c above for the GPA and Paid categories. Be sure to delete the blank line left when the category name is removed.
    e. Move the cursor to the blank line between First Name and Address and press `Open-Apple D`. The format now contains three lines.

Check - Your report format should be similar to:

```
/File: Ivy Student              REPORT FORMAT            Escape: Report Menu\
 Report: Student Label
 Selection: All records


 ==============================================================================
 First Name       Last Name
 Address
 City        State    Zip
 ----------------------------Each record will print  3 lines------------------




 ------------------------------------------------------------------------------
\Use options shown on Help Screen                            @-? for Help/
```

5) PREVIEW A SAMPLE LABEL

    a. Press `Open-Apple Z` to preview a label.

    b. Return to the format display using `Open-Apple Z`.

6) PRINT AND SAVE THE REPORT

    a. Press `Open-Apple P`.

    b. Select your printer, enter the date and number of copies. Press Escape to terminate the printing after the first page has been printed.

    c. After the report has been printed, press `Open-Apple S` to save the format and the data base on disk.

6.6 A Better Labels Report

Three changes would make the label report printed in Practice 3 easier to read and use: printing a title describing the contents of the report, eliminating the extra space between categories printed on the same line and printing a blank line between each record's data. AppleWorks has options to allow for each of these. Note that if this format were used to print on mailing labels the title would not be necessary.

To add a title to a report, `Open-Apple N` (for **N**ame) is pressed from the report format screen. First, you will be given a chance to either change the report format's name or press Return to keep the same name. You may then enter a title of up to 78 characters which describes the contents or purpose of the report. This title is printed at the top of each page of the report along with the data base file name, date and page number. Although both the report format name and the title are changed using `Open-Apple N`, you should be careful not to confuse them: the report <u>name</u> is used when the format is loaded or saved; the <u>title</u> is simply a line of text that is printed as part of the heading of the report.

As you have seen in the label report printed in the last Practice, having extra space between categories printed on the same line makes a report less readable. The process of removing the spaces between categories is called "justification" and is performed using `Open-Apple J`. Pressing `Open-Apple J` makes a category "left-justified"; that is, the data printed for that category will start exactly one space from the end of the data printed for the previous category, no matter what its length. AppleWorks identifies justified categories by placing a less than sign (<) before their names in the report format. For example, printing the data "Jane" for First Name and "Caputi" for Last Name with the non-justified format

```
First Name          Last Name
```

produces:

```
Jane                Caputi
```

Printing the same data with the following justified format (note the less than sign)

```
First Name          <Last Name
```

produces:

```
Jane Caputi
```

Normally when more than one category appears on the same line in a format, any following categories should be justified. For example, in the current Student Label format both State and Zip should be justified to make the report more readable.

Finally, reports can be made more readable by leaving a blank line between records to help show where one record's data ends and the next begins. This is accomplished by moving the cursor to the last line of the format and pressing down-arrow. A blank "spacing line" will then be inserted into the format. When the report is printed, spacing lines appear as blank lines, making it easy to distinguish between the end of one record and the beginning of the next.

Practice 4

In this Practice you will modify the Student Label report format to include a title, justify three categories and print a spacing line after each record. Start AppleWorks and load Ivy Student if you have not already done so.

1) LOAD THE STUDENT LABEL FORMAT

    a. Press `Open-Apple P` to display the Report Menu.
    b. Select the 'Get a report format' option.
    c. Choose Student Label from the list of formats.

2) ADD A TITLE TO THE REPORT

    a. Press `Open-Apple N`.
    b. The prompt

`Type new report name or press Return: Student Label`

is shown at the bottom of the screen. Press Return to keep the same report name (Inventory List).

    c. The prompt

`Type title line at cursor position`

is shown at the bottom of the screen. Enter the title `Student Mailing Labels` and press Return.

3) JUSTIFY LAST NAME, STATE AND ZIP

    a. Move the cursor to the "L" in Last Name.
    b. Press `Open-Apple J`. A less-than sign appears before Last Name to indicate that this category is left-justified.
    c. Move to the "S" in State and press `Open-Apple J`.
    d. Move to the "Z" in Zip and press `Open-Apple J`.

4) ADD A SPACING LINE AT THE BOTTOM OF THE FORMAT

With the cursor on the last line of the format press down-arrow. A spacing line is shown and each label is now 4 lines long.

5) PRINT THE NEW REPORT

    a. Make sure the printer is properly connected and press `Open-Apple P`.
    b. Choose your printer, enter today's date and accept the default of 1 copy. Press Escape to terminate the printing after the first page has been printed.

6) SAVE THE NEW FORMAT

After the report has printed, press `Open-Apple S`. The new format and the data base are saved on disk. The next time the Student Label report is printed it will have a title, spacing line and justified categories.

6.7 Arranging (Sorting) Records in a Data Base

Data stored in a data base can be made easier to use if the records are in order based on the data stored in a certain category, called the "key category." For example, it is easy to locate students in the Ivy Student data base because the records are in order alphabetically by Last Name. In AppleWorks placing a data base in order is called "arranging" or "sorting" and is accomplished using the `Open-Apple A` command (for **A**rrange). To arrange a data base the cursor is first moved to the desired key category, the category that contains the values on which to base the ordering. Version 3 prompts:

`Arrange (sort) on?` **Category (GPA)** `Several categories`

Arrange then gives options as to how you wish the records to be ordered. For example:

```
/‾‾‾‾‾‾‾‾‾‾‾‾‾‾‾‾‾‾‾‾‾‾‾‾‾‾‾‾‾‾‾‾‾‾‾‾‾‾‾‾‾‾‾‾‾‾‾‾‾‾‾‾‾‾‾‾‾‾‾‾‾\
| File: Ivy Student        ARRANGE (SORT)       Escape: Review/Add/Change |
|                                                             |
| Arrange on Category: GPA                                    |
|                                                             |
|                                                             |
| ============================================================|
|                                                             |
|                                                             |
|        Arrangement order:                                   |
|                                                             |
|           1. From A to Z                                    |
|           2. From Z to A                                    |
|           3. From 0 to 9                                    |
|           4. ▌From 9 to 0▐                                  |
|                                                             |
|                                                             |
|                                                             |
| -----------------------------------------------------------|
| Type number, or use arrows, then press Return    348K Avail.|
\‾‾‾‾‾‾‾‾‾‾‾‾‾‾‾‾‾‾‾‾‾‾‾‾‾‾‾‾‾‾‾‾‾‾‾‾‾‾‾‾‾‾‾‾‾‾‾‾‾‾‾‾‾‾‾‾‾‾‾‾‾/
```

Should the key category be a date or time category, two other options are automatically available for the arrangement order:

```
5. Chronological
6. Reverse chronological
```

Chronological means earliest to latest (Jan, Feb, Mar... Dec, or 1AM, 2AM, etc.) and reverse chronological is latest to earliest (Dec, Nov,...Jan, etc.).

Once an arrangement order has been selected, AppleWorks changes the order in which the records are displayed based on the contents of the key category. If arranged using the example menu shown above, a student record with a GPA of 4.0 would be moved before any records with a GPA of 3.9, and so on. If the data base is then saved on disk, the records are stored in the newly arranged order, so that the next time the file is loaded it will be sorted.

Sorting a data base file affects not only the order in which the records are displayed on the screen but also the order in which they appear in printed reports. This makes it possible to have one report sorted by Last Name, another by GPA, etc. In addition, it is possible to specify the arrangement order and key category from the REPORT FORMAT screen, making it easy to generate different versions of the same report. However, the arrangement is not saved with the format. Should a report format specifying arrangement by Last Name be saved and the data base then sorted by GPA, the next time the report format is loaded it will print the records in order by GPA.

Practice 5

In this Practice you will print a sorted version of the Student List report. Start AppleWorks and load Ivy Student if you have not already done so. Note that Ivy Student is already in order by Last Name.

1) LOAD THE STUDENT LIST REPORT

    a. Press `Open-Apple P`.
    b. Get the Student List report format.

2) ARRANGE THE RECORDS ON THE GPA CATEGORY

    a. Move the cursor to GPA.
    b. Press `Open-Apple A`.
    c. Press Return to accept the default of 'Category (GPA)'.
    d. Select the arrangement order 'From 9 to 0' which will arrange the records in descending order (high to low) based on the GPA.

3) PRINT THE NEW REPORT

    a. Press `Open-Apple P`.
    b. Choose your printer, enter the date and number of copies.
    c. Compare this report with the previous version of Student List. Note how the records are ordered differently.

4) SORT THE DATA BASE ON THE LAST NAME CATEGORY

    a. Press Escape twice to return to the Review/Add/Change screen.
    b. Move the cursor to Last Name using Tab.
    c. Press `Open-Apple A`, select 'Category (Last Name)' and 'From A to Z'. Note how the order of the records changes.

5) RETURN TO THE STUDENT LIST REPORT FORMAT

    a. Press `Open-Apple P` and get the Student List report format.
    b. Print the report. Note that the ordering by GPA has been lost and the file is again ordered by Last Name.

6) SAVE THE FILE

    a. Press Escape to return to the Review/Add/Change screen.
    b. Press `Open-Apple S` to save the file on disk. The file is saved in alphabetic order by Last Name.

6.8 Using Selection Rules to Create Reports

Selection rules were used in the last chapter to limit the number of records displayed to only those which met certain criteria. When a selection rule is applied, the records printed in a report are also limited.

This allows special reports to be printed which show, for example, only students with GPA's greater than 3.5 or only students from Maine or Vermont.

Unlike arrangement, selection rules are stored with the report format so that each time the report is loaded the selection rule will be applied. Applying a selection rule to a report format has no effect on the Review/Add/Change screen, and vice versa.

6.9 Duplicating a Report Format

Many printed reports have similar features. For this reason, AppleWorks allows a previously created report to be duplicated under a new name and then modified and saved.

To copy a format, the 'Duplicate an existing format' option is selected from the Report Menu. A list of current formats is given from which you may select and then enter a new name for the copy. The new format will have all of the characteristics of the old and may then be modified, printed and saved like any other format.

Practice 6

In this Practice you will create a new report named Honors by modifying the current Student List format. Honors will use a selection rule to print only students with a GPA greater than 3.5. Start Apple-Works and load the Ivy Student data base if you have not already done so.

1) DUPLICATE THE STUDENT LIST REPORT FORMAT UNDER THE NAME HONORS

    a. Press Open-Apple P to display the Report Menu.
    b. Select option 4, 'Duplicate an existing format'.
    c. Select Student List.
    d. Press Open-Apple Y to delete the old name and enter Honors. The Honors report format is displayed.

2) APPLY A SELECTION RULE TO HONORS

    a. Press Open-Apple R.
    b. Select the GPA category from the menu.
    c. Select 'is greater than' from the list of comparisons.
    d. Enter the comparison text 3.5 and press Return.
    e. Press Escape to apply the rule. All of the records printed in the report will have GPA's greater than 3.5.

3) CHANGE THE REPORT TITLE

    a. Press Open-Apple N.
    b. Press Return to retain the current format name.
    c. Press Open-Apple Y to delete the old title.
    d. Enter the new title: Students with Honors GPAs and press Return. Remember, the format name is used when loading or saving a report, and the title is simply a line of text printed in the heading.

4) PRINT AND SAVE THE NEW REPORT

    a. Press Open-Apple P.
    b. Select your printer, enter the date and number of copies.

    c. After the report has printed, press `Open-Apple S` to save the Honors report format with the data base. Note that the selection rule is not applied to the Review/Add/Change screen, but is stored with the Honors format.

5) RETURN TO THE MAIN MENU

    Press Escape.

6.10 Calculated Categories in Reports

Reports can do more than just list the information stored in a data base in an organized manner. It is possible to have a report perform calculations using the data contained in a record and print the result as part of the report in what is called a "calculated category". For example, AppleWorks can be told to print the result of the value stored in one category times the value in another for each record in the report.

Calculated categories are created by pressing `Open-Apple K` (for **K**alculated) from the REPORT FORMAT screen. AppleWorks then adds a new category named "Calculated" to the current report. Calculated is just a default name - it can be changed to whatever you wish. This type of category is useful for reports about data bases which deal with numeric values, such as an inventory data base or a bank's records. The value printed in the calculated category is expressed as a "formula" or "calculation rule" which refers to the other categories in the report. For example, suppose the following report format is used:

```
File: Ivy Bookstore               REPORT FORMAT             Escape: Report Menu
Report: Inventory List
Selection: All records


================================================================================
   --> or <--   Move Cursor                @-J  Right justify this category
    >  @  <     Switch category positions  @-K  Define a calculated category
   --> @ <--    Change column width        @-N  Change report name and/or title
   @-A  Arrange (sort) this category        @-O  Printer options
   @-D  Delete this category                @-P  Print the report
   @-G  Add/remove group totals            @-R  Change record selection rules
   @-I  Insert a prev. deleted category    @-T  Add/remove category totals
--------------------------------------------------------------------------------
School Store Inventory
Item Name          Department  In Stock  Price     L
-A--------------- -B--------- -C------ -D------  n
Avocado Dip          F           6        .99      5
Ball point pen       P          150       .89      1
Chips                F           77       .65
------------------------------------------------------------------ More -->
Use options shown above to change report format            348K Avail.
```

This is a report for the Ivy University Bookstore data base which contains only the four categories shown above. Each record stores the following information about one item available for sale in the store:

Item Name	-	The name of an item for sale
Department	-	The department the item is sold in
In Stock	-	How many of the item are currently available for sale
Price	-	How much the item sells for

The rest of this chapter will use this data base, named Ivy Bookstore, to demonstrate certain features of the AppleWorks data base which deal with numeric quantities.

When creating a calculated category a formula must be given which describes how the value to be stored in that category is to be calculated. Formulas may use the following mathematical operators:

Operator	Action
+	Add
−	Subtract
*	Multiply
/	Divide

Formulas usually refer to a value stored in another category. This is done by specifying the category's column letter (A through D in the Bookstore report format shown above) in the formula. When the report is printed, the actual value stored in that entry will be used.

As an example, it would be possible to determine the value of the inventory by multiplying the number of items in stock (column C) by the price per item (column D). Thus the formula for a calculated category showing the value of an inventory item would be C * D, meaning multiply the value stored in column C by the value stored in column D and print the results in the calculated category. It is also possible to include numeric constants in a formula. For example, the formula D * 0.05 could be used to calculate a five percent sales tax on the Price category.

When a calculated category is added to a report, AppleWorks allows you to specify the number of decimal places that should be included when that category is printed. Money amounts should usually have two places (for cents) but other categories will vary with the information being calculated. You may also specify the number of spaces to leave before printing the calculated category on the report. These formatting options help make a report easier to read.

It is important to note that the value printed for a calculated category is determined when the report is printed, not when the format is created. This allows the report to print the correct value when changes are made to the data base after the format has been created. Note also that the calculated values are not stored in the data base.

Practice 7

In this Practice you will modify a report format for the bookstore's data base, named Ivy Bookstore, to include a calculated category which displays the value of inventory as described in Section 6.10. Start AppleWorks if you have not already done so.

1) ADD THE IVY BOOKSTORE DATA BASE TO THE DESKTOP

Add Ivy Bookstore from your data disk to the Desktop.

2) LOAD THE INVENTORY LIST REPORT FORMAT

a. Press `Open-Apple P` to display the Report Menu.
b. Choose the 'Get a report format' option.
c. Get Inventory List from the list of already created report formats.

3) ADD A CALCULATED CATEGORY TO THE REPORT

    a. Press right-arrow four times to move the cursor to the right end of the report.

    b. Press `Open-Apple K` to insert a calculated category. Apple-Works shows all 9's in the format to show that this category contains values that will be calculated when the report is printed.

    c. Press `Open-Apple Y` to delete the default category name.

    d. Enter `Value` and press Return.

    e. At the prompt

`Type calculation rules (Example: A+B+C/5.75):`

       type `C*D` and press Return.

    f. At the prompt

`Decimal places for this category: 0`

       type 2 and press Return.

    g. At the prompt

`Blank spaces after this category: 1`

       press Return to accept the default of 1. The 9's are reformatted to show the decimal places.

<u>Check</u> - Your report format should be similar to:

```
/ File: Ivy Bookstore             REPORT FORMAT             Escape: Report Menu \
| Report: Inventory List                                                         |
| Selection: All records                                                         |
|                                                                                |
|                                                                                |
| ===============================================================================|
|   --> or <-- Move Cursor              @-J  Right justify this category          |
|    >  @  <   Switch category positions @-K  Define a calculated category        |
|   --> @ <-- Change column width        @-N  Change report name and/or title     |
|   @-A  Arrange (sort) this category    @-O  Printer options                     |
|   @-D  Delete this category            @-P  Print the report                    |
|   @-G  Add/remove group totals         @-R  Change record selection rules       |
|   @-I  Insert a prev. deleted category @-T  Add/remove category totals          |
| ------------------------------------------------------------------------------ |
| School Store Inventory                                                         |
| Item Name          Department In Stock Price    Value        L                 |
| -A--------------- -B-------- -C------ -D------ -E---------- n                  |
| Avocado Dip        F           6        .99     999999999.99 6                  |
| Ball point pen     p           150      .89     999999999.99 4                  |
| Chips              F           77       .65     999999999.99                    |
|                                                                                |
| -----------------------------------------------------------------------More --> |
| Use options shown above to change report format            348K Avail.          |
\                                                                                /
```

4) PRINT THE REPORT

    a. Press `Open-Apple P`.

    b. Choose your printer, enter the date and number of copies.

5) SAVE THE MODIFIED FORMAT

    Press `Open-Apple S` to save the data base and the modified format on the disk. The next time that Inventory List is printed it will include the calculated Value category. If Price or In Stock entries are changed in the data base, the number printed in the Value column will also be changed.

<u>Check</u> - Your printed report should be similar to:

```
School Store Inventory
File:   Ivy Bookstore                                      Page 1
Report: Inventory List                                     12/10/90


Item Name            Department In Stock Price          Value
------------------   ---------- -------- --------    ------------
Avocado Dip          F             6       .99               5.94
Ball point pen       P           150       .89             133.50
Chips                F            77       .65              50.05
Class Ring           C            50    212.50           10625.00
Dictionary           B            22     12.95             284.90
           . . .  Etc.
```

6.11 Adding Totals to Reports

In addition to printing calculated categories AppleWorks reports can also keep track of the total of all of the values printed in a category. This value is then printed at the bottom of the category with an asterisk (*) to note that it is the total.

To add a total to a category column in a report format, Open-Apple T (for **T**otal) is pressed when the cursor is on the desired column. The contents of that category are then shown on the screen as a series of 9's to indicate that this is a numeric category. The last line of that category is shown as equals signs (=), which indicates that a total will be calculated and printed for this category. For example, the Value category in the format below will be printed with a total:

```
School Store Inventory
Item Name            Department In Stock Price   Value           L
-A---------------    -B-------- -C------ -D------ -E---------- n
Avocado Dip          F             6       .99   999999999.99 6
Ball point pen       P           150       .89   999999999.99 4
Chips                F            77       .65   999999999.99
                                                 ============

----------------------------------------------------------------More -->
Use options shown above to change report format          348K Avail.
```

As with calculated categories, you are asked to supply the number of decimal places you wish to see printed for the total as well as how many spaces to skip after printing the total. Pressing Open-Apple T for a category which already has a total removes the total from the report.

Practice 8

In this Practice you will add a total to the Value category in the Inventory List report. Start AppleWorks and load Ivy Bookstore if you have not already done so.

1) LOAD THE INVENTORY LIST REPORT FORMAT

    a. Press Open-Apple P to display the Report Menu.
    b. Get Inventory List from the previously created formats.

2) HAVE APPLEWORKS PRINT A TOTAL FOR THE VALUE CATEGORY

a. Move the cursor to the Value column.
b. Press `Open-Apple T` to calculate the column's total.
c. At the prompt

    `Decimal places for this category:` **2**

    press Return to accept the default of 2.
d. At the prompt

    `Blank spaces after this category:` **1**

    press Return to accept the default of 1. A line of equals signs is shown at the bottom of the format below the Value category, indicating that a total will be printed for this category.

3) PRINT THE REPORT

a. Press `Open-Apple P`.
b. Choose your printer, enter the date and number of copies.

4) SAVE THE MODIFIED FORMAT

Press `Open-Apple S` to save the data base and the modified format on disk. The next time that Inventory List is printed it will have a total printed for the Value category.

<u>Check</u> - Your printed report should be similar to:

```
School Store Inventory
File:   Ivy Bookstore                                    Page 1
Report: Inventory List                                12/10/90


Item Name            Department In Stock Price         Value
------------------   ---------- -------- -------- ------------
Avocado Dip          F          6        .99              5.94
Ball point pen       P          150      .89            133.50
Chips                F          77       .65             50.05
Class Ring           C          50       212.50       10625.00
Dictionary           B          22       12.95          284.90
      . . .
Three-Hole Paper     A          200      1.98           396.00
Three-Ring Binder    A          122      3.50           427.00
                                                      19111.52*
```

6.12 Where can you go from here?

The last three chapters introduced you to the concepts of data bases; their design, creation and use. The AppleWorks data base has a number of other options not discussed in this text which you may want to explore on your own. One of the best places to begin is by reading the data base sections of the AppleWorks manuals.

Larger, more powerful data base programs have even more options for generating reports and performing various operations with the data. Several of the most widely used packages on microcomputers are dBASE III, Paradox, and R:Base. Because you have learned how to use the AppleWorks data base it will be easier to learn a new package such as one of the ones listed above.

As the use of computerized data bases becomes more widespread the knowledge of what a data base is and what it can be used for will be an important skill. There are many job opportunities for people to work with computer data bases. More information about careers involving computers and data bases is given in Chapter 11.

Chapter Summary

This chapter covered one of the most important aspects of the computerized database: its ability to produce printed reports detailing the information stored in its records. AppleWorks has two different report styles, the tables report and the labels report. A tables report shows the data for only a few categories of each record and is useful for comparing records to one another. The labels report can display all of the data for a single record in a format similar to a mailing label. In the labels report, printing category names is an option.

Both report formats are created by pressing `Open-Apple P` from the Review/Add/Change screen. The Report Menu is then displayed and gives the option of retrieving a previously created report, creating a new tables or labels report, or duplicating a current format. Reports are then created or modified from the REPORT FORMAT screen where the categories to be included in the report, their widths and placements are decided. When a data base file is then saved, any report formats created are saved with it and may be modified or printed again later.

With longer reports it is often necessary to organize the data in the report so that the desired information is easy to find. This may be done by arranging (sorting) the data in the report or applying selection rules to it. When a data base file is arranged using `Open-Apple A` its records are placed in order according to the data stored in a specific field called the key field. When a report is then printed, the records are displayed in order according to that field. If a data base is saved after it has been arranged, the next time it is accessed the records will be in the arranged order. Selection rules applied using `Open-Apple R` limit the number of records displayed when a data base is printed based on certain criteria such as GPA greater than 3.5 or State equals ME. Selection rules defined from the REPORT FORMAT screen are saved with the format, but arrangements are not.

Reports have many different options designed to make them more readable. Categories may be left-justified to eliminate extra space between them when printed. Spacing lines can be placed between records when they are printed. Titles and dates may be printed so that a report is easy to identify.

AppleWorks reports have a number of options for producing reports dealing with numeric categories. A calculated category can be created which prints a value based on the values stored in other categories. This value is calculated by specifying a mathematical formula such as C * D to print the product of the value stored in the category in column C times the value stored in column D. The sum of all the entries in a numeric category can be calculated and printed as a total by pressing `Open-Apple T` when the cursor is on that category in the REPORT FORMAT screen.

Vocabulary

Calculated category - Numeric report category which is calculated based on the value(s) stored in other categories using a calculation rule: `Open-Apple K`.

Calculation rule - Mathematical statement which describes how the value printed in a calculated category is determined.

Formula - See "calculation rule".

Justification - Placing the data from two categories on the same line, one space apart. Used in label reports: `Open-Apple J`.

Key category - Category which stores the data used when determining the order during a sort.

Label report - Report which prints the categories in a format which could be used to produce mailing labels.

Report - Printed description of the information stored in a data base. Created using `Open-Apple P`.

Report category - The information from one category which appears in a report format.

Report format - Description of the order and placement of categories in a report.

Spacing line - Blank line printed between records in a report to make it more readable.

Table report - Report which prints only a few categories from each record in columns.

Reviews

Sections 6.1-6.5

1. a) What is the difference between a table-style and label-style report?
   b) Give examples where each type of report might be used.

2. Once a table-style report format has been defined, may it be used again at a later time? If yes, explain how this may be done.

3. A data base file named Savings Account contains the following categories:

   First name - 15 characters
   Last name - 20 characters
   Street address - 20 characters
   City - 15 characters
   State - 4 characters
   Zip code - 5 characters
   Open date - 8 characters
   Account number - 8 characters
   Last deposit - numeric value
   Last withdrawal - numeric value
   Account balance - numeric value

   a) List the steps required to produce a table-style report named Balance of the data base. Have the report display only Last name, Zip code, and Account balance.
   b) What additional steps are required to add City to the report so that it appears after Zip Code?
   c) List the steps required to produce a label-style report named Savings Label that will display records in the form:

   ```
   First Name          Last Name
   Street Address
   City                State      Zip code
   Account Balance
   ```

Sections 6.6-6.9

4. a) List the steps required to properly left justify the categories in the label-report named Savings Label produced in Review 3c.
    b) What additional steps are required to leave 3 blank lines between each label?

5. a) What is meant by "arranging" records?
    b) Give 3 examples of how the Ivy Student data base could be arranged.

6. Explain how the Savings Account data base in Review 3 could be arranged:

    a) by account balance from highest account to lowest account.
    b) chronologically by the dates accounts were opened.
    c) If the data base is saved after it has been arranged chronologically, how will it be arranged when next accessed from disk?

7. List the steps necessary to create a new report named High Balance which is a modification of the table-style report named Balance produced in Review 3a. High Balance should display only those accounts with balances which exceed $5,000.

8. What are formulas used for when producing data base reports?

Sections 6.10-6.12

9. Explain the steps required to add a calculated category to the Balance table-style report produced in Review 3a, that displays the interest on each account. Interest is calculated by multiplying the account balance by .08, which is 8%.

10. Explain the steps required to display the total of all account balances in the report Balance produced in Review 3a.

Exercises

1. Load the Car Price data base from your data disk.

    a) Arrange the records is ascending order by base price and answer the following:

    > Name the three most expensive cars.
    > Name the three least expensive cars.

    b) Arrange the records in ascending order by price with stereo and answer the following:

    > Name the three most expensive cars with stereo.
    > Name the three least expensive cars with stereo.

    c) Create a new table report named Inexpensive which lists the Make, Model and Base price for all cars with a base price less than $9,000.

    d) Print a copy of the Inexpensive report on the printer.

    e) Modify Inexpensive to print all cars with stereos which cost less than $10,000. Print a copy of the new report.

2. Load the Address data base created in Chapter 5 exercise 1.

    a) Arrange Address in alphabetic order by last name.

    b) Create a new table report named Presents which lists all people in Address who have a birthday either this month or next month.

    c) Print a copy of the Presents report on the printer.

    d) Create a new labels report named Summer which prints the name and full mailing address of each person born in June, July or August. Use justified categories to create realistic mailing labels.

3. Load the Inventor data base from your data disk.

    a) Arrange Inventor in ascending order based on invention date.

    b) Create a new table report named French which lists the date, invention and inventor for each inventor from France.

    c) Print a copy of the French report on the printer.

    d) Duplicate the French report format under the name New French.

    e) Modify the New French report to list only French inventions from the 20th century. Print a copy of New French.

4. Load the Fantasy data base created in Chapter 5 exercise 3.

    a) Create a new table report named Car Profit which shows the make, price paid and asking price for each car in inventory.

    b) Create a calculated category named Profit which displays the profit on each sale (asking price minus the price paid).

    c) Have the computer print the total of the Profit and asking price categories at the bottom of the report.

    d) Arrange Fantasy in ascending order by year.

    e) Print a copy of the Profit report on the printer.

    f) Create a new label report named Sticker which could be used to produce the price sticker for a car. Include the year, make, accessories and asking price for each car on the lot.

    g) Print a copy of the Sticker report on the printer.

5. Load the Weather data base created for exercise 6 in Chapter 5.

    a) Create a new table report named Good Days which lists the date and time for each observation that had a temperature above 65 and no rain.

    b) Add a title to Good Days which describes the criteria for being a good day.

    c) Print a copy of the Good Days report on the printer.

    d) Duplicate a copy of Good Days under the name Bad Days. Bad Days should print only cloudy days with a temperature below 40. Be sure to change the report title.

    e) Print a copy of Bad Days on the printer.

Chapter 7

Introducing the Spreadsheet

Open-Apple B

Open-Apple P

Open-Apple S

Open-Apple U

Open-Apple ?

Objectives

After completing this chapter you will be able to:

1. Understand what a spreadsheet is and define its vocabulary.

2. Plan a spreadsheet.

3. Create a simple spreadsheet on the computer and enter data into it.

4. Perform and display the value of spreadsheet calculations using formulas and functions.

5. Store and retrieve spreadsheets from the disk.

6. Print a spreadsheet.

*T*he final AppleWorks application is the spreadsheet. This chapter will explain what a spreadsheet is and how to use one. We will first concern ourselves with the vocabulary of a spreadsheet and then with the specific commands needed to produce a simple one on the computer. The next chapter will explain how AppleWorks is used to make larger and more powerful spreadsheets.

7.1 What is a Spreadsheet?

A spreadsheet is simply rows and columns of data. The term comes from the field of accounting where accountants keep track of business activities on large sheets of paper that spread out to form a "spreadsheet". These spreadsheets contain rows and columns of figures with totals and other calculations that relate to the flow of money in a business, but they can also be used to organize any type of numeric data.

Spreadsheets are record keeping tools that work primarily with numbers. An example of a simple non-computerized spreadsheet is the grade book used by Ivy University's chemistry professor, Dr. Sulfuric. In her grade book the names of her students run down the left side of the page, while labels running across the top of the page indicate each test and the date on which it was given:

Name	Test 1 9/10	Test 2 10/20	Test 3 11/15	Test 4 12/12
J.Smith	50	83	68	64
W.Freitas	86	89	78	88
M.Porter	78	100	90	89
B.Presley	45	78	66	78
H.Crane	66	76	78	55
M.Lee	85	74	83	66

Dr. Sulfuric's grade book

The grade book is organized into rows and columns. A row runs horizontally and stores both the name and grades for any one student. The name J. Smith and the grades 50 to 64, which run across the page, form a row. A column runs vertically and stores a title and all of the grades for a single test. The title Test 1 and its grades run down the page from a grade of 50 to 85 forming a column.

Computerized spreadsheets appear similar to manual ones with the added capability of using the computer to perform calculations on the data stored in the spreadsheet. If instead of storing her grades in a gradebook, Dr. Sulfuric were to use a computerized spreadsheet she would be able to have the computer calculate averages on her grades. Then if she were to change one of the grades the computer would automatically redo the calculations. This is the primary advantage of a computerized spreadsheet; the ability of the computer to perform calculations on the data stored in it and to redo the calculations when changes are made to the data.

7.2 Cells, Labels, and Values

Computerized spreadsheets store data in a grid of columns and rows. Columns are identified by letters which run along the top of the spreadsheet. In AppleWorks these letters run from A to Z, and then AA to AZ, BA to BZ, CA to CZ, and DA to DW. This allows for a maximum of 127 columns. Rows are numbered on the left-hand side of the spreadsheet from row 1 to row 9,999 (999 in version 2). In most instances a much smaller number of rows and columns will actually be used to store data. Due to memory limitations some computers would not be able to store a spreadsheet as large as the maximum allows.

The diagram below shows an empty AppleWorks spreadsheet. Note the column letters running horizontally across the top and the row numbers running down the left hand side of the screen:

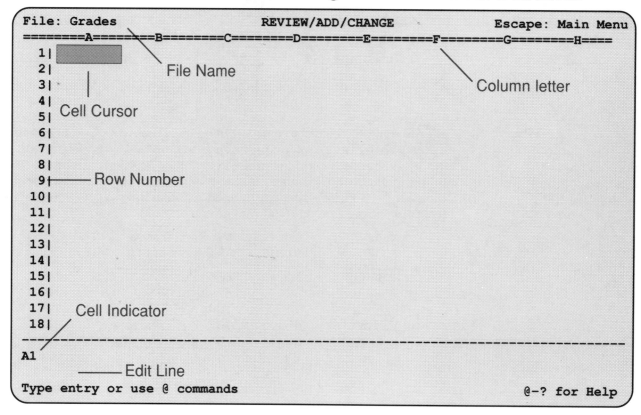

Where a row and column intersect is called a "cell". A single cell is identified by its column letter followed by its row number. Therefore, the third cell from the top in column C is named C3. Each cell can store a single item of data. This system is similar to mailboxes at the post office where each "box" or cell has a name and can store information. On this screen you will enter data into a spreadsheet. The white rectangle located at coordinate A1 is called the "cell cursor". Data can be entered from the keyboard into the cell where the cell cursor is located. The "cell indicator" at the bottom of the screen shows the current location of the cell cursor, in this case A1. Directly below the cell indicator is the "edit line". Normally blank, the edit line displays data as it is entered from the keyboard and when changing the contents of a cell.

Note that the screen only displays columns A to H and rows 1 to 18. The other columns and rows can be displayed by using the arrow keys to "scroll" the screen. When this is done columns and rows move off the screen and new ones appear. The old columns and rows are not lost, just not displayed. In this way the screen can be considered a window on a very large spreadsheet. Scrolling moves the window around the spreadsheet without affecting any of the data stored in the cells.

Spreadsheets can store two types of data in cells: "labels" and "values". Labels are entries which store data that cannot be used in calculations, including words or letters. Values are entries that have numeric values and can be used in calculations. The student names and the headings for each column of grades (i.e. J.Smith and Test 1) are labels, while a grade such as 50 is a value. When setting up a computerized spreadsheet it will be important to first determine what data will be stored as labels and what data as values. Be careful not to confuse the name of the cell and the data it stores.

7.3 Creating a New Spreadsheet

To create a new spreadsheet the 'Add Files to the Desktop' option of the Main Menu is selected and then the 'Spreadsheet' option from the Add Files Menu. This displays the Spreadsheet menu from which the 'From scratch' option is used to create a new spreadsheet. The other spreadsheet option will not be used in this chapter.

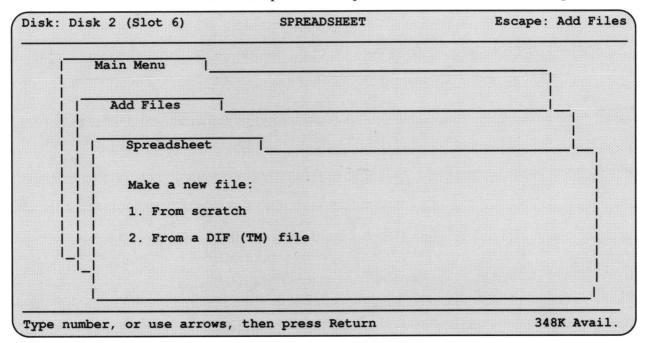

```
Disk: Disk 2 (Slot 6)          SPREADSHEET          Escape: Add Files


     ___Main Menu_____|_____
     |                                                        |
     |  ___Add Files_____|_____|
     |  |                                                     |
     |  |  ___Spreadsheet_____|_____
     |  |  |                                                 |
     |  |  |                                                 |
     |  |  |  Make a new file:                               |
     |  |  |                                                 |
     |  |  |  1. From scratch                                |
     |  |  |                                                 |
     |  |  |  2. From a DIF (TM) file                        |
     |__|  |                                                 |
        |__|                                                 |
           |                                                 |
           |_____|

 Type number, or use arrows, then press Return          348K Avail.
```

A new spreadsheet must be given a valid filename before it may be used. It is best to pick a name which describes the contents of the spreadsheet. For example, a spreadsheet storing Dr. Sulfuric's grades would best be named Grades or Grade Book.

Once a new spreadsheet has been created there are several ways to move the cell cursor through it. Pressing the right-arrow key moves the cell cursor one cell to the right, into the next column. Pressing the left-arrow moves it one cell to the left. The up and down-arrows move the cell cursor one cell to the top or bottom, into the next row. Because spreadsheets can get large, there are several keys which move the cell cursor more than one row or column at a time. Open–Apple 1 moves the cell cursor directly to row 1 and Open–Apple 9 directly to the last row in the spreadsheet that contains data. Open–Apple > jumps to the last column in the current row which contains data and Open–Apple < moves to the first column in the current row.

Practice 1

In this Practice you will create a new spreadsheet named Grades, move the cell cursor around the empty spreadsheet, and scroll through the spreadsheet.

1) BOOT PRODOS AND START APPLEWORKS

2) SELECT THE 'ADD FILES' OPTION FROM THE MAIN MENU

Press Return to accept the default.

3) SELECT THE 'SPREADSHEET' OPTION FROM THE ADD FILES MENU

Type 5 and press Return.

4) SELECT 'FROM SCRATCH' FROM THE SPREADSHEET MENU

Press Return to accept the default.

5) NAME THE SPREADSHEET FILE

In response to the prompt

Type a name for this new file:

type Grades and press Return. An empty spreadsheet is shown.

6) MOVE THE CELL CURSOR TO CELL D8

a. Press the right-arrow key 3 times. The cell cursor is now located at cell D1 as shown by the cell indicator on the screen.
b. Press the down-arrow key 7 times. The cell cursor is now located at cell D8.

7) SCROLL THE SCREEN

a. Hold the right-arrow key down until the cell cursor is on cell Z8. Note how the columns on the left disappear off the screen.
b. Hold the down-arrow key down until the cell cursor is on cell Z100. Note how the rows on the top disappear off the screen.

8) RETURN THE CELL CURSOR TO CELL A1

a. Press Open–Apple 1. The cell cursor is now located in row 1.
b. Press Open–Apple < to move the cell cursor to cell A1.

7.4 Entering Data into the Spreadsheet

To enter data into a cell in the spreadsheet the cell cursor is moved to that cell and the data entered from the keyboard. As the data is typed it will appear on the edit line at the bottom of the screen. If the first character of data is numeric the word Value: will appear followed by the data you type. If the first character of data is a letter of the alphabet or a quote mark (") the word Label: will appear followed by the data typed. When the data entry is complete, pressing Return will transfer the data from the edit line to the cell in the spreadsheet. The contents of the cell is then shown in the cell indicator. For example

        C3: (Value) 50

indicates that the cell cursor is currently on cell C3 which stores the value 50. The cell indicator shows the contents of a label cell as well:

        A3: (Label) J.Smith

This indicates that the cursor is currently on cell A3 which stores the label J.Smith.

If the data to be entered into a cell is a label that does not begin with a letter of the alphabet, it is necessary to first type a quote mark. This informs AppleWorks that the characters that follow are to be considered a label rather than a value. For example, to adjust a label over a column it is sometimes necessary to start the entry with blank spaces. To do this a quote mark is typed, then the blank spaces, followed by the label. The label will then be displayed with the leading spaces, but without the quote mark.

Another example where a quote mark is needed is when a label begins with a number. If a date such as 9/10 is entered in a cell, the value .9 will be displayed because AppleWorks divides the numbers. If a quote mark is typed first, followed by the date, it will be displayed properly.

If a mistake has been made in entering data into a cell it may be corrected by returning the cell cursor to the cell, typing the correct data and pressing Return. The new data will then replace the incorrect data in the cell. If the mistake is noticed before Return is pressed the Delete key may be used to erase data from the edit line, and the correction typed. When changing the contents of a cell, the new data is first shown on the edit line while the cell indicator displays the old value. Pressing Return will replace the contents of the cell with the data on the edit line. Pressing Escape instead of Return will erase the edit line, leaving the contents of the cell unchanged.

AppleWorks will automatically display up to 9 characters stored in a single cell. In order to display the contents of cells containing more than 9 characters formatting commands explained in the next chapter must be used.

7.5 Saving a Spreadsheet on Disk

To save a spreadsheet Open-Apple S is pressed. This will transfer a copy of the spreadsheet from the computer's memory to the disk. Each time Open-Apple S is pressed when a spreadsheet is in the computer's memory, the latest version of the spreadsheet will be saved replacing any earlier version. For this reason it is necessary to press Open-Apple S again after making changes to a previously stored spreadsheet.

The procedure used to transfer a previously saved spreadsheet file from diskette to the computer's memory is the same as that used for word processor or data base files. From the Main Menu the 'Add files' option is selected, followed by 'The current disk' option from the Add Files menu. All AppleWorks files will then be listed. The cursor is moved down past the word processing and database files to the desired spreadsheet file name. Pressing Return transfers a copy of the spreadsheet from the diskette into the computer's memory.

Practice 2

In this Practice you will enter the data from Dr. Sulfuric's grade book into the Grades spreadsheet created in the last Practice.

1) ENTER THE COLUMN TITLES IN ROW 1

    a. Move the cell cursor to cell A1.

    b. Type Name and Return. Note that the word Label: appears on the cell indicator at the bottom of the screen when the "N" is pressed to indicate that non-numeric data has been entered. When Return is pressed the label Name appears in cell A1.

    c. Move the cursor to cell C1. Column B is skipped to make the spreadsheet easier to read.

    d. Type a quote mark ("), press the space bar twice and then type Test 1 and Return. The spaces are necessary to place the heading properly over the row of numbers.

    e. Move the cursor to cell D1.

    f. Type a quote mark, press the space bar twice and then type Test 2 and Return.

    g. Continue this procedure to place the headings for Test 3 and Test 4 in cells E1 and F1.

2) ENTER THE TEST DATES

    a. Move the cell cursor to cell C2.

    b. Type a quote mark, press the space bar 3 times and then type 9/10 and Return.

    c. Move the cell cursor to cell D2.

    d. Type a quote mark, press the space bar 3 times and then type 10/20 and Return.

    e. Continue this procedure to place the date 11/15 in cell E2 and 12/12 in cell F2.

3) ENTER THE STUDENT NAMES

    a. Move the cell cursor to cell A4. Row 3 is skipped to make the spreadsheet more readable.

    b. Type the name J.Smith and press Return. Do not place a space between the period after the initial and the last name when entering these names.

    c. Move the cursor cell to cell A5.

    d. Type the name W.Freitas and press Return.

    e. Continue this process to place the names:

        M.Porter   into cell A6
        B.Presley into cell A7
        H.Crane   into cell A8
        M.Lee   into cell A9

4) ENTER THE GRADES

Using the arrow keys move the cell cursor to cell C4 to enter the first grade for J. Smith, a 50. Continue entering the grades until your spreadsheet looks like the one below:

```
File: Grades                    REVIEW/ADD/CHANGE              Escape: Main Menu
========A=======B========C========D========E========F========G========H====
   1|Name             Test 1   Test 2   Test 3   Test 4
   2|                  9/10     10/20    11/15    12/12
   3|
   4|J.Smith              50       83       68       64
   5|W.Freitas            86       89       78       88
   6|M.Porter             78      100       90       89
   7|B.Presley            45       78       66       78
   8|H.Crane              66       76       78       55
   9|M.Lee                85       74       83       66
  10|
  11|
  12|
  13|
  14|
  15|
  16|
  17|
  18|
-------------------------------------------------------------------------------
F10

Type entry or use @ commands                                @-? for Help
```

5) SAVE THE SPREADSHEET ON DISK

Press Open-Apple S.

6) RETURN TO THE MAIN MENU

Press Escape.

7.6 Using Formulas to Perform Calculations

We have stated that the primary benefit of a computerized spreadsheet is its ability to perform calculations. To perform these calculations "formulas" are used. Formulas are mathematical statements used to calculate values. For example, the formula 25 * 38 can be entered in a cell and when Return is pressed, the value 950 will be shown in the cell. If we want to store the product of the values stored in cells A5 and B7 in a cell all we need do is enter the formula +A5 * B7 in that cell. The computer will then automatically calculate the product of the two stored numbers and place it in the cell. Note that all formulas in AppleWorks must begin with a digit or mathematical operator, such as a + sign or parentheses.

The following mathematical operators may be used in writing a formula:

Addition	+
Subtraction	−
Multiplication	*
Division	/
Exponentiation	^

Exponentiation means raised to a power and uses the caret (^) symbol. For example, 2^2 = 4 and 5^3 = 125. Below are some examples of formulas that could be stored in cells:

```
3 * C5 + D15
25 + (D19 / 22)
+B10 * 2
+A3^3
```

Because cell names begin with a letter, a mathematical operator (such as the plus shown above) must start any formula which begins with a cell name.

When AppleWorks evaluates a formula it reads it from left to right. For example, the formula 2^2 + 3 equals 7, and the formula 2^2 + 3*2 equals 14. Note in the last example that 2 is first squared which gives 4, then 3 is added to make 7 and the result is then multiplied by 2 to give 14. To add the result of 2^2 to the product of 3*2 parentheses must be used: (2^2) + (3*2). AppleWorks will perform the calculations inside the parentheses first and then evaluate the formula from left to right. Here are a number of formulas and the results they will yield:

```
2 * 2 + 3 * 2            = 14
(2 * 2) + (3 * 2)        = 10
25 * 8 / 4               = 50
35 + 12 / 3              = 15.66666
35 + (12 / 3)            = 39
```

If cell B3 stores the value 20 and cell C2 the value 50, the formulas below would produce the following:

```
+B3 / C2                 = .4
+B3 * C2                 = 1000
+B3 - C2                 = -30
2 * B3 + 5 * C2          = 2250
2 * B3 + (5 * C2)        = 290
(2 * B3) + (5 * C2)      = 290
```

If cells C1 to C6 store values the sum of the values can be calculated with the formula:

```
+C1 + C2 + C3 + C4 + C5 + C6
```

The average of the values in cells C1 to C6 can be calculated with the formula:

```
(C1 + C2 + C3 + C4 + C5 + C6) / 6
```

If you enter an illegal formula into a cell, AppleWorks displays ERROR in that cell. For example, it is illegal to attempt to divide a number by zero because this result is undefined in mathematics. Therefore, entering 10/0 in a cell will cause AppleWorks to display ERROR in that cell when Return is pressed.

7.7 Editing Entries

When a mistake has been made in a formula or a change is desired, the complete formula can be retyped and entered, but this is unnecessary. AppleWorks allows a cell's entry to be edited by placing the cell cursor on the cell and pressing Open-Apple U. The cell formula will then appear on the edit line at the bottom of the screen with a blinking cursor located at its leftmost character. The cursor can then be moved with the right-arrow key to the position where an insertion will be made and the insertion typed.

Characters may be deleted by moving the cursor one character to the right of the character to be deleted and pressing the delete key. For example, to delete the multiplication sign in the formula +B1^*C8 the cursor is moved to the C and the delete key pressed.

7.8 Blanking Cells

To erase whatever is stored in a cell, whether it is a value, label or formula, the blank command `Open-Apple B` is used. The cell cursor is first placed on the cell to be blanked and the command given which results in the question:

`Blank?` **Entry** `Rows   Columns   Block`

To blank a single cell select the default Entry. The contents of whole rows, columns or blocks can be blanked by selecting these options. Note that it is not necessary to blank a cell to change its value to another value, only if it is to be left blank.

Practice 3

In this Practice you will enter values and formulas into the cells of a new spreadsheet and perform calculations. Boot ProDOS and start AppleWorks if you have not already done so.

1) CREATE A NEW SPREADSHEET FROM SCRATCH NAMED TEST

    a. Press Return to accept the default option 'Add files to the Desktop'.
    b. Select the 'Spreadsheet' option.
    c. Select 'From scratch'.
    d. Name the spreadsheet `Test` and press Return.

2) ENTER FORMULAS INTO THE SPREADSHEET

    a. Move the cell cursor to cell B5.
    b. Type `35 + 12 / 3` and press Return. The result 15.66666 is shown in cell B5. Note that the formula is shown on the cell indicator.
    c. Type `35 + (12 / 3)` and press Return. The result 39 is shown in cell B5, replacing the old value. The new formula is shown on the cell indicator.

3) ENTER VALUES INTO THE SPREADSHEET

    a. Move the cell cursor to cell B3.
    b. Enter the value `20` and press Return.
    c. Move the cell cursor to cell C2.
    d. Enter the value `50` and press Return.

4) ENTER FORMULAS

    a. Move the cell cursor to cell D5.
    b. Enter each of the following formulas in cell D5 followed by Return. Note the resulting values:

Formula	Resulting value
`+B3 / C2`	`.4`
`+B3 * C2`	`1000`
`2 * B3 + 5 * C2`	`2250`
`(2 * B3) + (5 * C2)`	`290`
`+B3^2 + C2^2`	`202500`
`(B3 + C2)^2`	`4900`
`B3 + C2`	`B3 + C2` (this is a <u>label</u>)
`10 / 0`	`ERROR`

5) BLANK EACH CELL

> Move the cell cursor to each cell displaying a value and press Open-Apple B and Return to accept the 'Entry' default to erase the values.

6) ENTER NEW VALUES

   a. Move the cell cursor to cell C1 and enter a value of 50.
   b. Move the cell cursor to cell C2 and enter a value of 85.
   c. Continue entering the values:

75	in cell C3
83	in cell C4
34	in cell C5
55	in cell C6

7) CALCULATE THE SUM OF THE VALUES IN COLUMN C

   a. Move the cell cursor to cell C8.
   b. Enter the formula:

   ```
   +C1 + C2 + C3 + C4 + C5 + C6
   ```

   The sum of the values stored in cells C1 through C6 is shown in cell C8: 382.

8) CALCULATE THE AVERAGE OF THE VALUES IN COLUMN C

   a. Move the cell cursor to cell C10.
   b. Enter the formula:

   ```
   (C1 + C2 + C3 + C4 + C5 + C6) / 6
   ```

   The average of the values, 63.66666, is shown in C10.

9) CALCULATE AVERAGE OF FIRST 3 CELLS ONLY

   a. Make sure the cell cursor is still on cell C10.
   b. Press Open-Apple U to edit the formula stored in C10. The formula will now be shown on the edit line at the bottom of the screen with a blinking cursor.
   c. Move the cursor to the right hand parentheses and press Delete 9 times.
   d. Move the cursor one space to the right of the 6 and press Delete and then type a 3.
   e. Press Return. The average of the first three cells only, 70, is shown in cell C10.

10) SAVE TEST ON DISK

> Press Open-Apple S. A copy of the Test spreadsheet is saved on disk.

<u>Check</u> - The spreadsheet should look like the following:

```
File: Test                    REVIEW/ADD/CHANGE            Escape: Main Menu
========A========B========C========D========E========F========G========H====
   1|                        50
   2|                        85
   3|                        75
   4|                        83
   5|                        34
   6|                        55
   7|
   8|                       382
   9|
  10|                        70
  11|
  12|
  13|
  14|
  15|
  16|
  17|
  18|
-----------------------------------------------------------------------------
C10: (Value) (C1+C2+C3)/3

Type entry or use @ commands                                    @-? for Help
```

7.9 Using Functions to Perform Calculations

To produce commonly performed calculations AppleWorks contains built-in "functions" which may be used as part of a formula. For example, in Practice 3 we added the values of a column of numbers stored in cells C1 to C6 and stored the result in cell C8. Instead we could have used the AppleWork's built-in @SUM function. The formula in C8 could be replaced with:

    @SUM(C1...C6)

The computer will then automatically calculate the value of C1 + C2 + C3 + C4 + C5 + C6. Note that in AppleWorks all functions begin with the @ sign. The @SUM function requires that the first cell name and last cell name in the sum be entered. Three periods (...) are used to indicate a "range" of cells so that (C1...C6) refers to cells C1, C2, C3, C4, C5 and C6.

We could replace the formula in cell C10 used to average the column of grades in Practice 3 with

    @SUM(C1...C6) / 6

and obtain the same result. Note that we must still divide the sum by 6 to obtain the average.

Values stored in a row of cells may also be summed using the @SUM function. For example, to sum the cells in row 2 for the range of cells B2 to G2 and store the result in cell H2 we need only enter

    @SUM(B2...G2)

in H2. AppleWorks will then sum the values in cells B2, C2, D2, E2, F2, and G2. It is important to realize that either a row or a column can be used to define a range, but no combination of the two.

Above we averaged the values stored in cells C1 through C6 by summing the values and dividing by 6. There is an easier method of averaging the values using the @AVG function which averages all the values contained in the cells between the first and last cell name entered. To average the values for cells C1 through C6 we can use the function @AVG(C1...C6).

Practice 4

In this Practice functions will be used to sum and average rows and columns of values. Start AppleWorks and load the Test spreadsheet created in Practice 3 if you have not already done so.

1) ENTER FUNCTION TO SUM COLUMN C

   a. Move the cell cursor to cell C8.
   b. Enter the function:

      `@SUM(C1...C6)`

     The sum 382 is displayed.

2) ENTER FUNCTION TO AVERAGE COLUMN C

   a. Move the cell cursor to cell C10.
   b. Enter the function:

      `@AVG(C1...C6)`

     The average 63.66666 is displayed.

3) ENTER VALUES IN ROW 2

   a. Move the cell cursor to cell B2.
   b. Enter the following values into the cells in row 2 (note that C2 already has a value):

      `97.8`   into cell B2
      `109.4`   into cell D2
      `105.8`   into cell E2
      `0.983`   into cell F2

4) ENTER FUNCTION TO SUM ROW 2

   a. Move the cell cursor to cell H2.
   b. Enter the function:

      `@SUM(B2...F2)`

     The sum of the values, 398.983, is displayed.

5) ENTER FUNCTION TO AVERAGE ROW B

   a. Scroll the cell cursor to cell J2.
   b. Enter the function:

      `@AVG(B2...F2)`

     The average of the values, 79.7966, is displayed.

6) CHANGE THE VALUE IN CELL F2

   a. Move the cell cursor to cell F2.
   b. Enter the new value `1945.8`.
     Note that both the row's sum (cell H2) and average (cell J2) change automatically to reflect the new value.

7) SAVE TEST

Press `Open-Apple S`. The spreadsheet is saved on disk.

<u>Check</u> - The modified spreadsheet should look like:

```
/ File: Test                          REVIEW/ADD/CHANGE              Escape: Main Menu \
|  ========C========D=========E========F========G========H=========I========J====  |
|     1|        50                                                                  |
|     2|        85     109.4    105.8   1945.8              2343.8           468.76  |
|     3|        75                                                                  |
|     4|        83                                                                  |
|     5|        34                                                                  |
|     6|        55                                                                  |
|     7|                                                                            |
|     8|       382                                                                  |
|     9|                                                                            |
|    10| 63.66666                                                                   |
|    11|                                                                            |
|    12|                                                                            |
|    13|                                                                            |
|    14|                                                                            |
|    15|                                                                            |
|    16|                                                                            |
|    17|                                                                            |
|    18|                                                                            |
|  - - - - - - - - - - - - - - - - - - - - - - - - - - - - - - - - - - - - - - - -  |
|                                                                                   |
|  F2: (Value) 1945.8                                                               |
|                                                                                   |
\  Type entry or use @ commands                                     @-? for Help   /
```

7.10 Planning a Spreadsheet

It is important to first plan a spreadsheet carefully before using the computer. This is best done by answering the following questions:

1. What new information should the spreadsheet produce?

2. What data must the spreadsheet store to produce the new information?

3. How could the information be produced without a computer?

4. How should the spreadsheet be displayed on the computer?

We will use Dr. Sulfuric's grade book, shown in Section 7.1, to answer these questions:

1. Dr. Sulfuric wants to calculate each student's term average and the class average on each of her tests.

2. The data to be stored is the student names and grades.

3. Without using a computer Dr. Sulfuric could produce the class average on each test by adding all the grades for that test and dividing by the number of students (6). Each student's term average could be calculated by adding the four grades and dividing by 4.

4. How the spreadsheet should be formatted on the computer is easy in this case since we want it to look like Dr. Sulfuric's grade book. Later when we plan more complicated spreadsheets, especially those involving financial calculations, we will have to spend considerable time planning them.

Step 3 is especially important. In the process of planning how to solve a problem without the computer we must determine the sequence of steps the solution will require. Since the computer solution will usually require the same or very similar steps we can use our non-computer solution to assist us in developing the computer one.

Working out the details, as we have above, is very important before proceeding to the computer. In the next chapter we will expand our discussion of planning a spreadsheet.

Practice 5

In this Practice you will enter formulas to calculate the average grade on each test and the term averages for each of Dr. Sulfuric's six students. Start AppleWorks if you have not already done so and load the Grades spreadsheet created in Practice 2.

1) ENTER THE FORMULA TO AVERAGE GRADES FOR TEST 1

    a. Move the cell cursor to cell C11.
    b. Enter the function:

```
@AVG(C4...C9)
```

The average grade on Test 1, 68.33333, is displayed in cell C11.

2) ENTER THE FORMULAS TO CALCULATE THE OTHER TEST AVERAGES

    a. Move the cell cursor to cell D11.
    b. Enter the formulas:

```
@AVG(D4...D9)        into cell D11
@AVG(E4...E9)        into cell E11
@AVG(F4...F9)        into cell F11
```

3) CALCULATE EACH STUDENT'S TERM AVERAGE

    a. Move the cell cursor to cell H4.
    b. Enter the formula:

```
@AVG(C4...F4)
```

The average for J. Smith, 66.25, is displayed in cell H4.

    c. Repeat this process by entering the formulas:

```
@AVG(C5...F5)        into cell H5
@AVG(C6...F6)        into cell H6
@AVG(C7...F7)        into cell H7
@AVG(C8...F8)        into cell H8
@AVG(C9...F9)        into cell H9
```

4) ADD TITLES FOR THE NEW INFORMATION

    a. Move the cell cursor to cell H1 and enter the label `Student`.
    b. Move the cell cursor to H2 and enter the label `Average`.
    c. Move the cursor to cell B11 and enter the label `Average:`.

5) SAVE GRADES

Press `Open-Apple S` to save the revised version of Grades on disk.

<u>Check</u> - The averages for Dr. Sulfuric's class should now appear in the spreadsheet as shown below:

```
File: Grades                  REVIEW/ADD/CHANGE              Escape: Main Menu
========A========B========C========D========E========F========G========H====
   1|Name               Test 1    Test 2    Test 3    Test 4      Student
   2|                    9/10      10/20     11/15     12/12       Average
   3|
   4|J.Smith                 50        83        68        64        66.25
   5|W.Freitas               86        89        78        88        85.25
   6|M.Porter                78       100        90        89        89.25
   7|B.Presley               45        78        66        78        66.75
   8|H.Crane                 66        76        78        55        68.75
   9|M.Lee                   85        74        83        66           77
  10|
  11|          Average:   68.33333 83.33333 77.16666 73.33333
  12|
  13|
  14|
  15|
  16|
  17|
  18|
   ----------------------------------------------------------------------------
B11: (Label) Average:

Type entry or use @ commands                              @-? for Help
```

7.11 Printing a Spreadsheet

Before printing a spreadsheet it is important to first save it on disk using Open-Apple S. If something then goes wrong in the process of printing and the computer's memory erased, the spreadsheet can be retrieved from disk. Also check to make sure that the printer is on and properly connected to your computer before printing.

To print a spreadsheet Open-Apple P (for **P**rint) is used. Because many spreadsheets exceed the width of printer paper Apple-Works allows you to select and print only a portion of the spreadsheet. It is possible to print the whole spreadsheet, selected rows, selected columns, or a "block". A block is made up of adjacent rows and columns.

A print menu will appear which asks you to select which printer will be used:

```
Where do you want to print the report?

1. ImageWriter
2. The Clipboard (for the Word Processor)
3. A text (ASCII) file on disk
4. A DIF (TM) file on disk
```

You may have different printers available. Usually option 1, the default option, will be the printer your computer is connected to. You will also be asked to enter both the date and the number of copies to be printed.

A list of available Open-Apple commands can be displayed by using the Help command, Open-Apple ?. Pressing the Escape key removes the help screen and again displays the spreadsheet.

Practice 6

In this Practice you will print all of the Grades spreadsheet as well as selected portions. Start AppleWorks and load the Grades spreadsheet if you have not already done so. Make sure that your computer is connected to a printer before attempting this Practice. Check to determine which printer to select from the Print menu.

1) GIVE THE PRINT COMMAND

Press `Open-Apple P`.

2) SELECT ALL FROM THE PRINT PROMPT

From the prompt

`Print?` **All** `Rows   Columns   Block`

press Return to select 'All'.

3) CHOOSE YOUR PRINTER

The PRINT menu will appear. Select your printer.

4) ENTER TODAY'S DATE

At the prompt

`Type report date or press Return:`

enter today's date in the form *mm/dd/yy*

5) ENTER NUMBER OF COPIES TO PRINT

At the prompt

`How many copies?` **1**

press Return to select the default value of 1 copy. The spreadsheet is now printed on the printer.

6) PRINT ONLY THE FIRST THREE ROWS OF GRADES

a. Move the cursor to cell A4.
b. Press `Open-Apple P`.
c. Select the 'Rows' option from the prompt. The row containing J. Smith's grades will be highlighted.
d. The message

`Use cursor moves to highlight Rows, then press Return`

appears at the bottom of the screen. Press the down-arrow key two times to highlight the rows containing W. Freitas' and M. Porter's grades and press Return.
e. Press Return 3 more times to accept the default values. The highlighted rows will be printed.

7) PRINT A BLOCK OF THE SPREADSHEET

a. Move the cell cursor to cell A1.
b. Press `Open-Apple P`.
c. Select the 'Block' option.
d. The message

`Use cursor moves to highlight Block, then press Return`

appears at the bottom of the screen. Press the right-arrow key 3 times to highlight to Test 2 and then the down-arrow key 4 times to include W. Freitas.
e. Press Return 4 times to accept the defaults and the highlighted block will be printed.

7.12 The @ROUND Function

AppleWorks includes a number of functions which are listed in Appendix A. We have already discussed @SUM and @AVG and will now explain @ROUND which allows a number to be rounded. In the spreadsheet containing Dr. Sulfuric's grades the test averages are printed to 5 decimal places, but only 1 place is desired. For example, the class average on Test 1 appears as 68.33333, but Dr. Sulfuric wants it displayed as 68.3.

To round the number of decimal places of a stored value, the cell name is entered into the @ROUND function followed by the number of decimal places the result is to be rounded to. For example, to round a value stored in cell C16 to 2 places the formula is written:

```
@ROUND(C16,2)
```

If the value stored in C16 is 72.856 the rounded result will be 72.86.

To round the result of a formula, the formula is given followed by the number of decimal places the result is to be rounded to. J. Smith's average can be rounded to 1 place with the formula:

```
@ROUND(@AVG(C4...F4),1)
```

To round his average to the nearest integer a 0 is used to indicate no decimal places:

```
@ROUND(@AVG(C4...F4),0)
```

Practice 7

In this Practice you will round the averages in the Grades spreadsheet using the edit mode to edit the formulas. Start AppleWorks and load the Grades spreadsheet if you have not already done so.

1) ROUND THE FORMULA FOR TEST 1 TO 1DECIMAL PLACE

   a. Move the cell cursor to cell C11.
   b. Press Open-Apple U to enter the edit mode. The formula is shown on the edit line.
   c. Type @ROUND(
   d. Move the cursor one space beyond the end of the formula and type ,1) so that the formula on the edit line appears:

```
@ROUND(@AVG(C4...C9),1)
```

Press Return and note that the average is now rounded to 1 decimal place, 68.3.

2) ROUND ALL TEST AVERAGES TO 1 DECIMAL PLACE

Repeat step 1 for cells D11, E11, and F11.

3) ROUND J. SMITH'S AVERAGE TO 1 DECIMAL PLACE

   a. Move the cursor to cell H4.
   b. Press Open-Apple U to enter the edit mode. The formula is shown on the edit line.
   c. Type @ROUND(
   d. Move the cursor one space beyond the end of the formula and type ,1) so that the formula appears:

```
@ROUND(@AVG(C4...F4),1)
```

Press Return and note that the average is now rounded to one decimal place, 66.3.

4)   ROUND ALL STUDENT AVERAGES TO 1 DECIMAL PLACE

Repeat step 3 for cells H5, H6, H7, H8, and H9.

5)   SAVE GRADES

Press `Open-Apple S` to save the modified version of Grades on disk.

Check - When you are done your spreadsheet should be similar to:

```
/ File: Grades                   REVIEW/ADD/CHANGE              Escape: Main Menu \
| =======A========B========C========D========E========F========G========H==== |
|    1|Name                 Test 1   Test 2   Test 3   Test 4         Student     |
|    2|                      9/10    10/20    11/15    12/12         Average      |
|    3|                                                                          |
|    4|J.Smith                50       83       68       64            66.3       |
|    5|W.Freitas              86       89       78       88            85.3       |
|    6|M.Porter               78      100       90       89            89.3       |
|    7|B.Presley              45       78       66       78            66.8       |
|    8|H.Crane                66       76       78       55            68.8       |
|    9|M.Lee                  85       74       83       66              77       |
|   10|                                                                          |
|   11|         Average:     68.3     83.3     77.2     73.3                      |
|   12|                                                                          |
|   13|                                                                          |
|   14|                                                                          |
|   15|                                                                          |
|   16|                                                                          |
|   17|                                                                          |
|   18|                                                                          |
| ------------------------------------------------------------------------------ |
| H9: (Value) @ROUND(@AVG(C9...F9),1)                                            |
|                                                                                |
| Type entry or use @ commands                              @-? for Help         |
\                                                                                /
```

Chapter Summary

This chapter covered the basics of planning and creating a computerized spreadsheet. A spreadsheet is simply rows and columns of data with rows running horizontally and columns vertically. The primary advantage of a computerized spreadsheet is that it has the ability to perform calculations on the data it stores with the calculations automatically changing to reflect any changes in the data.

In an AppleWorks spreadsheet the rows are numbered on the left-hand side and the columns identified by letters which run along the top of the spreadsheet. Where a row and column intersect is called a cell. A single cell is identified by a column letter and row number. For example, C4 names the cell located in column C at row 4.

Spreadsheet cells can store two types of data; labels and values. Labels can be words or characters and cannot be used in calculations. Values are numeric and can be used in calculations.

A new spreadsheet is created on the computer by selecting the 'Spreadsheet' option from the Add Files menu. Data is entered into the spreadsheet by moving the cell cursor to a cell location, typing the data and pressing Return. The cell indicator at the bottom of the screen shows the current location of the cell cursor.

A spreadsheet is saved on disk by typing `Open-Apple S`. It is printed by typing `Open-Apple P`. The print command allows ALL of the spreadsheet to be printed or just ROWS, COLUMNS or BLOCKS.

Formulas are mathematical statements used to calculate values which can be stored in cells. The statement +B3*C4 is a formula which calculates the product of the value stored in cell B3 times the value in cell C4. All formulas must begin with a digit or mathematical operator. Functions are used by the computer to produce commonly performed calculations. The statement @SUM(B3...B8) is a function. All functions begin with the @ sign. B3...B8 is called a range which may define either a portion of a row or column, but not both. This chapter covered the following three functions:

@SUM

`@SUM(B3...B8)`

sums the values in the column of cells B3, B4, B5, B6, B7 and B8.

`@SUM(A5...E5)`

sums the values in the row of cells A5, B5, C5, D5 and E5.

@AVG

`@AVG(C3...C8)`

averages the values in the column of cells C3, C4, C5, C6, C7 and C8.

`@AVG(B7...F7)`

averages the values in the row of cells B7, C7, D7, E7 and F7.

@ROUND

`@ROUND(C5,2)`

rounds the value stored in cell C5 to 2 decimal places.

It is important to carefully plan a spreadsheet before using the computer. This is best done by first deciding what new information the spreadsheet will produce, what data it will store, how it can be produced without a computer, and what it should look like when displayed on the computer.

Vocabulary

Block - Selected group of adjacent rows and columns. May be copied, moved, formatted, etc.

Cell - Where a row and column intersect. A cell is identified by its column letter and row number, for example G8.

Cell cursor - White rectangle on the screen which is moved from cell to cell using the arrow keys. Data may be entered into a cell when the cell cursor is located on it.

Cell indicator - Shows the current location of the cell cursor at the bottom of the screen.

Column - Vertical line of data identified by a letter.

Edit line - Line at the bottom of the screen where data entered from the keyboard is displayed before it is entered into the cell.

Formulas - Mathematical statements used to calculate values which are stored in cells. The statement +C5+D7+E8 is a formula.

Functions - Used in formulas to perform common calculations. @SUM(B5...B10) is a function.
Label - Words or characters stored in a cell that cannot be used in calculations.
Range - Partial row or column of adjacent cells.
Row - Horizontal line of data identified by a number.
Scroll - Moving the cell cursor to view different parts of a spreadsheet.
Spreadsheet - Rows and columns of data on which calculations can be performed.
Values - Numeric data that can be stored in cells and used in calculations.

Reviews

Sections 7.1-7.3

1. What is the primary advantage of using a computerized spreadsheet rather than a spreadsheet produced using paper and pencil?

2. a) What is a cell in a spreadsheet?
   b) What is the difference between a row and a column?

3. a) What is the difference between a label and a value?
   b) How many labels are stored in the Grades spreadsheet shown in Practice 2?

4. a) What is the maximum number of cells permitted by an AppleWorks spreadsheet?
   b) How many value cells does the Grades spreadsheet in Practice 2 contain?

5. a) What is the difference between a cell name and the data stored in a cell? Give an example.
   b) Can the name of a cell be changed?
   c) Can the data stored in the cell be changed?

6. Draw a diagram that shows all of the cells in a spreadsheet containing three columns and five rows. Show the name of each cell and store the value 27 in the cell named B3.

7. a) How can spreadsheet columns that are off of the screen be moved on to the screen?
   b) What is this action called?

Sections 7.4-7.5

8. What is the maximum number of characters that may be displayed in a single cell without using special commands?

9. How is a label that begins with a number entered into a cell, for example the date 10/20/90?

10. If a mistake has been made entering data into a cell, how may it be corrected?

11. What steps would you take to enter the value 65 into cell C4 of the spreadsheet produced in Practice 2.

12. How do you transfer a copy of a spreadsheet from the computer's memory to disk?

Sections 7.6-7.8

13. What is the difference between a formula and a function?

14. Write a formula which calculates each of the following:

    a) The product of the numbers stored in cells A1, B3 and C4.
    b) The sum of the values stored in cells A3, A4, A5, A6, A7, and A8.
    c) The product of the values stored in cells B5, B6 and B7.

15. What value would be calculated by AppleWorks for each of the following formulas?

    a) 2 * 7 + 5 * 4
    b) (2 * 7) + (5 * 4)
    c) 5 + 10 / 5
    d) (5 + 10) / 5
    e) 2^3 + 4
    f) 15 + (12 / 4)

16. What value would be calculated by AppleWorks for each of the following formulas if cell C15 stores a value of 16 and cell D8 a value of 4?

    a) +C15 * D8
    b) +C15 + 5 + D8
    c) +C15 * 5 + D8
    d) +C15 * (5 + D8)
    e) +C15 / D8
    f) +C15 + 4 / D8
    g) +C15 + (4 / D8)

17. If a mistake has been made in a formula what are two ways it may be corrected?

18. a) How can all of the values in a column of cells be blanked?
    b) How can all of the values in a row of cells be blanked?

Section 7.9

19. Write formulas using functions that will calculate each of the following:

    a) The sum of the values stored in cells B4, B5, B6 and B7.
    b) The sum of the values stored in cells B4, C4, D4, and E4.
    c) The average of the values stored in the column of cells D7 to D35.
    d) The average of the values stored in the row of cells F3 to J3.

20. How could the average be found of the values stored in cells B3, B4, B5, C5, D5 and E5? Write the formula.

Sections 7.10-7.12

21. Answer the four questions presented in Section 7.10 to plan a spreadsheet that will list the name of each member of your class, his or her height in inches, and calculate the average height of your classmates. Produce a sketch of the spreadsheet on paper.

22. a) What options does the Print command allow?
    b) If the Block option is selected from the Print prompt, how does the user indicate the portion of the spreadsheet that will be printed?
    c) What must be done to print only the grades for Test 1 in the Grades spreadsheet?

23.   Using functions, write formulas to calculate each of the following:

a) The sum of the values in cells C5, C6, C7, C8 and C9 rounded to 2 decimal places.

b) The sum of the values in cells B5, C5, D5 and E5 rounded to the nearest integer.

c) The average of the values in cells A1, A2, A3, B1, B2, B3 rounded to 1 decimal place.

Exercises

1. The Ivy University Sports Car Club is testing different sports cars and storing the results in a spreadsheet named Track Test.

   a) Create and save a new spreadsheet named Track Test. Enter the following data exactly as shown below:

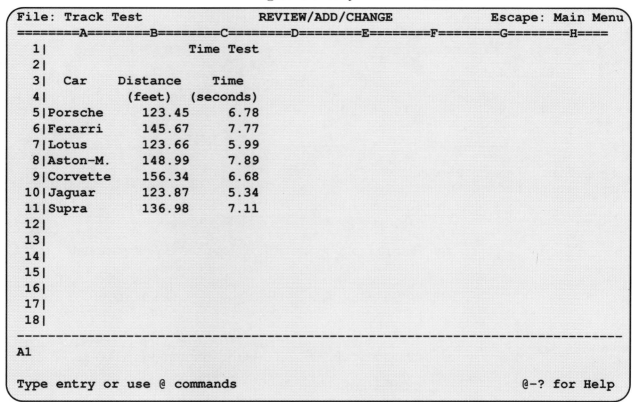

```
File: Track Test              REVIEW/ADD/CHANGE            Escape: Main Menu
========A========B========C========D========E========F========G========H====
  1|              Time Test
  2|
  3|  Car     Distance    Time
  4|          (feet)   (seconds)
  5|Porsche    123.45      6.78
  6|Ferarri    145.67      7.77
  7|Lotus      123.66      5.99
  8|Aston-M.   148.99      7.89
  9|Corvette   156.34      6.68
 10|Jaguar     123.87      5.34
 11|Supra      136.98      7.11
 12|
 13|
 14|
 15|
 16|
 17|
 18|
------------------------------------------------------------------------
A1

Type entry or use @ commands                              @-? for Help
```

   b) In column D add the title Velocity and calculate the velocity for each trial by dividing the distance by the time. Make sure that any change made to a distance or time will automatically change the corresponding velocity.

   c) In cell D13 have the spreadsheet calculate the average velocity for the trials. Be sure to include a label for the average.

   d) Edit the formulas for velocity and average velocity to display their values rounded to 2 decimal places. Save the modified spreadsheet on disk.

2. The term spreadsheet was originated by accountants who spread out large sheets of paper containing financial figures. Computerized spreadsheets are useful in keeping track of personal finances as well.

   a) Create and save a spreadsheet named Expenses that will record your expenses for a week. It should look similar to the following:

```
/ File: Expenses                    REVIEW/ADD/CHANGE              Escape: Main Menu \
|========A========B========C========D========E========F========G========H====|
|    1|                   Expenses                                               |
|    2|                                                                          |
|    3|Expense     Week 1                                                        |
|    4|                                                                          |
|    5|Lunch          4.52                                                       |
|    6|Snacks         3.75                                                       |
|    7|Movies         8.35                                                       |
|    8|Clothes       12.35                                                       |
|    9|Supplies       9.75                                                       |
|   10|                                                                          |
|   11|                                                                          |
|   12|                                                                          |
|   13|                                                                          |
|   14|                                                                          |
|   15|                                                                          |
|   16|                                                                          |
|   17|                                                                          |
|   18|                                                                          |
|     -------------------------------------------------------------------------- |
| A1                                                                             |
|                                                                               |
\ Type entry or use @ commands                                  @-? for Help    /
```

b) Add a row labeled TOTAL to the bottom of column B that calculates the total expenses for the week.

c) Edit the total formula to display the expenses rounded to 2 decimal places.

d) Add columns C, D and E for your expenses in weeks 2, 3 and 4. Be sure to include proper titles and the total for each column.

e) Add a column F which displays the average cost per week of each item and then the total expenses for an average week.

f) Edit the formulas in column F to round the averages to 2 decimal places. Save the modified spreadsheet on disk and print a copy.

When complete your spreadsheet should be similar to:

```
/ File: Expenses                    REVIEW/ADD/CHANGE              Escape: Main Menu \
|========A========B========C========D========E========F========G========H====|
|    1|                   Expenses                                               |
|    2|                                                                          |
|    3|Expense     Week 1   Week 2   Week 3   Week 4   Average                   |
|    4|                                                                          |
|    5|Lunch          4.52     2.75     3.45     6.78      4.38                  |
|    6|Snacks         3.75     6.89     2.47     4.55      4.41                  |
|    7|Movies         8.35        0     7.55     3.45      4.84                  |
|    8|Clothes       12.35     9.99    78.65        0     25.25                  |
|    9|Supplies       9.75      .56     2.34     2.13      3.69                  |
|   10|                                                                          |
|   11|TOTAL:        38.72    20.19    94.46    16.91     42.57                  |
|   12|                                                                          |
|   13|                                                                          |
|   14|                                                                          |
|   15|                                                                          |
|   16|                                                                          |
|   17|                                                                          |
|   18|                                                                          |
|     -------------------------------------------------------------------------- |
| A1                                                                             |
|                                                                               |
\ Type entry or use @ commands                                  @-? for Help    /
```

3. Create and save a spreadsheet named Multiply that displays a multiplication table. When a number is entered into cell B3 it is then shown multiplied by 1 through 10.

Your spreadsheet should be similar to the following:

```
File: Multiply                 REVIEW/ADD/CHANGE              Escape: Main Menu
========A========B========C========D========E========F========G========H====
   1|                    Multiplication Table
   2|
   3|Enter:           8
   4|
   5|        1      *         8      =         8
   6|        2      *         8      =        16
   7|        3      *         8      =        24
   8|        4      *         8      =        32
   9|        5      *         8      =        40
  10|        6      *         8      =        48
  11|        7      *         8      =        56
  12|        8      *         8      =        64
  13|        9      *         8      =        72
  14|       10      *         8      =        80
  15|
  16|
  17|
  18|
--------------------------------------------------------------------------------
A1

Type entry or use @ commands                              @-? for Help
```

Hint: Use the quotation mark to properly space the labels in columns B and D.

4. Mr. Horatio von Money, Ivy University's major benefactor, keeps track of his stock portfolio in a spreadsheet named Stocks. Load this spreadsheet from your data disk. Note that the spreadsheet displays the price of each stock and the number of shares Mr. von Money owns.

   a) You are to assist Mr. von Money by adding a column to his spreadsheet that calculates the value of each stock he owns. The value is calculated by multiplying the price of the stock by the number of shares he owns.

   b) Edit the formulas in column D to round the value to 2 decimal places.

   c) Mr. von Money has decided that he will donate 25% of his portfolio to Ivy University. Total the value of all of his stocks and then display the amount of the donation. Be sure to label both figures.

   d) Edit the spreadsheet to show the donation rounded to 2 decimal places. Save the modified spreadsheet on disk and print a copy.

5. Varsity baseball coach Slugger Ryan needs a spreadsheet to store the statistics on each of his players. Below are listed the names, times at bat, and number of hits for the players:

Player	At bats	Hits
Attis	10	3
Baker	11	3
Connelly	9	5
Doucette	12	4
Enders	15	2
Fritz	10	6
Gold	14	4
Hernandez	12	6
Li	11	5

a) Enter the above statistics into a new spreadsheet named Baseball. Be sure to include proper titles. Save Baseball on your data disk.

b) Add a column to Baseball that calculates and displays each player's batting average rounded to 3 decimal places. Batting averages are calculated by dividing the number of hits by the number of times at bat.

c) Coach Ryan would like to know the overall team batting average. Use the average function to produce the calculation for him. Be sure to include rounding and a proper label. Save the modified spreadsheet on disk and print a copy.

6. Spreadsheets can be used to keep track of any type of numerical data. You will produce a spreadsheet to help determine your caloric intake for a week.

a) Create and save a spreadsheet named Diet which keeps a record of the calories you consume each day. Your spreadsheet should be similar to the following:

```
File: Diet                    REVIEW/ADD/CHANGE              Escape: Main Menu
========A========B========C========D========E========F========G========H====
  1|                         Calories
  2|
  3|Meal         Mon      Tue      Wed     Thurs     Fri      Sat      Sun
  4|
  5|Breakfast    560      640      680      780      890      970        0
  6|Lunch        789      450      450     1100      670        0     1465
  7|Dinner      1250     1340      980      790      450     1350      745
  8|Snacks       560      200      460      450      900      440      430
  9|
 10|
 11|
 12|
 13|
 14|
 15|
 16|
 17|
 18|
----------------------------------------------------------------------------
A1

Type entry or use @ commands                              @-? for Help
```

b) Have the spreadsheet calculate the total number of calories consumed each day, the total for the week, and the average number of calories consumed per day. Be sure to include rounding and appropriate labels.

c) It has been determined that aerobic exercise burns 360 calories per hour. Have the spreadsheet calculate the number of hours for a workout to burn off 50% of the total calories consumed for each day. Include an appropriate label. Save the modified spreadsheet on disk.

7. Spreadsheets can be helpful in personal time management.

a) Create and save a spreadsheet named Activity which stores the number of hours you spend each day of the week at each of the following activities:

school classes
athletics
extra-curricular groups and clubs
studying and doing homework
eating
sleeping
watching television or listening to music
talking on the phone
doing chores at home
working at a part-time job

b) For each activity have the spreadsheet calculate the total hours spent each week on the activity. Also calculate the average number of hours spent per day on each activity for the week.

c) Most people's schedules do not exactly account for all 24 hours in a day. Add a row which calculates and displays the amount of unaccounted time in your schedule for each day. Save the modified spreadsheet on disk.

Chapter 8
Manipulating Data with the Spreadsheet

Open-Apple A

Open-Apple C

Open-Apple D

Open-Apple F

Open-Apple I

Open-Apple L

Open-Apple Z

Objectives

After completing this chapter you will be able to:

1. Plan a large spreadsheet including its layout.

2. Use the Copy command to copy labels, values and formulas.

3. Use the Find command to search for a particular cell or label.

4. Use the @MAX and @MIN functions.

5. Use the @IF function to make decisions.

6. Insert and delete rows and columns.

7. Arrange (sort) the data in a spreadsheet.

8. Use a spreadsheet to answer "What if?" questions.

*T*his chapter discusses how to plan a large spreadsheet and the techniques used to produce one on the computer. You will be taught how to format and manipulate data so that your spreadsheets are easy to read and use. Commands will be introduced which allow you to copy formulas from one set of cells to other cells, to arrange the data in a spreadsheet, and to make decisions. The chapter will end by teaching you how to ask and answer "What if?" questions so that predictions can be made based upon the data stored in a spreadsheet.

8.1 Planning a Large Spreadsheet

The spreadsheets produced in Chapter 7 required little planning because they were small and easy to understand. In this chapter planning will be more important as we develop large spreadsheets which will be continually modified and expanded.

As an example of the need for planning, we will produce a spreadsheet for Ivy University's accounting department to assist it in calculating its payroll. To do this we will follow the four steps for planning a spreadsheet presented in Chapter 7.

The first step in developing such a plan is to determine what new data the spreadsheet is to generate. This will be each employee's gross pay for the week. Gross pay is the pay earned before any deductions (such as taxes) are made.

The second step is to decide what data to include in the spreadsheet. This will be:

1. Employee name
2. Payrate per hour
3. Hours worked per day for each of 5 days

The third step is to decide what calculations must be performed to produce the desired new data. Ivy's employees work by the hour for an hourly payrate which differs from employee to employee. Multiplying the total number of hours worked for the week by the payrate produces the gross pay.

The fourth step is to determine how the spreadsheet will appear on the computer screen - its "layout". This is an important step. If we choose a proper layout the spreadsheet will not only be easy to use, but will be able to be expanded later to perform additional tasks.

We will begin planning the layout by determining what type of data will be placed in each column. The placement of columns is important since we want related data grouped by columns. Next we will decide how wide each column should be to display its longest entry. Because the 9 character default width may be either too small or too large, AppleWorks allows us to change column widths.

Before using the computer a sketch of the spreadsheet showing each column heading, the width of the column, and the type of data it will store should be drawn using paper and pencil. Here is a sketch of our plan for Ivy's payroll spreadsheet:

Name	Rate/hr	Mon	Tues	Wed	Thurs	Fri	Gross Pay
15 chars	*9 chars*	*9*	*9*	*9*	*9*	*9*	*12*
(label)	*(dollars)*		*(1 decimal place)*				*(dollars)*

Note that each column width is shown along with the type of data it will store. Later we will add columns to the spreadsheet that will contain other calculations.

8.2 Producing a Spreadsheet Layout

To change a spreadsheet layout the Open-Apple L command (for **L**ayout) is used. It allows single entries (one cell), rows, columns, or blocks to be formatted. When a selection is made the part of the spreadsheet to be formatted is highlighted. For example, if the Columns option is selected the column in which the cell cursor is currently located will be highlighted. You will then be given options of how that highlighted area is to be formatted. We will discuss three formatting options: column width, value formats and label formats.

The Column width option allows the width of the highlighted column to be changed. Pressing Open-Apple and the right-arrow key will increase the width and Open-Apple left-arrow will decrease it. Each time an arrow key is struck the width changes by one character. Note that all cells in any one column have the same width.

If a cell is not wide enough to display its value, AppleWorks displays pound signs (#) in the cell. The width of the column containing that cell should then be expanded to accommodate the value.

Another layout option allows cells to be formatted for dollar values. When this is done a dollar sign is displayed in front of the value and the option given as to how many decimal places are to be displayed, usually 2. A problem we will encounter is that when AppleWorks formats a column to contain value amounts, all cells in that column must store value amounts. Since the headings on our columns are labels, we must be careful to use the dollar format for only those cells in the column that will contain dollar values. This is done using the Block rather than Columns option.

A third layout option allows labels to be displayed as left-justified or right-justified. Cells containing labels are automatically left-justified while values are right-justified. For this reason they do not line up when displayed in the same column. To line up a label heading over a column of values the label can be right-justified using the Layout command.

It is important to realize that formatting options only effect the way that the data in a spreadsheet is displayed, and have no effect on the actual contents of the cells. For example, giving a dollar format to a cell which stores the value 5 will display $5.00. However, the contents of the cell can be seen to be only a 5 by checking the cell indicator.

The following spreadsheet contains examples of each of the options discussed above:

```
┌─────────────────────────────────────────────────────────────────────────┐
│ File: Payroll              REVIEW/ADD/CHANGE         Escape: Main Menu     │
│ =========A==========B=======C=======D=======E=======F=======G====        │
│   1|Employee Name   Rate/Hr    Mon     Tue     Wed    Thurs    Fri        │
│   2|                                                                      │
│   3|Connelly, B.     $4.75     6.0     7.5     3.0     8.0     7.0        │
│   4|Fritz, J.        $5.00     5.0     8.0     6.0     5.0     7.5        │
│   5|Wilson, N.       $7.65     6.5     7.0     0.0     8.0     8.0        │
│   6|                                              Right Justified Labels  │
│   7|Wide Column    Dollar Format                                          │
│   8|                                                                      │
│   9|                                                                      │
│  10|                                                                      │
│  11|                                                                      │
│  12|                                                                      │
│  13|                                                                      │
│  14|                                                                      │
│  15|                                                                      │
│  16|                                                                      │
│  17|                                                                      │
│  18|                                                                      │
│ ------------------------------------------------------------------------- │
│ A1: (Label) Employee Name                                                 │
│                                                                           │
│ Type entry or use @ commands                          @-? for Help        │
└─────────────────────────────────────────────────────────────────────────┘
```

Practice 1

In this Practice you will create a spreadsheet named Payroll which stores the names, hourly wages, and hours worked each day for three of Ivy University's employees. The spreadsheet will look like the one shown in section 8.2 above.

1) BOOT PRODOS AND START APPLEWORKS

2) CREATE A NEW SPREADSHEET NAMED PAYROLL

    a. Select the 'Add files' option from the Main Menu.
    b. Select the 'Spreadsheet' option to create a new file.
    c. Select 'From scratch'.
    d. Name the new spreadsheet `Payroll`.

3) FORMAT COLUMN A TO 15 CHARACTERS WIDE

    a. Place the cell cursor in column A and press `Open-Apple L`.
    b. From the prompt

`Layout?` **`Entry`** `Rows  Columns  Block`

press C to select the 'Columns' option. All of column A is highlighted.

    c. In response to the prompt

`Use cursor moves to highlight Columns, then press Return`

simply press Return to highlight only column A.

    d. From the prompt

`Layout?` **`Value format`** `Label format  Protection  Column width`

press C to select the 'Column width' option.

e. Holding down the `Open-Apple` key, strike the right-arrow key 6 times and then press Return. Six characters are added to the default width of nine characters, now making column A fifteen characters wide.

4) FORMAT CELLS B3 TO B5 TO DISPLAY DOLLAR AMOUNTS WITH 2 DECIMAL PLACES

a. Move the cell cursor to cell B3 and press `Open-Apple L`.
b. Select the 'Block' option because only a portion of column B will be formatted for dollar values.
c. Press down-arrow twice to move the cursor to cell B5 to highlight the block and press Return.
d. Press Return to select 'Value format'.
e. From the prompt

`Value format?` **Fixed** `Dollars  Commas  Percent Appropriate  Standard`

select 'Dollars'.

f. In response to the prompt

`How many decimal places? (0-7)` **0**

type 2 and press Return. Note that the cell indicator shows "Layout-D2" to indicate that the current cell is formatted for <u>D</u>ollar values with <u>2</u> decimal places.

5) FORMAT BLOCK CONTAINING THE VALUES PORTION OF COLUMNS C THROUGH G TO DISPLAY 1 DECIMAL PLACE

a. Place the cell cursor in cell C3 and press `Open-Apple L`.
b. Select the 'Block' option and press right-arrow 4 times to include columns D, E, F and G in the highlighted block.
c. Press down-arrow 2 times to include rows 4 and 5 and press Return.
d. Select 'Value format'.
e. Select 'Fixed'.
f. In response to the prompt

`How many decimal places? (0-7)` **0**

type 1 and press Return. Now all five daily hours columns have been formatted to display 1 decimal place each. The cell indicator shows "Layout-F1" for Fixed with 1 decimal place.

6) RIGHT JUSTIFY THE COLUMN HEADINGS

The column headings in your spreadsheet should be right-justified to line up with the numbers in the columns.

a. Place the cell cursor on cell B1.
b. Press `Open-Apple L`.
c. Select 'Block'.
d. Move the cell cursor to cell G1 and press Return.
e. Select 'Label format'.
f. Select 'Right justify'. Note that the cell indicator shows "Layout-R" to indicate that labels entered here will be right-justified.

7) ENTER DATA

Enter all of the data shown in the spreadsheet in Section 8.2, including names and column headings.

8) SAVE PAYROLL ON DISK

When all of the data has been entered and formatted properly, press `Open-Apple S` to save the spreadsheet on disk. Your spreadsheet should look like the one in section 8.2.

8.3 Entering Formulas

We will next calculate the Gross Pay column for Payroll. This calculation is done by multiplying the payrate by the total number of hours worked for the week. To calculate B. Connelly's gross pay we will use the formula:

```
+B3*@SUM(C3...G3)
```

A useful technique to employ when entering a formula which contains cell names is to let the computer enter the cell names in a process called "pointing". This is accomplished by typing the formula up to the point where the first cell name appears. The cell cursor is then moved to that cell, in this case B3, and the next character in the formula an asterisk (*) entered. When the asterisk is typed, AppleWorks enters the cell name B3 into the formula. When entering ranges, move the cursor to the first cell in the range, C3, and type a period (.). AppleWorks then automatically adds 2 more periods to the formula. Next move the cell cursor to the last cell in the range, in this case G3. This causes all of the cells contained in the range to be highlighted. Return is then pressed and the formula completed by typing a right parenthesis and pressing Return. The advantage of this technique is that in a large spreadsheet it helps to avoid the possibility of making a mistake by including the wrong cells in the formula. This is especially useful when the cells you wish to include in the formula are not currently shown on the screen.

Practice 2

In this Practice you will add a Gross Pay column to Payroll and calculate B. Connelly's gross pay for the week.

1) FORMAT COLUMN H TO 12 CHARACTERS WIDE

   a. Move the cell cursor to cell H1 and press `Open-Apple L`.
   b. Select 'Columns' and press Return to highlight column H.
   c. Select 'Column width'.
   d. Hold down the `Open-Apple` key and press `right-arrow` 3 times, then press Return. Column H is now 12 characters wide.

2) ENTER THE GROSS PAY HEADING AND RIGHT JUSTIFY IT

   a. Enter the label `Gross Pay` in cell H1.
   b. With the cell cursor still located on cell H1, press `Open-Apple L`.
   c. Select 'Entry'.
   d. Select 'Label format'.
   e. Select 'Right justify'. Note how the label moves to the right-hand side of the cell.

3) ENTER GROSS PAY FORMULA IN CELL H3

   a. Place the cell cursor on cell H3 and type:

   ```
   +B3*@SUM(
   ```

    b. Use the arrow keys to move the cell cursor to cell C3.

    c. Type a period. Note that AppleWorks adds two more periods to the formula on the edit line.

    d. Move the cell cursor to cell G3 and press Return.

    e. Type a right parenthesis to complete the formula and press Return. The calculated gross pay for B. Connelly is shown in cell H3.

4) FORMAT CELLS H3, H4 AND H5 TO DISPLAY DOLLARS

    a. Place the cell cursor on cell H3 and press Open-Apple L.

    b. Select 'Block'.

    c. Move the cursor down two rows and press Return.

    d. Select 'Value format'.

    e. Select 'Dollars'.

    f. Type 2 for the number of decimals and press Return. Note how the value displayed in the cell is changed to include dollar signs and decimal places. The actual contents of the cell is shown in the cell indicator.

5) SAVE PAYROLL ON DISK

    Press Open-Apple S to save the latest version of Payroll.

    <u>Check</u> - Your spreadsheet should be similar to:

```
/ File: Payroll                    REVIEW/ADD/CHANGE              Escape: Main Menu \
| ========B========C========D========E========F========G========H=========I=== |
|    1|  Rate/Hr     Mon      Tue      Wed     Thurs      Fri   Gross Pay          |
|    2|                                                                           |
|    3|  $4.75       6.0      7.5      3.0      8.0      7.0    $149.62            |
|    4|  $5.00       5.0      8.0      6.0      5.0      7.5                       |
|    5|  $7.65       6.5      7.0      0.0      8.0      8.0                       |
|    6|                                                                           |
|    7|                                                                           |
|    8|                                                                           |
|    9|                                                                           |
|   10|                                                                           |
|   11|                                                                           |
|   12|                                                                           |
|   13|                                                                           |
|   14|                                                                           |
|   15|                                                                           |
|   16|                                                                           |
|   17|                                                                           |
|   18|                                                                           |
|   --------------------------------------------------------------------------   |
| H3: (Value, Layout-D2) +B3*@SUM(C3...G3)                                        |
|                                                                                 |
| Type entry or use @ commands                                   @-? for Help     |
_____/
```

8.4 The Copy Command

Often the same label, value or formula should be stored in a number of different cells. We can of course type it over and over again, but AppleWorks makes such copying easy with the Copy command, Open-Apple C. Copying can be done within a spreadsheet or to other files. We will copy only within one spreadsheet in this Chapter. A simple use of Copy is to place a line of dashes across a spreadsheet to separate column headings from the rest of the spreadsheet.

The Copy command asks that a "Source" cell be identified from which the copy will be made as well as beginning and ending cells of the range to which copies will be transferred, the "Destination". For example, cell A2 can be identified as the source, cell B2 as the beginning destination cell and cell H2 as the ending. The cells B2 through H2 will then be highlighted. When Return is pressed, the contents of cell A2 will be copied into all cells in row 2 between cell B2 and H2 (B2, C2, D2, E2, F2, G2 and H2).

With Copy, it is also possible to specify more than one cell as the source. For example, cells A1, B1 and C1 could be specified as the source and cell A2 as the destination. When Return is pressed the contents of A1 will be copied to cell A2, the contents of B1 will be copied to B2, and C1 will be copied to C2. This technique is useful when copying data into new rows and will be demonstrated in Practice 8.

Practice 3

In this Practice you will place a line of dashes across row 2 of the Payroll spreadsheet using the Copy command. Start Appleworks and load the Payroll spreadsheet if you have not already done so.

1)   ENTER DASHES INTO CELL A2

Because the dash (–) is also used as a minus sign, it is necessary to first enter a quote mark (") to inform the computer that a label rather than a value will be entered.

a.   Move the cell cursor to cell A2.
b.   Type a quote mark followed by 15 dashes and press Return.

2)   ISSUE THE COPY COMMAND

a.   Press `Open-Apple C`.
b.   From the prompt

`Copy?` **`Within worksheet`** `To clipboard  From clipboard`

press Return to select 'Within worksheet'.

3)   SELECT SOURCE OF COPY

Make sure the cell cursor is still on cell A2. In response to the prompt

`Use cursor moves to highlight Source, then press Return`

select cell A2 as the Source by pressing Return.

4)   SELECT CELLS TO BE COPIED TO

a.   In response to the prompt

`Move to new location, then press "." or Return`

press right-arrow to move the cell cursor to B2, the first cell to be copied to.

b.   Press a period (`.`).
c.   In response to the prompt

`Use cursor moves to highlight Destination, then press Return`

move the cell cursor to the last cell to be copied to, cell H2. Note that the destination cells are highlighted. Press Return. A line of dashes now runs across the spreadsheet in row 2.

5) SAVE PAYROLL ON DISK

> Press `Open-Apple S` to save this latest version of Payroll on disk.

<u>Check</u> - The spreadsheet should contain a line of dashes in row 2:

```
/ File: Payroll                   REVIEW/ADD/CHANGE             Escape: Main Menu \
 ===========A===========B========C========D========E========F========G====
   1|Employee Name    Rate/Hr      Mon      Tue      Wed    Thurs      Fri
   2|-------------------------------------------------------------------------
   3|Connelly, B.     $4.75        6.0      7.5      3.0      8.0      7.0
   4|Fritz, J.        $5.00        5.0      8.0      6.0      5.0      7.5
   5|Wilson, N.       $7.65        6.5      7.0      0.0      8.0      8.0
   6|
   7|
   8|
   9|
  10|
  11|
  12|
  13|
  14|
  15|
  16|
  17|
  18|
   -------------------------------------------------------------------------
 A1: (Label) Employee Name

 Type entry or use @ commands                              @-? for Help
\                                                                            /
```

8.5 Copying and Displaying Formulas

Another useful application of the Copy command is in copying formulas. In our Payroll spreadsheet the formula to calculate B. Connelly's gross pay

    +B3*@SUM(C3...G3)

is stored in cell H3. To calculate J. Fritz's and N. Wilson's gross pay the formula will have to be entered into rows 4 and 5 with the cell names adjusted for the new row numbers. For example, because J. Fritz's data is stored in row 4, the gross pay formula must be changed to refer to the values stored in row 4 instead of row 3:

    +B4*@SUM(C4...G4)

AppleWorks includes a most useful way of copying a formula into cells with the computer automatically changing the cell references to apply to the new row or column. This is called "relative" copying.

To produce relative copies of a formula the Copy command is issued. The source cell and the destination's first and last cells are then selected. Before copying, AppleWorks will display the formula on the edit line at the bottom of the screen with the cursor placed on the first cell name. In the case of the first formula above this would be B3. You are then asked if the cell name in the copy should be left as is (No change), or have its row and column changed to reflect its new position (Relative). This process continues for each cell name until the end of the formula is reached. When Return is pressed, copies are made and entered into the selected cells, changing the cell names as requested.

If the formula in cell H3 to calculate B. Connelly's wage

```
+B3*@SUM(C3...G3)
```

is copied to cell H4 and Relative selected for each of the cell names, AppleWorks will change the resulting formula to correctly calculate J. Fritz's gross pay:

```
+B4*@SUM(C4...G4)
```

For N. Wilson's wages, calculated in cell H5, the copied formula will be:

```
+B5*@SUM(C5...G5)
```

Although this technique of copying formulas is useful for making copies into only two cells, think how much time it would save if the spreadsheet contained a larger number of employees. Another important advantage of this approach is that it avoids the possible errors that would be made if you were required to type each copy separately, changing the cell names each time.

When a spreadsheet becomes large it is helpful to view the many formulas it may contain at their cell locations. This can be accomplished by using the Zoom command, `Open-Apple Z`. When this command is issued AppleWorks displays the formula stored in each cell, rather than its value. To return to the regular screen press `Open-Apple Z` again.

Practice 4

In this Practice you will store relative copies of the wage formula in cell H3 in cells H4 and H5 for the Payroll spreadsheet. Start AppleWorks and load Payroll if you have not done so already.

1) ISSUE COPY COMMAND

a. Place the cell cursor on cell H3.
b. Press `Open-Apple C`.
c. Select 'Within worksheet'.
d. Press Return to select H3 as the source.
e. Press down-arrow to move the cell cursor to cell H4 and type a period.
f. Press down-arrow to move the cursor to H5 and press Return.

2) CHOOSE RELATIVE COPIES OF CELL NAMES

a. The formula in cell H3 will appear on the edit line at the bottom of the screen with its first cell name, B3, highlighted. In response to the prompt

    `Reference to B3?` **No change**   `Relative`

    press R to select 'Relative'.
b. The next cell name in the formula, C3, will be highlighted. In response to the prompt

    `Reference to C3?` **No change**   `Relative`

    select 'Relative'.
c. The third cell name in the formula, G3, will be highlighted. In response to the prompt

    `Reference to G3?` **No change**   `Relative`

    select 'Relative'. Relative copies of the gross pay formula are placed in the destination cells, and the gross pay displayed for all three employees.

3) VIEW FORMULAS

Press Open-Apple Z. The formulas stored in each cell are displayed, up to the column's width:

```
Gross Pay
------------
+B3*@SUM(C3.
+B4*@SUM(C4.
+B5*@SUM(C5.
```

The complete formula can be seen in the cell indicator.

4) RETURN TO REGULAR SCREEN

Press Open-Apple Z. The formulas are replaced on screen by the values they calculate.

5) SAVE PAYROLL ON DISK

Press Open-Apple S.

Check - The gross pay for J. Fritz and N. Wilson will now appear in cells H4 and H5:

```
File: Payroll                  REVIEW/ADD/CHANGE           Escape: Main Menu
========B=========C=========D=========E=========F=========G=========H==========I===
   1|   Rate/Hr      Mon       Tue       Wed      Thurs      Fri    Gross Pay
   2|----------------------------------------------------------------------------
   3|    $4.75       6.0       7.5       3.0       8.0       7.0    $149.62
   4|    $5.00       5.0       8.0       6.0       5.0       7.5    $173.25
   5|    $7.65       6.5       7.0       0.0       8.0       8.0    $225.68
   6|
   7|
   8|
   9|
  10|
  11|
  12|
  13|
  14|
  15|
  16|
  17|
  18|
--------------------------------------------------------------------------------
H3: (Value, Layout-D2) +B3*@SUM(C3...G3)

Type entry or use @ commands                                  @-? for Help
```

8.6 The Find Command

When working with large spreadsheets it is sometimes cumbersome to locate a particular cell or label. To assist in such a search, AppleWorks contains the Find command which is executed using Open-Apple F. Find has three options: find a specific cell (Coordinates), find a label (Text), or repeat the last Find command executed (Repeat last).

To move the cell cursor directly to a particular cell the cell name is entered at the Coordinates prompt. The cursor will then jump to the specified cell. If a second cell is to be searched for, Open-Apple Y can be used to erase the first cell name before the second name is entered.

To search for a label, the text is entered at the Comparison prompt. This will start a search from the current location of the cell cursor, across descending rows, until either the label is found or the end of the spreadsheet reached. To search the whole spreadsheet the cell cursor should first be moved to cell A1 before the Find command is issued. If a search is executed for another label, `Open-Apple Y` can be used to erase the first label before the second is entered. Searches are not case sensitive, which means that it does not matter if letters are typed in upper or lower case. Also, the search will stop if it finds the search text in any part of the labels. That is, specifying a search text of "P" will find both "Presley" and "Roper". Note that it is not possible to search for a specific value.

The Find command also allows a search to be done to find every occurrence of a label using the 'Repeat last' option. For example, if the cell cursor is moved to cell A1 and a letter "P" entered at the comparison prompt, AppleWorks will find the first label containing a "P". Each time the 'Repeat last' option is chosen the next label containing a "P" will be found. Again this feature may not be used to search for values.

Practice 5

In this Practice you will search a large spreadsheet using the Find command. Load the spreadsheet named Ivy Payroll from your data disk. This spreadsheet calculates the payroll for 25 Ivy University employees.

1) FIND CELL H29

    a. Press `Open-Apple F`.
    b. From the prompt

        `Find?` **Repeat last**   `Coordinates`   `Text`

        press C to select 'Coordinates'.
    c. In response to the prompt

        `Coordinates?`

        enter the cell name H29 and press Return. The cell cursor jumps directly to cell H29.

2) FIND CELL A1

    a. Press `Open-Apple F`.
    b. Select 'Coordinates'.
    c. Press `Open-Apple Y` to erase the old coordinates.
    d. Enter A1 and press Return. The cell cursor jumps to cell A1.

3) FIND THE TEXT "PRESLEY"

    a. Press `Open-Apple F`.
    b. Select 'Text'.
    c. In response to the prompt

        `Comparison?`

        enter `Presley` and press Return. The cell cursor will jump to cell A6 which contains the name Presley, B.

4) SEARCH FOR ALL OCCURRENCES OF THE LETTER P

   a. Move the cell cursor to cell A1.
   b. Press `Open-Apple F`.
   c. Select 'Text'.
   d. In response to the prompt, press `Open-Apple Y` to erase the old text, PRESLEY.
   e. Type a P and press Return. The cell cursor moves to the label "Gross Pay" which is the first cell in row 1 to contain a P.
   f. Press `Open-Apple F`.
   g. Select 'Repeat last'. The cell cursor moves to the label "Presley, B.", which is the next cell to contain a P.
   h. Press `Open-Apple F`.
   i. Press Return to select 'Repeat last'. The cell cursor moves to the label "Roper, M.", which is the next cell to contain a P. Note that it does not matter that the P is embedded in Roper or that it is in lower case.
   j. Press `Open-Apple F`.
   k. Select 'Repeat last'. The message

   `Couldn't find P`

   is displayed indicating that another P could not be found.
   l. Press Esc to terminate the search.

8.7 The @MAX and @MIN Functions

AppleWorks includes two functions which determine the maximum and minimum value stored in a range of cells. These functions are useful to the Ivy University accounting department in determining the highest and lowest salaries earned by its employees. The @MAX function takes the form:

   `@MAX (<range of cells>)`

For example

   `@MAX(C3...C10)`

displays the maximum value stored in the range of cells C3 to C10. The @MIN function takes the form:

   `@MIN (<range of cells>)`

For example

   `@MIN(C3...F3)`

displays the minimum value stored in the range of cells C3 to F3.

8.8 Expanding a Spreadsheet

Data can be added to the right side of a spreadsheet by simply making entries into unused columns, but this should be done with care. If data is added without thought to the overall plan, the spreadsheet will quickly become a jumble of unrelated data.

To make the Ivy Payroll spreadsheet more useful to the Ivy University accounting department we will modify it to calculate and deduct taxes and social security from each employee's gross pay. The taxes deducted will be 15% and the social security 6.5% of the gross pay. To display this data on the spreadsheet we will add three columns; Taxes, Soc. Sec., and Net Pay. Net pay is the actual pay an employee receives after deductions have been made, and is calculated by subtracting the taxes and social security from gross pay.

Practice 6

In this Practice you will add columns to Ivy Payroll which calculate taxes, social security and net pay for each of the 25 Ivy University employees. The maximum and minimum net pay will also be displayed. Start AppleWorks and load the Ivy Payroll spreadsheet if you have not already done so.

1) WIDEN COLUMNS AND ADD HEADINGS

    a. Move the cell cursor to cell I1.
    b. Press `Open-Apple L`.
    c. Select 'Columns'.
    d. Press right-arrow twice to highlight columns I, J, and K and press Return.
    e. Select 'Column width'.
    f. Hold down `Open-Apple` and press `right-arrow` 3 times. Press Return. Columns I, J, and K are now 12 characters wide.
    g. With the cell cursor on cell I1, enter the label `Taxes`.
    h. Move the cursor to cell J1 and enter the label `Soc. Sec.`
    i. Move the cell cursor to cell K1 and enter the label `Net Pay`.

2) RIGHT-JUSTIFY HEADINGS

    a. Move the cell cursor to cell I1.
    b. Press `Open-Apple L`.
    c. Select 'Block'.
    d. Press right-arrow twice to move the cell cursor to cell K1. Cells I1, J1 and K1 will be highlighted. Press Return.
    e. Select 'Label format'.
    f. Select 'Right justify'.

3) COPY THE LINE OF DASHES TO COLUMNS I, J AND K

    a. Move the cursor to cell H2 and press `Open-Apple C`.
    b. Select 'Within worksheet'.
    c. Press Return to accept H2 as the Source.
    d. Press right-arrow to highlight I2 and type a period.
    e. Press right-arrow two times to highlight the destination and press Return. The line of dashes now extends to column K.

4) FORMAT COLUMNS TO DISPLAY DOLLAR VALUES

    a. Place the cell cursor on cell I3.
    b. Press `Open-Apple L` and select 'Block'.
    c. Move the cursor to cell K30 and press Return.
    d. Select 'Value format'.
    e. Select 'Dollars', enter 2 for the number of decimal places and press Return.

5) ENTER FORMULAS FOR TAXES COLUMN

    a. Place the cell cursor on cell I3.
    b. Enter the formula

      `+H3 * .15`

    to calculate the taxes by taking 15% of the gross pay and press Return.
    c. With the cell cursor on cell I3, copy the relative formulas into cells I4 through I27 by typing `Open-Apple C`.

d. Select 'Within worksheet'.
e. Press Return to select I3 as the Source.
f. Move the cell cursor to cell I4.
g. Type a period.
h. Move the cell cursor to cell I27. Cells I4 through I27 will be highlighted. Press Return.
i. Select Relative. A 15% tax is now calculated for each employee.

6) ENTER FORMULAS FOR SOCIAL SECURITY COLUMN

a. Place the cell cursor on cell J3.
b. Enter the formula

```
+H3 * .065
```

to calculate the social security by taking 6.5% of the gross pay.
c. Repeat parts c through i from step 5 to copy the formula. Be careful to make the proper entries for column J.

7) ENTER FORMULAS TO CALCULATE NET PAY

a. Place the cell cursor on cell K3.
b. Enter the formula

```
+H3 - I3 - J3
```

to calculate the net pay by taking the gross pay minus the taxes and social security deductions.
c. Repeat parts c through i from step 5 to copy the formula. Be careful to make the proper entries for column K.

8) DETERMINE MAXIMUM AND MINIMUM NET PAY

a. Move the cell cursor to cell J29.
b. Type the label `Min pay =`.
c. Move the cell cursor to cell K29.
d. Enter the function:

```
@MIN(K3...K27)
```

Note that a value of $58.88 is displayed.
e. Move the cell cursor to cell J30.
f. Type the label `Max pay =`.
g. Move the cell cursor to cell K30.
h. Enter the function:

```
@MAX(K3...K27)
```

Note that a value of $273.38 is displayed.

9) SAVE IVY PAYROLL

Press `Open-Apple S` to save the modified version of Ivy Payroll on disk.

<u>Check</u> - The last 2 rows of Ivy Payroll should contain the values:

```
Total =    $4,941.01              Min pay =       $58.88
                                  Max pay =      $273.38
```

8.9 Using the @IF Function

It is sometimes desirable to have simple decisions made based upon the data stored in a spreadsheet. In AppleWorks such a decision is made using the @IF function. The decision is based on a comparison entered into the function. If the comparison is true one value is placed in the cell; if not, a second value is used. The @IF function has the form:

```
@IF (<comparison>, <value1>, <value2>)
```

For example,

```
@IF(C5 = E7, 10, 20)
```

will store a value of 10 in the current cell if the value in cell C5 equals the value in cell E7, and a 20 if it does not.

The comparison part of the @IF function can contain one of the following logical comparisons:

=	equals
<	less than
>	greater than
<=	less than or equal to
>=	greater than or equal to
<>	not equal to

The following are examples of valid @IFs:

```
@IF(N1 <= 25, 50, 100)
@IF(B2 < K25, 0, B2*.15)
@IF(C10 > @MIN(C3...C8), C12, C14)
@IF(D22 <> F25, 0, @SUM(E1...E10))
```

The @IF function can be used by Ivy University's accounting department to calculate two tax brackets rather than one in the Ivy Payroll spreadsheet. For example, if an employee's gross pay exceeds $250, 25% should be deducted for taxes. If the gross pay is less than or equal to $250, 15% should be deducted. To recalculate all of the salaries by hand for the two tax brackets would be quite a job. Happily this can easily be done using the @IF function. Another advantage of our computerized spreadsheet is that when the taxes are recalculated the net pay will also be recalculated automatically.

To calculate B. Connelly's taxes to take into account the two tax brackets we will replace the formula in cell I3 with

```
@IF(H3 > 250, H3*.25, H3*.15)
```

This formula states that if the gross pay stored in cell H3 is greater than 250, multiply it by .25. If the value stored in H3 is less than or equal to 250 multiply it by .15.

Practice 7

In this Practice you will change the formulas in column I to allow for two brackets in calculating each employee's taxes. Start AppleWorks and load Ivy Payroll if you have not already done so.

1) ENTER NEW TAX FORMULA

   a. Move the cell cursor to cell I3.

   b. Enter the formula:

```
@IF(H3 > 250, H3*.25, H3*.15)
```

2) COPY NEW FORMULA TO CELLS I4 THROUGH I27

   a. Make sure the cursor is on cell I3 and press `Open-Apple C`.
   b. Select 'Within worksheet'.
   c. Press Return to select cell I3 as the Source.
   d. Move the cell cursor to cell I4 and type a period.
   e. Move the cell cursor to cell I27 and press Return.
   f. Select 'Relative' 3 times for each of the cell names in the function.

Now all employees earning more than $250 a week are taxed at the rate of 25% while all others are taxed at the 15% rate.

<u>Check</u> - The last 2 rows of Ivy Payroll should contain the values shown below. The Max pay value changes because J. Sowers is now taxed at the higher rate (25%):

```
Total =   $4,941.01              Min pay =         $58.88
                                 Max pay =        $238.55
```

8.10 Sorting Data - Arrange

AppleWorks allows the data in a spreadsheet to be sorted, which means arranged in order, either alphabetically or numerically. This feature is especially useful in alphabetizing columns of names or values. It is important to realize that when a column is sorted, all the data in each row is also moved. In the Ivy Payroll spreadsheet if we arrange the names alphabetically, AppleWorks will automatically shift all of the data in each row. Arranging is accomplished using the Arrange command `Open-Apple A`.

The Arrange command will sort the spreadsheet based on the column the cell cursor is located in when the command is executed. A prompt will ask what rows are to be arranged and then whether to sort them alphabetically from A to Z or from Z to A, or numerically for values from 0 to 9 or 9 to 0. If the cell cursor is located in column A of Ivy Payroll when `Open-Apple A` is typed, the spreadsheet is sorted by name. If the cell cursor is located in column B, it is sorted by payrate, and so on. If the spreadsheet is saved after it has been sorted, it will retain the order the next time it is loaded.

There is, however, a problem when arranging spreadsheets which contain formulas that reference a column, or part of a column. When AppleWorks arranges a column, it also changes the cell references in any formulas which refer to that column. For example, in the small spreadsheet below

```
      |====A====
   1|           2
   2|           1
   3|           3
   4|
   5|           6
```

cell A5 contains the formula @SUM(A1...A3). After arranging, the spreadsheet will display

```
      |====A====
   1|           1
   2|           2
   3|           3
   4|
   5|           5
```

with the formula in cell A5 now reading @SUM(A2...A3). This is because AppleWorks adjusted the first cell reference in the formula to reflect that cell's new position. Because of this, it is important to check all column formulas after arranging and modify them if necessary.

8.11 Insert and Delete

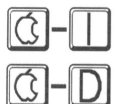

It is possible to insert or delete whole rows or columns in a spreadsheet. This is especially helpful to Ivy University when a new employee has been hired and a row must be inserted, or an old employee leaves and a row must be deleted. It is also useful when columns must be inserted between existing columns. For example, a new column to deduct pension plan contributions can be inserted between the Soc. Sec. and Net Pay columns in Ivy Payroll.

Inserting new rows or columns is accomplished using the insert command, `Open-Apple I`. Deleting is accomplished using the delete command, `Open-Apple D` and should be used with care. Once a row or column has been deleted it can not be recovered.

Practice 8

In this Practice you will first arrange the Ivy Payroll spreadsheet alphabetically. Then employee H. Crane, who says she has found a much better job, will be deleted, and a new employee, A. Nitrate, who cleans chemistry labs added. Start AppleWorks and load Ivy Payroll if you have not already done so.

1) SORT THE SPREADSHEET BY NAME

   a. Move the cell cursor to cell A3. Do not place the cell cursor on cell A1 because we do not want to include the column heading "Employee Name" in the sort.
   b. Press `Open-Apple A`.
   c. In response to the prompt

   ```
   Use cursor moves to highlight Rows, then press Return
   ```

   press down-arrow to move the cursor to row 27. All rows from 3 to 27 are highlighted. Press Return.
   d. From the menu

   ```
   Rows 3 through 27 will be arranged
   based on the contents of column A

   Arrangement order:

       1. Labels from A to Z
       2. Labels from Z to A
       3. Values from 0 to 9
       4. Values from 9 to 0
   ```

   press Return to select the default option of sorting alphabetically from A to Z. The spreadsheet will now appear with all the rows alphabetically ordered starting with Attis, B.

As described in Section 8.10, AppleWorks automatically changes the cell references in formulas when arranging rows.

   e. Change the references from row 7 to row 3 in the formulas stored in cells H29 (change H7 to H3), K29 and K30 (change K7 to K3) which were incorrectly modified by AppleWorks when the data was arranged.

2) DELETE EMPLOYEE CRANE, H.

   a. Move the cell cursor to the row containing H. Crane's data.
   b. Press `Open-Apple D`.
   c. In response to the prompt

      `Delete?` **Rows** `Columns`

      press Return to select Rows. The current row is highlighted.
   d. From the prompt

`Use cursor moves to highlight Rows, then press Return`

      press Return to delete only this row. H. Crane's data is now
      deleted and all other rows below it are moved up. All formulas
      are automatically recalculated.

3) INSERT ROW FOR NEW EMPLOYEE

   a. Move the cell cursor to row 17.
   b. Press `Open-Apple I`.
   c. In response to the prompt

      `Insert?` **Rows** `Columns`

      select Rows.
   d. In response to the prompt

      `Insert how many? (max 9)`

      type 1 and press Return. A blank row is inserted at row 17, and
      the other rows are moved down.

4) ADD AND FORMAT DATA FOR NEW EMPLOYEE

   a. Place the following data in the inserted row:

      `Nitrate, A.   5.5   6.5   7   8   2   1.5`

   b. Format the data in the new row to look like the rest of the
      spreadsheet: dollars for the pay and one fixed decimal place for
      each of the hours worked columns.

5) COPY FORMULAS TO THE NEW ROW

Note that the formulas needed to calculate A. Nitrate's salary and
deductions do not appear in the newly inserted row. The new row will
require the copying of the four formulas into columns H through K.
Rather than using four separate Copy commands, we can copy all of the
formulas at one time by defining them together as the source.

   a. Move the cursor to cell H16.
   b. Press `Open-Apple C`.
   c. Select 'Within worksheet'.
   d. Press right-arrow 3 times to highlight the Source and press
      Return.
   e. Press down-arrow to move the cursor to the Destination, cell
      H17, and press Return.
   f. For each of the cell references select 'Relative'. The new formu-
      las are copied into A. Nitrate's row and the values calculated.

6) SAVE IVY PAYROLL

      Press `Open-Apple  S` to save the modified version of Ivy
      Payroll.

<u>Check</u> - A. Nitrate's salary and deductions should be shown in row 17:

```
Gross Pay          Taxes         Soc. Sec.        Net Pay
   $137.50         $20.62           $8.94        $107.94
```

8.12 Asking "What If?"

One of the most powerful features of a spreadsheet is its ability to answer "What if?" questions. By making changes in a spreadsheet it is possible to perform calculations that make predictions based on the changes. Because spreadsheets perform such calculations rapidly, a number of different situations can be tested. This technique is widely used by businesses to predict their finances under a wide range of possible situations. For example, if an automobile manufacturer uses a spreadsheet to determine the cost of producing cars it could predict the cost under various price changes: What if the price of steel were to increase by 15%? What if the cost of labor were to increase by 6%? What if taxes were halved? The effects of such changes can be quickly calculated by entering the new information in the appropriate cell or cells. All formulas would then be automatically recalculated. It is in using a spreadsheet to produce such predictions that its calculation power is truly utilized.

Ivy University's employees have not had a raise in five years and have decided to strike if their demand for wage increases are not met. Since the budget at Ivy is already very tight, this threat has the administration concerned about how much the raises will cost. Using the Ivy Payroll spreadsheet the accounting department will do wage projections. The employees want an increase of 15% of their gross pay. Ivy plans to offer a 5% increase, but may have to compromise at 10% or may even be forced to accept the full 15%. To see how much each of these percentages will cost, three new columns will be added to the spreadsheet which calculate the new gross pay for each of the raises and the total payroll for all employees.

Practice 9

In this Practice you will answer the "What If?" question described in Section 8.12 by adding 3 columns to the Ivy Payroll spreadsheet which calculate raises of 5%, 10% and 15%. Start Apple-Works and load Ivy Payroll if you have not already done so.

1) FORMAT THE NEW COLUMNS

   a. Move the cell cursor to cell L1.
   b. Press Open-Apple L and change the width of columns L, M and N to 12 characters each.

    c. Right justify row 1 in the 3 new columns.

    d. Move the cursor to cell K2 and use `Open-Apple C` to extend the underline of dashes to include the 3 new columns.

    e. Format the block of cells from cell L3 to N30 to include dollar amounts with 2 decimal places.

2) CALCULATE 5% RAISES

    a. Enter the heading `5% Raise` into cell L1. Because this title begins with a digit, you must begin by typing a quote mark to inform the computer that a label is being entered.

    b. Enter the formula

```
+H3 * 1.05
```

    into cell L3. This formula calculates a new gross pay which is 5% higher than the original.

    c. Copy the formula from cell L3 into cells L4 through L27 using the Relative option.

3) CALCULATE 10% AND 15% RAISES

    a. Enter the heading `10% Raise` into cell M1.

    b. Repeat parts b and c of step 2 for column M using the formula `+H3 * 1.10` to properly calculate a 10% raise.

    c. Enter the heading `15% Raise` into cell N1.

    d. Repeat parts b and c of step 2 for column N using the formula `+H3 * 1.15` to properly calculate a 15% raise.

4) SUM THE NEW GROSS PAYS

    a. Blank the block of cells from J29 to K30 using `Open-Apple B`.

    b. Enter the label `Pay Raise =` into cell K29.

    c. Enter the formula

```
@SUM(L3...L27)
```

    into cell L29.

    d. Copy the formula in cell L29 to cells M29 and N29 using the Relative option.

5) CALCULATE THE INCREASED COST OF RAISES

    a. Enter the label `Raise Cost =` into cell K30.

    b. Enter the formula

```
+L29 - H29
```

    into cell L30.

    c. Copy the formula in cell L30 to cells M30 and N30 using the Relative option for the first reference, and No change for the second (H29) reference.

6) SAVE THE MODIFIED SPREADSHEET ON DISK

    Press `Open-Apple S` to save the modified Ivy Payroll on disk.

<u>Check</u> - The last two rows of the new columns should be:

```
Pay Raise  =    $5,118.70    $5,362.45    $5,606.20
Raise Cost =      $243.75      $487.50      $731.24
```

Advanced Spreadsheet Techniques

In the earlier part of this chapter we presented the most commonly used spreadsheet functions, but there are many other functions available to you. In this section we present additional functions which may be used to produce advanced spreadsheets. A complete list of functions is given in the AppleWorks Reference manual from Claris.

8.13 The @CHOOSE and @LOOKUP Functions

The @IF function allows a formula to be created which displays one value if a comparison is true, and another value if the comparison is false. The example given in Section 8.9 uses @IF to calculate tax withholdings using two different rates based on gross pay: 25% for those employees earning over $250 and 15% for all others. Suppose, however, that there were 10 or 15 different tax rates. The @IF required to calculate the tax would be extremely large and complex, and might exceed the maximum display length for formulas. To solve problems such as this, AppleWorks includes two functions which can be used to select one value from a list of many: @CHOOSE and @LOOKUP.

@CHOOSE:

The @CHOOSE function has the form

$$\text{@CHOOSE}(\text{<position>},\ \text{<value}_1\text{>},\ \text{<value}_2\text{>},\ \ldots\ \text{<value}_N\text{>})$$

where <position> is an expression that evaluates between 1 and N. @CHOOSE displays the <value> in the list which corresponds to <position>. If <position> is 1, @CHOOSE displays <value$_1$>, if it is 2 then <value$_2$> is displayed, and so on. For example, given the formula

$$\text{@CHOOSE}(A1,\ 10,\ 15,\ 20,\ 25)$$

AppleWorks displays 10 if the value stored in cell A1 is 1, 15 if the value stored in A1 is 2, 20 if the value is 3, and 25 if it is 4. If <position> is negative or greater than N (the number of possible <values>) NA is displayed, meaning that a corresponding value is not available. Note that only the integer portion of <position> is used to determine which <value> to display. If A1 stores 2.6, 15 is displayed because the 2.6 is truncated to 2. @CHOOSE could be used to calculate multiple tax rates by assigning each employee a numeric code between 1 and N which signifies which tax rate to use.

@LOOKUP:

@LOOKUP is similar to @CHOOSE except that the <values> to be displayed are stored in cells in the spreadsheet, not listed in the function itself. This has two advantages; first, because they are in cells, the values may be calculated instead of being constants. Second, the values may be printed with the spreadsheet showing the table used. @LOOKUP has the form

$$\text{@LOOKUP}(\text{<position value>},\ \text{<range>})$$

where <position value> is a numeric expression and <range> is the cell range where the values to be displayed by LOOKUP are stored. When evaluated, AppleWorks finds the largest number in <range> which is less than or equal to <position value>, and then displays the value which is stored adjacent to that cell. This is similar to the manual operation of looking up a value in a table: the first column is searched for the desired data, then the value read from the adjacent column. As an example, assume the following spreadsheet fragment:

	B	C
1	1	10
2	2	15
3	3	20
4	4	25
5	5	30

Given the function

```
@LOOKUP(A1, B1...B5)
```

if cell A1 stores the value 1, then 10 is displayed. This is because cell B1 stores the largest value which is less than or equal to 1 so @LOOKUP displays the value stored in the cell that is adjacent to B1, the 10 in cell C1. If A1 stores 3.5, this function would display 20, because cell B3 stores the largest value in <range> which is less than or equal to 3.5. (If A1 stored the value 0, NA would be displayed.)

Note that the values in <range> must be in ascending order for @LOOKUP to work correctly. If the <position value> is less than the first value stored in <range> NA is displayed. For this reason it is important to make the first value in <range> less than any value that will be looked up. If <position value> is larger than the last value in <range>, the last value in the lookup table is displayed. For example, if A1 stores 100, the function above would display 30. @LOOKUP differs from @CHOOSE in that the <position value> may be negative or zero as long as it is greater than or equal to one of the values stored in <range>.

Assume that a payroll spreadsheet is to calculate withholding using the 7 tax rates shown below:

Gross Pay	Tax Rate
under $150	0%
$150-$199	8%
$200-$249	10%
$250-$299	12%
$300-$349	17%
$350-$599	28%
$600-up	33%

If gross pay were calculated in cell H1, the function

```
+H1 * @LOOKUP(H1, Y1...Y7)
```

would properly calculate withholding if the tax lookup table was stored in the spreadsheet as:

	Y	Z
1	0	0
2	150	0.08
3	200	0.10
4	250	0.12
5	300	0.17
6	350	0.28
7	600	0.33

8.14 Splitting Windows and Freezing Titles

A problem encountered when working with large spreadsheets is that as you scroll across or down the spreadsheet the titles in row 1 or the labels in column A scroll off the screen making it difficult to determine what columns or rows displayed cells are in. Another problem with large spreadsheets is that it is sometimes difficult to compare data from distant parts of the spreadsheet. AppleWorks solves these problems by allowing you to "freeze" columns so they may not be scrolled off the screen and to split the spreadsheet screen into two different windows that can each view separate parts of the spreadsheet.

The Titles command, `Open-Apple T`, can lock columns or rows on the screen so that they will always be displayed - scrolling does not affect them. To freeze the top rows of a spreadsheet, place the cursor beneath the rows that are to be frozen and execute the Titles command. The following options are displayed:

`Titles?` **`Top`** `Left side   Both`

Selecting the 'Top' option eliminates scrolling of the upper rows; they will now remain on the screen. Similarly, columns to the left of the cursor can be frozen so that they are not scrolled off the screen by selecting 'Left', or a combination of rows and columns can be frozen using the 'Both' option. To remove frozen titles, execute the Titles command again and choose 'None'.

AppleWorks also allows you to split the screen into two windows so that you can view two separate parts of the spreadsheet at the same time. This is useful for viewing the results of calculations that use data entered in a distant portion of the spreadsheet. You can enter the data in one window and immediately see the results in the other window.

To split the screen into two windows execute the Windows command, `Open-Apple W`. AppleWorks then gives you two options:

`Windows?` **`Side by side`** `Top and bottom`

Selecting 'Side by side' creates a vertical line at the position of the cursor which splits the screen into two windows. Each shows the same spreadsheet, but the windows can be scrolled independently. Selecting 'Top and bottom' creates a horizontal line at the position of the cursor with one window above it and one below. These two windows can now be scrolled independently. To move the cursor from one window to the other, the Jump command, `Open-Apple J`, is executed.

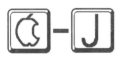

The new windows can be synchronized so that they are scrolled together. With two vertical windows (the result of selecting Side by side) this means that the rows in one window move with the rows in the other window. With two horizontal windows (the result of selecting Top and bottom) this means that the columns in both windows move together. Synchronizing windows is accomplished by executing the Windows command, `Open-Apple W`, again after the windows have already been split and selecting the 'Synchronized' option. Windows are unsynchronized by choosing 'Unsynchronized'. To remove the split and return to having only one window, press `Open-Apple W` and choose 'One'.

Practice 10

In this Practice you will modify the Ivy Payroll spreadsheet to include a retirement deduction which allows employees to contribute different percentages of their salaries. This will be done using the @CHOOSE function. An advantage to employees of contributing to the retirement plan is that they do not have to pay taxes on the contribution. The spreadsheet will also be modified to allow for seven tax rates using the @LOOKUP function. Frozen titles will be used to keep the employee names and column titles on the screen.

1) OPEN THE IVY PAYROLL SPREADSHEET

2) FREEZE EMPLOYEE NAMES

   a. Move the cursor to cell B3.
   b. Press `Open-Apple T` to execute the Titles command and select Both. The employee names to the left of the cell cursor and column titles above it will now remain on the screen when the spreadsheet is scrolled.

3) INSERT COLUMNS TO CALCULATE RETIREMENT

   a. Insert two new columns at columns I and J and increase their widths to 12.
   b. Title column I `Retire Code` and column J `Retirement`.
   c. Right justify the labels in cells I1 and J1.
   d. Extend the dashes in row 2 to cells I2 and J2 using the Copy command.

4) ENTER THE RETIREMENT CODES

   There are five retirement codes numbered 1 through 5 which determine the percentage of gross pay that will be deducted for each employee.

   Enter the following numbers in the cells indicated:

Cell	Code	Cell	Code	Cell	Code
I3	1	I12	4	I20	2
I4	3	I13	2	I21	3
I5	2	I14	1	I22	1
I6	4	I15	3	I23	4
I7	2	I16	2	I24	3
I8	2	I17	1	I25	2
I9	5	I18	5	I26	2
I10	3	I19	2	I27	5
I11	3				

5) ENTER THE @CHOOSE FUNCTION TO CALCULATE RETIREMENT

   Each of the codes above correspond to the following percentages which will be used to calculate the retirement deduction:

Code	Percentage
1	0%
2	2%
3	5%
4	8%
5	10%

a. Enter the following function in cell J3:

```
@CHOOSE(I3, 0, .02*H3, .05*H3, .08*H3, .1*H3)
```

b. Use the Copy command to produce appropriate functions for the rest of column J.

c. Format column J for dollars with two decimal places using the Layout command.

6) CALCULATE TAXES USING THE @LOOKUP FUNCTION

The following tax rates will be used in calculating taxes:

Salary	Tax Rate
under $150	0%
$150-$199	8%
$200-$249	10%
$250-$299	12%
$300-$349	17%
$350-$599	28%
$600-up	33%

a. The tax table will be stored in cells R2 through S8. Enter the label Tax Table in cell R1.

b. Enter the following values into the indicated cells to create the tax table:

Cell	Salary	Cell	Tax Value
R2	0	S2	0
R3	150	S3	0.08
R4	200	S4	0.1
R5	250	S5	0.12
R6	300	S6	0.17
R7	350	S7	0.28
R8	600	S8	0.33

c. Enter the formula

```
@LOOKUP(H3-J3, R2...R8) * (H3-J3)
```

into cell K3. Note that taxes are based on the gross pay minus the deduction for retirement.

d. Use Copy to complete the calculations in column K.

7) RECALCULATE NET PAY AND SAVE THE SPREADSHEET

a. Enter the formula:

```
+H3 - J3 - K3 - L3
```

into cell M3.

b. Use Copy to recalculate the cells in column M. The new net pay is displayed.

c. Press Open-Apple S to save the modified file on disk.

8.15 Amortization Tables

One of the most useful applications of a spreadsheet is to produce an amortization table which displays how much interest and principal is paid on each payment of an installment loan. Principal paid is the amount of a loan that has been paid back. For example, the payment made each month on a 30 year loan of $150,000 borrowed at an interest rate of 10% is $1,316.36. On the first payment made $1,250.00 goes to paying the interest on the loan and $66.36 goes to reducing principal (i.e., the amount owed). On the 50th payment $1,216.70 goes to paying interest and $99.65 to reducing principal.

The @PMT function is used to calculate the periodic payments for an installment loan when given the interest rate, the number of payments to be made, and the amount of the loan (principal). It takes the form:

@PMT (<rate>, <term>, <principal>)

where

rate: the interest rate per period

term: the number of payments to be made

principal: the amount of the loan

As an example, if you borrow $150,000 to purchase a home at an interest rate of 10% for 30 years the function will be:

@PMT(.1 / 12, 360, 150000)

Note the yearly interest rate is divided by 12 to calculate the monthly rate. The number of payments is 360, 30 years * 12 months. When calculated @PMT returns a value of approximately -1316.36, the negative sign indicating that payment is to be made rather than received.

Practice 11

In this Practice you will complete an amortization table in a spreadsheet named LOAN which displays the interest and principal paid on the payments made on a loan. Start Works if you have not already done so and open LOAN.

1) ADD THE LOAN SPREADSHEET TO THE DESKTOP

2) ENTER THE LOAN'S INFORMATION

  a. Enter the principal, 150000 in cell B3.
  b. Enter the yearly interest rate, .1 in cell B4.
  c. Enter the number of payments, 360 (30 years * 12 monthly payments) in cell B5.

3) CALCULATE THE MONTHLY PAYMENT

  Enter the formula

    -@PMT(B4 / 12, B5, B3)

  into cell B7. The division by 12 is needed to convert the yearly interest rate in cell B4 to a monthly value. The negative sign is used so that the amount of the payment will be positive.

4) ENTER THE FIRST PAYMENT DATA

  a. Enter the number 1 in cell A11.
  b. Enter +B3 in cell B11 to display the original principal.
  c. In cell C11, enter +B11 * (B4 / 12) to calculate one month's interest on the loan. The value 1250 is displayed.

    d. To calculate the amount of the payment which is applied to the principal, enter the formula +B7 — C11 in cell D11.

    e. To calculate the new principal, enter the formula +B11 — D11 in cell E11.

5) ENTER FORMULAS FOR THE SECOND PAYMENT

    a. Enter the formula +A11 + 1 in cell A12.

    b. To display the new principal, enter +E11 in cell B12.

    c. Use the Copy command (Open-Apple C) to copy the formulas in cell C11 through E11 into cells C12 through E12. Make sure that the references to cells B4 and B7 are not changed, but all others are relative.

    d. Format the block of cells from B11 to E12 to display dollar amounts with 2 decimal places. The new principal $149,866.73 should be displayed in cell E12.

6) COMPLETE THE TABLE USING COPY

Use the Copy command to copy cells A12 through E12 into rows 13 through 370. This can be done in one step by selecting A12 through E12 as the source and highlighting cells A13 to E370 as the destination. Make sure that the references to cells B4 and B7 are not changed, but all others are relative. Because of the large number of cells and formulas involved, it will take a moment for the computer to recalculate the spreadsheet.

7) SAVE THE TABLE ON DISK

Press Open-Apple S to save the modified LOAN spreadsheet on disk.

Check - The final rows in your spreadsheet should be similar to:

```
Total Payment  =   $473,888.65
Principal      =   $150,000.00
Total Interest =   $323,888.65      $323,888.65
```

Note that at the end of the 360th payment that the new principal is 0. Total Interest is calculated twice, once by subtracting the principal from the total amount paid, and once by summing the Interest column payments. The fact that these figures agree is a check of the validity of the spreadsheet.

This spreadsheet is now a "template" which may be used to calculate the payments on any 30 year loan. Experiment by changing the principal and interest rate values in cells B3 and B4 to see the effects on the monthly payment and the total amount of interest paid. What changes would have to be made to the template to have it calculate 10 or 20 year loans?

8.16 Where can you go from here?

The last two chapters introduced you to the concepts of a spreadsheet: how one is designed, created on the computer and used to produce calculations. There are other AppleWorks spreadsheet options we have not discussed which you may want to learn about. Reading the spreadsheet sections in the AppleWorks manuals is a good place to start.

Spreadsheets may be used to store laboratory data to produce scientific and statistical calculations as well as financial calculations. There are larger and more powerful spreadsheet programs available with names such as Lotus 1-2-3, Excel and Quattro which include many advanced calculating features. Although more complicated to use, these spreadsheet programs are similar to the AppleWorks program you have used and would look familiar to you in many ways. Because you have learned the AppleWorks spreadsheet, you will be able to easily learn and use other spreadsheet software.

There is little doubt that the use of spreadsheets will grow to include almost every type of endeavor that makes use of numbers. The introduction you have had should be helpful to you when you encounter these other applications, either in school or on the job.

Chapter Summary

Large spreadsheets require careful planning so that they can be modified and expanded. Consideration must be given to the placement of columns so that related data is located in adjacent columns. The layout of a spreadsheet is modified using the Layout command, Open-Apple L to change the width and display format of cells.

Often the same label, value or formula must be stored in a number of cells. The Copy command, Open-Apple C, can be used to copy what is stored in a cell across a row or down a column of cells. One of its most useful applications is in copying formulas. This can be done using the Relative copy option which changes the cell names in the copies to reflect the new rows or columns they are in.

The Find command, Open-Apple F, can be used to move the cursor to a particular cell by giving its cell name. It can also search for a label, a series of characters, or each occurrence of them.

The @MAX and @MIN functions display the maximum or minimum value stored in a range of cells.

Decisions can be performed based on data in a spreadsheet using the @IF command. If a comparison is true the first action in the command is taken, if not true the second action is taken.

Data in a spreadsheet can be arranged alphabetically or numerically using the Arrange command, Open-Apple A. When arranged all the data in each row is shifted automatically.

New columns or rows can be inserted into a spreadsheet using the Insert command, Open-Apple I. Old columns or rows can be deleted using the Delete command, Open-Apple D.

A spreadsheet can be used to answer What If? questions. By changing the data in a spreadsheet it is possible to produce calculations that make predictions based on the changes.

The @CHOOSE and @LOOKUP functions are used to select a value from a list. Choose includes the values as part of the function, while @LOOKUP uses a table stored in another part of the spreadsheet. The @PMT function calculates the periodic payment on an installment loan given the interest rate, principal and number of payments.

Vocabulary

Arrange - To organize (sort) rows of data based upon the value stored in one column, in either alphabetic or numeric order: `Open-Apple A`.

Destination - Where copied or moved data is placed.

Layout - The design of a spreadsheet including the placement of data in its rows and columns, column widths and the use of formatting: `Open-Apple L`.

Pointing - Moving the cell cursor to specify cell names in formulas.

Relative copy - Copying formulas in a spreadsheet so that the cell names reflect the new rows and columns they are in.

Sort - See arrange.

Source - Where the data to be copied is stored.

What If? question - Performing calculations to make predictions based upon the data stored in a spreadsheet.

Reviews

Sections 8.1-8.3

1. What factors should be considered when planning the layout of a spreadsheet?

2. Sketch a layout for a spreadsheet that will contain the inventory for an automobile dealership. The spreadsheet should include the names of the different automobile models, the number of each model in stock, and the price of each model. Show the width of each column and tell whether it stores a value or a label.

3. What will be displayed if a cell is not wide enough to display the value it stores?

4. a) What option of the Layout command must be used to format a column of dollar values that will have a label heading?
   b) Why must this option be used?

5. a) What is usually the best way to enter the range of a formula on a large spreadsheet?
   b) What is the primary advantage of using this method?

Section 8.4-8.6

6. What steps must be taken to copy the label PAID from cell C1 to the range of cells C20 through C32?

7. What is meant by the term "relative" copying? Give an example.

8. What steps must be taken to copy the formula

   `@AVG(C6...C20)`

   stored in cell C22, into the range of cells D22 to G22 so that the formula correctly calculates the average for each column?

9. What is the fastest way to move the cell cursor from cell A1 to cell Z14?

10. a) What steps must be taken to find each label in a spreadsheet that contains the name Harry?
    b) What is displayed if a search is performed for a label that does not appear in a spreadsheet?

11. Which of the following labels would be found in a repeated search for the characters PO?

```
pox
Oprah
Porter
opposite
Hoppy
```

Sections 8.7-8.9

12. a) Write a formula that will calculate the maximum value stored in the range of cells D5 to Y5.
b) Write a formula that will calculate the minimum value stored in the range of cells D5 to Y5.

13. Write formulas that perform each of the following:

a) Store 50 in the current cell if the value stored in D20 equals the value in C90, or 25 if they are not equal.
b) Store the value contained in B50 in the current cell if the sum of the range of cells C30 to C430 exceeds 1000, otherwise store a 0.
c) Store the value of X20 * 10 in the current cell if X20 is less than 30; otherwise store just X20's value.

Sections 8.10-8.12

14. What steps must be taken to arrange the Ivy Payroll spreadsheet so that the employees are listed in order by net pay, with the employee with the highest pay displayed first?

15. What steps must be taken to delete the Net Pay column from Ivy Payroll?

16. What steps must be taken to insert a column titled Sat into Ivy Payroll that follows the column titled Fri?

17. a) Explain what is meant by a "What if?" question.
b) How can a spreadsheet be used to answer "What if?" questions?

18. Make a list of 5 "What if?" questions that could be answered using the Ivy Payroll spreadsheet.

Sections 8.13-8.15

19. Write a CHOOSE function which displays 100 if cell B20 contains the value 0, 500 if it is a 1, 900 if a 2 and 1200 if a 3.

20. The Lawrenceville Widget company uses the following discount rate when large numbers of widgets are ordered:

Number of Widgets	Discount %
100 - 499	10%
500 - 999	30%
1000 - 1999	50%
2000 and over	70%

Write a LOOKUP function that can be used to display the proper discount percent if cell C12 stores the number or ordered widgets. In a labeled diagram show the contents of the lookup table.

21. Write a PMT function which returns the montly payment on a 5 year loan of $13,500 at an annual interest rate of 12%.

Exercises

1. The Ivy University Prom Committee has decided to use a spreadsheet to determine how much it must charge each student attending the Prom so that it will not lose money. Below are listed the costs of each item based upon 50 students attending the prom:

```
File: Prom                     REVIEW/ADD/CHANGE              Escape: Main Menu
===========A=============B============C=============D=============E======
   1|Expenses         50 students
   2|
   3|Band              $1,500.00
   4|Decorations         $185.00
   5|Print tickets        $73.15
   6|Electricity          $50.00
   7|Advertising         $182.00
   8|Clean up             $78.00
   9|Cake                 $56.00
  10|Sodas               $111.00
  11|Cookies              $34.50
  12|Ice cream           $150.00
  13|
  14|Cost/Student =       $48.39
  15|
  16|
  17|
  18|
-------------------------------------------------------------------------
A15

Type entry or use @ commands                            @-? for Help
```

a) Create a new spreadsheet named Prom similar to the one above which calculates the cost per ticket when 50 students attend the prom. All of the costs are summed and the total divided by the number of students to produce the cost per student. Save the spreadsheet on disk when complete.

b) In columns C, D and E calculate the cost per ticket when 100, 150 or 200 students attend. Consider the following when adding these columns:

(1) The expenses for Band through Clean up remain the same no matter how many students attend the prom. Be careful to set up these values in the new columns so that if the value in column A is changed it will also change in the other columns. For example, if Band is changed to $785.50 in column A, it should also appear as $785.50 in the three new columns.

(2) The values for Cake through Ice Cream change depending on how many students attend the prom. Therefore the cost for Cake for 50 students must be multiplied by 2 to calculate the cost for 100 students, by 3 to calculate the cost for 150 students, and so on. The values for Sodas, Cookies and Ice Cream are calculated similarly.

Your spreadsheet should be similar to the following:

```
/ File: Prom                    REVIEW/ADD/CHANGE              Escape: Main Menu
==========A============B============C============D============E=======
   1|Expenses      50 students  100 students  150 students  200 students
   2|
   3|Band            $1,500.00     $1,500.00     $1,500.00      $1,500.00
   4|Decorations       $185.00       $185.00       $185.00        $185.00
   5|Print tickets      $73.15        $73.15        $73.15         $73.15
   6|Electricity        $50.00        $50.00        $50.00         $50.00
   7|Advertising       $182.00       $182.00       $182.00        $182.00
   8|Clean up           $78.00        $78.00        $78.00         $78.00
   9|Cake               $56.00       $112.00       $168.00        $224.00
  10|Sodas             $111.00       $222.00       $333.00        $444.00
  11|Cookies            $34.50        $69.00       $103.50        $138.00
  12|Ice cream         $150.00       $300.00       $450.00        $600.00
  13|
  14|Cost/Student =     $48.39        $27.71        $20.82         $17.37
  15|
  16|
  17|
  18|
------------------------------------------------------------------------
A15

Type entry or use @ commands                              @-? for Help
```

c) Perform the following What if? questions using your prom spreadsheet and then save it on disk:

(1) The Ivy student body is unhappy about most of the prom plans. They hate the band, The Poison Ivy's. Many students want the Dreadful Greats instead, but they will cost $3,500. Calculate the cost per student with the new band.

(2) Many students think serving cookies at a prom is not very sophisticated. Calculate the costs with Cookies set to 0 and Cake and Ice Cream doubled.

(3) A group of students does not want to hold the prom in Ivy Hall which the school will let them use if they pay for electricity and clean up. These students want to hold the prom at the Newton Hilton which will cost $7,000. Add a row to your spreadsheet to include the new hotel cost and delete the rows for Electricity and Clean up because these costs are included in the Hilton's fee.

2. On your data disk is a spreadsheet named Stock2 which stores the names, purchase price and number of shares for stocks owned by Grace van Ivy, a relative of Ivy University's founder. Assist her by producing the following calculations in the spreadsheet. Note that columns D through G are 15 characters wide and formatted to display dollar values.

a) Add the title Original Value to column D and calculate the original value of each stock. The original value is calculated by multiplying the shares bought by the purchase price.

b) At the bottom of column D calculate the total paid for all stock.

c) Ms. van Ivy wants to know how much money she has made or lost on each stock. Below is listed the current price per share for each stock:

Alex Car Wash	$23.12
American Exp.	$120.45
Freitas Fries	$30.12
Giorgio Pizza	$89.78
International	$45.23
Ivy Newspapers	$14.00
Jane's Cakes	$56.89
Johnson Co.	$45.32
Lucky Stores	$20.67
Mad Music Co.	$67.39
Mercedes Birdfood	$79.50
Micheal's Auto	$45.35
Photo Magic	$1.20
Ronald Indust.	$10.45
Sam's Pancakes	$67.00
Taco Willies	$15.89
Tasco Foods	$90.00
Zanadu Clothes	$123.45

Add the title Current Price to column E and display the current price per share. Save the spreadsheet on disk.

d) Add the title Current Value to column F and calculate the current value of each stock. Current value is found by multiplying the number of shares by the current price. Sum column F to find the current total value of the stocks.

e) Ms. van Ivy wants to know what stocks have gained in value and which ones have lost in value. Add a column G titled Gain or Loss and calculate the gain or loss of each stock by subtracting the original value from the current value. Note that AppleWorks displays negative dollar amounts by enclosing them in parentheses.

f) Ms. van Ivy has decided that it would be best to sell the poorest performing stocks. She wants to know which stocks have lost more than 30% of their original value. Add a column H named Stock Status which uses @IF statements to display 0's for stocks that should be sold or 1's for stocks that should be retained. Be careful in creating the @IF statements.

g) When she sells stock, Ms. Ivy pays a commission to her stock broker based on the following scale:

Number of Shares	Commission %
0 - 29	5%
30 - 69	4%
70 - 99	2%
100 - 149	1%
150 and over	0.5%

The commission is calculated by multipying the current value of the stock by the commission percent. Add a column titled Commission which displays the sales commission on each of Ms. Ivy's stocks. Use a lookup table to calculate the commission.

h) Save the modified spreadsheet on disk.

3. Fantasy Wheels Used Cars wants to use a spreadsheet to keep track of its inventory. The spreadsheet should record the year and model of each car for sale, and the price Fantasy paid for it. Fantasy will use the spreadsheet to determine how much to charge for each car (the selling price). Here is a partial list of Fantasy's inventory. Be imaginative and add three of your own cars to the list:

1972 Corvette price paid: $8,500	1978 Rolls Royce price paid: $34,460
1984 Ferrari price paid: $22,340	1967 Mustang price paid: $11,230
1985 Porsche price paid: $31,000	1958 Cadillac price paid: $8,895
1955 Studebaker price paid: $950	1948 Bentley price paid: $49,500
1957 Bel Aire price paid: $1,250	1988 Jaguar price paid: $24,650
1975 Aston-Martin price paid: $56,700	1968 GTO price paid: $12,000
1978 Triumph price paid: $4,560	1985 DeLorean price paid: $28,999
1958 Thunderbird price paid: $14,000	1978 Bricklin price paid: $36,200

a) Carefully design your spreadsheet using paper and pencil. Take into consideration all of the ways the spreadsheet will be used. In your plan make separate columns for each of three possible selling prices: 10% markup over price paid, 20% markup and 35% markup.

b) Using the design from part (a) create a new spreadsheet named Cars and enter the above data. Use proper formatting and labels. Display the following on your spreadsheet:

(1) total of prices paid for inventory
(2) average price paid per car
(3) total of the selling prices for all three markups
(4) profit for each car when it sells at the 20% markup price.
(5) total profit if all of the cars were to sell at the 20% markup price.

c) The Corvette has been sold. Delete its row from the data base. Be sure to modify any formulas that might need to be changed.

d) Fantasy has acquired two new cars. Add the following data to the spreadsheet, being sure to modify any formulas that might need to be changed:

> 1987 Honda
> price paid: $6,500
>
> 1986 Jeep
> price paid: $5,350

e) Fantasy is having a sale on all cars built before 1970. Create a properly formatted column titled Sale which displays only a 7.5% markup on the price paid if the car is on sale, and 0 if it is not.

f) Create a properly formatted column titled Sale Profit which displays the <u>profit</u> that Fantasy would earn if all of the pre-1970 cars sold at the 7.5% markup price described in part (e). Total this column.

g) Fantasy has decided to determine the markup of its cars based on each car's condition. A rating system will be used of from 1 to 5. The rating for each car is shown below:

Type	Cars
1	Studebaker, Thunderbird, DeLorean, Bricklin
2	Mustang, Jaguar, Honda, Jeep
3	Ferarri, Aston-Martin, Triumph, GTO
4	Bel Aire, Rolls Royce, Cadillac
5	Porsche, Bentley

Create a column titled Rating which stores each car's rating.

h) The percent (%) mark up for each rating is listed below:

Rating	% markup
1	10%
2	20%
3	35%
4	50%
5	75%

Create a column titled Rating Markup which displays the price of each car after its markup. Use the @CHOOSE function to produce this column.

i) Save the modified Cars spreadsheet on your data disk.

4. Your friend, Mike Entrepreneurial, is opening a lawn mowing service and wants you to set up a spreadsheet named Lawn for his business.

a) Using paper and pencil, design the spreadsheet so that Mike can enter his customers' names, and the lengths and widths of their lawns in feet. Have the computer display lawn area and the price of cutting the lawn. Mike charges $0.002 per square foot. Be careful to properly format each column.

b)   Using the design from part (a), create the spreadsheet on the computer. Include data for a minimum of 15 customers. Display the total income Mike receives from mowing all his customer's lawns and the average income per lawn.

c)   Mike would like to increase his profit. He wants to ask "What if?" questions about raising his prices. Modify the spreadsheet so that he need only change one entry to raise his price per square foot. Determine what happens to his total income when he doubles and triples his prices.

d)   Mike's customers who have large lawns are complaining bitterly about his prices. In response to the complaints he has decided that all customers with lawns of less than 20,000 square feet will pay $0.003 per square foot and those with larger lawns will pay $0.002 per square foot. Use @IF statements to calculate the price each customer will pay.

e)   Mike must pay taxes on the price he charges so he wants the following tax table built into the spreadsheet:

Price in Dollars	Tax %
0 -- 14	0
15 -- 39	5
40 -- 59	7
60 -- 99	12
100 -- 199	15
200 and above	30

Add a column titled Taxes which displays the taxes Mike must pay for each of his customers. Use a lookup table to produce the calculations.

f)   Mike would like to give better service to his customers who pay the most. Arrange the spreadsheet in descending order (high to low) based on the price to cut each lawn.

g)   Save the spreadsheet on disk when complete.

5.   You have been given an assignment in science class to record the average yearly temperature for your city for the last 50 years. You can find this information in an almanac or at the town library or use the example data given below:

Year	Temp	Year	Temp	Year	Temp
1939	64	1956	49	1973	69
1940	73	1957	54	1974	74
1941	62	1958	65	1975	80
1942	51	1959	53	1976	76
1943	66	1960	55	1977	68
1944	55	1961	63	1978	59
1945	67	1962	75	1979	58
1946	78	1963	67	1980	67
1947	76	1964	76	1981	72
1948	65	1965	58	1982	65
1949	64	1966	69	1983	64
1950	53	1967	70	1984	58

1951	54	1968	65	1985	67
1952	65	1969	56	1986	68
1953	74	1970	57	1987	74
1954	73	1971	72	1988	73
1955	65	1972	70	1989	71

a) Create a spreadsheet named Temp which shows the year and average temperature for the last 50 years. Use proper formatting and labels. To save typing, use a formula and the relative Copy command to display the year.

Add formulas to the spreadsheet which calculate each of the following and then save the spreadsheet on disk. Use proper formatting and labels:

b) The average temperature over the past 50 years.

c) The average of the first 25 years only.

d) The average of the last 25 years.

e) The minimum and maximum temperatures for the first 25 years.

f) The minimum and maximum temperatures for the last 25 years.

6. The following figures represent the data for the last 10 years for Flat Technologies, a one-product manufacturer:

Year	**Expenses**	**Units Sold**	**Price/Unit**
Year 1	$50,000.00	6,000	$14.50
Year 2	$60,000.00	7,500	$15.50
Year 3	$65,000.00	8,000	$16.00
Year 4	$75,000.00	10,000	$17.00
Year 5	$77,500.00	15,000	$17.75
Year 6	$70,000.00	14,000	$19.00
Year 7	$65,000.00	11,500	$19.00
Year 8	$63,500.00	10,250	$18.50
Year 9	$60,000.00	10,750	$18.25
Year 10	$62,500.00	11,000	$18.50

a) Create a new spreadsheet named Flat and enter the above data into it. Be sure to use proper formatting.

b) Add a column titled Profit which calculates the profit (income minus expenses) for each year.

c) Add rows to the bottom of the spreadsheet which calculate the average of the yearly expenses, unit sales, price and profit columns. Be sure to include proper labels for these figures.

d) Flat's production department has estimated that expenses will rise by 5% each year for the next five years. Insert rows showing the expense costs for the next 5 years.

e) Flat's marketing department has estimated that the unit sales will increase by 3.5% each year for the next five years. Extend the unit sales column to include these figures.

f)   The marketing department has also determined that the product sells the most when it is priced at $18.45. Make this the selling price for years 11 through 15.

g)   Add rows which calculate the average, minimum and maximum profit for years 11 through 15 only. Include proper labels for these rows. Print a copy of the modified spreadsheet.

h)   The state in which Flat Technologies is located has a corporate tax based on the following rates:

Profit	Tax Rate
0 -- 19,999	2%
20,000 -- 39,999	4%
40,000 -- 59,999	5%
60,000 -- 99,999	6%
100,000 and above	8%

Create a column titled State Tax which displays the taxes Flat has paid for each of its 15 years. Use a lookup table to calculate the tax.

i)   Save the spreadsheet on disk when complete.

7.   You have been asked to get price quotes from several printers to have a small newsletter printed for your club:

Printer A: $.25 per copy up to 1000 copies
$.23 per copy for every copy over 1000

Printer B: $.27 per copy for up to 900 copies
$.15 per copy for every copy over 900

Printer C: $.28 per copy for up to 500 copies
$.20 per copy for every copy over 500

a)   Create a new spreadsheet named Printer which shows the cost for printing 500, 1000 and 1500 copies of the newsletter for each of the three printers. Use an @IF to calculate the prices.

b)   Add a row to the bottom of the spreadsheet which shows the minimum cost for printing each of the three numbers of copies.

c)   The club president would also like quotes for 750 and 1250 copies. Add two columns to the spreadsheet which calculate and display the costs for these numbers of copies. Note which printer is cheapest for each of the five numbers of copies. Save the spreadsheet when completed.

d)   Printer C has heard about the other printer's prices and has decided to change his quote to the following:

$.27 per copy for up to 500 copies
$.21 per copy for every copy over 500

Change the formulas for Printer C to reflect this new price. Save the modified spreadsheet on disk.

Chapter 9
Integrating the Word Processor, Data Base and Spreadsheet

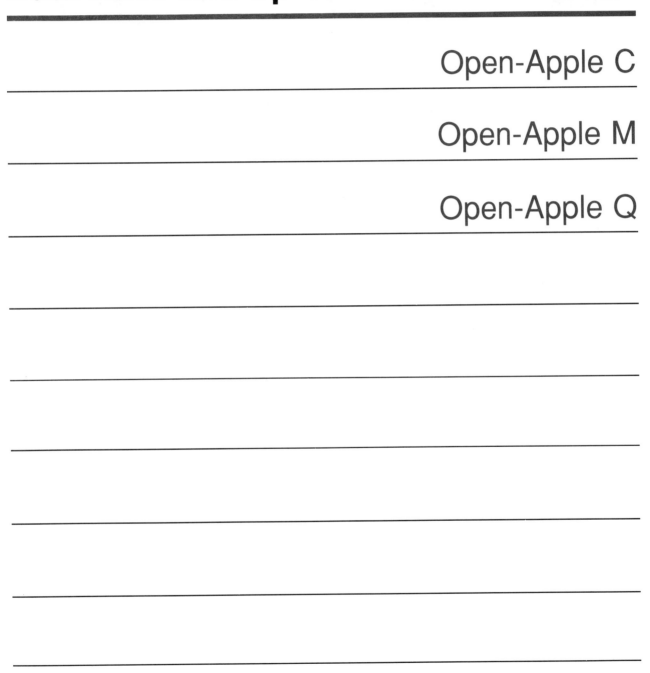

Open-Apple C

Open-Apple M

Open-Apple Q

Objectives

After completing this chapter you will be able to:

1. Load multiple files onto the Desktop and switch between them.

2. Use the Clipboard to transfer text between word processor files.

3. Merge data base information with a word processed document.

4. Integrate spreadsheet data with a word processed document.

5. Use the word processor to create a mail-merge document for use with the data base.

6. Share data between the data base and spreadsheet.

*A*ppleWorks is an "integrated" software package. That is, it is possible to use the three applications areas, word processing, data base and spreadsheet, by running only one program. There are two important reasons for using integrated packages. The first is that, because the applications are integrated, it is possible to share data between them. The second reason is that it is easy to learn and use such a package because it has similar commands in each of the different areas. For example, Open-Apple D is always the command for Delete whether you are using the word processor, data base or spreadsheet. This chapter will discuss the different ways of sharing data between the applications areas. It assumes that you have completed the previous chapters and are familiar with the word processor, data base and spreadsheet commands.

9.1 Expanding the Desktop

The terms and operations used in AppleWorks mimic the work done in an actual office: for example, a file is retrieved from storage and placed on a desktop before it may be used. It is unlikely in a real office that only one file would be worked on at a time. For this reason AppleWorks allows up to twelve files to be on its Desktop at any one time. This can include any mix of word processor, data base and spreadsheet files, but is limited by the amount of memory your computer has available.

When adding files to the Desktop, AppleWorks displays a list of the different files on your data disk. It is possible to load a single file by placing the cursor on its name and pressing Return. However, if the right-arrow key is pressed instead, an arrow will be displayed next to the file name and the cursor can then be moved down the list. Up to eleven more files can then be selected in this manner. When Return is now pressed all of the selected files are placed on the Desktop simultaneously. AppleWorks then lists the names of the selected files and asks which file you wish to see first:

```
┌─────────────────────────────────┐
│         Desktop Index           │
│ ─────────────────────────────── │
│  1.   Ivy Congrat      WP       │
│  2.   Ivy Deanslist    DB       │
│  3.   Grades           SS       │
│                                 │
└─────────────────────────────────┘
```

When a file is selected from the above Desktop Index menu, AppleWorks automatically switches to the proper application and displays that file. The two letters after the file's name indicate the type of the file: WP for Word Processor, DB for Data Base and SS for Spreadsheet.

9.2 Moving Between Files on the Desktop

When several files are placed on the Desktop it is possible to switch between them by pressing `Open-Apple Q` (for **Q**uick file change). The Desktop Index is then displayed allowing you to select the file you want to work with. AppleWorks will automatically switch to the proper applications area depending on the file you select. For example, if you are in the word processor and Quick change to a data base file, AppleWorks will switch to the data base screen and display that file.

There are many different reasons for switching between files. For example, you may be writing a letter in the word processor and wish to refer to some figures stored in a spreadsheet. With both files on the Desktop, you could call up the Desktop Index, Quick change to the spreadsheet file, view the figures and then change back to the word processed letter. Other reasons include integrating the data between applications which will be described below.

When working with more than one file on the Desktop Apple-Works maintains the current status of each file, including any changes made. This includes the position of the cursor and any options set, so that it is possible to work with one file, switch to another, and return to the first file, picking up exactly where you left off. A file does not have to be saved until you have finished working with it. However, it is a good idea to save modified files from time to time as a safety measure.

Practice 1

The Practices in this Chapter deal with problems that require several files on the Desktop at one time. We will start by adding several Ivy University files to the Desktop and switching between them.

1) BOOT PRODOS AND START APPLEWORKS

2) SELECT THREE FILES TO ADD TO THE DESKTOP

    a. Choose 'Add files' from the Main Menu.
    b. Select your data disk.
    c. Move the cursor to the Ivy Congrat word processor file and press the right-arrow key. Do not press Return yet.
    d. Move the cursor to the Ivy Deanslist data base file and press right-arrow only.
    e. Move the cursor to the Grades spreadsheet file created in chapter 7 and press right-arrow only.

3) ADD THE FILES TO THE DESKTOP AND DISPLAY IVY CONGRAT

    a. Press Return to add all three files to the Desktop.
    b. From the Desktop Index menu

```
+-----------------------------+
|       Desktop Index         |
| --------------------------- |
| 1.  Ivy Congrat       WP    |
| 2.  Ivy Deanslist     DB    |
| 3.  Grades            SS    |
+-----------------------------+
```

press Return to display Ivy Congrat, the default selected file. Because this is a word processor file the word processor screen is displayed.

    c. Use down-arrow to move the cursor to line five.

4) SWITCH TO IVY DEANSLIST

    a. Press `Open-Apple Q` to display the Desktop Index.

    b. From the Desktop Index choose Ivy Deanslist and press Return. The application switches to data base and displays the Ivy Deanslist file.

5) SWITCH TO GRADES

    a. Press `Open-Apple Q`.

    b. From the Index choose Grades and press Return. The application switches to spreadsheet and displays the Grades file.

6) SWITCH BACK TO IVY CONGRAT

    Press `Open-Apple Q` and select Ivy Congrat. The application switches to the word processor. Note that the cursor is still on line five, where it was placed in step 3 above.

<u>Check</u> - The Ivy Congrat word processor file should be displayed:

```
File: Ivy Congrat          REVIEW/ADD/CHANGE          Escape: Main Menu
=====<====<====<====<====<====<====<====<====<====<====<====<====<====<==
          Ivy University Announces Deans List Students

Dear Faculty and Staff:

Dean Bob Doucette is proud to announce the members of the
Dean's List for the Spring semester. Each of these students
should be congratulated heartily.

As you know, only students with an exceptional GPA are
eligible for this award. To quote the student handbook:


The following students are recipients of this semester's
Dean's List Award:


Dr. Sulfuric's Chemistry class once again led the school in
highest percentage of Dean's List students. Here is a
selection from her grade book showing the extraordinary
performance of her students:
------------------------------------------------------------------------
Type entry or use @ commands        Line 5  Column 1        @-? for Help
```

9.3 Removing Files from the Desktop

When work on a file is complete, it should be removed from the desktop to free memory for other files. Certain operations work faster when more memory is available. Also, should some accident occur that clears the computer's memory, limiting the number of files on the Desktop to only those necessary means that less data from modified files will be lost.

If changes have been made to a file, it should be saved on disk before it is removed from the Desktop. If you attempt to remove a file which has been modified before saving it, AppleWorks will warn you that your changes will be lost before it removes the file.

To remove files from the Desktop, select option 4 'Remove files from the Desktop' from the Main Menu. As when adding files, Apple-Works will display a list of possible files:

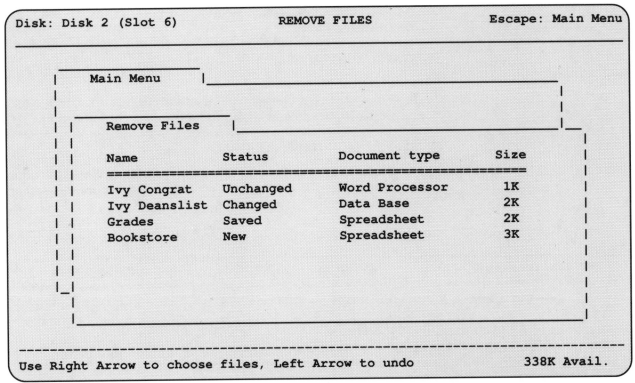

```
Disk: Disk 2 (Slot 6)            REMOVE FILES            Escape: Main Menu


      |     Main Menu     |
      |                                                                 |
      |                                                                 |
      | |     Remove Files     |                                       |_
      | |                                                               |
      | |  Name          Status        Document type     Size          |
      | |  ===========================================================  |
      | |  Ivy Congrat   Unchanged     Word Processor    1K            |
      | |  Ivy Deanslist Changed       Data Base         2K            |
      | |  Grades        Saved         Spreadsheet       2K            |
      | |  Bookstore     New           Spreadsheet       3K            |
      | |                                                               |
      | |                                                               |
      |_|                                                               |
       |                                                                |
       |                                                                |

 -----------------------------------------------------------------------
 Use Right Arrow to choose files, Left Arrow to undo        338K Avail.
```

The actual menu that you see here will depend on the files you have placed on the Desktop. If one file is to be removed, the cursor may be moved to that file's name and Return pressed. That file will then be removed from the Desktop, freeing memory for other files or operations. More than one file may be removed at a time by moving the cursor to the desired file names and pressing the right-arrow key. When all of the files to be removed have been selected, pressing Return removes them.

Note the Status column in the Remove Files menu above. "Changed" means that you have made some changes to the file, but have not yet saved it on disk. "New" means that you created this file but it has not been saved. If you try to remove a file with a status of Changed or New, AppleWorks prompts you to make sure that you really wish to do this. If you have tried to delete this file by mistake, you can press Escape to cancel the operation. "Unchanged" means that you have placed the file on the Desktop but not made any changes to it, and "Saved" means that you have done some work with the file and saved it on disk.

9.4 Using the Clipboard to Integrate Word Processed Documents

As you saw in the previous Practice, AppleWorks can keep several files on the Desktop at one time and switch easily between them. However, when one file is displayed it is not possible to see or use the data stored in another file, even if that file is also on the Desktop. To transfer data between different files and applications areas, AppleWorks uses a special area in memory called the "Clipboard".

You have seen the Clipboard mentioned on several menus as you have worked with the different applications areas. There are three steps required to use the Clipboard to transfer data between applications:

1. The data to be transferred is placed on the Clipboard.
2. The file to receive the data is displayed on the screen.
3. The data is taken from the Clipboard and placed in the current file.

Because it is the easiest to understand, we will start by moving data from one word processed document to another. This is a powerful tool, allowing lengthy or complex blocks of text to be entered into the word processor once, and then shared among different documents.

From the word processor, text may be placed on the Clipboard using two different methods: it may be copied to the Clipboard using the Copy command (Open-Apple C), or moved there with the Move command (Open-Apple M). Copying the text simply makes a copy of the marked block on the Clipboard; the original file is unchanged. Moving the block places a copy on the Clipboard, and then deletes the block from the original file. The correct method to use depends on your application. In most cases it is best to copy the block to the Clipboard, retaining the block in the original file.

Practice 2

In this Practice you will copy a paragraph from one word processed document into another. The three files Ivy Deanslist, Ivy Congrat and Grades should still be on the Desktop from the last Practice. We will copy a paragraph from Ivy Handbook into the Ivy Congrat letter.

1) REMOVE THE UNNEEDED FILES FROM THE DESKTOP

   a. Press Escape to return to the Main Menu.
   b. Select option 4, 'Remove files from the Desktop'.
   c. Move the cursor to Ivy Deanslist and press right-arrow only.
   d. Move the cursor to Grades and press right-arrow only.
   e. Press Return to remove both files from the Desktop.

2) ADD IVY HANDBOOK TO THE DESKTOP

Choose 'Add files' and select Ivy Handbook from your data disk. The Desktop now contains two files. Ivy Handbook contains a passage from the Ivy University student handbook.

3) COPY THE TEXT TO BE TRANSFERRED TO THE CLIPBOARD

   a. Move the cursor to the first paragraph in Ivy Handbook which begins "One of the most...".
   b. Press Open-Apple C to execute the Copy command.
   c. Select 'To clipboard'.
   d. Move the cursor the end of the paragraph. The entire paragraph is highlighted.
   e. Press Return to copy the block to the Clipboard.

4) COPY THE PARAGRAPH INTO THE IVY CONGRAT LETTER

   a. Press Open-Apple Q and switch to Ivy Congrat.
   b. Move the cursor to the position where the text should be inserted, the blank line after the sentence which reads "To quote the student handbook:".
   c. Press Open-Apple C for the Copy command.

d. Select 'From clipboard'. The paragraph from Ivy Handbook is copied from the Clipboard and placed at the current cursor position.
e. Press `Open-Apple S` to save the modified congratulations letter on disk.

<u>Check</u> - The paragraph should be inserted in the congratulations letter:

```
File: Ivy Congrat            REVIEW/ADD/CHANGE            Escape: Main Menu
=====<====<====<====<====<====<====<====<====<====<====<====<====<====<==
           Ivy University Announces Deans List Students

  Dear Faculty and Staff:

  Dean Bob Doucette is proud to announce the members of the
  Dean's List for the Spring semester. Each of these students
  should be congratulated heartily.

  As you know, only students with an exceptional GPA are
  eligible for this award. To quote the student handbook:

  "One of the most coveted academic honors is to be included
  in the Dean's List. To be considered for the Dean's List
  award, a student must possess an 'exceptional' GPA,
  exceptional being defined as in the upper 10% of the
  average school GPA for that semester."

  The following students are recipients of this semester's
  Dean's List Award:

  -----------------------------------------------------------------------
  Type entry or use @ commands        Line 19  Column  1      @-? for Help
```

9.5 Merging Data Bases with the Word Processor

Data from a data base may also be copied into a word processor document. This is done when a word processed report must contain information from a data base. The ability to copy records from a data base to a document is another important feature of AppleWorks.

The steps required to place data from an open data base into an open word processed document are:

1. The desired data base information is copied or printed to the Clipboard.
2. The word processor document is displayed.
3. The cursor is positioned and the data copied from the Clipboard.

(Note: records may be copied directly in version 3 only.)

Multi-record format is useful when copying records because it allows more than one record to be highlighted. Categories copied into a document are automatically separated by tabs. You may change the tab stops so that the data from the data base will better fit the document.

The data base information can also be printed as a table report to the Clipboard and then copied into the word processor document. This retains the formatting of the table report. Any tab characters in the report are replaced with spaces so that the tab stops in the word processor document do not affect the columns of the report. Also printing the data as a report retains any header information and allows calculated categories to be used. Since printing the information as a table report saves the formatting, it is often a better method than copying the information directly from the data base.

Practice 3

In this Practice a data base report will be printed to the Clipboard and then transferred into a word processor document. Ivy Handbook and Ivy Congrat should still be on the Desktop from the last Practice.

1) PREPARE THE DESKTOP

   a. Remove Ivy Handbook from the Desktop.
   b. Add the Ivy Deanslist data base to the desktop from your data disk. Ivy Deanslist is a list of students with high GPA's.

2) PRINT THE REPORT TO THE CLIPBOARD

   a. Press Open-Apple P and select the 'Get a report format' option.
   b. Load the Congrat format.
   c. Press Open-Apple P and select 'The clipboard (for the Word Processor)'.
   d. Press Return for the date. The report will be placed on the Clipboard.
   e. When AppleWorks displays the message

      `The report is now on the Clipboard.`

      press Space Bar to return to the REPORT FORMAT screen.

3) COPY THE REPORT FROM THE CLIPBOARD TO THE DOCUMENT

   a. Press Open-Apple Q and switch to Ivy Congrat.
   b. Move the cursor to the blank line after the sentence which begins "The following students...".
   c. Press Open-Apple C and select 'From clipboard'. The report is copied from the Clipboard and placed in the document at the current cursor position.
   d. Use Open-Apple D and delete the report header from the document, leaving only the column titles and student data.
   e. Press Open-Apple S to save the modified congratulations letter on disk.

Check - The Deans List report should be inserted into the letter:

```
/ File: Ivy Congrat           REVIEW/ADD/CHANGE            Escape: Main Menu \
| =====<====<====<====<====<====<====<====<====<====<====<====<====<====<== |
|                                                                           |
|    The following students are recipients of this semester's               |
|    Dean's List Award:                                                     |
|                                                                           |
|    First Name   Last Name      GPA                                        |
|    ----------   ------------   ---                                        |
|                                                                           |
|    Amy          Freitas        4.0                                        |
|    Alma         Lee            4.0                                        |
|    Roberta      Poisson        4.0                                        |
|    Jack         Lime           3.9                                        |
|    Vanna        Green          3.8                                        |
|    Bruce        Bonner         3.7                                        |
|    Nancy        Rohrman        3.6                                        |
|    Zack         Levow          3.5                                        |
|    Steve        Rohrman        3.5                                        |
|                                                                           |
|    -------------------------------------------------------------------    |
|    Type entry or use @ commands       Line 23   Column  1   @-? for Help  |
\                                                                           /
```

9.6 Merging Spreadsheets with the Word Processor

One of the options when printing a spreadsheet is to print the data to the Clipboard. Once on the Clipboard, the spreadsheet data can be transferred into the word processor like the data base report above. Businesses and offices must often send memos and letters which contain the figures from a spreadsheet. Usually the files produced by a separate (non-integrated) spreadsheet are not compatible with a separate word processor, requiring the figures to be entered by hand. This is a time consuming and error prone process. The ability to merge a spreadsheet with a word processed document is one of the most powerful features of an integrated package like AppleWorks.

The steps required to merge a spreadsheet with a word processed document are:

1. Print the desired spreadsheet information to the Clipboard.
2. Switch to the word processed document.
3. Copy the spreadsheet information from the Clipboard.

As in the data base, spreadsheet information can be either printed or copied (copied in version 3 only) to the Clipboard. Copying retains the tab characters between each column which can become a nuisance when the spreadsheet information is inserted into a word processed document with its own tab stops. Since printing retains formatting, it is usually the better method for transferring spreadsheet data into a word processed document.

Practice 4

In this Practice part of a spreadsheet will be printed to the Clipboard and then transferred into a Word Processor document. Ivy Congrat and Ivy Deanslist should still be on the Desktop from the last Practice.

1) PREPARE THE DESKTOP

   a. Remove Ivy Deanslist from the Desktop.
   b. Add the Grades spreadsheet to the Desktop from your data disk.

2) PRINT THE FIRST 6 COLUMNS TO THE CLIPBOARD

    a. Press `Open-Apple P` and select the 'Columns' option.
    b. Select the first 6 columns.
    c. Select the 'The clipboard (for the Word Processor)' option.
    d. Press Return for the report date.
    e. Press Space Bar to return to the spreadsheet.

3) COPY THE COLUMNS FROM THE CLIPBOARD TO THE DOCUMENT

    a. Press `Open-Apple Q` and switch to Ivy Congrat.
    b. Move the cursor to the blank line after the paragraph which begins "Dr. Sulfuric's Chemistry class...".
    c. Press `Open-Apple C` and select 'From clipboard'. The spreadsheet data is copied from the Clipboard into the document.
    d. Use `Open-Apple D` to delete the report header, leaving only the titles and student data.
    e. Press `Open-Apple S` to save the modified letter on disk.
    f. Print the letter using `Open-Apple P` and the 'Beginning' option.

<u>Check</u> - The spreadsheet showing Dr. Sulfuric's grades should be inserted into the letter:

```
/ File: Ivy Congrat              REVIEW/ADD/CHANGE              Escape: Main Menu \
 ====<====<====<====<====<====<====<====<====<====<====<====<====<====<====<==

   Dr. Sulfuric's Chemistry class once again led the school in
   highest percentage of Dean's List students. Here is a
   selection from her grade book showing the extraordinary
   performance of her students:

   Name                 Test 1    Test 2    Test 3    Test 4
                        9/10      10/20     11/15     12/12

   J.Smith                 50        83        68        64
   W.Freitas               86        89        78        88
   M.Porter                78       100        90        89
   B.Presley               45        78        66        78
   H.Crane                 66        76        78        55
   M.Lee                   85        74        83        66

          Average:      68.3      83.3      77.2      73.3


   -----------------------------------------------------------------------------
 Type entry or use @ commands          Line 42   Column  1          @-? for Help /
```

9.7 Sharing Data between two Spreadsheets

It is possible to share parts of two spreadsheets by placing the data on the Clipboard, and copying it into the new file. The Copy command allows complete rows or columns or blocks to be copied.

To transfer data between two spreadsheets, the following steps are taken:

    1. Copy the desired spreadsheet data to the Clipboard.
    2. Switch to the second spreadsheet.
    3. Copy the data from the Clipboard.

Practice 5	In this Practice you will copy a group of rows from one spreadsheet to another using the Clipboard. Start AppleWorks if you have not already done so. The data for a group of new employees will be added to the Ivy Payroll spreadsheet.

1) PREPARE THE DESKTOP

    a. Remove and add files as needed so that the Desktop contains only the Ivy Payroll and Ivy New Emp spreadsheets.

    b. Display Ivy New Emp.

2) COPY THE DATA TO THE CLIPBOARD

    a. Press `Open-Apple C` and select the 'To clipboard' option.

    b. Select the Rows option.

    c. Use the arrow keys to select all of the rows containing data.

    d. Press Return to copy the data to the Clipboard.

3) COPY THE DATA FROM THE CLIPBOARD TO THE PAYROLL SPREADSHEET

    a. Press `Open-Apple Q` and switch to Ivy Payroll.

    b. Move the cursor to the last row of employee data, row 27.

    c. Press `Open-Apple C` and select 'From clipboard'.

    d. From the prompt

`From clipboard?` **Formulas and values** `Values only`

press Return to copy both the formulas and values stored in the data on the Clipboard. The formulas in Ivy Payroll are updated to include the new data.

    e. Copy the formulas for Taxes and Net Pay into the columns for the new employees.

    f. Save the modified spreadsheet on disk.

<u>Check</u> - The new employees inserted into the spreadsheet change the payroll totals displayed at the bottom of the spreadsheet:

`Total =`   `$6,280.31`

9.8 Sharing Data between two Data Bases	It is possible to transfer data between two data bases by using the Clipboard. After placing both files on the Desktop, the desired records from the first file are copied to the Clipboard, and then into the second file.

However, the process of sharing records between data bases is made slightly more complex when the files contain different categories. When this occurs, the entries from the first category in the original file are copied to the first category in the second file, and so on, regardless of the category names. Therefore, care must be taken when transferring records from one data base to another to ensure that the entries are placed in the proper categories.

Practice 6	In this Practice you will use the Clipboard to transfer records between two data base files. Start AppleWorks if you have not already done so.

1) PREPARE THE DESKTOP

    a. Remove and add files as needed so that the Desktop contains only the Ivy Student and Ivy New Stu data bases.

    b. Display Ivy New Stu.

2) COPY THE RECORDS TO THE CLIPBOARD

    a. Press Open-Apple C and select the 'To clipboard' option.

    b. Use the arrow keys to highlight all of the records.

    c. Press Return to copy the data to the Clipboard.

3) COPY THE RECORDS FROM THE CLIPBOARD INTO THE IVY STUDENT DATA BASE

    a. Press Open-Apple Q and switch to Ivy Student.

    b. Press Open-Apple C and select 'From clipboard'. The new student records are copied from the Clipboard into the data base. Note that the ordering has been lost because inserting the new students destroyed the alphabetic order.

    c. Move the cursor to the Last Name field and sort the data base by Last Name using Open-Apple A and selecting 'Category (Last Name)' and 'From A to Z'.

    d. Save the modified data base on disk.

9.9 Mail Merge and Form Letters

One of the most powerful applications provided by an integrated package is the ability to use "mail merge" to create personalized form letters. You have undoubtedly received such letters that begin "The next winner of 10 Million dollars could be" followed by your name. This is an example of a mail merged form letter.

Mail merge takes advantage of the computer's ability to integrate information from a data base with a word processed letter and print the result. To create such a letter, a data base must be created which contains the names and addresses of the people you wish to write to. (Other personalized data which is to appear in the letter is also placed in the data base.) The letter is then entered into the word processor, leaving room for data base information. When completed, the computer prints one copy of the letter for each record in the data base, substituting the data in that record into the printed version of the letter.

To mail merge a letter, the following steps are required:

1. The desired data base records are copied to the Clipboard.
2. The letter is word processed, marking where you wish the data from the different categories to be printed.
3. The Print command is given and the Mail Merge option selected.

The data base information can also be printed to the Clipboard as a table report. One advantage of this method is the ability to save a selection rule with the report format which is automatically applied to limit the merged data. Another advantage is the ability to use calculated categories in a mail merged document.

When the Mail Merge option is selected from the Print menu, AppleWorks generates and prints a personalized copy of the letter for each record on the Clipboard. If there are 50 records on the Clipboard, 50 personalized letters will be printed.

The position of the merged data in the letter is specified by entering MM (for mail merge) from the Options menu, `Open-Apple O`. AppleWorks then displays a menu of the categories on the Clipboard. For example:

```
Select a data base category

    1.   First Name
    2.   Last Name
    3.   City
    4.   State
    5.   Zip
```

You select the desired category name from the menu. AppleWorks then inserts a marker into the text showing the name of the category that will be printed when the letter is mail merged. For example, selecting First Name from the above menu would place the marker

```
^<First Name>
```

in the document at the current cursor position. These markers can be positioned throughout the document until all the information required has been specified. When the letter is printed you are asked if you wish to print a plain or merged document. Printing a plain document shows the markers, allowing you to review the placement of the categories. A merged document prints the actual information from the data base in place of the markers.

Practice 7

In this Practice you will modify and print a mail merged letter. Although this letter contains only two categories, it is possible to create a mail merged document which contains data from any category in a data base report. Start AppleWorks if you have not already done so.

1) PREPARE THE DESKTOP

    a. Remove and add files as needed so that the Desktop contains only the Ivy Student data base and the Ivy Tuition letter.

    b. Display Ivy Student.

2) APPLY A SELECTION RULE TO THE DATA BASE

    a. Execute the Record Selection command by pressing `Open-Apple R`.

    b. Select Paid from the fields list.

    c. Select "equals" from the comparison list.

    d. Type N on the comparison information line and press Return.

    e. Press Escape to apply the selection rule. Note that only those students who have not paid their tuition are displayed.

3) COPY THE DESIRED RECORDS TO THE CLIPBOARD

    a. Press `Open-Apple C` and select the 'To Clipboard' option.

    b. Highlight all of the records that are currently displayed and press Return.

4) PREPARE THE TUITION LETTER TO BE MAIL MERGED

    a. Press `Open-Apple Q` and switch to Ivy Tuition.

    b. Place the cursor on the <u>second</u> space after "Dear".

    c. Press `Open-Apple O`, type MM and Return.

    d. Select First Name from the menu.

    e. From the prompt

`Omit line when all entries on line are blank?` **No**   `Yes`

        press Return to accept 'No'. A marker is inserted into the letter.

    f. Enter MM and select Last Name from the menu. Press Return to accept the 'No' default.

    g. Press Escape to return to the work area.

    h. Place the cursor on the space after the <Last Name> marker and type a colon (:).

<u>Check</u> - The First Name and Last Name markers should be inserted into the letter so that the first line appears on the screen as:

`Dear ^<First Name> ^<Last Name>:`

5) PRINT THE TUITION LETTER

    a. Press `Open-Apple P`, select 'Beginning' and press Return.

    b. Select your printer from the list of choices.

    c. Select 'Print document without merging' to print a plain (non mail-merged) copy of the letter. Note the position of the category markers in the text. Only one copy of the letter is printed and the word processor screen is again displayed.

    d. Press `Open-Apple P`, select 'Beginning' and press Return.

    e. Select your printer from the list of choices.

    f. Select 'Merge data base items with this document' to print a mail merged version of the letter. Note how the markers have been replaced by the different names from the data base information. A personalized copy of the letter is printed for each record on the Clipboard. Press Escape to terminate the printing after three or four letters have been printed.

    g. Press `Open-Apple S` to save the modified letter on disk.

9.10 Integrating the Data Base and Spreadsheet

It is often desirable to have information stored in a data base available for use in a spreadsheet. This allows users to employ the power of the spreadsheet to ask "What If?" questions and perform other calculations on numerical data base fields. For example, the Ivy University Bookstore data base could be transferred into a spreadsheet to determine the profit that would result from raising the cost of all items by 10 percent.

So far, we have used the Copy command to transfer data into a previously opened file, but it can also be used to transfer data to a new file. When this is desired, the new file can be created by selecting the type of the new file from the Add Files menu after the Copy command has been executed.

Creating a spreadsheet from a data base file is a 4 step process:

1. The Copy command is executed and 'To Clipboard' selected.

2. The desired entries are highlighted.

3. The 'Make a new file for the Spreadsheet' command from the Add Files menu is used to create a new, empty spreadsheet.

4. The Copy command is again used, this time with the 'From Clipboard' option to copy the fields into empty cells.

(Note: this is different in version 2 which requires the creation of a temporary DIF file.)

A data base can be created from a spreadsheet in a similar process. When this is done, each column of the spreadsheet data will appear as a different category in the data base, and each row will be a different record. First the desired spreadsheet information is copied to the Clipboard. Then a new data base is created from scratch with as many categories as there are columns of the spreadsheet data. Finally the spreadsheet data is copied from the Clipboard into the data base. If the spreadsheet data has more columns than the data base has categories, the excess data will be lost.

Practice 8

In this Practice you will create a new spreadsheet named Bookstore using the information from the Ivy Bookstore data base file. Start AppleWorks if you have not already done so.

1) PREPARE THE DESKTOP

   a. Return to the Main menu and close any open files with the 'Remove files from the Desktop' command.
   b. Open the Ivy Bookstore data base.
   c. If it is not already, switch to multi-record format using Open-Apple Z.

2) COPY THE DESIRED RECORDS TO THE CLIPBOARD

   a. Move the cursor to the first record in the data base.
   b. Press Open-Apple C and select 'To Clipboard'.
   c. Highlight all of the records by moving the cursor to the last record in the data base.
   d. Press Return to copy the records to the Clipboard.

3) COPY THE HIGHLIGHTED RECORDS INTO A NEW SPREADSHEET

   a. Select 'Make a new file' and 'Spreadsheet' from the Add Files menu to create a new, empty spreadsheet.
   b. Select the 'From scratch' option and name the new file Bookstore.
   c. With the cursor on cell A1, press Open-Apple C and select 'From Clipboard'. The highlighted records from the Ivy Bookstore data base are copied from the Clipboard and placed at the current cursor position, each field in a separate column.
   d. Press Open-Apple S to save the new spreadsheet.

Check - Data from the Ivy Bookstore data base has been translated into a spreadsheet. As the cell indicator shows, the entire item name was transferred, but only 9 characters (the default for any new spreadsheet) are currently displayed. Formatting commands could now be used to change the layout of the spreadsheet and formulas added to perform calculations. Your spreadsheet should be similar to:

```
File: Bookstore                    REVIEW/ADD/CHANGE              Escape: Main Menu
========A========B========C========D========E========F========G========H====
   1|Avocado DF                  6       .99
   2|Ball poinP                150       .89
   3|Chips    F                  77       .65
   4|Class RinC                 50    212.50
   5|DictionarB                 22     12.95
   6|Doritos  F                145      2.49
   7|Felt-tip P                 76       .98
   8|Logo T-ShC                250      9.99
   9|Pencil   P                200       .15
  10|Pepsi    F                444       .65
  11|School JaC                100     34.95
  12|School TiC                 15     17.50
  13|TheasauruB                 12     15.00
  14|Three-HolA                200      1.98
  15|Three-RinA                122      3.5
  16|
  17|
  18|
------------------------------------------------------------------------------
A1: (Label) Avocado Dip

Type entry or use @ commands                               @-? for Help
```

Chapter Summary

This chapter presented the commands necessary to share data between the applications areas and different files produced by the same application. The ability to share data between applications is the primary reason for using an integrated package such as AppleWorks.

The AppleWorks Desktop is capable of holding up to 12 different files. The files can be any mixture of word processor, data base and spreadsheet files. It is possible to switch between any file on the Desktop by pressing Open-Apple Q and selecting the file name from a menu called the Desktop Index. When work has been completed on a file, it may be saved and then removed from the Desktop to make room for other files.

To transfer data between different files, the files are opened and the following steps executed:

1. The Copy command, Open-Apple C, is executed and 'To Clipboard' is selected.
2. The data to be copied is highlighted and Return is pressed.
3. The Quick change command, Open-Apple Q, is used to switch to the document that will receive the copied data.
4. The cursor is placed at the position for the copied data, the Copy command is executed, and the 'From Clipboard' option is chosen.

Data from the data base or spreadsheet may also be printed to the Clipboard and then copied into a word processor document. Printing replaces the tabs in the data base and spreadsheet files with spaces so that they are not affected by the tab stops in the word processor document but retain their original format.

This chapter explained how data may be transferred between:

2 word processor documents (section 9.4)
a data base and a word processed document (section 9.5)
a spreadsheet and a word processed document (section 9.6)
2 spreadsheets (section 9.7)
2 data bases (section 9.8)
mail merging a data base and a word processed document (section 9.9)
a data base and spreadsheet (section 9.10)

One of the most powerful abilities of an integrated package is the ability to produce mail merge documents. In mail merge, a document is created in the word processor with several areas left blank. When the document is printed, the blank areas are automatically filled in with information from a data base report, creating a different copy of the document for each record in the report. In this way, the computer can produce personalized form letters.

Vocabulary

Clipboard - Place in the computer's memory used to store data being transferred between files.

Desktop Index - Listing of the files currently on the Desktop. Also acts as a menu when switching between Desktop files.

Integrated - Different applications that are part of one software package. Because AppleWorks is integrated, data may be shared between its three applications areas.

Mail merge - Using the contents of a data base report and a word processed document to have the computer produce personalized form letters.

Reviews

Sections 9.1-9.5

1. a) What is meant by an integrated software package?
   b) What are two advantages of using such a package?

2. What is the purpose of having more than one file on the Desktop at any one time?

3. What is the Desktop Index used for?

4. a) What command is used to switch between files on the Desktop?
   b) Give two reasons why you might want to switch between files.

5. a) How may files be removed from the Desktop?
   b) What is usually done to a file with a status of Changed before it is removed from the Desktop? Why?

6. What is the purpose of the Clipboard?

7. The file New President contains a paragraph which describes the inauguration of Ivy University's new president. Explain the steps required to copy this paragraph into a file named Alumni which contains a letter to be sent to all Ivy alumni.

8. Give three examples when you might want to merge part of a spreadsheet with a word processor document.

Sections 9.6-9.10   9. List the steps necessary to copy the name and GPA of each student from California or Oregon from the data base Ivy Student into a word processor document named Western.

10. a) What steps are required to copy two columns from a spreadsheet named Owed and insert them between two existing columns in a spreadsheet named Assets?
b) Must the formulas in Assets be changed to include the new columns?

11. Fantasy cars has just bought out Luxury Autos and wants to merge into a single file the data bases which contain both dealership's inventories. Explain the steps required to do this.

12. What must be watched for when transferring records between two data bases?

13. What does "mail merge" mean?

14. a) Where does the personalized data to be included in a mail merged letter come from?
b) How is the position of this data in the text specified?

15. a) Explain the steps required to mail merge the names and addresses of customers from Fantasy Cars customer data base into a letter to be sent to each customer.
b) What additional steps would be required to send the letters only to customers living in Boca Raton, Florida?

16. Give three examples where you might want to copy information from a data base into a spreadsheet. For each example explain what the spreadsheet would be used for.

Exercises

1. Ivy University must raise next semester's tuition in order to cover its increasing labor costs.

   a) Create and save a letter named Increase using the word processor which notifies students of the upcoming tuition increase. Increase should be similar to:

   Dear Student:

   We are sorry to inform you that due to rising labor costs we are forced to raise your tuition by $1,000 dollars. This increase is effective next semester.

   Sincerely,

   The Administration

   The administration has decided that students might take the news of a tuition increase better if it came in a personalized letter.

   b) Using the Ivy Student data base create a report named Students that contains only the first and last names for each student in the file. Print this report to the Clipboard for use with mail merge.

   c) Modify the Increase letter to mail merge the students' first and last names in place of the word "Student". Save the modified version on disk.

   d) Print mail merged letters for the first three students. Use Escape to cancel the printing.

   e) In order to keep its better students from transferring to less expensive schools, the Ivy administration has decided that the tuition increase should be on a sliding scale based on the student's GPA. Every student's tuition will increase by $500. An additional $100 will be charged for each tenth of a GPA point below 4.0, for example:

GPA	Increase
4.0	$500
3.9	$600
3.8	$700

   . . .

   Modify the Students report to contain a calculated category which displays the amount of the tuition increase. Print Students to the Clipboard for use with mail merge.

   f) Modify the Increase letter to merge the actual tuition increase from the report on the Clipboard in place of the "1,000".

   g) Using the new Increase, print mail merged letters for the first three students. Use Escape to cancel the printing. Save the modified version on disk.

2. The Fantasy Wheels pre-owned car company would like to transfer their inventory data base into a spreadsheet so that they can perform "What If?" questions with the data. This data base was created in Chapter 5 exercise 3.

    a) Copy all of the records in Fantasy data base to the Clipboard.

    b) Create a new spreadsheet named What If and copy the data from the Clipboard into it. Delete all of the categories except Year, Make, Paid, and Asking Price and format the spreadsheet, adding titles and labels.

    c) Add two columns to the spreadsheet. The first should calculate a new asking price which is a 10% increase of the current asking price. The second should display the additional profit gained by selling the cars at these new prices.

    d) Acting as the sales manager, use the word processor to write a letter named New Price to the owner of Fantasy Wheels describing your plan to raise prices.

    e) Place a copy of the What If spreadsheet on the Clipboard and copy it into the New Price letter. Print a copy of New Price.

3. When using a computerized data base to store inventory figures, the numbers stored in the file can be incorrect when items have been added or removed from inventory without notifying the computer operator to update the data base. To keep the figures up to date, a worker must periodically count the actual number on hand for each product and report this number to the operator who updates the data base.

    a) Using the Product data base created in Chapter 5 exercise 5 create a mail merged form that could be used by the worker to record the actual amount on hand for each item. An example form is shown below:

    ```
    Plasma-Tech Industries
    Manual Inventory Update Form

    Product ID: A1000
    Product Name: Widgets
    Presumed amount on hand: 920

    Actual amount on hand:  _____
    ```

    b) Using the Product data base, prepare a report listing the product ID, name and amount on hand for those items with less than 100 units on hand. Print the report to the Clipboard and copy it into a word processed letter informing the purchasing manager that these items must be reordered.

4. In Chapter 7 exercise 4 Mr. Horatio von Money used a spreadsheet named Stock to calculate his donation to Ivy University. Print the spreadsheet to the Clipboard and copy it into a word processed letter informing the I.U. Board of Trustees of the donation.

5. Using the Ivy Student data base create a selection rule to display only those students with a GPA of 3.3 or higher. Copy all of the selected records to the Clipboard and mail merge them with a word processed document congratulating each student for above average performance. Print a copy of the letter for each student in the report. Use Escape to interrupt the printing if you wish.

6. Your friend Jill is searching for a new car and has written to you for information.

   a) Using the Car Price data base, create a report showing the name and price for all cars which cost less than $15,000 with air conditioning. Print the report to the Clipboard and copy it into a word processed letter informing Jill of her choices.

   b) Jill has written back for more information. Prepare a new word processed letter which contains two reports: one showing all cars with stereos which cost between $10,000 and $12,000 and all cars with sunroofs which cost less than $11,500.

7. You have been asked to gather some statistics about car prices for your economics class.

   a) Create a new spreadsheet named Prices from the Car Price data base which contains all of the data about new car prices.

   b) Using the Prices spreadsheet, calculate the following:

      average base price of a new car
      average price for a new car with air
      average price for a new car stereo
      average price for a new car with sunroof
      maximum base price of a new car
      minimum price of a new car with air conditioning

   c) Using the word processor, create a report detailing your findings for the class. Use the Clipboard to include the actual figures from Prices in the report.

8. Use the word processor to create the following file named Memo:

   ```
   Memo to: Steve Munger, Asst. Headmaster
   From: Bob Doucette, Dean

   Steve:

   The following students have received Dean's
   List status:


   Please update their records. Thank you.
   ```

   Using the Clipboard, copy the table of Dean's List students from the Ivy Congrat letter created earlier in this chapter into this memo.

9. You have moved. Using the Address data base created in Chapter 5 exercise 1, prepare and print a personalized mail merged letter to each of your friends which gives your new address. Use Escape to interrupt the printing if you wish. An example letter is shown below:

```
Amy Eppelman
343 Nenue Street
Honolulu, HI 08033

Dear Amy:

This is just a short note to let you know
my new address:

    1389 Southwest Drive
    Atlantic, FL 76800

Of course, we'll still get together on
your birthday, Jul 5, 65, or I'll call you
at (767) 145-5937.

See you soon,


A. Friend
```

10. In Practice 8 you created a spreadsheet named Bookstore by transferring records from the Ivy Bookstore data base file. Load Bookstore and make the following changes to it:

   a) Insert rows at the top of the spreadsheet and add proper column titles.

   b) Increase the item name column width to 20 characters.

   c) Format all prices using the 'Dollars' option with 2 decimal places.

   d) Calculate and display the average price of all items available. Use proper formatting and include a label for this value.

   e) Format the department column, making it right justified and decrease its width.

   f) In column E create a formula which will display the value of the items in stock for each item (price per item times the number of items in stock).

   g) At the bottom of column E calculate and display the total value of all items available.

   h) Format column E and include a proper title and label for the total.

   i) Save the modified spreadsheet on disk and print a copy.

11. In Practice 7 you modified a letter named Ivy Tuition to include mail merge data from the Ivy Student data base.

   a) Load Ivy Student and modify the Not Paid report format to include the students' full mailing address.

   b) Print Not Paid to the Clipboard for use with mail merge.

   c) Load Ivy Tuition and modify it so that the student's mailing address is mail merged at the top left-hand side of the letter.

   d) Save the modified letter on disk and print a mail-merged copy.

Chapter 10

An Introduction to Programming Using Applesoft

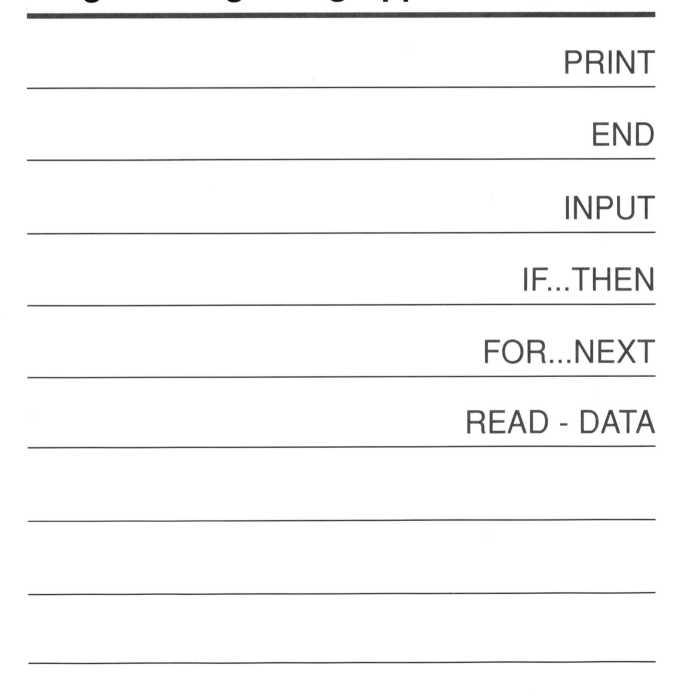

PRINT

END

INPUT

IF...THEN

FOR...NEXT

READ - DATA

Objectives

After completing this chapter you will be able to:

1. Start the computer and load Applesoft BASIC.

2. Use immediate mode to perform calculations.

3. Write and run an Applesoft program.

4. Locate and correct programming errors.

5. Use the RUN, LIST, SAVE, LOAD, CAT and NEW commands.

6. Assign values to numeric and string variables.

7. INPUT numbers and strings.

8. Use the IF...THEN conditional statement.

9. Produce FOR...NEXT loops.

10. Assign values to variables using READ - DATA.

*I*n Chapter 1 a computer program was defined as a list of instructions written in a special language that tells the computer which operations to perform and in what sequence to perform them. You have been using a very sophisticated program written by professional computer programmers when using the word processor, data base and spreadsheet applications of Appleworks. It is possible to write your own programs using the computer language BASIC (Beginner's All-purpose Symbolic Instruction Code), which was originally developed by John Kemeny and Thomas Kurtz at Dartmouth College. One of the reasons for naming it BASIC was because it uses simple English words as commands which are easy to learn. The version of BASIC you will use on the Apple is named Applesoft. In this chapter you will be given a brief introduction to programming in Applesoft.

10.1 Using Immediate Mode

Insert a disk containing Applesoft into disk drive 1 and turn on the computer. The disk light will flash and Applesoft will be transferred from the disk into the computer's memory. You will see the following message on your screen:

```
PRODOS BASIC 1.1
COPYRIGHT APPLE, 1983-84

]
```

The square bracket (]) shown on the screen is called the "prompt". Applesoft displays the prompt whenever it is ready to accept an instruction from you. It is possible to have the computer follow a BASIC instruction immediately by typing the instruction at the prompt and then pressing Return; this is called using the computer in "immediate mode". The computer can also receive instructions through programs, which will be explained later in this chapter.

PRINT

PRINT is the BASIC command used to display numbers, characters and words on the screen. Using immediate mode, the following example prints the results of a math operation when it is typed at the prompt and Return pressed:

```
]PRINT 12 + 5          <press Return>
17
```

PRINT followed by a mathematical operation tells the computer to print the result of that operation. Notice that only the result and not the mathematical statement is printed. It is important to remember to press Return after giving the computer any command. This instructs BASIC to execute the command. In BASIC the following symbols are used for each of the five mathematical operations:

Operation	Symbol
Addition	+
Subtraction	-
Multiplication	*
Division	/
Exponentiation	∧

PRINT with Quotation Marks

The computer can print both numbers and words. To the computer a number is a symbol that can be used in a mathematical calculation. A character or word, on the other hand, cannot be used to do any of these things.

PRINT followed by quotation marks instructs the computer to print whatever appears between the quotation marks. Using immediate mode, the following example prints a message on the screen when Return is pressed:

```
]PRINT "Go Go Ivy!"
Go Go Ivy!
```

Note that the word PRINT and the quotation marks are not displayed in the output.

?SYNTAX ERRORs

The computer will only act when it recognizes a command or instruction that is in its language. Anytime the computer does not recognize an instruction, it prints an error message and stops to wait for the programmer to correct the error. One of the most common error messages is the ?SYNTAX ERROR:

```
]PRUNT "Go Go Ivy!"
?SYNTAX ERROR
```

Because the computer cannot think for itself, it does not realize that the programmer meant to type "PRINT". Since the BASIC language does not contain the word PRUNT, the computer displays an error message and does not carry out the instruction.

Correcting Errors

If an error is detected before Return has been pressed it can be easily corrected by using the left-arrow key to bring the cursor back to the location of the error, where typing the correction replaces it. The cursor must then be returned to the end of the line using the right-arrow key and Return pressed.

If an error occurs after Return is pressed and the ?SYNTAX ERROR message printed, simply retype the entire line correctly and press Return.

Practice 1

This Practice demonstrates loading Applesoft into the computer's memory, using immediate mode to print the results of a series of mathematical calculations and the use of quotation marks in a PRINT statement.

1) LOAD APPLESOFT

Place a disk containing Applesoft in disk drive 1 and turn on the computer.

2)   USE IMMEDIATE MODE TO PRINT THE RESULTS OF CALCULATIONS

Press Return after typing each of the following calculations:

```
a.  PRINT 25 * 57
b.  PRINT 218 / 32
c.  PRINT 25 + 6 - 5 / 7
d.  PRINT 25^2 + 12^3
```

3)   ENTER EACH OF THE FOLLOWING LINES EXACTLY AS SHOWN

```
PRNT "Most Ivy students are not brilliant!"
```

Press Return. Note that the syntax error may not be corrected with the left-arrow key if Return has been pressed. Retype the whole line, being careful to spell PRINT correctly. Next type the line:

```
PRINT "But they are motvated."
```

Do not press Return. Correct the spelling of "motivated" using the arrow keys, then return the cursor to the end of the line and press Return.

10.2 Writing a Program

As we have noted, immediate mode instructs the computer one command at a time, immediately after the command has been typed. A program, on the other hand, gives the computer a series of instructions written as numbered lines. These lines are stored in memory until the computer is given the command to execute the program. The computer then finds the lowest numbered line, executes the instructions on that line, and continues to read the lines and carry out the instructions until the highest numbered line is completed.

Entering Programs

There are a few simple rules about program lines and line numbering that should be kept in mind when writing a program:

1.   Each line in a program must begin with a number. If you forget to type the number, the computer will execute the command in immediate mode when Return is pressed.

2.   To enter a program line into the computer's memory, press Return when the line is completed:

```
]10 PRINT 2 + 2          <press Return>
```

3.   When writing a program, it is best to use line numbers that are units of ten (10, 20, ...100, 110, 120, etc.). This leaves room to insert nine possible lines between any two in case it becomes necessary to add lines later.

4.   It is not necessary to enter the program lines in order. Line 20 can be entered first, then line 10 and later line 30. The computer automatically puts the lines in numerical order. Any time a new instruction is to be added, just type the new line number, the instruction and press Return. The computer will then put the line into its proper sequence. Were the program lines

```
]20 PRINT "with a computer:"
]10 PRINT "Mathematics"
]30 PRINT "2 + 2 ="
]40 PRINT 2 + 2
```

entered, the computer would execute them in the proper order (10,20,30,40) when the program is run.

END

The END statement should be the last statement in a program, and is used to halt program execution. For example,

```
50 END
```

causes the execution of a program to stop when line 50 is reached. It is a good programming practice to place an END statement in all programs since it helps ensure that the program will terminate properly. The following is an example of a complete program:

```
]10 PRINT "This is a program."
]20 PRINT "Instructions are written"
]30 PRINT "on separate lines. Each line"
]40 PRINT "has a line number."
]50 END
```

RUN

The RUN command instructs the computer to execute the program stored in its memory. Type the word RUN and press Return when you have completed typing your program. It is important to realize that the command RUN is not part of the program, does not get a line number and is typed only after the program is complete.

Program 10.1

Note that when RUN is typed and Return pressed, the computer executes the program lines that are stored in its memory in numerical order, beginning at line 10:

```
]10 PRINT "Who at Ivy University"
]20 PRINT "can solve the following?"
]30 PRINT "5 * 3 ="
]40 PRINT 5 * 3
]50 PRINT "24 / 4 = " 24 / 4
]60 END

]RUN
Who at Ivy University
can solve the following?
5 * 3 =
15
24 / 4 = 6
```

When a line is executed, PRINT works the same as it does in immediate mode. The message "Who at Ivy University" is printed by line 10 because those characters are between quotation marks, as are the messages on lines 20 and 30. Notice that the word PRINT and the quotation marks are not printed when the program is executed. Line 40 prints the results of the mathematical calculation because it is not enclosed in quotations. Note how line 50 prints 24 / 4 = and then the result, 6, on the same line. This is because the first part of the line is enclosed in quotation marks and the second part is not.

10.3 LIST

The LIST command is used to display the program currently in the computer's memory. If LIST is typed after Program 10.1 has been entered into the computer's memory, the following output will appear:

```
]LIST
10 PRINT "Who at Ivy University"
20 PRINT "can solve the following?"
30 PRINT "5 * 3 ="
40 PRINT 5 * 3
50 PRINT "24 / 4 = " 24 / 4
60 END
```

LIST is especially useful when you are in the process of editing a program and want to continually check to see what lines the program contains.

Correcting Errors

Typing errors and other mistakes in a program can be corrected in several ways. The following examples refer to Program 10.1:

1. If the error is detected while the line containing it is being typed, the left-arrow key can be used to move the cursor back to the error. The correction can then be typed and the cursor moved to the end of the line using the right arrow key and Return pressed.

2. RETYPING A LINE: A program line can be changed by simply retyping it using the same line number. If Program 10.1 is stored in memory and the line

   ```
   ]20 PRINT "takes math?"
   ```

   is typed, only the output produced by line 20 will be changed.

3. ERASING A WHOLE LINE: An entire line of a program can be erased by typing the line number and pressing Return:

   ```
   ]50
   ```

4. ADDING A NEW LINE: To add a line between other lines of a program, type the new line and press Return. The computer then enters the line in its proper place:

   ```
   15 PRINT "is a genius who"
   ```

A LIST of Program 10.1 with the changes made in steps 2, 3 and 4 followed by a RUN produces:

```
]LIST
10 PRINT "Who at Ivy University"
15 PRINT "is a genius who"
20 PRINT "takes math?"
30 PRINT "5 * 3 ="
40 PRINT 5 * 3
60 END

]RUN
Who at Ivy University
is a genius who
takes math?
5 * 3 =
15
```

Practice 2

This Practice demonstrates the writing, editing and running of a simple program. Start the computer and load Applesoft if you have not already done so.

1) TYPE THE FOLLOWING PROGRAM

Remember to press Return at the end of each line. Correct any mistakes you may make by either using the arrow keys or retyping the entire line.

```
]10 PRINT "This program performs"
]20 PRINT "calculations using 8 and 2."
]30 PRINT "8 + 2 = " 8 + 2
]40 PRINT "8 - 2 = " 8 - 2
]50 PRINT "8 * 2 = " 8 * 2
]60 PRINT "8 / 2 = " 8 / 2
]70 PRINT "8 ^ 2 = " 8 ^ 2
]80 END
```

2) RUN THE PROGRAM

Type RUN and press Return. You will see the following output:

```
This program performs
calculations using 8 and 2.
8 + 2 = 10
8 - 2 = 6
8 * 2 = 16
8 / 2 = 4
8 ^ 2 = 64
```

3) REPLACE THE FOLLOWING LINES AND RUN THE PROGRAM

Enter the following lines exactly as shown:

```
]60 PRINT "So what!"
]30 PRINT "This is a lot of work."
]50

]RUN
```

Note how the output produced by the program has changed:

```
This program performs
calculations using 8 and 2.
This is a lot of work.
8 - 2 = 6
So what!
8 ^ 2 = 64
```

4) LIST THE MODIFIED PROGRAM

Type LIST. The program is shown with the corrections you made:

```
]10 PRINT "This program performs"
]20 PRINT "calculations using 8 and 2."
]30 PRINT "This is a lot of work."
]40 PRINT "8 - 2 = " 8 - 2
]60 PRINT "So what!"
]70 PRINT "8 ^ 2 = " 8 ^ 2
]80 END
```

10.4 System Commands

The following commands are called "system commands" and may be entered whenever the prompt is shown on the screen. System commands are not used within programs, but instead store, retrieve and erase programs on the disk.

SAVE

The SAVE command is used to store a program on disk. The statement

```
]SAVE CALCULATE
```

will save the program currently in memory on the disk and give it the name CALCULATE. If there is already a program on the disk with that name, the new program will replace it, erasing the original.

LOAD

Programs previously stored on disk can be recalled using the LOAD command.

```
]LOAD CALCULATE
```

will load the program CALCULATE into memory from the disk. Any program previously in memory will be erased. It is important to note that this procedure does not remove the program from the disk. An exact copy of the program is transferred to the computer's memory where it can be modified or run.

CAT

Typing the command CAT (for catalogue) produces a list of all the programs and files stored on a disk:

```
]CAT

/SYSTEM.DISK

NAME              TYPE      BLOCKS      MODIFIED

PRODOS            SYS       32          6-SEP-86
BASIC.SYSTEM      SYS       21          18-SEP-84
CALCULATE         BAS       1           20-MAR-89
```

NEW

The NEW command is used to erase the computer's memory. Before entering a new program into memory, it is a good programming practice to type NEW to insure that any program lines from a previous program will not affect the new program. Typing

```
]NEW
```

followed by

```
]LIST
```

will show that there is now no program in the computer's memory. Be sure that you really want your program erased from the computer's memory before typing NEW. Once a program is erased, it is lost, unless it has been previously saved on disk.

Practice 3

This Practice demonstrates saving a program on disk, clearing the computer's memory and then loading the program back into memory from the disk. It assumes that the program entered in Practice 2 is still in the computer's memory.

1)   SAVE THE PROGRAM TO DISK NAMING IT CALCULATE

Type `SAVE CALCULATE` at the prompt and press Return. A copy of the program in the computer's memory is placed on disk and named "CALCULATE".

2)   CHECK THAT CALCULATE IS SAVED ON THE DISK

Type `CAT` and press Return. CALCULATE is listed as one of the files stored on disk.

3)   ERASE THE COMPUTER'S MEMORY

Type `NEW` at the prompt and press Return.

4)   CHECK THAT THE MEMORY IS ERASED

Type `LIST` and press Return. Because the program has been erased from memory nothing is listed.

5)   LOAD CALCULATE FROM THE DISK

Type `LOAD CALCULATE` and press Return. The light on the disk drive will flash showing that the program is being copied from disk to the computer's memory.

6)   RUN CALCULATE

Type `RUN` and press Return. Because CALCULATE has been transferred back into memory from disk it can be executed.

10.5 Using Numeric Variables

Because data used in a program may change, BASIC allows for the use of "variables". A variable is a name which is used to represent a value. For example,

```
A = 5
```

assigns the number 5 to the variable named A, which can then be used in place of the number 5.

To the computer there are two kinds of data: numbers and characters. Therefore, in order to use a variable, the computer must be told both the name of the variable and the type of data, either number or character, that will be assigned to it.

Assigning a Numeric Variable

An assignment statement is one way of giving a value to a variable. For example,

```
10 A = 5
```

instructs the computer to set aside a place in its memory named A where the number 5 is stored. The computer's memory is like a post office with its memory divided into many boxes with a variable name used to represent the address of a single box. When the computer executes the above assignment statement, it sets aside a box in its memory, names it A and puts 5 in it:

A

```
5
```

Whenever the computer is told to use A, it looks in the box named A and uses the value that A represents, in this case, 5. Note that this statement may not be entered as 5 = A because this would cause an error.

The value stored by a variable can change as the name "variable" implies; however, it is important to realize that a variable can hold only one value at a time. Suppose a later statement such as

```
50 A = 7
```

is entered. When line 50 is executed the value stored in the box named A changes from 5 to 7:

A

```
7
```

The old value of A is lost and may not be retrieved again.

When using variables, Applesoft only considers the first two characters of a variable name to differentiate it from any other variable name. For example, the names TALL and TAXES would represent the same variable (TA). For this reason we will use only one or two character variable names.

Program 10.2

This program demonstrates how variables are used in a program:

```
]NEW
]10 A = 5
]20 B = 3
]30 PRINT A * B
]40 A = 7
]50 B = 12
]60 PRINT A * B
]70 END

]RUN
15
84
```

Line 10 assigns the value 5 to variable A, and line 20 assigns the value 3 to variable B. Line 30 instructs the computer to print the product of A and B.

A   B

```
5                                    3
```

A variable can only hold one value at a time. If a different number is put in the box, then the first number is erased and lost. This happens when line 40 assigns the value of 7 to variable A, and line 50 assigns 12 to variable B.

A   B

```
7                                    12
```

10.6 Using String Variables

A character is any letter, number, punctuation mark or mathematical symbol which can be found on the computer's keyboard. For example, A, !, and 5 are all characters. Even a blank space is a character. A "string" is a single character or series of characters that are strung together to form a word, number or sequence of symbols. Numbers can be made part of a string, but they cannot be used in a mathematical operation since the computer thinks of them as symbols rather than numbers when they are stored in a string variable.

When a string variable is given a name, the variable name must be followed by a dollar sign ($) so that the computer knows that this variable stores a string. A letter, a letter and single digit, or two letters followed by a dollar sign instructs the computer that the variable is a string variable. A$, N$, P1$, and TA$ are all legal string variable names.

Assigning a String Variable

When a string variable is given its value by an assignment statement the characters that make up the string must be enclosed by quotation marks:

```
10 N$ = "Harry"
```

This statement assigns the string Harry to the variable N$.

If we think of boxes again, the computer names one of its boxes N$ and places the string Harry in it when line 10 is executed:

```
  N$
┌───────┐
│ Harry │
└───────┘
```

As with numeric variables, it is possible to change the value assigned to the variable N$. For example,

```
50 N$ = "Jane"
```

changes the value of N$ from Harry to Jane when line 50 is executed:

```
  N$
┌──────┐
│ Jane │
└──────┘
```

Program 10.3

This program shows the string variable N$ being assigned two different values:

```
]NEW
]10 N$ = "Judy"
]20 PRINT N$
]30 N$ = "George"
]40 PRINT N$
]50 END

]RUN
Judy
George
```

10.7 INPUT: a number

The INPUT statement allows a value to be assigned to a variable directly from the keyboard so that it may be changed each time the program is run. The assignment statement, on the other hand, assigns the same value to a variable each time the program is run. A program that calculates a savings account balance provides a good example of these two situations. Each time money is deposited or withdrawn from the account the amount is likely to be different, but the rate of interest that the bank pays its depositors changes infrequently. Therefore, a deposit or withdrawal is best entered with an INPUT statement while the interest rate is best assigned to a variable.

The statement

```
10 INPUT A
```

allows a value to be assigned to A directly from the keyboard. When the computer executes the INPUT statement, it prints a question mark on the screen and then waits for data to be typed in and Return pressed.

Program 10.4

This program inputs a number, N, and prints the result of that number multiplied by 5:

```
]NEW
]10 INPUT N
]20 PRINT "5 * " N " = "
]30 PRINT 5 * N
]40 END

]RUN
?7
5 * 7 =
35
```

When line 10 is executed, the computer prints a question mark on the screen and then waits for the user to enter a number. When 7 is typed after the question mark and Return pressed, the computer sets aside a box in it memory, names it N, and places a 7 in it:

N

```
┌───┐
│ 7 │
└───┘
```

The value stored in N is then printed by line 20 and used in the calculation in line 30.

INPUT Errors

Be careful when using an INPUT statement not to use commas when entering large numbers because commas will cause the computer to print an ?EXTRA IGNORED error and ignore any numbers typed after the command. A second run of Program 10.4 illustrates this:

```
]RUN
?3,500
?EXTRA IGNORED
5 * 3 =
15
```

The computer accepted only the 3 (not 3,500) because of the comma.

?REENTER

If a letter or word is typed when the computer is expecting a number, it prints a ?REENTER error message and waits for appropriate input. Running Program 10.4 again illustrates this:

```
]RUN
?Six
?REENTER
?6
5 * 6 =
30
```

To prevent the ?REENTER error, the program user should be given a message indicating the kind of data expected. The message can be made part of an INPUT statement by combining the INPUT with the message enclosed in quotation marks:

```
10 INPUT "Type a number: "; N
```

A semicolon (;) must follow the quotation marks that end the message to separate it from the variable name; otherwise a ?SYNTAX ERROR will halt the program. Here is a run of the modified Program 10.4:

```
]RUN
Type a number: 7
5 * 7 =
35
```

The message makes it clear to the user as to what type of information should be input.

10.8 INPUT: a string

An INPUT statement can also be used to assign a string of characters to a variable, for example:

```
10 INPUT A$
```

Letters, symbols and numbers can be assigned to the variable A$. When the computer is expecting a value for a string variable the ?REENTER error message will not appear because the computer can accept numbers as part of a string.

Program 10.5

This program prints the string input by the user for A$:

```
]NEW
]10 INPUT "Enter a string: "; A$
]20 PRINT "This is what you typed:"
]30 PRINT A$
]40 END

]RUN
Enter a string: I am a 1990 Ivy graduate!
This is what you typed:
I am a 1990 Ivy graduate!
```

Line 10 instructs the computer to set aside a box in its memory named A$ and then assigns data to it typed in from the keyboard:

```
                A$
```
```
┌─────────────────────────────┐
│ I am a 1990 Ivy graduate!   │
└─────────────────────────────┘
```

As you can see, both the numbers 1990 and the exclamation mark symbol are stored in the string.

Program 10.6

This program, which calculates Ivy University's usually inflated grades, illustrates the use of all of the statements covered so far. It asks the user for a student's name and four grades, then prints the name and the student's average:

```
]NEW
]10 INPUT "Student's name: "; N$
]20 INPUT "English grade: "; E
]30 INPUT "History grade: "; H
]40 INPUT "Mathematics grade: "; M
]50 INPUT "Science grade: "; S
]60 PRINT
]70 A = (E + H + M + S) / 4
]80 PRINT "The average for " N$ " is " A
]90 END

]RUN
Student's name: Mike Porter
English grade: 78
History grade: 85
Mathematics grade: 71
Science grade: 50

The average for Mike Porter is 71

]RUN
Student's name: Suzie Jones
English grade: 92
History grade: 72
Mathematics grade: 86
Science grade: 90

The average for Suzie Jones is 85
```

Note how parentheses are used in line 70 so that the sum of the variables is divided by 4 rather than only the variable S. Also note how the PRINT statement at line 60 is used to print a blank line before the average, making the output easier to read.

10.9 IF...THEN

The IF...THEN statement is called a "conditional statement". When a condition is met, a specified response is carried out; when not met, the statement is ignored. This is in contrast to the statements introduced so far (PRINT and INPUT) which are executed whenever they are read by the computer.

To describe a condition to the computer, an IF...THEN statement is used:

```
IF <condition> THEN <statement>
```

In the <condition> part of the IF statement a comparison is made. If the comparison is true, the computer then executes the <statement> following THEN; if false, it ignores the statement and proceeds to the next line in the program. By using one of the symbols shown below, two quantities can be compared:

Symbol	Meaning
=	equal to
>	greater than
<	less than
>=	greater than or equal to
<=	less than or equal to
<>	not equal to

The following are examples of IF...THEN statements:

```
20 IF N$ = "Mike" THEN PRINT "Hello Mike!"
```

When the condition N$ = "Mike" is true, the computer prints Hello Mike! and goes on to the next line; if the condition is false (N$ is not equal to "Mike") it prints nothing and goes on to the next line.

```
30 IF A <> 10 THEN PRINT "Not equal to 10"
```

When the condition A is not equal to 10 is true, the computer prints Not equal to 10; if variable A stores 10, the condition is false and nothing is printed.

Program 10.7

This program determines whether the value input for variable X is the solution to the equation $2 * X = 6$:

```
]NEW
]10 INPUT "Type a number: "; X
]20 IF 2 * X = 6 THEN PRINT X " is the solution."
]30 END

]RUN
Type a number: 5

]RUN
Type a number: 3
3 is the solution.
```

In the first RUN, 5 is not the solution so the comparison is false and nothing is printed. In the second RUN, because 3 causes the comparison to be true the program prints "3 is the solution."

10.10 Comparing Strings

The IF...THEN statement can also compare letters of the alphabet as strings. When using strings, the comparison operators refer to alphabetical order rather than numeric order. Strings can be compared using variables or characters enclosed within quotation marks. The following examples illustrate this:

```
10 IF A$ < B$ THEN PRINT "Less than"
20 IF D$ > "M" THEN PRINT "Big letter"
```

In line 10 if A$ comes before B$ in the alphabet Less than is printed, if not, nothing is printed. For example, if A$ stores "A" and B$ stores "B" then Less than will be printed. In line 20 if the string stored in D$ comes after "M" alphabetically (is greater than) then Big letter is printed, if not, nothing is printed. For example, if D$ stores a "P" then Big letter will be printed, if D$ stores "L" nothing will be printed.

Program 10.8

The following program decides whether the string input for variable A$ is alphabetically before, equal to, or after the one input for variable B$:

```
]NEW
]10 INPUT "Enter first word: "; A$
]20 INPUT "Enter second word: "; B$
]30 IF A$ < B$ THEN PRINT A$ " is before " B$
]40 IF A$ > B$ THEN PRINT A$ " is after " B$
]50 IF A$ = B$ THEN PRINT A$ " is equal to " B$
]60 END
```

```
]RUN
Enter first word: sky
Enter second word: blue
sky is after blue

]RUN
Enter first word: Jimmy
Enter second word: Joanie
Jimmy is before Joanie

]RUN
Enter first word: crickets
Enter second word: crickets
crickets is equal to crickets
```

10.11 FOR...NEXT Loops

Often it is desirable to repeat a set of instructions a number of times by adding a loop to a program. The loop will then execute the program lines contained within it over and over again a set number of times. To do this a FOR...NEXT loop is used which takes the form:

```
FOR <variable> = <starting value> TO <ending value>
    <statements>
    .
    .
NEXT <variable>
```

Note that the <variable> after the FOR and the NEXT must be the same and that a string variable cannot be used. The first time through the loop the variable is given the <starting value>. Each time the loop is executed +1 is added to the current value of the variable until it reaches a value greater than the <ending value>. The following is an example of a valid FOR..NEXT loop:

```
10 FOR X = 2 TO 6
   .
   .
40 NEXT X
```

When this loop is executed X starts at line 10 with a value of 2 and retains this value until the NEXT X statement is encountered at line 40. At this point the value of X is increased by +1, changing from 2 to 3. All the statements in the lines occurring between lines 10 and 40 are executed in sequence during each consecutive pass through the loop. The program continues to return from line 40 to the line immediately following line 10 until X exceeds the specified limit of 6. At this point the program exits the loop and moves to the line following 40. During this process the loop is executed 5 times with X being assigned values of 2, 3, 4, 5 and 6.

Program 10.9

Here a FOR...NEXT loop is used to calculate and print the 5 times table from 0 to 10:

```
]10 FOR J = 0 TO 10
]20 PRINT J " * 5 = " J * 5
]30 NEXT J
]40 PRINT "Finished the loop"
]50 END
```

```
]RUN
0 * 5 = 0
1 * 5 = 5
2 * 5 = 10
3 * 5 = 15
4 * 5 = 20
5 * 5 = 25
6 * 5 = 30
7 * 5 = 35
8 * 5 = 40
9 * 5 = 45
10 * 5 = 50
Finished the loop
```

In line 10, J is initialized to 0 and increases by +1 each time the loop is repeated. Line 20 displays the multiplication table. The NEXT J on line 30 instructs the computer to increase the value of J by +1 if its value is less than or equal to 10; otherwise, it exits the loop and goes on to line 40.

STEP

By adding a STEP value at the end of a FOR...NEXT statement it is possible to make the loop count by values other than +1. For example the loop

```
30 FOR N = 3 TO 13 STEP 2
  .
  .
80 NEXT N
```

will execute 6 times with N being assigned the values 3, 5, 7, 9, 11 and 13. Each time the loop is executed the value of N is incremented by 2 because of the STEP 2.

```
120 FOR T = 10 TO 0 STEP -1
  .
  .
180 NEXT T
```

This loop counts backward because of the STEP -1. It will execute 11 times with T taking the values 10, 9, 8, 7, 6, 5, 4, 3, 2, 1 and 0.

Program 10.10

This program finds solutions to the condition $5 * X + 3 < 100$ for all odd integers from 7 to 25:

```
]NEW
]10 FOR X = 7 TO 25 STEP 2
]20 IF 5 * X + 3 < 100 THEN PRINT X
]30 NEXT X
]40 PRINT "Done"
]50 END

]RUN
7
9
11
13
15
17
19
Done
```

Lines 10 and 30 create a loop for testing the condition located at line 20. The loop starts at line 10 with X = 7 and each time the program reaches the NEXT X statement at line 30, X is incremented by a STEP value of 2. The program then returns to line 20 unless the value of X has exceeded 25, at which time the loop is exited and Done printed.

10.12 READ - DATA

So far we have had two methods of assigning a value to a variable; either using an assignment statement or an INPUT statement. Often it is desirable to build the values into a program using READ and DATA statements. Each time a READ statement is executed it assigns a value to a variable which it reads from DATA statements. The data is read in sequence item by item.

Program 10.11

This program allows Ivy chemistry professor Dr. Sulfuric to check a list of names to determine if a student is in her chemistry class:

```
]10 INPUT "Enter name for search: "; N$
]20 FOR S = 1 TO 9
]30 READ C$
]40 PRINT "Checking name "; S, C$
]50 IF N$ = C$ THEN PRINT C$ " is in the class."
]60 NEXT S
]70 PRINT "Done."
]80 DATA Appleby, Broadus, Couser
]90 DATA Jackson, Keith, Lombardi
]100 DATA Mulberry, Newman, Perez
]110 END

]RUN
Enter name for search: Lombardi
Checking name 1       Appleby
Checking name 2       Broadus
Checking name 3       Couser
Checking name 4       Jackson
Checking name 5       Keith
Checking name 6       Lombardi
Lombardi is in the class.
Checking name 7       Mulberry
Checking name 8       Newman
Checking name 9       Perez
Done.
```

When this program is run Dr. Sulfuric enters the student name, Lombardi, which is assigned to the variable N$. Then the FOR...NEXT loop formed by lines 20 to 60 is executed 9 times. On the first execution, for S = 1, line 30 reads the first element of data, Appleby, and assigns it to the variable C$. Line 40 prints both the values of S and C$. Line 50 checks whether N$ = C$. It does not so nothing is printed. The program then goes to line 60 where S is assigned a value of 2 and then to line 30. Line 30 now reads the second element of data, Broadus. Since N$ does not equal C$ line 50 again prints nothing. This process continues until S = 6 and Lombardi is read from the DATA statements. Now since N$ = C$ the message "Lombardi is in the class." is printed. The loop continues to be executed until S = 9. At this point the loop is exited, "Done." is printed and the program ends.

10.13 Learning More Programming

We hope that this brief introduction to programming has made you realize how interesting and rewarding writing programs can be. It is indeed challenging to make the computer do exactly what you want it to do. To become a competent programmer it is usually necessary to take courses which will teach you how to write long programs that can perform complex tasks. Chapter 11 discusses different careers in computing which you might consider; becoming a programmer is one of them.

Chapter Summary

Computers do not understand regular English and must be told what to do with a program written in a special language. Applesoft is a version of the BASIC programming language which is easy to learn and use. A program is a list of instructions that tells the computer which operations to perform and in what sequence to perform them.

Single instructions can be executed immediately by entering them in immediate mode. PRINT is the instruction used to display numbers, characters and words on the screen in either immediate mode or within a program.

Errors in a program line can be corrected by using the arrow keys before Return is pressed or by retyping the whole line after Return is pressed. Each line of a program must begin with a number. When the program is run the computer executes the program lines in sequence beginning with the lowest number and proceeding to the highest number.

The END statement should be the last statement in a program. RUN instructs the computer to execute the program stored in memory. LIST displays the program currently in the computer's memory. Both RUN and LIST are not part of a program.

SAVE stores a program on disk and LOAD recalls it from disk. CAT produces a list of all the programs and files stored on disk. NEW erases the computer's memory so that a new program may be entered.

Variable names are used to represent values. There are two types of variables; numeric variables, which can be assigned numbers, and string variables, which can be assigned characters, symbols and digits. A string is defined as any set of characters. The values assigned to variables may be changed at any time.

```
A = 35
```

is an example of a numeric variable being assigned a value.

```
F1$ = "Tod"
```

is an example of a string variable being assigned a value. Note that string variable names must end with a $ to distinguish them from numeric variable names.

INPUT allows a value to be assigned to a variable directly from the keyboard. An input statement may contain a message:

```
10 INPUT "Enter your name: "; N$
```

IF...THEN is called a conditional statement. If a condition is met, a specified response is carried out; if not met, the statement is ignored:

```
20 IF P$ = "Itch" THEN PRINT "Poison Ivy"
```

prints Poison Ivy only if P$ = "Itch"; otherwise, nothing is printed.

A FOR...NEXT loop allows instructions to be repeated a set number of times. The lines

```
10 FOR X = 1 TO 10
20 PRINT X
30 NEXT X
```

print the numbers from 1 to 10. Each time the loop is executed the value of X is increased by 1. Adding a STEP value produces increments of other than 1:

```
10 FOR X = 10 TO 1 STEP -1
20 PRINT X
30 NEXT X
```

These lines print the numbers in reverse order from 10 down to 1.

READ - DATA allows data to be stored in a program. The READ statement sequentially reads values from a DATA statement and assigns them to a variable.

Vocabulary

Applesoft - Version of the BASIC programming language which runs on Apple computers.

Assign - To give a variable a value.

BASIC - Popular computer programming language. Its name is an acronym for Beginner's All-Purpose Symbolic Instruction Code.

Bug - An error in either the design or the instructions of a program.

CAT/CATALOG - Command for producing a list of files and programs stored on disk.

Command - Instruction to the computer in a language the computer understands.

Conditional statement - Statement executed only when a condition is true. (See IF...THEN)

DATA - Statement that allows a list of data to be stored in a program. (See also READ)

Debugging - The process of finding and removing "bugs" (errors) in a program.

Edit - To make changes in a program.

END - Statement that halts program execution.

Execute - To carry out a command or instruction in a program.

FOR...TO - Statement used to define a loop.

IF...THEN - Conditional statement that instructs the computer to take a specified action if a comparison is found to be true, and no action if it is false.

Immediate mode - Mode in which the computer executes commands and instructions immediately when the Return key is pressed.

INPUT - Statement used for entering data into the computer directly from the keyboard.

Line number - Number in front of each program line that is used to place the line in its proper sequence within the program.

LIST - Command that displays the lines of the program currently in memory.

LOAD - Command for recalling a program previously stored on disk.

Loop - Section of a program designed to be executed repeatedly.

NEW - Command that erases the program currently in memory so that a new one can be entered.

NEXT - Statement that ends a loop started with a FOR...TO.

Numeric operator - A symbol (+, -, *, /, ^) used to express a mathematical operation.

Numeric variable - Variable which stores a numeric value.

PRINT - Statement that causes the computer to display information on the screen.

Program - Series of instructions written in a special language directing the computer to perform specific operations and in what order to perform them.

Program line - One line of instructions in a program. Each line is preceded by a line number.

Prompt - Square bracket (]) displayed by Applesoft when it is ready to accept instructions.

READ - Statement that takes data from a DATA statement and assigns it to a specified variable.

Relational operator - A symbol (=, <, >, <>, <=, >=) used to indicate the comparison of two values.

Reserved word - Word such as PRINT or FOR that is part of the programming language and therefore cannot be used as a variable name.

RUN - Command that starts program execution.

SAVE - Command that instructs the computer to save the program in memory on disk under the name specified.

Statement - All the elements that combined carry out an instruction, i.e., a PRINT instruction can be followed by quotation marks, variable names, semicolons, commas, etc., to make an entire PRINT statement.

String - A sequence of letters, numbers and/or special characters such as punctuation marks. Strings may not be used in mathematical calculations.

String variable - Variable that stores a string. All string variable names end with a dollar sign and may not be used in mathematical calculations.

Syntax - The correct rules or "grammar" of a programming language.

Syntax error - Statement or command which the computer does not understand because it does not fit the rules of the programming language.

Variable - Name used to represent a value that is stored in the memory of the computer by a program. The value assigned to a variable can be changed.

Reviews

Sections 10.1-10.4

1. What is the difference between writing a command in immediate mode or making it a part of a program?

2. a) How can an error be corrected in a program line if Return has not been pressed?
   b) How can an error be corrected in a program line if Return has been pressed?

3. What is a syntax error?

4. Why is it better to number the lines of a program by units of ten (10, 20, 30...) rather than by units of one (1, 2, 3...)?

5. What statement should always be the last statement in a program?

6. What output is produced when the following program is RUN?

```
10 A = 20
20 B = A + 10
30 PRINT B
40 END
```

7. Find and correct the errors in the following program. Show the output when the corrected program is run.

```
10 64 = B
20 32 = A
30 C = A + B
40 PRINT C
50 END
```

8. What output is produced when the following program is RUN?

```
10 PRINT "Going to Ivy"
30 PRINT "is a lot"
20 PRINT "of fun"
15 PRINT "especially if"
35 PRINT "you like to study."
50 END
```

9. What will be displayed if the LIST command is typed while the program in Review 8 is in the computer's memory?

10. Briefly explain what each of the following commands does:
    a) NEW
    b) SAVE
    c) LOAD
    d) CAT

Sections 10.5-10.7

11. What output is produced when the following program is RUN?

```
10 PRINT 25 * 2
20 PRINT "25 * 2"
30 PRINT "25 * 2 = " 25 * 2
40 END
```

12.   What output is produced when the following program is RUN?

```
10 A = 20
20 B = 30
30 C = 40
40 D = A + B + C
50 PRINT D * B
60 C = 12
70 PRINT D * B
80 END
```

13.   What output is produced when the following program is RUN?

```
10 N1$ = "Tommy"
20 N2$ = "Trisha"
30 PRINT "Who has seen " N2$ " or " N1$ "?"
40 PRINT "I saw " N2$
50 END
```

14.   What is the difference between assigning a variable its value using an assignment statement and using an INPUT statement?

15.   What output is displayed on the lines when the following program is RUN and the data shown entered?

```
10 INPUT N
20 PRINT N * 10
30 INPUT N
40 PRINT 30 * N
50 END

RUN
? 50
```
_____
```
? 50,000
```
_____

_____

Sections 10.8-10.9   16.   a) What happens if a number is typed when the following statement is executed:

```
10 INPUT N$
```

b) What happens if the string Happy is typed when the following statement is executed:

```
10 INPUT N
```

17.   What output is produced when each of the following programs is RUN?

a)
```
10 A = 100
20 B = 20
30 IF B >= A/3 THEN PRINT "Big!"
40 IF A < B^2 THEN PRINT "Small!"
50 IF A <> 2 * B THEN A = 5
60 PRINT A * B
70 END
```

b)
```
10 X$ = "Matilda"
20 Y$ = "Hortense"
30 IF X$ < Y$ THEN PRINT Y$
40 IF X$ >= Y$ THEN PRINT X$
50 END
```

Sections 10.10-10.11   18. What output is produced when each of the following programs is RUN?

a)
```
10 FOR J = 1 to 10
20 PRINT J - 5
30 NEXT J
40 FOR K = 2 TO 10 STEP 2
50 PRINT K * 2
60 NEXT K
70 END
```

b)
```
10 FOR N = 1 TO 6
20 READ C
30 PRINT N + C
40 PRINT N * C
50 NEXT N
60 DATA 5, 4, 7, 8, 12, 7
70 END
```

c)
```
10 FOR X = 5 TO 20 STEP 5
20 READ N$
30 PRINT N$ " is a good student."
40 NEXT X
50 DATA Arlene, Bobby, Marcia, Jim, Jane
60 DATA Harry, Roberto, Winston, Willy
70 END
```

d)
```
10 FOR X = 1 TO 9
20 READ N$
30 IF X / 2 < 2 THEN PRINT N$
40 NEXT X
50 DATA Arlene, Bobby, Marcia, Jim, Jane
60 DATA Harry, Roberto, Winston, Willy
70 END
```

Exercises

1. Perform each of the following computations on paper. Check your answers using immediate mode:

    a) 5 + 16   d) 239 * 27
    b) 33 - 16   e) 250 / 5
    c) 13 * 3   f) 999 / 11

2. Write a program that first prints the results of 275 times 39, and then 275 divided by 39.

    ```
    ]RUN
    275 * 39 = 10725
    275 / 39 = 7.05128
    ```

3. Write a program which assigns the value 10 to variable A, and 35 to B and then prints the results of A + B, A - B, A * B, and A / B.

4. Write a program that uses the asterisk symbol (*) to draw the letters I U on the screen:

    ```
    ]RUN

    * * * * * * * *        *           *
            *              *           *
            *              *           *
            *              *           *
            *              *           *
            *                 *     *
    * * * * * * * *           * * * * *
    ```

5. Write a program that uses INPUT to assign values to two variables A and B and then calculates their sum and product. A RUN of the program should look like this:

    ```
    ]RUN
    ?45
    ?10
    45 + 10 = 55
    45 * 10 = 450
    ```

6. Write a program in which the price of a loaf of bread (P) and the number of loaves purchased (N) is INPUT from the keyboard. The total spent for the bread is then printed:

    ```
    ]RUN
    Enter price of a loaf: .89
    Enter number of loaves: 6
    Total spent = $ 5.34
    ```

7. A piece of pizza normally contains about 375 calories. Jogging one mile burns about 100 calories. Write a program that asks the user how many pieces of pizza were eaten and then tells how many miles must be jogged to burn up the calories consumed.

    ```
    ]RUN
    How many pieces of pizza did you eat? 4

    You consumed 1500 calories
    and must jog 15 miles.
    ```

8. Write a program that computes the volume of a room given its length, width and height in cubic meters.

    ```
    ]RUN
    Enter length: 12
    Enter width: 4
    Enter height: 3
    144 cubic meters
    ```

9. Professional musicians have succeeded in making staggering sums of money through careful negotiations. Of course, the real winner is Uncle Sam, who does not negotiate at all. Write a program which asks for a musician's name and salary and then prints the name, take home pay and taxes assuming the tax rate for that income bracket is 30 percent:

    ```
    ]RUN
    Enter musician's name: Michael Jackson
    Enter musician's wage: 50000

    Michael Jackson would keep $35000
    Michael Jackson would pay $15000 in taxes.
    ```

10. A state has a 7% sales tax. Write a program which allows you to INPUT the name and price (before taxes) of an item found in a department store and then prints the item name, tax and the total cost of the item including the sales tax.

    ```
    ]RUN
    Enter name of item: Coat
    Enter price: 65

    Coat has a tax of $4.55 and costs $69.55
    ```

11. Write a program that allows two numbers A and B to be entered. Have the computer compare them and print a message stating whether A is less than, equal to, or greater than B.

```
]RUN
Enter first number: 12
Enter second number: 45

12 is less than 45


]RUN
Enter first number: 650
Enter second number: 650

650 is equal to 650
```

12. Allow a string A$ to be entered. Print the string and the message "is below" if A$ comes before the string "down" alphabetically; otherwise, print nothing.

```
]RUN
Enter a string: broke
broke is below down


]RUN
Enter a string: jump
```

13. Write a program which asks for a person's age. If the person is 16 years or older, have the computer print "You are old enough to drive a car!". Otherwise, have the computer indicate how many years the person must wait before being able to drive.

```
]RUN
Enter your age: 17
You are old enough to drive a car!


]RUN
Enter your age: 12
You may drive in 4 years.
```

14. Write a program that employs a FOR...NEXT loop to print the following values:

```
]RUN
5
10
15
20
25
```

15. Write a program that prints all integers with values between 1 and 100 which solve the condition $3 * X^2 + 5 * X + 3 < 200$.

16. Print the cubes of the odd integers from 11 to -11, inclusive, in descending order.

17.   Print all integers which end in 4 from 4 to 84, inclusive.

18.   Write a program that allows a player to play a number guessing game with the computer. The computer stores six numbers between 1 and 100 in a data statement. When the player enters a guess the data statements are searched for the number. If it is found the computer prints "You Win!"; otherwise, nothing is printed.

```
]RUN
Enter your guess: 38

]RUN
Enter your guess: 27
You Win!
```

Chapter 11
The Future of Computing: Social and Ethical Implications

Objectives

After completing this chapter you will be able to:

1. Define telecommunications and describe its uses.

2. Describe artificial intelligence and its use in expert systems and natural language processing.

3. Understand how robots may be used to automate tasks.

4. Describe different careers in computing and their educational requirements.

5. Understand the ethical responsibilities of computer use and programming.

6. Describe several objectives for the future of computing.

*I*n this concluding chapter we discuss the future of computing, including the effects on computers of various technological developments, the career possibilities created by computers, and the social and ethical consequences of living in a computerized society. After having studied the previous chapters you should have a good understanding of how useful and powerful a computer is. In the first chapter of this text we stated that computers, unlike people, could not actually think but could store huge amounts of data and process it at very high speeds. This chapter will describe how these capabilities will be exploited in the future to perform an ever increasing and varied number of tasks.

11.1 Tele-communications

One of the most important advances made in computing has been in the field of "telecommunications". By telecommunications we mean the sending of computer data over telephone lines. To do this an additional piece of hardware called a "modem" is required to translate the binary data of the computer into waves which can then be transmitted over phone lines. To receive data a modem must also have the capability of translating the waves back into binary form. This process involves what is called signal _mo_dulation and _dem_odulation, hence the name modem. In addition to the modem, special telecommunications software is required so that the computer can transmit and receive data.

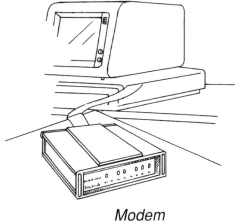

Modem

With a modem a microcomputer is capable of transmitting and receiving data between any two locations connected by phone lines. The rate at which each character of data is sent is measured in "baud", one baud representing the transmission of one character per second. Currently the most common rates are 300, 1200 and 2400 baud which means 300, 1200 and 2400 characters per second. However, newer modems are being created which are capable of communicating at 9600 baud and higher.

Any type of data that a computer is capable of storing can be sent and received by modem. Using a modem it is possible to access and search very large data bases which might store financial data, news reports, travel information or a company's sales data. If you go to a travel agent to book a flight, the agent will most likely use a computer to check the availability of flights and then make your reservation. The agent's computer will be hooked by modem to a large computer that contains a data base of flight information. This data base is similar to the ones you created using AppleWorks, only much larger.

Because of telecommunications it is now possible for many people to work at home rather than in an office. News reporters and writers often write their stories at home on a word processor and then transmit their word processing files to a central office many miles away. Financial consultants, accountants and travel agents are sometimes able to work at home accessing needed data bases using a computer and modem.

In many states it is possible to do your banking by computer, paying bills and making deposits from your home. Companies are also establishing computer services that allow you to shop at home, make your own travel reservations, even play a game of chess with someone in another state or country all by using a computer and modem. As you can see it is becoming increasingly apparent that the impact of telecommunications on our society will be significant.

11.2 Electronic Bulletin Boards and Mail

One of the most popular forms of telecommunication is the "electronic bulletin board" or "BBS". People who subscribe to a bulletin board service can call another computer and transmit messages to it which are then stored. When other subscribers of the service call the bulletin board it allows them to list all of the messages that have been "posted". Many companies and other organizations maintain bulletin boards to keep their employees aware of important events. For example, the Ivy University Alumni Association has an electronic bulletin board which lists the month's events including athletic events and alumni reunions. All an Ivy alumnus need do to get a list of all of the events is call up the bulletin board using a modem and computer.

Electronic mail or "E-Mail" is similar to an electronic bulletin board, but is used instead to send and receive messages meant for one person or a small group. The person sending the message contacts the electronic mail service using a computer and modem, and then types in the name of the recipient and the message. When the recipient calls the electronic mail service he or she receives the message. The advantage of this system is primarily speed. Often letters sent through the mail take days to receive, even when sent across a town, while electronic mail can be received instantly. Another advantage of this service is that recipients can receive messages when they want them rather than when they are sent. This is especially useful when messages are sent around the world. A message sent from New York at 9 A.M. will be immediately received and stored by a computer in Tokyo at 1 A.M. Tokyo time, but the person in Tokyo need not call the electronic mail service until a more convenient time.

To keep electronic mail private a password system is employed. When first calling to receive messages, a person is asked to enter a secret password which must then be verified by the computer before the messages are transmitted.

It is possible to create a copy of a message left on a BBS or E-Mail system on your computer. This is called "downloading" and involves having the system's computer send a copy of the message file to your computer, where it is stored on disk. Similarly, the process of sending files to a BBS or E-Mail system is called "uploading".

Electronic mail is especially popular in universities where students and faculty can easily send messages to each other. If Ivy University chemistry instructor, Dr. Sulfuric, wants to change her homework assignment she can send the new assignment to each member of her class using the university's electronic mail system. She can also find out if the messages have been received (downloaded) because the system keeps a record of when each member of her class has checked for messages. It would be possible to complete the assignment using a word processor and send the answers as another message (upload).

A growing number of universities now require all of their students to purchase microcomputers and modems. Among many other advantages, it has allowed everyone on their campuses to make use of electronic mail services.

11.3 Future of Computing

In Chapter One we traced the history of computing and discovered that, as technology improved, computers increased in speed, stored more data, decreased in size and most importantly became less expensive. This trend will, in all probability, continue. As it does, one of the advances will be the continued development of small microprocessors which will be found in an ever increasing number of appliances and devices. Microprocessors can already be found in telephone answering machines, cameras, television sets, refrigerators, washing machines and automobiles.

One example of the use of a microprocessor is in the anti-lock braking system (ABS) found on many cars. A computer connected to sensors on a car's wheels detects when, as the brakes are applied, the car begins to skid. The computer then takes over control of the brakes, pumping them rapidly to keep the wheels from locking. This process avoids the skidding which often results when brakes are applied on wet roads. Other microprocessors are being developed which increase the efficiency of an automobile engine or control how safety devices will perform in case of an accident.

Microprocessors are also found in auto-focusing cameras which both focus themselves and set the proper exposure. To focus the camera a high frequency sound is sent from the camera to the subject. The sound then bounces off of the subject and back to a receiver on the camera. A microprocessor measures the time for the sound to return and then calculates the distance, setting the focus accordingly. To set the proper exposure the camera uses a photocell to measure the intensity of light and then, using a microprocessor, calculates the correct exposure.

One of the most promising areas of microprocessor development is in the diagnostic systems of complex electronic devices. Many devices such as computers and photocopiers have become so complicated that it is difficult to determine what is wrong when they malfunction. Therefore microprocessors have been developed which pinpoint what component is not working properly and then alerts the user. These types of systems will soon be commonly found on automobiles, aircraft or any device which contains a large number of complicated parts. Undoubtedly many new applications for microprocessors will be found in the future in areas which we cannot begin to imagine.

Besides the development of better microprocessors, software will also improve. Most software developers are attempting to make their software increasingly "user friendly", which means easier to use. In learning the three applications areas you were required to familiarize yourself with a number of commands. By making the commands have similar effects in each of the applications areas, the program was made easier to learn. This process will continue to become less complicated as better software is written. Later in this chapter we will discuss attempts to produce computers that will allow the user to use voice rather than typed commands.

11.4 Artificial Intelligence

Although computers cannot think, one of the major areas of research continues to be the development of software programs that are capable of making increasingly complex decisions. The concept of using computers to make decisions which would normally be made by human beings is called "artificial intelligence". Herbert Schorr, a computer scientist at IBM, has declared that the development of artificial intelligence is the "second wave" of the information revolution. The first wave was the development of automated data processing which you studied when producing data bases and spreadsheets. According to Schorr "the second wave will automate decision making".

In a recent newspaper article the Internal Revenue Service (I.R.S.) defined artificial intelligence as "the science of making machines do things that would require intelligence if done by man". As an example, there are currently computers which can play chess so well that they can beat all but the best players. Universities actually challenge each other's computers to play chess to determine which has the best chess playing program. Are these computers really intelligent? Most computer scientists would say no. They are simply programmed to make a series of decisions in response to the moves made by their opponents. It is merely their speed and ability to access huge amounts of stored data which make them appear to be intelligent.

In 1950 the brilliant English mathematician Alan Turing wrote a paper entitled "Computing Machinery and Intelligence" in which he raised the question "Can machines think?". To answer the question he invented the "Imitation Game". Briefly summarized, the game involves placing a person and a computer in separate rooms and an interrogator in a third room. Communicating by typed questions and answers the interrogator questions the human and computer to determine which is the computer. If the interrogator cannot tell the difference between the responses then, according to Turing, the machine has human thought capabilities. Since not even psychologists can agree on a definition of intelligence, this is probably as good a test as any. Currently, no computer or software package has been shown to be capable of passing Turing's test.

11.5 Expert Systems

One of the most promising areas of research into artificial intelligence is the development of what is called "expert systems". An expert system is programmed to produce the same solution a human expert would if asked to solve the same problem. The concept was first employed in research done in the 1960's at Stanford University by Professor Edward Feigenbaum and Doctor Edward Shortliffe. They developed a computer program named "Mycin", named for a group of antibiotics, which was designed to perform medical diagnosis of infectious diseases and suggest possible treatments. The program worked by asking questions about a patient's symptoms. A diagnosis was then given based upon the answers. Was this program actually thinking? Again, we answer no. The program was making its decisions based upon over 500 rules given it by human experts. For example, such a rule might specify that if a patient had a low-level infection and was allergic to penicillin, then the antibiotic Erythromycin should be prescribed.

Mycin, which took more than 20 man-years to develop, turned out to be more accurate than the human experts against whom it was tested. In one test Mycin prescribed the correct treatment 65% of the time, in contrast to the experts who were right in 42% to 62% of the cases. One of the problems with Mycin was that it did not know whether it was diagnosing a human being or not. In fact, it was capable of prescribing penicillin to fix a broken window.

Since the experiment at Stanford, many expert systems have been developed in fields as diverse as accounting, medicine, law and automobile repair. Although expert systems can be helpful in reducing the time it takes a professional to analyze and solve a problem, it has so far been apparent that a computer is sometimes a poor substitute for a human expert. This is because human experts may use "intuition" to solve a problem. In making a diagnosis a doctor uses intuition when making a decision which is not based on systematic logic. By looking at a patient and discussing his or her feelings and moods, a doctor is often able to ascertain important information which could not be used by a computer. We consider these to be "human" or "psychological" factors which, while very important, can not be programmed into a computer.

An example of an expert system that works quite well is one installed by the credit card division of American Express. In the past when a store called to get approval for a large charge, a trained credit expert would have to decide if approval should be given. By asking a series of questions about the amount being charged, the type of item being purchased, and so on, the expert would then make a decision. Now if an American Express card holder wants to make a large purchase, for example a $10,000 oriental rug, in many cases the computer will decide whether or not to approve the purchase.

Another useful expert system involves the repair of automobiles. In the past when Ford automobile dealers were confronted by a hard-to-diagnose engine problem they called expert Gordy Kujawski. Now they simply access a computer system developed to duplicate the reasoning Kujawski uses to solve a problem. Creating the expert system involved describing Kujawski's thought processes in terms of rules, like the Mycin program. Programmers watched Kujawski at work and asked "Why did you test the battery?" and "How did you know to look at the carburetor?" and programmed the computer to act the same way.

One of the more secretive uses of expert systems is that used by U.S. intelligence agents to avert terrorist acts. Programmed with the knowledge of a handful of terrorism agents, the system has proven surprisingly accurate in its ability to predict when and where terrorist activities will occur. Another similar system is used by the F.B.I. to predict the activities of criminals. Both systems have been programmed with rules that experts have developed based on many years of experience.

We earlier referred to the I.R.S. definition of artificial intelligence. They have developed an expert system which analyzes tax returns to determine if a person is correctly reporting income or making improper deductions. Programmed to look for suspicious patterns, the I.R.S. computer decides when a human agent should consider initiating a tax audit.

Currently there are about 3,000 expert systems in use with the number increasing at the rate of 50% per year. To date the expert systems that work the best are those for which a series of rules can be used to make a decision. When specific rules do not apply, as when intuition must be used, expert systems are usually not successful.

11.6 Natural Language Processing

Designing a computer system that can recognize human speech has long been a goal of computer scientists. After almost three decades of slow progress, machines are now being developed that can recognize spoken words and then translate them into digital form. This is called "speech recognition" and involves "natural language processing", a field of artificial intelligence which attempts to translate a sentence into its separate parts and understand its meaning.

The difficulties in producing natural language processing systems are many. First, many words have different meanings based upon the context in which they are used. The word "change", for example, could mean money as in "Here's your change" or a different order as in "Change my order to a hot dog". Second, there are almost an unlimited number of ways of giving the same instructions. And finally, a speech recognizing computer needs to be able to understand many different voice patterns and accents.

Solving these problems highlights the difference between human and machine "intelligence". A person would have little problem overcoming the difficulties mentioned above, but to a machine, which is programmed to follow instructions in a logical sequence, the difficulties are considerable.

A recent advance in natural language processing has been the development of the Sphinx software package by Carnegie-Mellon graduate student Kai-Fu Lee. It is an experimental system capable of recognizing continuous speech based on a vocabulary of almost 1,000 words. Most previous systems have been limited to individual words or words separated by pauses. One of the major advances made by Sphinx is its ability to recognize speech from many different speakers.

The potential applications for natural language processing systems are numerous. One such development will allow users of car telephones to dial their phones by speaking the numbers. Other potential uses include allowing people to dictate letters to their word processors or ordering airline tickets over a telephone connected to a computer. Voice messages might also be sent in digital form to computers as electronic mail.

One very useful application of natural language processing would be in language translation. A person calling France could speak in English with the computer translating and speaking in French at the other end. Although systems have already been developed which allow the user to type in English and have the output printed in French, machines which can handle spoken language appear to be well off in the future.

A major problem faced by language translation programs is that most languages such as French, German, and especially Asian languages such as Japanese and Chinese are structured differently than

English. Also, as you have learned if you have studied a foreign language, many words have a number of different meanings. For all of these reasons even the best translation programs are at present not very accurate, often producing humorous results. A computer asked to translate the biblical passage "the spirit is willing, but the flesh is weak" from English into Russian and then back into English produced the result "the wine is agreeable, but the meat is spoiled".

Many computer scientists believe that future advances in artificial intelligence will depend upon the development of radically new technologies. To be truly useful as artificial intelligence machines, computers will have to possess some form of "common sense". They will have to be able to distinguish, for example, between a person and a window, as Mycin cannot. Until this is accomplished we will be wise to give artificial intelligence systems only limited trust, being on guard against the errors in judgement they may make.

11.7 Robotics

Another application of artificial intelligence is in "robotics". To be defined as a robot a machine must be able to be programmed and also be able to move. Most robots, unlike an R2D2 or C3PO, are simply moveable arms that can be directed to perform a task by moving. Because they can be programmed, robots can make simple decisions and then act upon them.

Of the robots currently "employed", most are used in the automobile industry to spot weld and spray paint cars. As robots become capable of performing increasingly complicated tasks, they will undoubtedly be used in many more industries.

There are a number of advantages to using robots. One is their ability to perform tasks too dangerous for humans. Robots have been developed which can defuse and remove bombs, work in highly radioactive environments, or under conditions of extreme noise or temperatures. Their use in aiding handicapped people is also a very promising area. A major advantage of robots is that they can perform their tasks tirelessly, willing to work twenty-four hour days without rest or vacations.

To date robots have been used only to perform simple, repetitive tasks. They have often been both expensive and unreliable. A task as simple as picking up an egg has proven extremely difficult for them to perform. The eye-hand coordination which we take for granted requires an extremely complex set of actions which are difficult to duplicate mechanically. Even a task as simple as moving through a room without hitting objects is currently difficult for today's robots.

We have all seen science fiction movies where a robot becomes so human-like that it exhibits emotions and temperament, but so far no real robot has been developed which has any of these traits. In all probability such a robot is a very long way off if indeed one can ever be invented.

When natural language processing and artificial intelligence programs are perfected, the use of robots will undoubtedly increase. The dream of having a machine you can order around like a personal servant may then become a reality.

The factory of the future will probably contain numerous robots performing a wide variety of tasks. As manufacturers produce an increasing number of highly complicated products, robots will be easier to train than human beings.

11.8 Careers in Computing

As computers become more powerful they will play an ever increasing role in the world in which we live. Consequently most people, no matter what field they are employed in, will encounter computers. It is estimated that by the end of the 1990's over 90% of all office personnel will have a computer terminal or PC at their desks.

Doctors, lawyers, accountants, business people, educators, farmers and almost any profession you can think of are currently using or will soon make use of computers. It is the purpose of this text to introduce you to the many varied tasks that a computer can perform to help and prepare you for almost any career you might consider.

If you have become especially interested in computers you might consider a career in computing. According to recent government projections the computer field will continue to hire people at an increasing rate. In this section we will discuss some of the careers that you might consider and the education required to enter them.

Data Processing

The area of computing that employs the largest number of people is data processing. Data processing, as you have already learned, involves the electronic storage, manipulation and retrieval of data. Banks, businesses, educational institutions - almost any organization requires large amounts of data and therefore people capable of data processing. Careers in data processing are usually divided into the following six categories:

1. System Analyst
2. System Developer -Programmer
3. System Manager
4. Computer Operator
5. Data-entry Operator
6. Computer Science and Research

We will consider each area separately, outlining the qualifications expected of a person entering the area.

System Analyst

Before a data processing system can be set up a system analyst must first analyze and design the system. The analyst must determine how an organization will use their computer system, what data they will store, how they will access it, and how they expect the system to grow in the future. The success or failure of the data processing system will be primarily determined by how well the analyst does his or her job. The data base chapters emphasized the importance of carefully planning how a data base is to be structured. This type of planning gave you an introduction to what a system analyst does.

The following are characteristics a system analyst should possess:

(1) A good knowledge of the organization installing the data processing system including its goals and objectives.

(2) A comprehensive knowledge of both data-processing methods and the current software and hardware available.

(3) A knowledge of programming languages and how they might be used to produce required software.

(4) The ability to work well with both technical and nontechnical personnel.

Most system analysts are college graduates who have majored in computer science or business administration or both. A good way to start preparing yourself to be a system analyst is to take the programming courses offered by your school in languages such as BASIC and Pascal and business courses such as management and accounting.

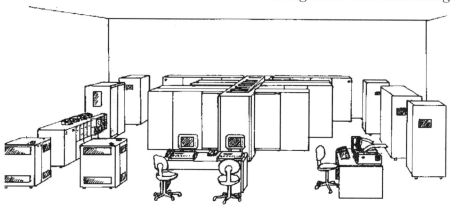

Large Computer Installation

System Developer - Programmer

After the system analyst has determined what type of system should be installed, it is the job of the system developer to provide the necessary software. This is accomplished by writing three types of programs:

1. system programs - are programs that operate the system's hardware. The disk operating system booted on your microcomputer is an example of a system program.

2. applications programs - are programs that solve specific problems. In a business these might be problems such as customer billing or inventory control. The word processing, data base and spreadsheet programs you have used are applications programs.

3. program maintenance - many businesses need their programs expanded or changed to meet new demands or to correct errors. This is called program maintenance.

The following are characteristics a programmer should possess:

(1) A detailed knowledge of the programming language being used.

(2) A detailed knowledge of the organization for which the program is being written.

(3) An ability to reason analytically and pay close attention to details.

(4) Creativity to develop problem-solving strategies.

(5) Considerable patience needed to work out the fine details of a program and to discover the "bugs" it may contain.

(6) Knowledge of how the programs and computer hardware will interact

The education required to be a programmer is usually determined by the needs of the employer. Many businesses employ programmers who have taken only technical school or junior college programming courses. Large or specialized companies, which need highly sophisticated programming, usually require college graduates. A good way to start in preparing for a career as a programmer is to take the programming and computer science courses as well as the mathematics courses offered by your school.

System Manager

Companies with large data processing requirements usually employ a manager who is responsible for running the Management Information Systems department (MIS). The MIS manager must organize the computer and human resources of the department in order to best achieve the organization's goals.

The following are characteristics a system manager should possess:

(1) A detailed understanding of the organization's goals.

(2) The ability to motivate and work closely with technical personnel.

(3) A detailed understanding of data-processing methods, hardware, and software.

A college degree in business administration with a concentration in information systems is desirable to be a system manager. Since a system manager is an administrator he or she will usually possess previous management experience.

Computer Operator

A computer operator is responsible for setting up equipment, mounting and removing tapes and disks, and monitoring the computer's operation. Often the computer operator must help the programmers and users of a computer when problems arise.

The following are characteristics a computer operator should possess:

(1) A good understanding of how the computer equipment operates.

(2) The ability to read and understand technical manuals.

(3) Be able to detect and correct operational errors.

(4) Good communication skills to explain to computer users problems they may encounter.

Most computer operators have technical school or junior college educations. Because of the many different types of computers, the majority of their training is usually received on the job. A good way to prepare for a career as a computer operator is to take computer courses in school and assist, if possible, in the operation and maintenance of the school's computers.

Data-Entry Operator

It is the job of a data-entry operator to type data into a computer. This is usually done at a computer terminal which is much like the computer you have been using. Data-entry operators may work for banks entering cancelled checks, department stores entering inventory figures, or educational institutions entering student records.

Often data is entered from various locations and then sent over phone lines to a central computer. Because of this it is sometimes possible for data-entry operators to work at home.

The following are characteristics a data-entry operator should possess:

(1) The ability to type fast and accurately.

(2) Attention to detail in order to pick up errors that may occur.

Usually a high school diploma is sufficient to gain a job as a data-entry operator. Often several weeks of on the job training will be offered by the employer. To begin to prepare for a position as a data-entry operator it is advisable to take courses in typing and word processing.

Computer Scientist   The study of computer science is a very broad field involving many disciplines including science, electronics and mathematics. A computer scientist often works in research at a university or computer manufacturer developing new computer applications software and hardware. It is computer scientists who first design robots, natural language processors, or any of the other many applications that we have mentioned.

The following are characteristics a computer scientist should possess:

(1) A sense of curiosity.

(2) An aptitude for science and mathematics.

(3) Patience to perform experiments that may take years to perfect.

A computer scientist usually has both undergraduate and graduate school degrees. To prepare to be a computer scientist it is advisable to take science courses, especially physics, mathematics courses including calculus, and programming and computer science courses.

11.9 The Social and Ethical Consequences of Computers

The society in which we live has been so profoundly effected by computers that historians refer to the present time as "the information age". This is due to the computer's ability to store and manipulate large amounts of information (data). Computers have become such a dominant force that if all of them were to disappear much of our society would be unable to function. Because of computers we are evolving out of an industrial into an information society much as over a hundred years ago we evolved from an agricultural into an industrial society. Such fundamental changes in society cause disruptions which must be planned for. For this reason it is crucial that we consider both the social and ethical consequences of our increasing dependence on computers.

We have already mentioned the impact of telecommunications. By allowing people to work anywhere that telephones or satellite communications are available, we are likely to become a more diversified society. Large cities with their centralized offices will no longer be as necessary. This diversification could reduce traffic congestion, air pollution and many of the other consequences of an urban society. Stock brokers or writers, for example, can now consider the benefits of working outside a city and yet still have all of the facilities they need readily available to them through a computer. Because of this, Alvin Toffler in his book "The Third Wave" called this the age of the "electronic cottage".

In our discussion of robots we mentioned their ability to work twenty-four hour days without vacations. While this is obviously a major benefit to an employer, it could have a negative impact on employees. Manufacturers are increasingly able to replace factory workers with machines, thereby increasing efficiency and saving money. This trend, however, also leads to increased unemployment of those factory workers who lack technical skills.

The argument is often used that new technologies such as robotics create jobs for the people who design, build, install and service them. While this is true, these new jobs require well educated, highly trained people. For this reason it is important to think carefully about the educational requirements needed for employment. As we become an increasingly "high-tech" society, those properly prepared for technical jobs will be the most likely to find employment. In response to this problem many states have instituted programs to train laid-off factory workers so that they may enter technical fields.

One of the probable benefits of our information society will be a reduction in the work week. In the agricultural age people often worked 80 or more hours per week just to grow enough food to feed their families. During the early part of the industrial age most factory workers worked 60 hours per week. Presently most people work less than 40 hours per week, and with increased technology the work week will likely continue to decrease.

11.10 The Right to Privacy

With computers impacting on our lives in an ever increasing number of ways, serious ethical questions arise. By ethical questions we mean asking what are the right and wrong ways to use computers. As human beings we want to insure that our rights as individuals are not encroached upon by the misuse of these machines.

Probably the most serious problem created by computers is in invading our right to privacy. Because, as we have learned, computers can store vast amounts of data we must decide what types are proper to store and what types improper. Every time you use a credit card, make a phone call, withdraw money from the bank, reserve a flight on an airplane, or register to take a course at school a computer records the transaction. Using these records it would be possible to learn a great deal about you - where you have been, when you were there, and what you have done.

Computers are also used to store information dealing with your credit rating, which determines your ability to borrow money. If you want to buy a car and finance it at the bank, the bank first checks your credit records on a computer to determine if you have a good credit rating. If you are able to purchase the car and then apply for automobile insurance, another computer will check to determine if you have traffic violations or have been involved in any activities which would make you a poor risk. How do you know if the information being used is accurate? To protect both your privacy and the accuracy of data stored about you, a number of laws have been passed.

The Fair Credit Reporting Act of 1970 deals with data collected for use by credit, insurance and employment agencies. The act gives individuals the right to see information maintained about them. If a person is denied credit they are allowed access to the files used to make the credit determination. If any of the information is incorrect, the person has the right to have it changed. The act also restricts who may access credit files to only those with a court order or the written permission of the individual whose credit is being checked.

The Privacy Act of 1974 restricts the way in which personal data can be used by federal agencies. Individuals must be permitted access to information stored about them and may correct any information that is incorrect. Agencies must insure both the security and confidentiality of any sensitive information. Although this law applies only to federal agencies, many states have adopted similar laws.

The Financial Privacy Act of 1978 requires that a government authority have a subpoena, summons, or search warrant to access an individual's financial records. When such records are released, the financial institution must notify the individual of who has had access to them.

Laws such as the three mentioned above help to insure that the right to privacy is not infringed by data stored in computer files. Although implementing privacy laws has proven expensive and difficult, most people would agree that they are needed.

11.11 Protecting Computer Software and Data

Because computer software can be copied electronically it is easy to duplicate. Such duplication is usually illegal because the company producing the software is not paid for the copy. This has become an increasingly serious problem as the number of illegal software copies distributed by computer "pirates" has grown. Developing, testing and marketing software is an expensive process. If the software developer is then denied rightful compensation, the future development of all software is jeopardized. Suppose for example that a programmer has written a piece of software which you like. If you illegally make copies and distribute them to your friends, that programmer loses income and may not be able to continue developing new software. Because most software is continually being updated and improved you could be denied these better versions.

Software companies are increasingly vigilant in detecting and prosecuting those who illegally copy their software. Therefore, when using software it is important to only use legally acquired copies, and to not make illegal copies for others.

Another problem that is growing as computer use increases is the willful interference with or destruction of computer data. Because computers can transfer and erase data at high speeds, it makes them especially vulnerable to acts of vandalism. Newspapers have carried numerous reports of home computer users gaining access to large computer data bases. Sometimes these "hackers" change or erase data stored in the system. These acts are usually illegal and can cause very serious and expensive damage.

One especially harmful act is the planting of a "virus" into computer software. A virus is a series of instructions buried into a program which cause the computer to destroy data when given a certain signal. For example, the instructions to destroy data might wait until a certain time or date is reached before being executed. Because the virus is duplicated each time the software is copied it spreads, hence the name virus. This practice is illegal and can result in considerable damage being done.

Most people are becoming aware that the willful destruction of computer data is no different than any other vandalization of property. Since the damage is done electronically the result is often not as obvious as destroying physical property, but the consequences are much the same. It is estimated that computer crimes may cost the nation as much as 30 billion dollars a year and be rising each year.

11.12 The Ethical Responsibilities of the Programmer

Increasingly computers are being used to make decisions in situations which can threaten human life. In one incident a patient being treated for cancer received five times the prescribed amount of radiation due to an error in the computer program operating the radiation machine. The consequences were a serious hazard to her life and health. As the use of computers to control medical equipment increases, this type of error may become more common.

It is extremely difficult, if not impossible, for a computer programmer to guarantee that a program will always operate properly. The programs used to control complicated devices contain millions of instructions and as the programs grow longer the likelihood of errors increases. What is a special cause for concern is the increased use of computers to control potentially dangerous devices such as aircraft, nuclear reactors, military weapons or sensitive medical equipment. This places a strong ethical burden on the programmer to insure, as best he or she can, the reliability of computer software.

The Defense Department is currently supporting research aimed at detecting and correcting program errors. Because it spends an estimated 18 billion dollars annually developing software, much of it for use in situations which can be life threatening, the department is especially interested in having reliable programs.

As capable as computers have proven to be, we must be cautious in allowing them to replace human beings in areas where judgement is crucial. Because we are intelligent, humans can often detect that something out of the ordinary has occurred and then take actions which have not been previously anticipated. Computers, on the other hand, will only do what they have been programmed to do, even if it is to perform a dangerous act.

We must also consider situations in which the computer can protect human life better than humans. For example, in the space program astronauts place their lives in the hands of computers which must continuously perform complicated calculations at very high speeds. No human being would be capable of doing the job as well as a computer. Computers are also routinely used to monitor seriously ill patients. Since computers are able to work 24-hours a day without becoming distracted or falling asleep, they probably perform such tasks better than most humans would.

11.13 Computers and Biological Systems

Computer scientists are now researching the possibility of developing computer circuits made from living proteins and enzymes. The chips created from these circuits are called "biochips". Signals would be sent through the biochips the same way as signals are sent through the human brain, but at speeds many thousands of times faster. The potential would then exist to create computers with reasoning power approaching that of the human mind.

Although the development of useful biochips is probably well in the future, it is both exciting and frightening to ponder their possibilities. It has been suggested that biochips could be implanted into the human brain. Thus, a person could become an instant expert in any field of interest. Obviously if such a possibility were to be realized, the social and ethical questions that would be raised would dwarf the problems we have considered.

11.14 Computing at Home

Most of the examples given in this text have involved using computers to help run a business or in the classroom. Personal computers are inexpensive enough that many people have them at home. As such, software has been created for the home user. Below we discuss several personal (non-business) applications for home use.

Games and Entertainment

Perhaps the most popular use for home computers is in the field of entertainment. As an example, software is available to produce graphics which can be recorded on a VCR. This allows the home user to produce professional-looking titles and animation for home videos. Other software can help organize a record collection or print labels for cassettes. There is even a program which turns the computer monitor into a "fish tank" by displaying images of coral, plants and swimming fish.

Many people enjoy playing computer games at home. There are several different types available, but they generally fall into two categories: "simulations" and "role-playing." In simulations, the computer uses graphics to simulate an action such as driving a car. The most popular simulation is Flight Simulator in which the computer is used to fly a plane. By giving different commands, the "plane" can be made to take-off, accelerate, turn, land, etc. Flight Simulator is so realistic that pilots use it to practice flying techniques at home. Many arcade-style games are also available to the home user. There are also other forms of simulations available- card games such as bridge and poker, or sports like baseball and football.

Role-playing or fantasy games involve solving a complex puzzle by directing the actions of a character described on the screen. This is similar to reading a book, but being able to tell the character what to do. In role-playing games the user enters commands such as "look up" or "open the door" which the character follows. The player could be looking for treasure, or seeking information about a crime. Several popular role-playing games are named Zork, King's Quest and Ultima. One of the first of this type of game is called Adventure, and was first written for the mainframe computer.

Art and Music

The computer can be used by hobbyists in the arts. Artists can use drawing and painting software to produce pictures. Special input devices called "scanners" can read drawings and pictures into a file, which can then be modified using the computer. Photographers can use similar software to retouch slides and produce special effects.

Today's musicians are using a special type of computer output called "MIDI"- Musical Instrument Digital Interface. MIDI permits a computer to control synthesizers, allowing entire scores to be composed, edited and performed using the computer. MIDI can also control recording and sound processing equipment, making the home recording studio easier to run.

Productivity

Other software helps personal computer users to be more productive. For example there are several packages for administering home finances. These help develop a budget, keep track of expenses, and prepare taxes. Some even print checks for bills. Software can provide opportunities for home study in a variety of different fields: math, science, reading, and for specialized courses such as the SAT or real estate examination. This is called "computer aided instruction." Some students find that the ability to work at home at their own pace increases their understanding of the topic.

Computers have always been used by professional investors in an attempt to get an edge on the market. Home computer users can now have the same type of software for managing their investments. Modems can be used to download the latest stock prices immediately as they become available. Some brokerage firms allow home users to conduct transactions such as buying and selling stock using their computer.

These are not, of course, the only home applications for a computer. The AppleWorks software that you have learned could be used to create a family budget spreadsheet, keep recipes in a data base, or write personal letters in the word processor.

11.15 Networking

In Chapter One, we discussed the time-sharing technique used by mainframe computers- many people using the same computer at the same time. It is also possible to link several minicomputers together, so that each person has access to the other's computer in what is called "networking."

In a network, microcomputers are connected by wires. Usually these computers are all in the same building. Data is transmitted between the computers over the wires in a process similar to telecommunications. Networking is especially important to businesses which have computers in different departments. As an example, suppose that you are preparing a report with a co-worker. If you are not using networked computers, the report file must be stored on a diskette and carried to the co-worker. When they are done with it, they must bring the diskette back to you. On a network, you could both have access to the file at the same time. This is especially helpful for large projects which require, for example, a spreadsheet from the accounting department's computer, a data base from the marketing group and a letter from the advertising department. On a network, each could be transmitted over the wires which link the computers, saving time and effort.

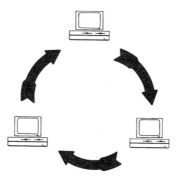

Networked computers can share files and send messages

There are several different types of networks, the most common being the LAN or Local Area Network. In a LAN, the networked computers are within a short distance of each other. The LAN operating system provides capabilities for sharing files, assigning passwords, and data security- preventing unauthorized users from reading or editing certain files. Some LANs have E-mail services built-in, making it possible to send messages between computers.

Desktop Publishing, Presentations and Graphics

The popularity of computers has spawned a new generation of software applications geared to the presentation of information. This has made it possible for computers to be used to produce and manipulate art work, pictures and the layout of documents in much the same way as word processors manipulate text. These applications, for example, allow a small business, educational institution, or individual to produce professional looking documents without the use of artists, designers or typesetters. Below we discuss three of the most popular applications, and the technology that has made them available.

11.16 Laser Printers and Output Devices

Probably the most important advance which made these applications possible was the creation of a low-cost, dependable *laser printer*. The printer that you have most likely used is called an "impact" printer. Like a typewriter, impact printers require that an inked ribbon be pressed against paper to produce an image of the character. The most common impact printer is the "dot matrix" which prints characters as a series of small dots. Because the characters are made up of dots, dot matrix print can appear jagged, especially on curved letters:

```
This is an example of dot matrix print.
```

Examining the print closely shows how the dots are used to create a character:

A character produced by a dot-matrix printer is composed of small dots

Because they are not very precise, dot matrix printers are not very good at printing graphics, and their output often appears sloppy or unfinished.

A laser printer, on the other hand, uses a beam of light to draw each character on the page, employing a process similar to a photocopier. This allows the characters to be fully formed, eliminating the use of dots. A close examination of a character produced by a laser printer illustrates this:

A character produced by a laser printer is smoother

Laser printers are also able to produce graphics such as pictures and diagrams with the same level of clarity.

11.17 Desktop Publishing

One of the most popular uses for laser printers is in the field of "desktop publishing", or DTP. In desktop publishing, special software is used to allow persons not trained in art or layout to create professional looking documents using a personal computer and a laser printer. It is the purpose of desktop publishing software to combine text (created in a word processor) with illustrations (created by a graphics program) to produce the final document. Before desktop publishing existed, creating a document such as an advertising brochure was a complicated procedure, often involving many people:

1. A writer to create the text of the brochure.
2. An artist to produce the illustrations.
3. A typesetter to print the text.
4. A layout person to combine the text and illustrations into the completed brochure using scissors and glue.

Now a single person can perform all of these tasks using a computer. A major advantage of using desktop publishing software is that changes can be made to a document in much the same way as changes are made to text using a word processor. Illustrations and text can be added or deleted, changed in size or the whole layout redone - all on a computer screen.

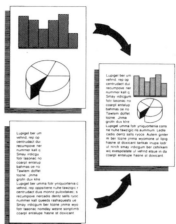

DTP software combines graphics and text into one file

By performing the layout of a document on the computer screen instead of on paper, changes may easily be made. Different layouts can be created and printed until the desired combination is found. Once completed, the final version can be printed and the document saved on disk so that it can be edited or reprinted at any later time.

Three of the most commonly used desktop publishing programs are *PageMaker*, *Ventura Publisher* and *Quark Express*. Less powerful and inexpensive programs such as Publish It!, First Publisher and PrintShop allow DTP documents to be created and printed on dot matrix printers. Often these packages contain collections of prepared illustrations called "clip art" which can be included in whatever document is produced, often eliminating the need for an artist.

11.18 Elements of Desktop Publishing

It must be remembered that the primary purpose for producing a desktop published document is to convey information to the readers of that document. For this reason, publishers must consider the appearance of the information and determine whether it is appropriate to the type of document being produced. The document could be a sales flyer, technical manual, or corporate report - it is unlikely that each would use the same format. One of the most powerful features of DTP is that it gives the user the opportunity to experiment with different formats until the one which best fits the information they are trying to communicate is produced.

Elements of format

There are several different elements which contribute to a document's format. In the word processing chapters of this text you learned about margins, indents, bold and italic text, and other formatting options. Documents produced using DTP software have these, and several other formatting options to consider.

Typeface
One of the first and most important decisions that must be made is to determine what *typeface* will be used in producing a document. The typeface is a description of how the text characters are formed. Laser printers have hundreds of typefaces which they can print while professional typesetting equipment has thousands. Some typefaces are better than others, however, when used for certain tasks. For example, a typeface which is good when used for a headline may not be as good when used in long paragraphs. Many laser printers and typesetting machines operate using a system called PostScript which is used to identify typefaces. Below we show examples of several PostScript typefaces along with descriptions of what each typeface is best used for.

The following faces are well suited for use in the paragraphs which make up the body of a document:

Bookman: ABCDEF abcdef 123456789 *ABCD* **ABCD**

New Century Schoolbook: ABCD abcd 123456 *ABC* **ABC**

Times-Roman: ABCDEF abcdef 123456789 *ABCD* **ABCD**

Palatino: ABCDEF abcdef 123456789 *ABCD* **ABCD**

The following faces are well suited for headlines and captions, and other short pieces of text such as a menu or table:

Avant Garde: ABCDEF abcdef 123456789 *ABCD* **ABCD**

Helvetica: ABCDEF abcdef 123456789 *ABCD* **ABCD**

Helvetica Narrow :ABCDEF abcdef 123456789 *ABCD* **ABCD**

There are several typefaces which are designed to be used in special applications such as displaying computer output, or to add decorative flair to a publication:

Zapf Chancery: ABCDEF abcdef 123456789 "?!&$(%#*

Courier: ABCDEF abcdef 123456789 *ABCD* **ABCD**

Symbols: ABXΔEΦ αβχδεφ 123456789 !≅#∃%⊥&*()–=

Zapf Dingbats: ✚✜☎★✱✲✦ ①❖✎◯➥❑▼❙ ∞✝✔✗☞✗✚✠✄

Usually a document will have several typefaces, one for the body, another for titles, etc. Again, the DTP software makes it easy to experiment, trying typefaces in different combinations until the most pleasing combination is found.

Graphics
Another element to consider when creating a DTP document is the use of graphics, which often determine how a document will be perceived. Questions involving graphics include where to place them, how large they should be and whether to use photographs or drawings. The proper use of graphics can often make the difference between a professional looking document and one that looks amateurish.

One of the most popular uses for DTP is the creation of newsletters. In an Exercise of Chapter 3 you were asked to create a newsletter with two columns. Because the Works word processor can not do this automatically, it is a tedious task to produce the columns. Desktop publishing software can create multi-column pages automatically making column text easy to read. The software can also draw horizontal and vertical lines called "rules."

Besides the options described above, DTP programs can perform such additional tasks as printing text in color, drawing boxes around paragraphs, rotating type so that it appears on an angle, and controlling the space between lines, words and letters.

11.19 Graphics and Illustration Software

Using specialized software it is possible to create graphic images on the computer. By graphic images, we mean non-text items such as drawings, photographs, charts, logos, etc. The advantage of using a computer rather than drawing on paper is that the image can then be manipulated; changed in size, rotated, etc. When an artist wants to make a change to a picture drawn on paper, he or she must either use an eraser or start from scratch. Using graphics software, the artist could instead draw the picture on a computer screen. If changes were then desired, they could be made to the picture stored in the computer's memory. When the final version had been created, it could be printed in black and white using a laser printer, or in color using a special, color printer.

There are several powerful programs available for creating and editing graphics images. Several of these are *Adobe Illustrator*, *Aldus Freehand* and *Corel Draw*. Most require the use of a specialized input device to aid in the drawing. The most popular of these devices are the mouse and the drawing tablet. These devices are used to translate the movements of the artist's hand onto the computer screen.

In addition to allowing the easy modification of a graphic, illustration software often has a variety of advanced tools that would be difficult or time consuming to duplicate manually. For example, suppose a business hires an artist to design a logo. Using pen and paper, the artist would then sketch the logo and add any colors using paint. Suppose the artist choose green as the color for the logo and painted it on paper. If the company then wanted to see what the logo looked like in red, the artist would have to start from scratch, drawing the outline, and painting it red. If the logo was instead prepared using illustration software, the artist could move the cursor to the desired location on the screen, issue a command which said "Change this green area to red" and print the version. Other examples of editing options include changing line widths, erasing lines and objects in a diagram, and changing the size or position of objects. Once complete, the final graphic can be saved in a file on disk, similar to a data base or spreadsheet, that could be edited or reprinted at a later date.

Another advantage to using illustration software is that any graphics produced can easily be placed in a desktop-published document. Most DTP software packages can read the files produced by illustration software, and place a graphic directly into a DTP document. Some DTP packages can even perform basic editing on the image, allowing it to be scaled (made larger or smaller), rotated, or clipped (choosing to display only part of the graphic).

11.20 Desktop Presentations

Many business people are required to give presentations; new employees must be trained, financial information disseminated, advertising campaigns tested, etc. These presentations often require the use of visual aids such as slides and charts. One of the fastest growing areas for personal computer use is in the field of *desktop presentation* where the computer is used to create and display such visual aids.

Suppose that a business hires 10 new employees, all of whom must be trained to perform certain tasks. One of the most common ways to train employees is to give them a series of lectures explaining the tasks they will perform. Visual aids such as charts or slides will probably help the new employees to learn the information being presented. With desktop presentation software, a personal computer could be used to prepare and present the visual aids.

Most desktop presentation software has two parts, an editor where graphics are created and manipulated (similar to the illustration software described above), and a display controller where the created graphics may be displayed in sequence on the computer's screen. Many packages are also able to display graphics which were created using separate illustration software.

There are several ways to use presentation software. The first is for the creation of slides. Graphics are created and then output to a "film recorder" which produces a photographic slide capable of being projected. Because the film recorder hardware is expensive, smaller companies often send a diskette containing their graphic files to a "service bureau"; a company that owns a film recorder and makes slides for customers.

A second way to use presentation graphics is to store the graphics on a diskette, and then use a computer screen to display them to an audience. Often the computer will be connected to a large monitor or projection system. Two advantages of this method is that the computer can be used to easily change the order of a presentation and to produce animated sequences by changing the displayed images very quickly.

The third use is to print black and white copies of the graphics on a laser printer for use by the audience as handouts. This is often done in conjunction with one of the other two methods, giving the audience take-home notes which they may review after the lecture.

11.21 How Do We Face the Future?

In this text we have presented the history of computing, showed you how to word process, use a database and a spreadsheet, and have considered the future of computing. Our hope is that you are excited by computers and realize the tremendous potential they have to serve us in a wide variety of ways. We also hope that you have been made aware of how computers might be misused. It is therefore the duty of each one of us, as responsible citizens, to insure that the awesome power given to us by computers be used only to benefit mankind.

Chapter Summary

This chapter began by discussing the future of computing. One of the most important advances in the field of computing has been in telecommunications, which means the sending of computer data over phone lines. Modems are used both to transmit and receive computer data. Because of telecommunications many people may be able to work at home.

A popular form of telecommunications is the electronic bulletin board which allows users to transmit and receive messages. A similar form of telecommunications is electronic mail (E-mail) where single users are able to receive messages meant only for them.

The continued development of microprocessors will effect many products including automobiles and home electronic devices. With their ability to make simple decisions, microprocessors can automate many of the functions performed by these devices.

Using computers to make decisions normally made by human beings is called artificial intelligence. Although computers cannot think, they can be programmed to make decisions which, for example, will allow them to play chess. Expert systems are a form of artificial intelligence where a computer is programmed with a set of rules that can solve a problem - producing the same solution a human expert would. Credit card companies, automobile manufacturers and hospitals are a few of the organizations currently using expert systems.

Recognizing spoken words and translating them into digital form is called speech recognition which involves natural language processing, a field of artificial intelligence that attempts to translate a sentence into its separate parts and understand its meaning. Numerous problems face the successful development of language processing systems.

A robot is a machine that can be programmed and also move. Robots are currently used to perform simple manufacturing tasks. When natural language processing and artificial intelligence programs are perfected, the use of robots will increase.

Careers in computing were discussed in this chapter and the educational requirements needed to pursue them. Careers which required only a high school education as well as those requiring a college education were presented.

Historians refer to the present time as the "information age" due to the computer's ability to store and manipulate large amounts of data. As the use of computers increases they will profoundly effect society including what jobs will be available and the length of the work week.

A problem created by computers is their potential for invading our right to privacy. Laws have been passed to protect us from the misuse of data stored in computers.

Because computer software is easy to copy, illegal copies are often made, denying software manufacturers of rightful compensation. Another problem has been the willful destruction of computer files by erasing data or planting a "virus" into programs that can spread when the programs are copied.

As computers are increasingly used to made decisions in situations which can threaten human life it becomes the responsibility of programmers to do there best to insure the reliability of the software they have developed. We must continue to be cautious not to replace human beings with computers in areas where judgement is crucial.

The use of personal computers in the home has become popular. These computers are often used to play games and to run applications such as AppleWorks.

In a network, microcomputers are connected by wires that transmit data between them. The most common network is the Local Area Network (LAN) which allows files to be shared between a number of computers.

Desktop publishing software has made it possible for computers to produce and manipulate art work, pictures and the layout of documents. The elements which contribute to a document's format are typeface and graphics. Laser printers, which employ a beam of light to draw characters on a page, are often used in desktop publishing applications.

Special software is used to create graphics images such as drawings, photographs, charts, etc. on the computer. This software allows the images to be easily manipulated and modified. Desktop presentation software creates and displays visual aids.

Vocabulary

Artificial intelligence - Using computers to make decisions which would normally be made by a human being.

Biochips - Computer circuits made from proteins and enzymes.

Baud rate - Rate at which characters of data are transmitted. One baud represents the transmission of one character per second.

Desktop presentation - Using a computer to create and display visual aids.

Desktop publishing - Using special software to create professional looking documents on a computer.

Download - To transfer a message or computer file from a bulletin board or E-Mail service computer to another computer.

Electronic bulletin board - (BBS) Telecommunications service which allows subscribers using a computer and modem to transmit messages that can be received by all the other subscribers.

Electronic mail - (E-Mail) Telecommunications service which allows a person using a computer and modem to send a message to another person's computer.

Expert systems - System programmed to produce the same solution a human expert would if asked to solve the same problem.

Graphics - Drawings, photographs, charts, etc. used in a document.

Hacker - Person who uses a computer and modem to enter a computer system without authorization.

Laser printer - Printer that employs a beam of light to draw characters.

Local Area Network (LAN) - Common method of networking microcomputers so that they can share data.

Modem - Device which translates binary data into waves and waves back into binary data so that computer data can be sent over telephone lines.

Natural language processing - Using a computer to recognize spoken words and then translate them into digital form.

Network - Connecting computers by wires so that data can be transmitted between them.

Pirate - Person who illegally copies computer software.

Robot - Machine which can be programmed and is also capable of motion.

Telecommunication - Sending of computer data over telephone lines.

Typeface - Description of how text characters are formed.

Upload - To transfer a message or computer file from a computer to a bulletin board or E-Mail service computer.

Virus - Program which hides within another program for the purpose of destroying or altering data.

Reviews

Sections 11.1-11.2

1. Name four databases that you would like to be able to access using telecommunications. State why each of them would be useful to you.

2. Besides those listed in the text, list three occupations where people would be able to work at home rather than in an office using telecommunications.

3. What is the difference between an electronic bulletin board and electronic mail?

4. If all of the students in your school had computers and modems at home, in what ways could they be used by teachers and students?

Sections 11.3-11.4

5. What tasks do you think automobile microprocessors may perform in the future?

6. What is artificial intelligence?

7. What devices owned by your family contain microprocessors and what are they used for?

8. State three questions you would ask to determine which was the human and which the computer when playing Turing's Imitation Game. Asking "Are you the computer?" is not fair!

Sections 11.5-11.7

9. What did the computer program Mycin do?

10. List four jobs where you think expert systems could be used to help the person performing the job. Explain why the system would be helpful.

11. List four jobs where expert systems could probably not be used, and explain why.

12. Would an expert system be helpful to you in selecting clothes to buy? Explain why or why not.

13. What are some of the difficulties being encountered in the development of natural language processing?

14. Why should we be careful in trusting expert systems? What do they lack that humans possess?

15. If you could have a robot built to your own specifications, what would you have it be capable of doing?

Section 11.8

The six computer careers mentioned include:

    (1) system analyst
    (2) system developer - programmer
    (3) system manager
    (4) computer operator
    (5) data-entry operator
    (6) computer scientist

16. Which of the above careers require only a:

    a) high school diploma
    b) college diploma
    c) college and graduate school degrees

17. For each of the following students list the careers above that he or she should consider:

    a) a student who likes mathematics.
    b) a student who wants to be involved in the management of a business.
    c) a student who wants to work in the development of rocket guidance systems.
    d) a student who likes to think through problems in a methodical, logical way.

Sections 11.9-11.13

18. Alvin Toffler named his book "The Third Wave". What were the first two waves?

19. What is meant by the term "high-tech" society?

20. a) How do you believe society will benefit from the information age?
    b) What might be the negative aspects of the information age?

21. How can a computer be used to invade your privacy?

22. What can you do if you are turned down for credit at a bank and believe that the data used to deny credit is inaccurate?

23. What is necessary for a federal government authority to access an individual's financial records? What must the authority do after accessing the records?

24. What ethical responsibilities does a programmer have when writing a program that will be used to design a bridge? Can the programmer absolutely guarantee that the program will operate properly? Why?

25. Do you think the development of biochips will benefit mankind? Why?

Sections 11.14-11.20

26. Describe how 3 organizations might make use of computer networks.

27. How does a laster printer differ from a dot matrix printer?

28. a) What are 4 advantages of using desktop publishing?
    b) Describe 3 organizations that might make use of desktop publishing.

29. What is graphics software used for?

30. What is desktop presentation and who might use it?

Appendix A
AppleWorks Commands

Open-Apple Commands

The following commands are grouped by applications area.

Word Processor

Command	Keyword	Description
Open-Apple C	**C**opy	Copies a block of text within a document or to and from the Clipboard.
Open-Apple D	**D**elete	Deletes a block of text or option marker from within a document.
Open-Apple E	**E**dit	Switches between insert mode (underline cursor) and overwrite mode (block cursor).
Open-Apple F	**F**ind	Searches for specified text, page or option marker.
Open-Apple H	**H**ard copy	Prints copy of current screen on the printer.
Open-Apple K	**K**alculate	Calculates page breaks.
Open-Apple M	**M**ove	Moves a block of text within a document or to and from the Clipboard.
Open-Apple N	**N**ame change	Changes a document's file name.
Open-Apple O	**O**ptions	Displays the Options menu for setting character formats, margins, mail merge, etc.
Open-Apple P	**P**rint	Prints all or part of a document.
Open-Apple Q	**Q**uick change	Displays the Desktop Index to switch to a different file on the Desktop.
Open-Apple R	**R**eplace	Replaces search text with different text.
Open-Apple S	**S**ave	Saves current document on the data disk.
Open-Apple T	**T**abs	Sets and clears tab stops.
Open-Apple Y	**Y**ank	Deletes all text from current cursor position to the end of the line.
Open-Apple Z	**Z**oom	Switches between Zoom mode which displays all option markers and regular mode.
Open-Apple ?	**H**elp	Displays help screen.

Cursor Movement

`Open-Apple 1...9`	Moves cursor to top of file (1), middle of file (5), bottom of file (9) or proportionately (2-8).
`Open-Apple ←`	Moves cursor one word to the left.
`Open-Apple →`	Moves cursor one word to the right.
`Open-Apple ↑`	Scrolls up one screen.
`Open-Apple ↓`	Scrolls down one screen.

Data Base

Command	Keyword	Description
`Open-Apple A`	**A**rrange	Arranges (sorts) the records in the current data base.
`Open-Apple C`	**C**opy	Copies current record or records to and from the Clipboard.
`Open-Apple D`	**D**elete	Deletes a record or group of records from the current data base or hides a report category.
`Open-Apple E`	**E**dit	Switches between insert mode (underline cursor) and overwrite mode (block cursor).
`Open-Apple F`	**F**ind	Searches for specified text in a record.
`Open-Apple G`	**G**roup	Creates or removes group totals for a report category.
`Open-Apple H`	**H**ard copy	Prints copy of current screen on the printer.
`Open-Apple I`	**I**nsert	Inserts a new record, or a previously deleted report category.
`Open-Apple J`	**J**ustify	Justifies a report category.
`Open-Apple K`	**K**alculated	Creates a calculated report category.
`Open-Apple L`	**L**ayout	Modifies the record layout.
`Open-Apple M`	**M**ove	Moves records to and from the Clipboard.
`Open-Apple N`	**N**ame change	Changes a data base's file name, a category name, a report format name or a report's title.
`Open-Apple O`	**O**ptions	Displays printer Options menu for setting margins, line spacing, etc. from the Report Format screen.
`Open-Apple P`	**P**rint	Displays the Report menu from the data base screen or prints the current report from the Report Format screen.

Open-Apple Q	**Q**uick change	Displays Desktop Index to switch to a different file on the Desktop.
Open-Apple R	**R**ules	Creates or changes a selection rule.
Open-Apple S	**S**ave	Saves current data base on the data disk.
Open-Apple T	**T**otals	Creates or removes totals for a report category.
Open-Apple V	**V**alues	Sets standard values for empty categories.
Open-Apple Y	**Y**ank	Deletes all data from current cursor position to the end of the entry.
Open-Apple Z	**Z**oom	Switches between single and multi-record display.
Open-Apple ?	**H**elp	Displays help screen.

Cursor Movement

Open-Apple 1...9		Moves cursor to top of file (1), middle of file (5), bottom of file (9) or proportionately (2-8).
Open-Apple ←		Decreases size of current category by one character from Change Record Layout screen.
Open-Apple →		Increases size of current category by one character from Change Record Layout screen.
Open-Apple ↑		Scrolls up one screen.
Open-Apple ↓		Scrolls down one screen.

Spreadsheet

Command	Keyword	Description
Open-Apple A	**A**rrange	Arranges (sorts) selected rows in the worksheet.
Open-Apple B	**B**lank	Blanks out (removes) the contents of a cell or group of cells.
Open-Apple C	**C**opy	Copies cell entries and formulas.
Open-Apple D	**D**elete	Deletes rows or columns.
Open-Apple E	**E**dit	Switches between insert mode (underline cursor) and overwrite mode (block cursor).
Open-Apple F	**F**ind	Searches for text in cells, or moves to a specific cell.
Open-Apple H	**H**ard copy	Prints copy of current screen on the printer.
Open-Apple I	**I**nsert	Inserts new rows or columns.
Open-Apple J	**J**ump	Jumps between windows.

Open-Apple K	**K**alculate	Recalculates all formulas.
Open-Apple L	**L**ayout	Modifies the cell, row or column layout.
Open-Apple M	**M**ove	Moves rows or columns within a worksheet or to and from the Clipboard.
Open-Apple N	**N**ame change	Changes a spreadsheet's file name.
Open-Apple O	**O**ptions	Displays printer Options menu for setting margins, line spacing, etc.
Open-Apple P	**P**rint	Prints all or part of the worksheet on the printer.
Open-Apple Q	**Q**uick change	Displays Desktop Index to switch to a different file on the Desktop.
Open-Apple S	**S**ave	Saves current worksheet on the data disk.
Open-Apple T	**T**itles	Sets or removes titles for scrolling.
Open-Apple V	**V**alues	Sets standard values for formats, column width, recalculation and protection.
Open-Apple Y	**Y**ank	Deletes all data from current cursor position to the end of the cell.
Open-Apple Z	**Z**oom	Switches between Zoom mode which displays formulas and regular mode.
Open-Apple ?	**H**elp	Displays help screen.

Cursor Movement

Open-Apple 1...9	Moves cursor to top of file (1), middle of file (5), bottom of file (9) or proportionately (2-8).
Open-Apple ←	Scrolls one screen to the left.
Open-Apple →	Scrolls one screen to the right.
Open-Apple ↑	Scrolls up one screen.
Open-Apple ↓	Scrolls down one screen.

Spreadsheet Operators and Functions

The AppleWorks spreadsheet contains a number of mathematical operators and built-in functions that may be used in formulas. These are summarized below.

Operators

+ (plus)	Addition
− (minus)	Subtraction
* (asterisk)	Multiplication
/ (slash)	Division
^ (caret)	Exponentiation, raise to a power

Functions

The examples below use following notation to describe function arguments:

`<value>` A single value such as 5.4, a cell reference such as A1, or any formula which results in a single numeric value.

`<range>` A series of adjacent cells, either part of a row such as (A1...A9) or column (A1...F1).

`<list>` A list of values or ranges separated by commas. For example: (A1, B2, C3...C5, H1)

`@ABS(<value>)`
Returns the absolute value of <value>.

`@AVG(<list>)`
Returns the average (arithmetic mean) of values stored in <list>.

`@COUNT(<list>)`
Returns the number of non-blank values in <list>.

`@ERROR`
Displays ERROR in current cell.

`@INT(<value>)`
Returns the integer portion of <value>.

`@MAX(<list>)`
Returns the largest value of the values stored in <list>.

`@MIN(<list>)`
Returns the smallest value of the values stored in <list>.

`@NA`
Displays NA in current cell for "not available".

`@ROUND(<value1>,<value2>)`
Rounds <value1> to <value2> decimal places.

`@SQRT(<value>)`
Returns the square root of <value>. <value> may not be negative.

`@SUM(<list>)`
Returns the total of the values stored in <list>.

`@IF(<logical>,<value1>,<value2>)`
Displays <value1> in current cell if <logical> is true, and <value2> if it is false. <logical> is a comparison using the following operators:

<	Less than
>	Greater than
=	Equal to
<=	Less than or equal to
>=	Greater than or equal to
<>	Not equal to

`@OR(<logical1>,<logical2>)`
Returns true if either <logical1> or <logical2> is true. Returns false only when both are false.

`@AND(<logical1>,<logical2>)`
Returns true only when both <logical1> and <logical2> are true, false otherwise.

Integrating using the Clipboard

The Clipboard is a place in memory used to store data being transferred from one file to another. Data may also be transferred between files created by different applications using the Clipboard.

To share data between files created by the same application:

1. Display the original data.
2. Place the data to be shared on the Clipboard using Open-Apple C or Open-Apple M.
3. Display the file to receive the data.
4. Transfer the data from the Clipboard into the file using Open-Apple C or Open-Apple M.

Data may be shared between the data base or spreadsheet and the word processor by "printing" it to the Clipboard:

1. Display the original data.
2. Print the data to the Clipboard.
3. Display the word processor file to receive the data.
4. Transfer the data from the Clipboard into the document using Open-Apple C or Open-Apple M.

Sharing data between a data base and spreadsheet requires that a DIF file be created on disk:

1. Display the original data.
2. "Print" the data to a DIF file on disk.
3. Create a new file from the DIF file.

For more information about integration, please see Chapter 9 in this text and your AppleWorks user manuals.

Appendix B
Using the 'Other Activities' Menu

About 'Other Activities' and ProDOS

Before the computer may be used, it is first necessary to load the ProDOS disk operating system as described in Chapter 2. Your STARTUP disk does this automatically each time it is booted. Because ProDOS controls all access to the disk, there are times that you must have access to its commands. For this reason, AppleWorks includes the 'Other Activities' menu, option 5 from the Main Menu:

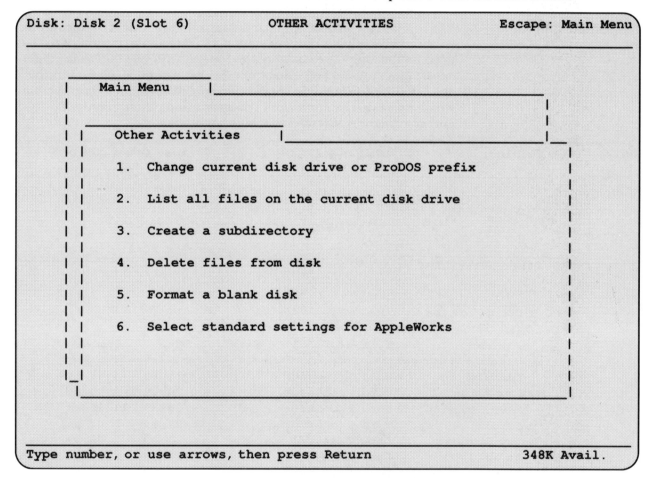

```
Disk: Disk 2 (Slot 6)          OTHER ACTIVITIES          Escape: Main Menu


        _____
       | Main Menu      |_____
       |                                                             |
       |  _____                                     |
       | | Other Activities     |_____ |
       | |                                                          | |
       | |  1.  Change current disk drive or ProDOS prefix          | |
       | |                                                          | |
       | |  2.  List all files on the current disk drive            | |
       | |                                                          | |
       | |  3.  Create a subdirectory                               | |
       | |                                                          | |
       | |  4.  Delete files from disk                              | |
       | |                                                          | |
       | |  5.  Format a blank disk                                 | |
       | |                                                          | |
       | |  6.  Select standard settings for AppleWorks             | |
       | |                                                          | |
       | |                                                          | |
       |_|                                                          | |
         |_____| |
       |_____|


Type number, or use arrows, then press Return          348K Avail.
```

Although not needed for most everyday work, the 'Other Activities' option is required for some special operations described below.

Option 1: 'Change current disk drive'

By default, AppleWorks looks to the "current disk drive" when searching for or saving files. This is normally the location of your DATA disk and is listed at the top left-hand corner of the screen after the word Disk: -- Disk 2 (Slot 6) in the example menu above. There are times when you would like AppleWorks to use another drive. Selecting the 'Change current disk drive' option displays a menu of possible drives:

```
Disk drives you can use:

1. Disk 1 (Slot 6)
2. Disk 2 (Slot 6)
3. Disk 1 (Slot 5)
4. RAMDisk (Slot 5)
5. ProDOS directory
```

The actual menu displayed here will depend on the number and location of the drives attached to your system. Selecting one of these options will change which drive is designated as the current disk drive, and the line at the top of the screen will be updated. Pressing Escape will terminate this option.

Option 2: 'List all files'

The 'List all files' option displays a listing of all of the files stored on the current disk drive (see option 1). This listing is similar to that used by the Main Menu's 'Add files' option with two important differences: files may not be loaded from this listing and all files on the disk are listed, not just those created by AppleWorks, including the files which make up the AppleWorks program, and others such as ProDOS and any DIF or ASCII files that you might create:

```
╭──────────────────────────────────────────────────────────────────────╮
│ Disk: Disk 2 (Slot 6)          LIST ALL FILES        Escape: Other Activities │
│ ──────────────────────────────────────────────────────────────────── │
│                                                                        │
│    ┌─────────────────────┬──────────────────────────────────────────┐ │
│    │   Main Menu         │                                          │ │
│    │                     │                                        │ │ │
│    │   ┌─────────────────┴───┬────────────────────────────────────┴─┐│ │
│    │ │ Other Activities    │                                      │ ││ │
│    │ │                     │                                      │ ││ │
│    │ │ ┌───────────────────┴───┬──────────────────────────────────┴┐ ││
│    │ │ │ List All Files        │                                   │ ││
│    │ │ │ Disk volume /APPLEWORKS has 361K available                │ ││
│    │ │ │    Name            Type of file    Size    Date     Time  │ ││
│    │ │ │ ================================================================ │ ││
│    │ │ │ Example         Word Processor    1K    9/11/90    8:47 am │ ││
│    │ │ │ Ivy Promo       Word Processor    4K    6/27/89    1:00 pm │ ││
│    │ │ │ News Story      Word Processor    3K    9/23/89   11:12 am │ ││
│    │ │ │ Scroll          Word Processor    2K    6/27/89    1:00 pm │ ││
│    │ │ │ Ivy Student     Data Base         3K    6/27/89    1:00 pm │ ││
│    │ │ │ Bookstore       Data Base         1K    6/27/89    1:00 pm │ ││
│    │ └─┤ Car Price       Data Base         5K    6/27/89    1:00 pm │ ││
│    │   │ Grades          Spreadsheet       3K    6/27/89    1:00 pm │ ││
│    │   │ Ivy Payroll     Spreadsheet       4K    6/27/89    1:00 pm │ ││
│    │   └─┤ APLWORKS.SYSTEM  Other          13K    8/03/89    4:01 pm │ ││
│    └─────────────────────── More ──────────────────────────────────┘ │
│                                                                        │
│ ──────────────────────────────────────────────────────────────────── │
│ Use up/down arrows to move through list                   346K Avail. │
╰──────────────────────────────────────────────────────────────────────╯
```

The list you see here will depend on the number and type of files stored on your disk. "More" at the bottom of the listing indicates that there are other files stored on the disk that may be listed by using the arrow keys.

Option 3: 'Create a subdirectory'

We have previously stated that AppleWorks mimics the functions of an office, and that the disk plays the role of a filing cabinet, storing files for later use. ProDOS allows a disk to be broken into smaller, named sections called "subdirectories" which act as the different drawers in a filing cabinet. For example, one subdirectory on a disk may store all of the files for your physics class, another your personal files, and another for the files you use at work.

Before it can be used, a subdirectory must be created. Selecting option 3 displays the prompt:

```
Type the subdirectory's pathname.
```

```
Pathname?
```

You then type the name of the disk followed by the new subdirectory name, separated by a forward slash (/). For example, typing the pathname /APPLEWORKS/PHYSICS will create a new subdirectory named PHYSICS on the disk named /APPLEWORKS. (The disk's name is listed on the 'List all files' screen, option 2.) The files stored in a subdirectory are made accessible by setting the current disk drive to that directory using the 'ProDOS directory' option from the 'Change current disk drive' menu (see option 1).

Subdirectories are important because they allow more files to be stored on a disk. Even if there is room, AppleWorks allows only 50 files to be stored on a disk without the use of subdirectories.

Option 4: 'Delete files from disk'

Because the number of files that may be stored on a disk is limited, it is sometimes necessary to delete old files from a disk to make room for new ones. This can be dangerous because once a file is deleted from the disk, it cannot be recovered. The 'Delete files from disk' option displays a menu similar to that used when removing files from the Desktop:

```
Disk: Disk 2 (Slot 6)          DELETE FILES          Escape: Other Activities


    ┌─── Main Menu ────┐
    │  ┌─── Other Activities ──┐
    │  │  ┌─── Delete Files ──────┐
    │  │  Disk volume /APPLEWORKS has 361K available
    │  │      Name          Type of file      Size     Date       Time
    │  │  ==============================================================
    │  │      Example       Word Processor     1K     9/11/90    8:47 am
    │  │      Ivy Promo     Word Processor     4K     6/27/89    1:00 pm
    │  │      News Story    Word Processor     3K     9/23/89   11:12 am
    │  │      Scroll        Word Processor     2K     6/27/89    1:00 pm
    │  │      Ivy Student   Data Base          3K     6/27/89    1:00 pm
    │_ │      Car Price     Data Base          5K     6/27/89    1:00 pm
      │      Grades        Spreadsheet        3K     6/27/89    1:00 pm
     _│      Ivy Payroll   Spreadsheet        4K     6/27/89    1:00 pm
                               More

Use Right Arrow to choose files, Left Arrow to undo          346K Avail.
```

Files are selected for deletion by moving the cursor to the appropriate file name and pressing right-arrow. When all of the files to be deleted have been selected, pressing Return removes them from the disk. For each file, AppleWorks will provide a prompt allowing the deletion to be continued, or the file left intact:

```
You are about to PERMANENTLY
remove this file from disk.

Do you really want to do this?  No   Yes
```

Pressing Return at this point will terminate the operation and the file will be left intact. Pressing the Y key will delete the file from the disk.

It is important to realize that in addition to the files you have created there are several AppleWorks and ProDOS files which are required to be on your disk. These files are listed at the end of the 'List all files' screen and have names such as APLWORKS.SYSTEM, SEG.EL and PRODOS, and have the type 'Other'. These files must not be deleted. A good rule of thumb is not to delete any file which you did not create, and never delete files with the type 'Other'.

Option 5: 'Format a blank disk'

Before a blank disk can be used by AppleWorks it must first be "formatted". Formatting checks the new disk for errors and prepares it to receive data. The STARTUP and DATA disks you have been using were formatted before they were given to you. Should you run out of room on your data disk, or wish to keep a backup copy of your files on another disk, you will need to use this option to format a blank disk.

Selecting this option displays the following prompt:

```
The formatter will use the disk drive
shown on the top line of the screen.

A disk name consists of up to 15 letters,
numbers, and periods. The first character
must be a letter.

Type a disk name:
```

If the current disk drive does not contain the disk that you want formatted, press Escape and use option 1 'Change current disk drive' to select the proper drive. You should select a disk name that describes the information that will be stored on it such as DATA.DISK.2 or BACKUP.DISK. After typing the disk name, place the blank disk in the current drive and press Return. AppleWorks will prompt you to be sure that the disk is to be formatted. Pressing Escape at this point will cancel the operation. Pressing the Space Bar will format the disk.

Formatting a disk removes all data from it and any files stored on it will be lost. For this reason, always be sure that you are formatting a blank disk, or one that does not contain needed files. As a safety measure you may wish to remove all important disks from their drives before executing this option.

Option 6: 'Select standard settings for AppleWorks'

AppleWorks has several default values which may be changed to better fit your computer system. These are listed on the Standard Settings menu displayed by selecting option 6 from the 'Other Activities' menu. The two most important of these are 'Select standard location of data disk' and 'Specify information about your printer(s)'.

Select standard location of data disk

By default, Appleworks sets the current disk drive to the drive that was used to boot the computer. If this is not where you would like to keep your data disk, a new drive may be permanently selected using this option. While the 'Change current disk drive' option temporarily changes the current drive, the drive selected from this option will be used each time AppleWorks is loaded. Selecting option 5 from the Standard Settings menu displays a list of available drives for the data disk:

```
Disk drives you can use:

1. Disk 1 (Slot 6)
2. Disk 2 (Slot 6)
3. Disk 1 (Slot 5)
4. RAMDisk (Slot 5)
5. ProDOS directory
```

The actual menu displayed will depend on the number and location of the drives attached to your system. Selecting one of these options will determine which drive AppleWorks will use when saving or loading files. Pressing Escape will terminate this option, leaving the standard data disk location unchanged.

Specify information about your printer(s)

Once a printer has been selected, there is usually little need for this option unless you are changing printers. AppleWorks allows up to three different printers to be used at any one time. These printers are listed on the various print menus. In order to work correctly, each printer must be properly configured to work with AppleWorks -- AppleWorks must be told where each printer is connected to your computer, what code to send to the printer to create boldface letters, what code to send for underlined text, etc. AppleWorks has the information for several common printers predefined, so it is easy to install one of these printers. For complete information about changing printers, please consult your AppleWorks manuals from Claris.

Glossary

Add Files option - Main Menu option used to create new files or load previously saved files from the disk.

ALU - Arithmetic Logic Unit, the part of the CPU that handles math operations.

Applesoft - Version of the BASIC programming language which runs on Apple computers.

Arrange, data base - Organize (sort) the records stored in a data base in order based on the value stored in one category.

Arrange, spreadsheet - Organize (sort) a block of rows in a spreadsheet based upon the value stored in one column.

Arrow keys - Four keys that move the cursor up, down, right and left on the screen without changing any data. The arrow keys are also used to select options from menus.

Artificial intelligence - Programming computers to make decisions which would normally be made by a human being.

ASCII - American Standard Code for Information Interchange, the code used for representing characters in the computer.

Assign - To give a variable a value.

BASIC - Popular computer programming language. It is an acronym for Beginner's All-Purpose Symbolic Instruction Code.

Baud rate - Rate at which characters of data are transmitted. One baud represents the transmission of one character per second.

Biochips - Computer circuits made from proteins and enzymes.

Bit - Binary Digit, a single 0 or 1 in a binary number.

Block Copy - Creates an exact copy of a high-lighted block in a new location: Open-Apple C.

Block Delete - Removes a highlighted block or option marker from a document: Open-Apple D.

Block Move - Removes a highlighted block from its current position and places it in a new one: Open-Apple M.

Block, spreadsheet - Selected group of adjacent rows and columns. May be copied, formatted, etc.

Block, text - Highlighted section of text which may contain anything from a single letter or phrase to a paragraph or several pages. Once highlighted, operations such as Copy and Move may be performed using the block.

Boldface - Darker letters, used for emphasis.

Boot - To turn on the computer and load the operating system (ProDOS).

Bug - An error in either the design or the instructions of a program.

Byte - A group of 8 bits.

Calculated category - Numeric data base report category which is calculated based on the value(s) stored in other categories using a calculation rule.

Calculation rule - Formula which describes how the value printed in a calculated category is determined.

CAT/CATALOG - Programming command for displaying a list of files and programs stored on disk.

Category - One specific piece of information stored in a record.

Category name - Name by which the computer identifies the different pieces of information in a record.

Cell - Where a row and column intersect in a spreadsheet. A cell is identified by its column letter and row number, for example G8.

Cell cursor - White rectangle on the screen which is moved from cell to cell using the arrow keys. Data may be entered into a cell when the cell cursor is located on it.

Cell indicator - Shows the current location of the cell cursor at the bottom of the spreadsheet screen.

Centered - Text positioned evenly between the left and right margins.

Character - Any letter, number or symbol which can be displayed on the computer screen or typed on the keyboard.

Character category - A category which stores only characters such as a name or address.

Clipboard - A place in the computer's memory used to store data being transferred between files.

Column - Vertical line of data identified by a letter in a spreadsheet.

Command - Instruction to the computer in a language the computer understands.

Comparison text - Text entered by the user during Find or Record selection which data is compared to.

Conditional statement - Programming statement executed only when a condition is true. (See IF...THEN)

CPU - Central Processing Unit, the device which electronically controls the functions of the computer.

Cursor - Blinking line on the screen which indicates where characters entered from the keyboard will be placed.

Cursor control keys - Keys used to move the cursor without having any effect on the text. See Arrow keys.

Data - Information either entered into or produced by the computer.

DATA - Programming statement that allows a list of data to be stored in a program. (See READ)

Data base - A collection of related information.

Data base file - A file on disk which is created by the data base application and which stores a computerized data base.

Date category - Any category with the word "date" in its name. AppleWorks automatically converts numbers entered into this category into dates.

Debugging - The process of finding and removing "bugs" (errors) in a program.

Default - Option that is selected automatically by pressing Return if no other option is chosen.

Delete key - Key that erases the character to the left of the current cursor position.

Delete record - To remove a record from a data base: Open-Apple D.

Delete text - The removal of a character or group of characters from a document.

Desktop - An area in the computer's memory holding files that may be used by AppleWorks.

Desktop Index - A listing of the files currently on the Desktop. It also acts as a menu when switching between Desktop files.

Destination - Where copied or moved information is placed.

DIF file - Short for "data interchange format", a DIF file is used as an intermediate file when transferring data between the data base and spreadsheet in AppleWorks.

Document - Data that can be typed in the word processor, such as a letter, paper or story.

Double Space - Leaving a blank line between each line of text when a document is printed.

Download - To transfer a message or computer file from a bulletin board or E-Mail service computer to another computer.

Edit - To make changes in a file or program.

Edit line - Line at the bottom of the spreadsheet screen where data entered from the keyboard is displayed before it is placed into a cell.

Electronic bulletin board - (BBS) Telecommunications service which allows subscribers using a computer and modem to transmit messages that can be received by all the other subscribers.

Electronic mail - (E-Mail) Telecommunications service which allows a person using a computer and modem to send a message to another person's computer.

END - Programming statement that halts program execution.

Entry - Information stored in one category in one record.

Esc key - Key used to terminate (escape from) an option or to quit a menu.

Exchange mode - Option used to switch between insert and overwrite modes, Open-Apple E.

Execute - To carry out a command or instruction in a program.

Expert systems - System programmed to produce the same solution a human expert would if asked to solve the same problem.

Field - Another name for category.

File - Information created by AppleWorks which is stored on a disk.

File name - A name for a file stored on disk.

Find - The computer searches a file for specified text: Open-Apple F.

Footer - Line which is printed at the bottom of each page.

FOR...TO - Programming statement used to define a loop.

Format, data base - How the records in a data base are displayed, single-record (one at a time) or multiple-record (up to 15 at a time).

Format, word processor - The way that text appears on a page, including options such as margins, emphasized text, and headers and footers.

Formula, report - See "calculation rule".

Formula, spreadsheet - Mathematical statements used to calculate values which are stored in cells. The statement +C5+D7+E8 is a formula. Functions - Used in formulas to perform common calculations. @SUM(B5...B10) is a function.

Get Files option - Option used to place a previously created disk file on the Desktop.

Hacker - Person who uses a computer and modem to enter a computer system without authorization.

Hardware - Physical devices which make up the computer and its peripherals.

Header - Line which is printed at the top of each page.

IF...THEN - Conditional programming statement that instructs the computer to take a specified action if a comparison is found to be true, and no action if it is false.

Immediate mode - Programming mode in which the computer executes commands and instructions immediately when the Return key is pressed.

Input - Data entered into the computer.

INPUT - Programming statement used for entering data into the computer directly from the keyboard.

Insert record - Adds a new, empty record to the data base above the current cursor position: Open-Apple I.

Insert text - Adding words or characters to a document.

Integrated - Different applications that are part of one software package. Because AppleWorks is integrated, data may be shared between its three applications areas.

Justification - Placing the data from two categories on the same line, one space apart. Used in data base label reports.

Justified - Word processor paragraph format in which each line of text is made to extend from the left margin to the right by adding extra space between words.

K, kilobyte - Measurement of computer memory capacity, 1024 bytes.

Keyboard - Device resembling a typewriter used for inputting data into a computer.

Key category - Category which stores the data used when determining the order during a sort.

Label report - Data base report which prints the categories in a format which could be used to produce mailing labels.

Label - Words or characters stored in a spreadsheet cell that cannot be used in a calculation.

Layout, data base - The arrangement and width of categories in a record (form). Open-Apple L.

Layout, spreadsheet - The design of a spreadsheet including the placement of data in its rows and columns, column widths and the use of formatting. Open-Apple L.

Line number - Number in front of each program line that is used to place the line in its proper sequence within the program.

LIST - Programming command that displays the lines of the program currently in memory.

LOAD - Programming command for recalling a program previously stored on disk.

Loop - Section of a program designed to be executed repeatedly.

Mail merge - Using the contents of a data base report and a word processed document to have the computer produce personalized form letters.

Main Menu - Menu containing options for manipulating different files and the Desktop.

Make New File option - Option to create a new file.

Margin - Blank spaces on a printed page which surround text.

Memory - Electronic storage used by the computer.

Menu - A list of options that are available at a particular point in a program.

Microprocessor - CPU on a single chip.

Modem - Device which translates binary data into waves and waves back into binary data so that computer data can be sent over telephone lines.

Modify - To change the contents of a cell or entry.

Monitor - Television-like device used to display computer output.

Multi-record format - Displays the first few categories for up to 15 records. Used when comparing records to one another.

Natural language processing - Using a computer to recognize spoken words and then to translate them into digital form.

NEW - Programming command that erases the program currently in memory so that a new one can be entered.

NEXT - Programming statement that ends a loop started with a FOR...TO.

Numeric category - A category which contains only numbers.

Numeric operator - Symbol (+, -, *, /, ^) used to express a mathematical operation.

Numeric variable - Variable which stores a numeric value.

Open-Apple commands - Commands executed directly from an applications screen by holding down the Open-Apple key and pressing another key. Some Open-Apple commands are shortcuts for menu options, others do not appear on any menu.

Open-Apple key - Key on the lower-left of the keyboard marked with an apple. Used to execute Open-Apple commands.

Option marker - Marker placed by AppleWorks in the text to indicate the beginning or ending of a formatting option. Markers are not printed.

Options menu - Menu from which formatting options such as bold, underline and margins are set from: Open-Apple O.

Output - Data produced by a computer program.

Pagination - The computer calculates and displays markers showing where text will be broken into pages when printed.

Paragraph alignment - How text is printed in relation to the margins: unjustified, justified, or centered.

Paragraph format - Use of options effecting a paragraph including alignment, spacing, tabs and margins.

PC - Personal Computer, a small computer employing a microprocessor.

Peripheral - Secondary hardware device connected to a computer such as a printer, modem or disk drive.

Pirate - Person who illegally copies computer software.

Pointing - Moving the cell cursor to specify cell names in formulas.

PRINT - Programming statement that causes the computer to display information on the screen or printer.

Print command - Command which prints the file currently on the screen, Open-Apple P.

ProDOS - Disk operating system programs that the computer needs to start up.

Program - Series of instructions written in a special language directing the computer to perform certain tasks.

Program line - One line of instructions in a program. Each line is preceded by a line number.

Prompt, AppleWorks - A message displayed on the screen by AppleWorks asking for information to be typed.

Prompt, BASIC - Square bracket (]) displayed by Applesoft when it is ready to accept instructions.

Query - See Selection.

Quit option - Main Menu option used to exit AppleWorks.

RAM - Random Access Memory, memory which the computer can both read and write

Range - Partial row or column of adjacent cells.

READ - Programming statement that takes data from a DATA statement and assigns it to a specified variable.

Record - A complete collection of information for one item in a data base.

Relational operator - Symbol (=, <, >, <>, <=, >=) used to indicate the comparison of two values.

Relative copy - Copying formulas in a spreadsheet so that the cell names reflect the new rows and columns they are in.

Replace command - The computer replaces one specified section of text with another: Open-Apple R.

Report - Printed description of the information stored in a data base.

Report category - The information from one category which appears in a report format.

Report format - Description of the order and placement of categories in a report.

Reserved word - Word such as PRINT or FOR that is part of a programming language and therefore cannot be used as a variable name.

Return key - Key used to indicate the end of an entry such as an option or response to a question, or to choose from a menu. In word processing Return is used at the end of each paragraph.

Robot - Machine which can be programmed and is also capable of motion.

ROM - Read Only Memory, memory from which the computer can read only.

Row - Horizontal line of data identified by a number in a spreadsheet.

RUN - Programming command that starts program execution.

SAVE - Programming command that instructs the computer to save the program in memory on disk under the name specified.

Save command - Command used to save the current AppleWorks file on disk, Open-Apple S.

Scale - Line at the top of the Word Processor work area showing placement of tab stops.

Screen scroll - Moving through a file, the screen acts as a window showing only part of the file at any one time.

Search - See Find and Selection.

Search text - Text entered by user to be found or replaced.

Selection - Limiting the number of records in a data base that are displayed by using rules to define criteria that displayed records must meet. Selection is based on rules which contain comparisons such as 'less than' or 'not equal to'.

Selection rule - Criteria for displaying records which refers to the contents of specific categories. For example, "GPA less than 2.0". Defined using Open-Apple R.

Single-record format - All of the categories for a single record displayed on the screen at one time. Used when updating a record.

Software - Computer programs.

Sort - See Arrange.

Source - Where the information to be copied is stored.

Spacing line - Blank line printed between records in a data base label report to make it more readable.

Spreadsheet - Rows and columns of data on which calculations may be performed using formulas.

Statement - All the elements that combined carry out a programming instruction, i.e. a PRINT instruction can be followed by quotation marks, variable names, semicolons, commas, etc., to make an entire PRINT statement.

String - Sequence of letters, numbers and/or special characters such as punctuation marks. Strings may not be used in mathematical calculations.

String variable - Variable that stores a string. All string variable names end with a dollar sign and may not be used in mathematical calculations.

Subscript - Text printed slightly below the normal line.

Superscript - Text printed slightly above the normal line.

Syntax - The correct rules or "grammar" of a programming language.

Syntax error - Programming statement or command which the computer does not understand because it does not fit the rules of the programming language.

Tab stop - Position(s), shown on the scale, where the cursor jumps to when the Tab key is pressed. Used to create columns or indent text.

Table report - Data base report format which prints only a few categories from each record in columns.

Telecommunications - Sending computer data over telephone lines.

Text - Any character or group of characters in a document.

Text alignment - See paragraph alignment.

Time category - A category which contains the word "time" in its name. AppleWorks automatically converts numbers entered into these categories to times.

Unjustified - Left-aligned text, with the right side jagged.

Update - See Modify.

Update a record - Changing the contents of an entry or entries in a record.

Upload - To transfer a message or computer file from a computer to a bulletin board or E-Mail service computer.

Values - Numeric data that can be stored in cell and used in calculations.

Variable - Name used to represent a value that is stored in the memory of the computer by a program. The value assigned to a variable can be changed.

Virus - Program which hides within another program for the purpose of destroying or altering data.

What If? question - Performing calculations to make predictions based upon the data stored in a spreadsheet.

Word processor - A computer application that allows text to be manipulated and stored.

Word wrap - When the computer decides whether to keep a word on the current line, or move it to the next based on the amount of space left on the line.

Zoom mode, data base - Used to switch between single and multiple-record formats: Open-Apple Z.

Zoom mode, spreadsheet - Used to switch between the contents and formulas stored in cells: Open-Apple Z.

Zoom mode, word processor - Used to display Option and Return markers on the screen: Open-Apple Z.

Index